HELPING YOUR STRUGGLING TEENAGER

This book is invaluable. Its practical advice built on sound research will meet a desperate need.

TONY CAMPOLO
AUTHOR OF *GROWING UP IN AMERICA*

Unique and urgently needed is the best way to describe this practical book.

H. NORMAN WRIGHT
AUTHOR OF *RAISING KIDS TO LOVE JESUS*

Dr. Parrott has furnished a brilliant handbook for all who work with teens.

DONALD M. JOY
ASBURY THEOLOGICAL SEMINARY

Les Parrott has put his sensitive finger on the pulse of adolescent problems and has come up with an array of practical, effecting helping techniques. His advice comes from his heart as well as from his extensive research.

PHILIP G. ZIMBARDO
STANFORD UNIVERSITY

This is an excellent tool. Dr. Parrott has an easy style that facilitates understanding the heart of the problem and how to assist each struggling child.

STEPHEN ARTERBURN
FOUNDER, NEW LIFE CLINICS

Only on rare occasions does a book come across my desk that is intriguing, practical, and theoretically insightful. This is one of those rare books.

G. KEITH OLSON
AUTHOR OF *COUNSELING TEENAGERS*

Les Parrott speaks from a platform of professional understanding and practical experience. This book will provide very practical help.

JAY KESLER
PRESIDENT, TAYLOR UNIVERSITY

Les Parrott understands adolescents and what troubles them. This is a practical and biblically based handbook.

STEPHEN A. HAYNER
INTERVARSITY CHRISTIAN FELLOWSHIP

Dr. Parrott has assembled a compassion-based approach to helping young people in very practical and effective ways. I highly recommend this book.

DUB AMBROSE
YOUTH PUBLICATIONS FOR UNITED METHODIST CHURCH

This book is well researched and documented. Dr. Parrott's warmth and poignant examples make this a supremely readable book.

ROBERT S. MCGEE
FOUNDER, RAPHA HOSPITAL TREATMENT CENTERS

HELPING YOUR STRUGGLING TEENAGER

A Parenting Handbook on Thirty-Six Common Problems

DR. LES PARROTT III

ZondervanPublishingHouse
Grand Rapids, Michigan

A Division of HarperCollinsPublishers

Helping Your Struggling Teenager
Copyright © 1993, 2000 by Les Parrott III

Helping Your Struggling Teenager has been adapted from *Helping the Struggling Adolescent,*
a book for counselors, pastors, and youth workers.

Requests for information should be addressed to:

📖 ZondervanPublishingHouse
Grand Rapids, Michigan 49530

Library of Congress Cataloging-in-Publication Data

Parrott, Les.
    Helping your struggling teenager : a parenting handbook on thirty-six common
problems / Les Parrott.
       p.   cm.
    Includes bibliographical references and index.
    ISBN: 0-310-23402-6
    1. Parenting. 2. Parent and teenager. 3. Adolescent psychology. 4. Parenting—Religious
aspects—Christianity. 5. Teenagers—United States—Family relationships. I. Title.
HQ755.8 .P3945 2000
649'.125—dc21
00-057217
CIP

This edition printed on acid-free paper.

Interior design by Amy Langeler

Printed in the United States of America

00 01 02 03 04 /❖ DC/ 10 9 8 7 6 5 4 3 2 1

To the two people who provided me
with boundless hope during my adolescent years.
I dedicate this work to my mom and dad,
Les and Lora Lee Parrott,
with love and affection

CONTENTS

ACKNOWLEDGMENTS

The first words of this book were written on an airplane as I was return-ing home to Seattle from Indianapolis, where I had addressed a gather-ing of parents, ministers, and counselors. They had come from across the country to talk about helping struggling adolescents. Their dedication, com-passion, and enthusiasm were self-evident, and a company of people never encouraged a writer more than they did me. *Helping Your Struggling Teenager* was inspired by these people and written for thousands like them.

I am indebted to my colleagues at Seattle Pacific University who under-stand and encourage my calling to integrate spiritual values with human understanding. I am especially thankful for the prayerful support of my col-leagues in the School of Social and Behavioral Sciences and the Department of Psychology.

The pages of this book represent the combined effort and expertise of many professionals who reviewed and critiqued particular chapters. The following specialists deserve not only acknowledgment, but my profound gratitude: Dub Ambrose, Roy Barsness, Alan Basham, Charles Bombardier, John Court, Wendy Fisher, Stan Gaede, Joy Hammersla, Dan Hartman, Donald Joy, James Mallory, David Massey, Steve Moore, Thanne Moore, Carol Parrott, Cliff Penner, Cindy Perrin, Robin Perrin, Kim Lampson-Reif, Michael Roe, Randy Rowland, Denny Rydberg, Suzanne Shelton, JoAnne Smatlan, James Scott Smith, Pat Springle, Les Steele, Scott Willis, Mitch Woltersdorf, Michael Vitiello, and Philip Zimbardo. The discerning questions and thoughtful input of these people have been immensely helpful. Although none of these individuals can be held responsible for weaknesses that remain, they have all made contributions to whatever strengths this book contains.

A debt of thanks is also owed to the people who have helped me improve my craft of writing. Luke Reinsma and Rose Reynoldson generously gave of their time to help me rework the first draft of this manuscript while it still suffered from "the disease of clutter." I am indebted to Lori VandenBosch, Sandy Vander Zicht, and Jim Ruark, my editors at Zondervan, for their personal touch and heartfelt desire to help those who work with struggling adolescents. I am also grateful for Stan Gundry's vision and confidence in this project. The library work of my research assistants—Jon Anderson, Sarah Timmons, and Steve Scott—was invaluable. Janice Lundquist and Mindy Galbreath, as usual, helped me keep the details of my life running smoothly during this project.

The long, lonely hours in front of my computer were compensated for by the energizing support of friends who put up with my "struggling adolescent obsession." Special thanks go to my pastor, Tharon Daniels, for the cathartic talks while jogging around Green Lake, and to my friend, Steve Moore, for affirming the dream.

To my wife, Leslie, I owe more than gratitude. It is difficult for me to imagine how any human being could give more to another than she has given to me. Her positive spirit helped create an environment that made this book possible. Her patience, vision, and unswerving dedication to our relationship know no bounds. Nor does my love for her.

Finally, I want to thank the adolescents who trusted me with the personal struggles that have defined their pilgrimage. They have taught me much.

HOW TO USE THIS BOOK

Helping Your Struggling Teenager is a practical resource tool for parents who want to be in the know. As a psychologist who has worked with numerous adolescents in a variety of settings, I am hoping to give you a behind-the-scenes look at how professionals view the problems your son or daughter may have. I also want to show how you—when necessary—can work alongside a professional counselor who is helping your child. As an informed parent, you deserve to know what professionals know about these problems. You need to know what we think about why a child struggles with a specific problem and what we can do to help him or her overcome it. In a sense, you can consider this book as a kind of crash course in helping today's youth with thirty-six of their most common problems.

Part One is designed to give a conceptual overview of how to help struggling adolescents in general. These introductory chapters may be read consecutively before delving into the remainder of the book. In Part Two, I deal with specific problems and how to address them. They are listed alphabetically for ease of access as you use the book as a handy reference. The design of the topical sections will enable you to quickly and easily find vital information for particular problems. Each section, indicated by the symbol ✔, succinctly answers several fundamental questions:

✔ *What* does a specific struggle look like?

✔ *Why* did it happen?

✔ *How* can a counselor help?

✔ *When* should a counselor refer the adolescent to another professional, and *where* can a counselor find additional resources for helping?

Additional resources are listed in each chapter to avoid the hazard of believing that this handbook can answer every question, and the danger of believing that you can work with every struggle your adolescent has.

In this volume I have tried to summarize the best information we have on solving kids' problems. I have intentionally approached the material as a Christian and as a clinical psychologist. The many helping techniques and practices are based on a thorough review of hundreds of scientific studies, and I carefully chose them to highlight strategies that have proved to be the most therapeutic and consistent with Christian understanding. Each section provides the latest technical knowledge in nontechnical language and demonstrates intervention strategies that a competent parent and/or counselor should consider.

No universal or simple formulas for resolving the complex problems of young people are available. Therefore, I have followed a pragmatic rather than a dogmatic approach to helping the struggling adolescent. When asked how he worked, Einstein once replied, "I grope." I hope that in your work with a struggling adolescent, this book will help you grope in the right direction.

All case material is real but disguised, originating from my clinical practice or from that of colleagues.

PART ONE

Effective Helping

1

ADOLESCENCE: A STRUGGLE FOR IDENTITY

During World War II, Erik H. Erikson coined a phrase that stuck—*identity crisis*. He used it to describe the disorientation of shell-shocked soldiers who could not remember their names. Through the years, this phrase has become a useful tool to describe the struggle of growing up.

Achieving a sense of identity is the major developmental task of teenagers. Like a stunned soldier in a state of confusion, sooner or later, young people are hit with a bomb that is more powerful than dynamite—puberty. Somewhere between childhood and maturity their bodies kick into overdrive and fuel changes at an alarming rate. With this acceleration of physical and emotional growth, they become strangers to themselves. Under attack by an arsenal of fiery hormones, the bewildered young person begins to ask, *"Who am I?"*

While achievement of a meaningful answer to this question is a lifelong pursuit, it is the burning challenge of adolescence. According to Erikson, having an identity—knowing who you are—gives adolescents a sense of control that allows them to navigate through the rest of life.

Without identities, awkward adolescents carry a "how'm-I-doing?" attitude that is always focused on their concern about impressions they are making on others. Without self-identities they will be or do whatever they think others want. They will flounder from one way of acting to another, never able to step outside of a preoccupation with their own performance and genuinely ask others, "How are you doing?" Erikson calls this miserable state "identity diffusion."[1]

The successful formation of self-identity follows a typical pattern. Teens identify with people they admire. Whether in real life or through magazines and TV, they emulate the characteristics of people they want to be like. By the end of adolescence, if all goes as it should, these identifications merge into a single identity that incorporates and alters previous identifications to make a unique and coherent whole.

The quest for identity is scary. Somewhere between twelve and twenty years of age, adolescents are forced to choose once and for all what their identity is to be. It is a formidable task. Uncertain which of their mixed emotions are really their true feelings, they are pushed to make up their minds. Their confusion is complicated further when they begin to guess what others, whose opinions they care about, want them to be.

For adolescents who never achieve an integrated identity, "all the world's a stage." In their adult years they will play the part of human beings who change roles to please whoever happens to be watching. Their clothes, their language, their thoughts, and their feelings are all a part of the script. Their purpose will be to receive approval from those they hope to impress. Life will become a charade, and players will never enjoy the security of personal identity or experience the strength that comes from a sense of self-worth.

HOW ADOLESCENTS SEARCH FOR IDENTITY

Young people look for identity in uncounted ways. In this section, seven common paths are examined: family relations, status symbols, "grown-up" behavior, rebellion, others' opinions, idols, and cliquish exclusion.

Through Family Relations

Adolescents' families have significant impact on identity formation. To assert individuality and move out of childhood, teenagers will wean themselves from their protecting parents. But individuality may also be found in reaction to the identities of one's brothers and sisters. If the first child, for example, decides to be a serious intellectual, the second may seek individuality in becoming a jokester. Seeing these places already taken, the third child may choose to be an athlete.

In some cases, when young people feel they possess no distinctive talents, they may rebel by separating themselves from the "white sheep." They may become delinquents or prodigals and gain identity by causing trouble.

Through Status Symbols

Adolescents try to establish themselves as individuals through prestige. They seek out behavior or possessions that are readily observable. They purchase sports cars, hairstyles, lettermen's jackets, skateboards, guitars, stereos, and designer clothes in hope of being identified as people who belong. Their status symbols help teens form self-identity because they themselves have what others in their group have: "the jocks," "the brains," "the Ravers," "the Straight Edgers," "the White Caps," "the Motherheads," "the Ram-Rams," or "the Goths." Owning status symbols, however, is not enough to achieve identity. Adolescents quickly recognize a struggling teen who is attempting to carve out an identity by buying the right symbols. In fact, they enjoy detecting these imposters and reinforcing their own identities by labeling them as "wanna-be's" or "posers."

To be authentic, appropriate behavior must accompany the status symbol. A "party girl," for example, must not only wear the right clothes, have the right hairstyle, and buy the right music, she must do the things a party girl does. Soon the behavior will earn the adolescent a reputation—something she must live up to if she is to maintain her identity, and something she must live down if she is to change it.

Through "Grown-Up" Behavior

Adolescents have a strong desire to be like adults. The more mature they appear, the more recognition they receive and the closer they get to feeling that they have achieved identity. Because real maturity is not always visible, young people often resort to behavior that is symbolic of adults. They engage in *tabooed pleasures*—the things parents, preachers, and teachers say they are too young to do.

The most common of these tabooed pleasures are smoking, drinking, drugs, and premarital sex. By the time adolescents reach high school, smoking is a widespread practice. Drinking has become a status symbol for girls as well as for boys, often beginning in the junior high school years. As with drinking, doing drugs usually begins as a group activity. Recent statistics on the number of sexually active adolescents are staggering.[2] Teens engage in these behaviors to gain independence from family restrictions, to increase their social acceptance, or even for adventure or curiosity.[3] Nearly every adolescent will experiment with these "adult" behaviors at some point, but certain adolescents will struggle intensely in these areas. Their problems are addressed more specifically in other sections of this book.

Through Rebellion

Rebellion is a logical consequence of young people's attempts to resolve incongruent ideas and find authentic identity. Rebellion results from a desire to be unique while still maintaining the security of sameness. "But, Dad, I gotta be a nonconformist," the teenager said to his father. "How else can I be like the other kids?"

A rebellious attitude is frequently accompanied by an idealism that prompts adolescents to reject the values of family, school, society, and church. However, their oversimplified and unrealistic ideals are often eventually found to be impractical and rarely held for any significant duration.

Through Others' Opinions

Essential to identity formation is the validation of one's self-image by other people's opinions. Adolescents' perceptions of themselves change, depending on what they believe others think about them. For example, if a young person sees himself as a talented actor but is not offered the lead role in the school play, his identity as an actor may be weakened and he may try to find his identity in academics or sports. If, however, he hears that others believe it was a mistake not to cast him as the lead, his identity may be maintained.

Adolescents do not always fall in line with what others think of them. On the contrary. Because adolescent identity is shaped by their perception of how others see them, they may change in order to contradict their perceptions, even if those perceptions are positive. It may be harmful to tell young people they won't have any problems, that they are the best, or that they will someday be the greatest. Aware of their weaknesses, they feel uncomfortable with an affirmation that leaves no room for error. They will go out of their way to prove parents and counselors wrong and to relieve themselves of the burden of being perfect. For some, relief will come only in identifying with what they are least supposed to be, not in being something that is unattainable.[4]

Through Idols

Especially in their early years, adolescents will often overidentify with famous people to the point of apparent loss of their own individuality. In our star-conscious society, literally thousands of rock stars, professional athletes, movie actors, and television personalities are available for teenagers to idolize.

Celebrities become "models" because adolescents are looking for a way to experiment with different roles. In their search for identity they latch onto notable personalities in order to explore different aspects of themselves. Idols allow them to test out new behavior and attitudes before incorporating them into their own identity. Idolizing celebrities does not necessarily mean that adolescents endorse idols' lifestyles or values.

Through Cliquish Exclusion

In their search for identity, adolescents may become remarkably intolerant and even cruel as they exclude others on the basis of minor aspects such as dress. They persistently try to define, overdefine, and redefine themselves in relation to others. If they see something in peers that reminds them of what they don't want to be, they will scorn and avoid those people and feel not an ounce of remorse. Teens strengthen their sense of self through ruthless comparisons and persistent exclusions.

Erikson sees the cliquishness of adolescence and its intolerance of differences as a defense against identity confusion.[5] Usually in the late teens adolescents realize that it takes a well-established identity to tolerate radical differences.

WHY ADOLESCENTS STRUGGLE

The establishment of a personal identity is not easy. The danger of identity confusion lurks around every bend. Erikson points out that some confused young people take an excessively long time to reach adulthood.[6] They may regress into a childish state and thus avoid having to make decisions on confusing issues. Other adolescents express their confusion through premature commitments and impulsive actions. They give themselves to poorly thought-out ways of being and end up fighting needless battles.

Adolescence is a period of stress and turmoil for many young people.[7] While the difficulties that occur in adolescence are due in part to lack of experience, at least five common experiences may exacerbate or create significant struggles: physical, sexual, social, religious, and moral changes.

Physical Changes

A fourteen-year-old tried to excuse his poor report card by saying, "My problem is not tests, but testosterone." He had a legitimate argument. The biochemical changes in adolescence may cause more apprehension than studying for an exam. Waking up with pimples, having your voice crack in public, wearing new jeans that are already too short, growing new facial hair, or beginning menstruation and breast development are all traumatic. As hormones set in motion the chain of physiological events that usher in adulthood, nice kids seem to turn into moody, rebellious adolescents. In fact, some parents with well-behaved teenagers worry that their kids aren't developing properly.

Sexual Changes

As the adolescent's body begins to take on the characteristic shape of his or her sex, new behaviors, thoughts, and physiological processes occur. Each reacts to the cultural stereotype of sexual changes. The adolescent boy encounters locker-room comparisons and wonders if his genitals are too small and why he hasn't begun to shave yet. If he gets an erection while dancing with a girl or while reading or merely thinking, he may suffer from a sense that his body has betrayed him. He might resent the lack of control he has over his body and feel he is "doing something wrong."

The adolescent girl also experiences confusion and shame about her sexual maturation. Menstruation is a serious concern, one often compounded by fear and ignorance. It may cause physical discomfort, weight gain, headaches, mood swings, and so on. Because it is commonly referred to as "the curse," a girl's period may encourage her to play the passive role of a martyr. It is not surprising that even the anticipation of this change contributes to other common struggles.

Social Changes

While the biological changes of puberty are dramatic, they are no more significant than the social changes that occur during adolescence. Between the sixth and eighth grades, the structure of school becomes a very different experience. Most young adolescents move from a relatively small neighborhood elementary school to a much larger, more impersonal junior high school. This move has many social ramifications. It disrupts the old peer-group structure, exposes students to different achievement expectations by teachers, and provides new opportunities for different extracurricular activities.

Family relations also shift as boys and girls turn into teenagers. Conflicts in family discussions increase. Male adolescents become more dominant in conversations—especially with their mothers. Feelings of affection toward their parents decline from the sixth to the eighth grades. This does not mean feelings necessarily become negative, but that the change is from very positive to less positive.

Religious Changes

Contrary to popular opinion, adolescents are genuinely interested in religion and feel that it plays an important role in their lives. While forty-eight percent of adolescents say that they pay more attention "to God and religious teachings" in deciding how to conduct their daily lives, almost as many, forty-five percent, say that they pay more attention to their "own views and the views of others."[8]

However, adolescence is a time when young people question the religious concepts and beliefs of their childhood. They may become skeptical of religious forms, such as prayer, and later begin to doubt the nature of God, but they are on a genuine spiritual quest. This is sometimes mistakenly interpreted as skepticism or doubt. In reality it is sincere questioning. Adolescents investigate their religion to make their faith their own rather than that of their parents. They question, not because they want to become agnostic or atheistic, but because they want to accept religion in a way that is meaningful to them. Still, the quest is often frightening, and the search for faith may lead to involvement in destructive religious cults or other potential problems.

Moral Changes

An important change occurs in adolescents when they realize that their behavior must conform to social expectations without the constant guidance, supervision, and threats of punishment they experienced as children. To become adults, they must replace specific childhood rules with their own moral principles.

Several basic changes occur in the moral thinking of adolescents:

- They become more abstract and less concrete.
- They become more concerned with what is right and less concerned with what is wrong.
- They become more cognitive and less emotional.
- They become more altruistic and less egocentric.
- They become more willing to exert emotional energy on moral issues.[9]

During adolescence, according to Lawrence Kohlberg, teens reach a stage of moral development that is based on respect for others rather than on personal desires.[10] While adolescents are intellectually capable of making this change and creating their own moral code, the task is difficult.[11] Every day adolescents see inconsistencies in moral standards. As they interact with peers of different religious, racial, or socioeconomic backgrounds, they recognize that people have different codes of right and wrong. Some fail to make the shift to adult morality during adolescence and must finish the task in early adulthood. Others not only fail to make the shift but build a moral code on socially unacceptable moral concepts.

Physical, sexual, social, religious, and moral changes all contribute to adolescent struggle for identity and may contribute to potential complications and possible problems.

WHAT ADOLESCENTS DO WITH THEIR STRUGGLES

It is difficult to predict exactly how a specific adolescent will attempt to manage his or her problems. A number of personality traits and environmental factors influence the struggling adolescent's coping style. There are, however, at least three common ways young people contend with their struggles. They either hold them in, act them out, or work them through.[12]

Hold Them In

Many adolescents cope with their difficulties by keeping them to themselves. Like Adam and Eve hiding in the bushes, these adolescents camouflage their struggles, hoping they will eventually disappear. Some adolescents conceal their anxiety by *blocking*—allowing unconscious conflicts to interrupt their flow of thought. Tony, for example, is troubled by having sexual fantasies about a girl he was assigned to work with in his social studies class. At the dinner table he begins to tell his parents about the project. He suddenly gets confused and "forgets" what it is.

Another way adolescents hide their problems is through *sublimation*—transforming unacceptable impulses into behaviors that are more socially acceptable. Angry at his alcoholic father, a young man might disguise his hostility by investing a tremendous amount of energy into basketball.

Adolescents who feel hurt sometimes hide their struggles through *emotional insulation,* keeping potential pain at bay. For example, Carla, a junior in high school, has just been asked to the prom by the boy of her dreams. In order to avoid any possibility of being disappointed, she feels no excitement or joy. She becomes numb for fear that he might drop her at the last minute.

Related to emotional insulation is *intellectualization*—interpreting a situation only at a cognitive level in order to avoid dealing with uncomfortable feelings. When asked how he was doing after being cut from the school drama tryouts, Kevin, who actually hurt very deeply, responds, "I think it is all for the best. God is in charge and he is really teaching me to be a better person through this. It is probably the best thing that could have happened to me."

Perhaps the most common form of hiding one's struggles is through *repression*—pushing thoughts, feelings, impulses, desires, or memories out of awareness. Take Mike, seventeen, who has grown up in the church and is sincerely seeking answers to some of life's difficult questions. He begins to doubt God's existence, but quickly forces this questioning from his awareness because it is "bad." Later this repressed doubt shows up as an inability to be genuine with other feelings. He fails to show normal expressions and becomes legalistic in his spirit.

Act Them Out

Some adolescents cope with struggles by *acting out*—expressing their feelings through impulsive actions to reduce tension. The anxiety they feel about failing a class, for example, is temporarily released through skipping classes, harassment, or vandalism. The tension they feel over not being accepted by their peers may be acted out through sexual promiscuity. Adolescents act out in several different ways.

Young people will sometimes act out their struggle by *displacement*—transferring feelings to a more neutral object. The fifteen-year-old who is angry at his mom might kick over a neighbor's garbage can on his way to school. The payoff is obvious. Telling off one's parents may have costly side effects, but kicking garbage cans vents the hostility for free.

Another way of acting out struggles comes in the form of *regression*—retreating to an earlier developmental period that was less stressful. If Wendy, fourteen, is denied her desire to stay out with her friends past midnight, she may regress to childish behavior and relieve some of her frustration by sulking, crying, or throwing temper tantrums.   .

Adolescents who are afraid of their own thoughts or impulses may act them out through *projection*—putting them into another person. Neal, a sixteen-year-old "jock," becomes convinced that Craig is a homosexual. To ward off fears of his own sexuality, Neal transfers his sexual confusion onto Craig and acts out his anger by ridiculing him in front of other teammates.

Another common way of warding off uncomfortable emotions is through *denial*—refusing to accept reality. Wayne, seventeen, does this by partying. Regardless of the problem—poor grades, a broken home, depression, anger, and so on—Wayne denies the reality of his pain through two words: "Let's party!" He avoids having to face up to his struggles by simply pretending they don't exist, "celebrating" by truant behavior, hanging out at the park, and drinking.

Work Them Through

Adolescents who hide their struggles and the ones who act them out have at least one characteristic in common. Both are avoiding *responsibility*—the freedom to consciously choose their actions and attitudes. Both are hung up, at some level, on thinking that says, "Why don't they . . . ?" In other words, both suffer from a tendency to wonder why others do not reduce their own problems. William Glasser sees this lack of responsibility as the central cause of adolescent struggles and even juvenile delinquency.[13] He claims that young people have problems in proportion to the degree they avoid taking responsibility for their actions or attitudes.

By holding their struggles in or acting them out, adolescents avoid having to confront them head-on. It is not that they do not have the capacity to take responsibility. Most psychologists agree with the developmental expert Jean Piaget that by adolescence young people are moving beyond concrete thinking and reaching a stage he calls "formal operations." They are able to look past what seems unchangeable, weed out irrelevant issues, and consider ramifications of choices they were unable to distinguish as children. Adolescents are capable of understanding the present and imagining the future. They can think abstractly and consider the consequences of their actions. Adolescents have the capacity to say, "The trouble with me is me, and I am going to do something about it."

Like most abilities, responsibility is best seen on a continuum. There are extreme cases of psychosis when people are simply unable to recognize that they have a choice. For example, the paranoid schizophrenic, who believes someone is out to get him, believes he can do absolutely nothing to change his situation.

At the other extreme, some take on too much responsibility. They are the ones who feel guilty about things for which they have no responsibility—the teenager, for example, who feels guilty about her father's death because she was away at school when he died.

The majority of young people, however, are somewhere between these extremes. Lead them to see that they are sometimes responsible for the things that happen to them and that, even when they aren't, they are free to choose attitudes that will help them transcend debilitating struggles.

This book is designed to help you guide the adolescents for whom you care to a place where they squarely face their struggles and choose to work through them. The techniques outlined in the sections of Part Two are designed to help you allow adolescents to become their own counselors.

When adolescents are able to solve their problems with reasonable success and feel increasingly confident in their abilities to cope, periods of struggle gradually become less frequent and less intense. Only then will fulfillment begin to outweigh struggle.

Notes

1. E. H. Erikson, *Identity: Youth and Crisis* (New York: Norton, 1968).

2. J. McDowell and D. Day, *Why Wait? What You Need to Know About the Teen Sexuality Crisis* (San Bernardino, Calif.: Here's Life Publishers, 1987, 1994).

3. G. M. Smith and C. P. Fogg, "Teenage Drug Use: A Search for Causes and Consequences," *Personality and Social Psychology Bulletin* 1 (1974): 426–29.

4. Erikson, *Identity: Youth and Crisis*.

5. E. H. Erikson, *The Challenge of Youth* (New York: Anchor, 1965).

6. Ibid.

7. J. J. Arnett, "Adolescent Storm and Stress, Reconsidered," *American Psychologist* 54 (1999): 317–26.

8. F. Newport and G. Gallup, *Gallup Poll* (December 24, 1999): www.gallup.com.

9. J. Mitchell, "Moral Growth During Adolescence," *Adolescence* 10 (1975): 221–26.

10. L. Kohlberg, *Stages in the Development of Moral Thought and Action* (New York: Holt, 1969). Kohlberg calls this stage "postconventional morality."

11. J. Piaget "The Intellectual Development of the Adolescent," in *Adolescence: Psychosocial Perspectives*, ed. G. Caplan and S. Lebovici (New York: Basic Books, 1969), 22–26. Piaget describes the adolescent as entering a stage of "formal operations."

12. G. K. Olson, *Counseling Teenagers: The Complete Christian Guide to Understanding and Helping Adolescents* (Loveland, Colo.: Group Books, 1984). Olson provides an excellent discussion of defense mechanisms. I have relied upon much of his work in this section.

13. W. Glasser, *The Identity Society* (New York: Harper & Row, 1972).

2

CHARACTERISTICS OF EFFECTIVE HELPING: A SELF-INVENTORY

The most important instrument you have to help adolescents is you.[1] Who you are as a person is critical in determining the effectiveness of your ability to really help. This understanding, however, does not diminish the importance of the Holy Spirit. The point is that your attitude and behavior either help or hinder any healing work the Holy Spirit is prepared to do through you.

Many researchers have attempted to identify the qualities that contribute to successful helping relationships. They have discovered the importance of sensitivity, hope, compassion, control, awareness, knowledge. The list could fill several pages. However, beginning in 1967 Carl Rogers and his colleagues conducted a four-year study that seemed to cut to the bone.[2] It has been supported by subsequent research and is cited in nearly every text on counseling. The findings are unequivocal. People are more likely to improve when they are with someone who is (1) warm, (2) genuine, and (3) empathic. Without these traits a person's condition may actually worsen regardless of other factors.

Warmth

Paul Tournier, the renowned Swiss counselor, said, "I have no methods. All I do is accept people." The key to nonpossessive warmth is acceptance. It is an attitude that does not evaluate or require change. It simply accepts the thoughts, feelings, and actions of the child. This warmth helps a teen develop a base of self-worth: "If my parents care about me, maybe I *am* valuable."

A Self-Inventory

Directions: For each statement indicate the response that best identifies your beliefs and attitudes. Keep in mind that the "right" answer is the one that best expresses your thoughts at this time. Use the following code:

5 = I strongly agree

4 = I agree

3 = I am undecided

2 = I disagree

1 = I strongly disagree

_____   1.   Giving advice has little to do with helping my child.

_____   2.   I can accept and respect my child when he or she disagrees with me.

_____   3.   I can make a mistake and admit it to my child.

_____   4.   I take a serious look at my child's side of a disagreement before I make a decision.

_____   5.   I tend to trust my intuition even when I'm unsure of the outcome.

_____   6.   I don't need to see immediate and concrete results in order to know progress is occurring.

_____   7.   Who you are in a helping relationship is more important than what you do.

_____   8.   My presence frees my child from the threat of external evaluation.

_____   9.   In a tense emotional situation I tend to remain calm.

_____   10. I know my limits when it comes to helping my child.

_____   *Total Score*

Total your responses to determine the degree to which you
have the qualities necessary to be an effective helper:

40–50   You are well on your way to being an effective
helper with your child; take special care to maintain the qualities you have.

30–39   You have what it takes to be effective, but you will
need to exert special effort to groom the traits described
in this chapter.

Below 30 You will want to seek objective assistance in the
help you attempt to give to your struggling son or daughter.[3]

Nonpossessive warmth is not necessarily approving of everything a child
does. Gary Collins recounts how Jesus showed warmth to the woman at the
well: "Her morals may have been low, and he certainly never condoned sinful
behavior. But Jesus nevertheless respected the woman and treated her as a person of worth. His warm, caring attitude must have been apparent wherever
he went."[4]

Nor is this warmth a kind of smothering sentimentality. It does not skip
through the day whistling a happy tune and tossing out platitudes and contrived
emotion. Through unconditional warmth we invite struggling adolescents to
catch glimpses of God's grace. And grace is the bedrock of growth. When adolescents feel sure they will not be condemned for who they are and that their
mom or dad will make no judgment of them, the power of God's grace begins
to turn the wheels of change.

Unconditional warmth frees adolescents from attempting to win their parents' approval. Young people no longer wonder whether they are loved for who
they are or for what they do. Why does this matter? Because teenagers who feel
a need to perform to get approval will be troubled by a nagging uncertainty
about whether their parents genuinely accept them.

Nonpossessive warmth provides a springboard for struggling adolescents
to accept themselves and become strong individuals who do not compulsively
conform their personalities to what others wish them to be.

Genuineness

Without honesty there is no way to touch hurting teenagers. Adolescents
have built-in radars that spot phoniness even at a distance. They are experts at
detecting fabricated feelings and insincere intentions. To every overture of help
they apply their own polygraph test. Honest thoughts and authentic feelings

may be verbally expressed at appropriate times, but it is just as important for genuineness to come through in all of its subtle forms, in parents' eyes and posture, for example.

Genuineness cannot be faked. Either you sincerely want to help or you are simply playing the sterile role of a "helper"—hiding behind masks, defenses, or facades. In other words, authenticity is something you *are,* not something you do. Genuineness has been described as a lure to the heart. Jesus said, "Blessed are the pure in heart." Or, to put it another way, "Consider the parent in whom there is no guile." When genuineness is present, a hesitant and skeptical adolescent is likely to stay with you and invest energy in the healing process.

Empathy

The best way to avoid stepping on adolescents' toes is to put yourself in their sneakers. I don't know who said that first, but it's surely true. Empathy lets struggling adolescents know you hear their words, understand their thoughts, and sense their feelings. This does not mean you necessarily understand all that is wrong with them. It means you understand what they feel and think. Empathy is void of judgment and says, "If I were you, I would act as you do; I understand why you feel the way you feel."

> To maintain the qualities of warmth, genuineness, and empathy, routinely ask yourself these questions:
>
> - Do I honestly accept this adolescent without requiring change? Do I value this person in spite of his thoughts, feelings, or behavior?
> - Am I more concerned with doing the right things as a parent than being who I am as a person? Am I aware of my emotions when I am with others?
> - How would I act, think, and feel if I were in this adolescent's situation? Do I understand him so accurately that I have no desire to judge him?

Two important distinctions about empathy are helpful. First, empathy is not identification. You don't need to wear faded jeans and blare rock and roll on your car radio to enter the adolescent's world. In fact, teenagers want to be seen as unique and complex. They resent blatant attempts by adults to identify with them. To say "I know exactly how you feel" to a struggling adolescent is like telling a Vietnam veteran that his post-traumatic stress is easy and simple to understand.

Second, empathy is deeper and stronger than sympathy. Sympathy is standing on the shore and throwing out a lifeline while empathy is jumping into the water and risking one's safety to help another. And the risk is real. In empathy we risk change. Understanding the aching heart of a struggling adolescent *will* change you in spite of the human tendency to resist change. Yet when we have the courage to enter the pain of a hurting teenager, we begin to build a relationship in which healing can occur.

For struggling adolescents, the best conditions for growth occur when they (1) feel they are accepted unconditionally; (2) feel they are with one who is trustworthy and real; and (3) feel they are deeply understood.

NECESSARY BUT NOT SUFFICIENT

Although these three traits are critical for effective helping, they do not assure success. They are necessary but not sufficient. Persons who possess these qualities will still vary in their effectiveness to truly help. For instance, crucial to effectual parenting is the practice of active listening, which I describe in the next chapter. A second important factor is a working knowledge of when and how to use practical techniques that have proved helpful in alleviating specific struggles. Part Two provides many of the practical components often overlooked when it comes to helping teenagers with specific problems.

Beware of excessive emphasis on techniques. This book is not a box of gimmicks and quick fixes. The methods and techniques recommended in this book must be enhanced by a parent's warmth, genuineness, and empathy. The result will be meaningful expressions of love for your child.

Notes

1. L. Parrott, *Counseling and Psychotherapy* (New York: McGraw-Hill, 1997), 24.

2. C. R. Rogers, G. T. Gendlin, D. V. Kiesler, and C. B. Traus, *The Therapeutic Relationship and Its Impact* (Madison: University of Wisconsin Press, 1967).

3. This self-inventory was designed by the author to provide a quick and rough estimate of a person's helping traits.

4. G. Collins, *Christian Counseling: A Comprehensive Guide, Revised Edition* (Waco, Tex.: Word, 1988), 24–25.

3

THE HEART OF HELPING

John, thirteen, confessed to his mother that he was having difficulty at school and wouldn't do his homework.

> JOHN: I don't care what they do to me. I'm not going to do another assignment.
> MOM: [With great concern] Do you know you can't graduate if you don't do your homework?
> JOHN: I don't care.
> MOM: [In a compassionate tone] I bet you'll care when you start looking for a job.
> JOHN: Big deal.
> MOM: [Desperately wanting to help] It is a big deal. It will affect the rest of your life.
> JOHN: I don't care.

This endless circle of conversation does not move John one inch closer to doing homework, and it does next to nothing to build a therapeutic relationship. The parent is rational and is obviously concerned. Why isn't it working?

The missing component is the most important and fundamental skill required for a successful helping relationship—active listening. Adolescents do not readily lay out their thoughts and feelings even for a compassionate parent. Mothers and fathers who build a helpful relationship with adolescents do it the old-fashioned way: They earn it. An adolescent's real concerns are often closed off and opened only by continued and careful listening. Like a safe-cracker, a parent who listens with skill can spin off the combination that gets through the door of silent pain. "The road to the heart," wrote Voltaire, "is the ear." Look at this brief interaction again with a parent who is hearing more than just words.

> JOHN: I don't care what they do to me. I'm not going to do another assignment.
> MOM: Sounds as if you've made up your mind.
> JOHN: Yep. Those teachers are idiots, especially Mr. Wilson.
> MOM: They're not too smart, huh?
> JOHN: Well, I'm sure they're smart and everything, but they aren't very nice.
> MOM: They're kind of mean?
> JOHN: Yeah. The last time I handed in my paper, Wilson read it aloud. I didn't write that for the whole world to hear.

Like marriage, a helping relationship can be for better or it can be for worse. Artful listening determines the difference.

LISTENING IS THE HEART OF HELPING

Aristotle observed that while an injury to the head can make one unconscious, a wound to the heart is invariably fatal. Active listening—listening with "the third ear" as Theodore Reik called it—is the heart of helping. It is vital to the life of a helping relationship. Without active listening compassion dies.

Jesus understood the importance of listening. Even as a young boy he was sitting with the teachers in the temple, "listening to them and asking them questions [and] everyone . . . was amazed at his understanding" (Luke 2:46–47). The apostle Paul understood that listening requires diligent work. When he was before Agrippa, he said, "I beg you to listen to me patiently" (Acts 26:3). The book of James tells us to "be quick to listen, slow to speak" (James 1:19). And the book of Proverbs says, "He who answers before listening—that is his folly and his shame" (Proverbs 18:13). The word *listen* occurs more than two hundred times in the Bible.

Two major ingredients go into active listening: reflection and clarification.

Active Listening Requires Reflection

Understanding comes through empathic reflection—responding sensitively to the emotional rather than the semantic meaning of a person's expression. Jesus responded on the basis of what he "heard" people *feeling*. After a short exchange, Nathanael declared Jesus to be the Son of God. Jesus reflected Nathanael's meaning and said, "You believe because I told you I saw you under the fig tree" (John 1:50; see vv. 43–51).

Active listening does not mean saying, "I understand." A classic cartoon shows an exasperated teenager telling her mother, "For Pete's sake, will you stop understanding me and just listen?"

Many believe that sincerity assures understanding. But sincerity ignores the fact that we communicate in ways that severely limit our ability to get our real messages across. Between what a person intends to communicate and what others hear stands an unavoidable filter of preconception. "I'm not going to do another assignment" may mean "I was terribly embarrassed by Mr. Wilson for reading my assignment to the whole class." "I won't go" may mean "I don't want to go." Or "Do you really think so?" may mean "I disagree."

The goal is to target one of three aspects of a message in your reflections: (1) the content of the message, (2) the thinking behind the message, and (3) the feeling behind the message. Each is equally valid and useful. Here is an example of how a single statement may be reflected at each level.

> ADOLESCENT: I couldn't believe he was accusing me for what *he* did.
>
> PARENT: [Reflecting content] He blamed you.
>
> ADOLESCENT: Yeah. He said I was the one responsible because I was there.
>
> PARENT: [Reflecting thinking] You thought he was unfair.
>
> ADOLESCENT: Yeah. I didn't deserve to be blamed.
>
> PARENT: [Reflecting feeling] It must have made you angry.
>
> ADOLESCENT: I was furious. I also felt bad.

By reflecting the content of the message, parents allow adolescents to elaborate further on what happened. By reflecting the thinking behind the message, parents allow adolescents to understand their evaluation of what happened. And by reflecting the feeling behind the message, parents invite adolescents to become aware of emotions resulting from what happened. Here are more examples.

> ADOLESCENT: [Sitting down, looking at the floor, hunched over, and silent]
>
> PARENT: [Reflecting content] You've had a bad day.
>
> ADOLESCENT: My coach wouldn't let me play today.
>
> PARENT: [Reflecting thinking] I wonder whether you would rather be left alone.
>
> ADOLESCENT: No, I just wish my coach had treated me better.
>
> PARENT: [Reflecting feeling] Looks as if you don't feel so good.
>
> ADOLESCENT: I guess I'm mad at the coach.

By reflecting the content, thinking, or feeling of a struggling adolescent, we are not evaluating or advising. We are saying, "I am with you and want to understand you better." Here is another example:

> ADOLESCENT: I got accepted to all three schools!
>
> PARENT: [Reflecting content] You got just what you wanted.
>
> ADOLESCENT: Yeah, every one of them sent me a letter.
>
> PARENT: [Reflecting thinking] Your hard work really paid off.
>
> ADOLESCENT: Yeah, I guess I didn't need to worry the way I did.
>
> PARENT: [Reflecting feeling] You got just what you wanted. You must be happy.
>
> ADOLESCENT: I've never been so relieved. I feel great.

However, reflecting comments can be overdone. Eager to build rapport with an adolescent, sometimes parents reflect everything that rolls across the kid's tongue. Continual "uh-huhs" and constantly nodding or parroting a young person's comments interfere at best, and may show superficiality and insincerity at worst. Go easy.

Active Listening Requires Clarification

```
Love
isnowhere
```

How do you read the two lines above? Some see "Love is no where." Others read "Love is now here." In the same way, we may see an entirely different meaning from the one the adolescent intends.

When absurd misunderstandings happened between Abbott and Costello, the famous comedy team, the whole nation chuckled. But in a helping relationship, being misunderstood is no laughing matter. Misunderstanding does not result from not hearing the words but from our not clarifying the meaning of the words. The five hundred most commonly used words in the English language carry over fourteen hundred different meanings—an average of nearly three meanings for each word!

In addition, some adolescents have personalized meanings for the words they use. I once heard an adolescent say he was "bailin' for a loc fiesta that's fully amped with no ancients." Translation: he was leaving for an exciting neighborhood party with no adults. Here are some more examples: *da bomb* means the greatest, *all that* means "all that much," *air out* means to leave somewhere and walk somewhere else (locomotion by legs), *ace* is a term for main man or good friend, *boogler* means any individual who is a party animal, *bunked* means somewhere between lightly drunk and buzzed off of alcohol, *crib* means one's house or place of residence, *Daddy-O* is a name exchanged between friends for bonding purposes, *dope* means great or very cool, *faded* or *damaged* means to be inebriated to the point of mental lapse, to *give lip* means to back talk, *kick it* means to relax, *phat* means great or very cool. No wonder clarification is necessary!

Clarification serves two basic purposes: (1) to gather additional information; and (2) to help explore an issue more thoroughly—to discover, for example, whether a problem is a greater concern to the adolescent or to you.

One obvious point: Clarification is necessary when you are not sure you heard correctly. Another cartoon says it beautifully: A king in the backseat of his Rolls-Royce is being carried by a group of longhaired guys with no shoes. He leans out the window and says, "I said 'radials,' not 'radicals'!"

An Exercise in Active Listening

Important feelings are often hidden behind the words of a struggling adolescent. Reflecting an adolescent's feelings is

one of the most helpful and difficult listening techniques to implement. Following are some typical adolescent statements. Read each separately, listening for feelings. Make note of the feeling you hear and write a response that reflects the feeling of each statement.

1. I practice all the time, but it doesn't make any difference.
2. Every girl has a date but me.
3. I shouldn't have slammed the door, but she shouldn't have said that.
4. I should be able to stay out past midnight if I want. Jim does.
5. Do you think I did the right thing?
6. I'd like to punch his lights out!
7. I don't want to talk about it anymore.
8. What's the use?
9. What if she laughs at me? I'm not going to ask her.
10. I don't feel anything about it.

Compare your list of reflective statements with those listed below to see how accurately you recognize feelings. Give yourself a *2* on items where your choice matches closely, a *1* on items where your choice only partially matches, and a *0* if you missed altogether.

How you rate on recognizing adolescents' feelings:

16–20   Above average recognition of feelings

11–15   Average recognition of feelings

0–10   Below average recognition of feelings

Possible Responses to the Exercise in Active Listening

1. I practice all the time, but it doesn't make any difference.—*Sounds as if you feel discouraged.*
2. Every other girl has a date but me.—*It feels as if you got left out.*
3. I shouldn't have slammed the door, but she shouldn't have said that.—*You feel kind of guilty but, at the same time, justified for what you did.*

4. I should be able to stay out past midnight if I want. Jim does.—*I wonder if you feel that we are being overly protective.*

5. Do you think I did the right thing?—*It sounds as if you're not very sure of yourself.*

6. I'd like to punch his lights out!—*You must be really angry.*

7. I don't want to talk about it anymore.—*It sounds as if you're feeling overloaded, as if it is all just too much.*

8. What's the use?—*As you say that, I get a picture of a guy who is discouraged and is crying uncle.*

9. What if she laughs at me? I'm not going to ask her.—*I get the sense that you're a little afraid and that your mind is made up.*

10. I don't feel anything about it.—*I'm wondering whether you have some idea of what you should be feeling and because you do not, you register it as not feeling anything.*

WHAT ACTIVE LISTENING DOES

Listening Unearths Hidden Feelings

Active listening allows teenagers' hidden feelings to percolate to the top. Struggling adolescents do not often broadcast their pain. They want someone to sense their hurt without their having to admit it. The cry of fear, for example, sometimes hides behind a fuming face. Pain is sometimes muted by wordy anger. And depression may lurk behind a stiff smile.

To help adolescents, a parent needs a sensitive internal seismograph to feel the tremors beneath the external calm. In effect, that is what active listening is—a way to sense the quaking of adolescence. If we have a hunch that Brian, a fourteen-year-old, is not so apathetic as he seems but actually angry because he didn't make the team, we don't blurt out, "You are denying how angry you really are." Instead we may probe gently: "I get the feeling you're angry and you aren't sure that's okay." A statement like this allows Brian to own his buried anger without losing face.

Listening Takes Away the Fear of Feeling

Free from evaluation, active listening creates a safe environment. It provides a place where trembling adolescents may shed defenses and own up to previously feared emotions—and know that their feelings are acceptable. When adolescents are guarded, it is as if they are pressing the accelerator all the way to the floor but keeping the car in neutral and a foot on the brake—using valuable fuel and going nowhere. Parents' active listening gives struggling adolescents new energy and helps them begin to move in positive directions.

Listening Helps Adolescents Be Their Own Counselors

Parenting isn't rescuing. Too often we mistake help with throwing out a line of advice. The problem with solving people's problems is that external solutions foster unhealthful dependence. If you solve a problem for a young person who comes back with a similar problem the next week, you put out the same fire over and over. When we listen to another person, we are saying, "I believe in you." But giving advice says, "I don't trust you to come up with your own solution." Active listening boosts the confidence of struggling adolescents and teaches them to depend on God and themselves for problem solving.

Listening Facilitates True Learning

The only people who really want somebody else to change them are wet babies. The goal of helping is not to change people. It is to provide a relationship in which persons learn to change themselves—a relationship in which people mature.

True learning, the kind that significantly influences behavior, for the most part is self-discovered. And active listening helps struggling adolescents to discover how they can best cope with their situations. Active listening generates the principle of participation: People are motivated to act or follow through on decisions they have had a part in making. The motivation to act on advice that has been imposed is minimal at best.

TWO COMMON MISTAKES IN ACTIVE LISTENING

In *The Healing Heart*, Norman Cousins reports that medical students usually score higher on measures of empathy when they are entering medical school than they do upon graduation.[1] Somewhere in the process of learning medicine, they shift their focus away from the patient and look solely at the disease. As a result, Cousins believes, many medical students have become superbly trained but poorly educated. Parents may fall into the same trap. We may become so overly confident of our ability to listen that we lose interest in practicing it. Or we may work so diligently at being sophisticated listeners that we miss what is most evident. To be effective in the art of listening, parents must not lose their desire or their ear for the obvious.

Desire to Listen

Since most people talk at the rate of 120 words per minute, and since most spoken material can be comprehended equally well at rates up to 250 words per minute, plenty of extra time is available for mental activity.[2] This means that parents have at least two options: We may use our surplus time for deepening our comprehension of the message, or we may wonder what we are going to have for dinner. If we are to remain effective in understanding struggling adolescents, we must maintain a genuine desire to listen. A lack of desire may be a symptom of burnout.

Useful Leads for the Active Listener

It sounds as if you're feeling . . .   It seems as if . . .

I get a picture of . . .   What I hear you saying is . . .

Could it be that . . .   It must have been . . .

I wonder if you're thinking . . .   You must feel . . .

An Ear for the Obvious

While active listening requires an eye for subtleties, it doesn't neglect the obvious—"the last thing a fish will discover is water." In our search for the hidden emotion, we sometimes lose sight of the most visible.

Harold Kushner tells a story that illustrates this point.[3] A factory was having problems with employee theft. Every day, it seemed, somebody stole a valuable item. So the plant hired a security guard to search each employee as he left the building. Most men carried only a lunch pail. But every day one man took out a wheelbarrow filled with trash, which the exasperated security guard had to dig through to determine whether the employee was making off with anything of value. The guard never found anything in the trash, but one day he couldn't stand it any longer. "Look," he howled, "I know you're up to something, but I can never find anything worth stealing in all that trash you carry out. It's driving me crazy. Just tell me what it is and I promise not to report you." The man shrugged and said, "Wheelbarrows. I'm taking wheelbarrows."

WHY ADVICE TURNS SOUR

Too often advice cuts the heart out of helping. A little advice, like a little garlic, goes a long way. The following reminders may help you keep from overdoing it.

Advice Is Often Self-Centered

When we dole out advice before we have truly actively listened, we may believe we are being skillfully helpful. After all, isn't it the loving thing to relieve adolescents of suffering by helping them see the light? Actually, attempts to change adolescents by giving advice is not only naïve and ineffective but often self-serving. It hurts to see adolescents struggle with psychic pain, so by doing our part—giving advice—we feel better. The driving motivation behind the practice is often a desire to feel good about oneself. Don't be surprised by the chaos that results from self-serving advice.

Advice May Make Young People Feel Worse

Offering advice may set young people up to feel worse because they cannot or are not ready to follow through on it. This may instill terrible pangs of guilt. The advice that Job's friends gave him in his time of affliction, for example, served only to make poor Job more miserable. The only way a parent can know when and whether an adolescent is ready for advice is through persistent and sensitive listening.

Advice May Be Threatening

Sometimes giving advice may call a kid's beliefs and attitudes into question. This practice may reflect a parent's insecurity and uncertainty regarding his or her own beliefs. It is uncomfortable for us to be uncertain of our own values on certain issues. So, we reason, if we convert adolescents to our way of thinking, our discomfort is relieved, and we have reinforced the validity of our convictions. Further, we have once again proved that we are all-knowing parents. This is much easier than putting ourselves out in an effort to understand adolescent perspectives.

Advice May Be Boring

Being forced to sit through an unrewarding or even irritating monologue causes people to turn off the one-sided "conversation" and put their minds on something else. Bored listeners simply suppress impulses to walk out by taking a mental vacation and sitting it out. They may feel like the bored youngster in church who said to his mom, "Pay the man and let's go home." Advice given without active listening causes boredom. And as Proverbs 18:13 says, advice without listening is the advice giver's "folly and his shame."

Advice May Be Costly

Advice is effective only when it fulfills the salient needs of the listener. Too often, advice is given without considering how the person will feel about it. Those who give advice without listening enjoy the luxury of an opinion without the labor of a thought.

Because a parent is ready to give advice does not mean a young person is ready to receive it. Trigger-happy advice is costly. When the price of listening to advice outweighs any gain from it, all of us turn it off. Upon hearing advice that is not given out of active listening, a teenager may say, "I don't want to talk about it anymore!" Even good advice isn't worth that price.

The point is obvious. It is difficult to make a mistake with active listening, but advice and recommendations may clog the flow of genuine feelings. Or, to put it another way, active listening will nearly always help a person clear out the clutter.

MAKING ADVICE HELPFUL

Carl Jung, the pioneering psychologist, said that advice seldom hurts any of us because we so rarely take it seriously. That may be true, but there are ways to help people take good advice to heart. The key is knowing when and how to give it. The Bible states, "Let your conversation be always full of grace, seasoned with salt, so that you may know how to answer everyone" (Colossians 4:6).

By now it should be clear that advice will usually backfire if the parent has not earned—through active listening—the right to give it. Before giving advice, a parent must understand what the struggling adolescent is really needing. Philosophers have always said it is more important to find someone who knows what the question is than it is to find someone who knows a pat answer to a question. The same holds true in helping. Listening is not icing on the cake; it *is* the cake.

With the importance of listening in mind, here are some specific ways to minimize the possible negative consequences of giving advice to adolescents, *even when it is appropriate to do so.*

- Advice is heard best by a person who is calm and rational. When a person is drowning, it is not a good time to try to teach him to swim.

- Help adolescents to give the advice themselves. It is sometimes help-ful to say, "What would you tell someone in your predicament?"
- Advice will have more impact if it is not given routinely. Like a telegram from Western Union, infrequent advice will stand out in importance.
- Ask what they hear you saying. Ask them to state in their own words what you have said.
- If the young person does not understand or accept the advice, don't push it. A parent I know has a plaque in her home that reads, "Lord, fill my mouth with good stuff, and nudge me when I've said enough."

Notes

1. N. Cousins, *The Healing Heart: Antidotes to Panic and Helplessness* (New York: Norton, 1983), 26.

2. E. Foulke, "Listening Comprehension as a Function of Word Rate," *Journal of Communication* 18 (1968): 198.

3. H. Kushner, *When All You've Ever Wanted Isn't Enough: The Search for a Life That Matters* (New York: Summit Books, 1986), 152.

4

COMMON PITFALLS IN HELPING ADOLESCENTS

A promising junior executive at IBM was involved in a risky venture for the company and managed to lose more than $10,000,000. The results were disastrous. When IBM's founder and president, Tom Watson, called the nervous executive into his office, the young man blurted, "I guess you want my resignation?" Watson said, "You can't be serious. We've just spent ten million dollars educating you!"

Fortunately, most mistakes are not as costly as the one this young executive made. And most companies can't absorb ten-million-dollar mistakes. But when it comes to helping teenagers, every error has the potential for devastating results. We are not doomed to repeat mistakes, however. We can learn to avoid the pitfalls others have encountered.[1]

This chapter is designed to help you sidestep some of the most common pitfalls in helping teenagers. It is not meant to serve as an exhaustive listing of blunders. Nor is it a catalog of the worst possible errors. Rather, this list is representative of some of the most common mistakes made when helping adolescents.

PREMATURE PROBLEM SOLVING

Trying to solve a young person's problem before the problem is fully understood is a common mistake.[2] It takes patience and time to unwrap the salient features of a teenager's problem. Like a complex jigsaw puzzle with hundreds of interlocking pieces, a young person's struggle cannot be solved in a matter of minutes.

Consider a counseling situation where even a trained professional can easily make this mistake. Tracy, a high school senior with a 3.8 GPA, who says, "I'm really depressed, and I think it's because I bombed my English midterm." Her counselor checks out her symptoms and quickly recognizes that her self-assessment seems accurate. Tracy expects to receive high marks, and failing an important exam is traumatic for her. Her counselor wonders whether the expectations Tracy holds for her academic performance are unrealistic. The counselor gently searches, asking questions that may or may not enforce his hypothesis. Tracy admits she is impatient with herself and wants to be valedictorian. The counselor seems to have nailed the problem squarely on the head and is ready to dispute her unrealistic self-talk. The counselor spends five sessions trying to whittle away at Tracy's overachieving standards and believes he is making progress. Then he receives a message on his answering machine from one of Tracy's concerned friends, saying, "I know I probably shouldn't be calling you, but I was afraid that Tracy hadn't told you she's bulimic." All of a sudden, the counselor's "overachieving theory" seems silly.

An effective helper never jumps to conclusions. It is not easy to zero in on key issues quickly. Effective counselors—and parents—are continually asking themselves, "Is there something else I may be missing?"

FEAR OF SILENCE

Parents are often afraid of silence. We feel a need to fill in the quiet gaps of communication. Silence, however, is not a signal that the parent needs to say something. Silence is not a sign of doing something wrong. When you see the adolescent's wheels of thought and feeling turning, allow the process to happen without interruption. If a parent is feeling nervous about silence, the results can be damaging. Interrupting young people before they have finished talking, cutting off productive thought, missing what they are actually saying because you are mentally rehearsing what to say next, and so on, can all result from trying to avoid moments of silence.[3]

INTERROGATING

Some parents rely too much on asking questions—lots of questions. Learn to refrain from subjecting your child to an ongoing barrage of inquiries. Excessive probing can push a young person toward feeling "on the spot" or beleaguered. The result can be a superficial defensiveness. Information can be obtained without interrogation. For example, suppose a teenager says, "My coach was angry at me for most of the afternoon." A natural line of questioning would be...

"How often does your coach become angry?"

"What does he do when he is angry?"

"How does that make you feel?"

You can obtain much of this information and more by saying something like, "I get the impression you have experienced your coach's anger more than once." A statement like this lets your child know he or she is understood and invites further disclosure without the risk of putting him or her on the spot.

The skilled parent can elicit information without a long list of questions. Actively trying to understand the teenager's experience helps him or her feel less defensive, and important information will become more readily available.

IMPATIENCE

All parents of struggling teenagers watch carefully for signs of progress. We want to see our children improve—the sooner, the better. A parent who is eager for this to happen, however, may subtly push unprepared teens into behavior before the time is right. Gradual change is not a reflection of poor parenting. A child's readiness for genuine renewal or transformation takes time. A young person who is grieving the loss of a loved one, for example, cannot be forced to "snap out of it." A teenager struggling with an eating disorder cannot be expected to change her exercise and eating patterns radically over the course of a couple of weeks.

Young people who are rushed into making rapid changes will be set up for further failure. Being "forced" to do something they are not adequately prepared for may result in extreme defensiveness or regression. Parents must be sensitive to issues of personal impatience. Most young people cannot and will not make dramatic changes quickly.

RELUCTANCE TO SEEK HELP

Some parents feel they are failing if they cannot meet the needs of their own children. No parent, however, is really expected to go it alone. Referral to a competent counselor is a part of being a good parent to a teenager in need. This may mean joining in the therapeutic process yourself. Each of the thirty-six "struggle" chapters in Part Two contains specific information on when you should refer to a counselor for help.

CONCLUSION

Fear of failure is one of the greatest obstacles parents face. All parents, regardless of experience and training, make mistakes. Even parenting "experts" are not immune to blunders. And no one expects you to be a "perfect" parent. So give yourself permission to make mistakes, learn from them, and don't give up.

The inventive genius Thomas Edison was faced one day with two dejected assistants, who told him, "We have just completed our seven hundredth experiment, and we still don't have a light bulb. We have failed."

"We haven't failed," said Edison. "We have made progress. Now we know seven hundred things not to do. We are becoming experts." Edison then told his colleagues, "With each 'mistake,' we are one step closer to reaching our goal."

Edison's wisdom makes sense in learning how to parent a struggling adolescent. It is hoped that you will avoid the mistakes summarized in this chapter and will journey closer to the quality of effectiveness.

Notes

1. E. Gambrill, *Critical Thinking in Clinical Practice: Improving the Accuracy of Judgments and Decisions about Clients* (San Francisco: Jossey-Bass, 1990).

2. A. Combs, "What Makes a Good Helper," *Person-Centered Review* 1 (1986): 51–61.

3. J. Brams, "Counselor Characteristics and Effective Communication in Counseling," *Journal of Counseling Psychology* 8 (1961): 25–30.

5

A Parent's Guide to Professional Help

Research indicates that adolescents often go first to parents when they are struggling. Mom and dad rank higher than peers, relatives, pastors, teachers, or counselors as resources for advice or help. Research also suggests that when parents are concerned about a serious problem in their adolescent children, they are most likely to turn to their extended family for advice. A trained counselor is consulted only after a number of repeated failures. This book will help parents know how to help more effectively and when to take that next step.

A growing body of evidence indicates that parents, with a little guidance from professionals, can successfully help resolve a number of struggles for their adolescents. For example, with help parents can deal with anger control, critical attitudes, God's will, grief, guilt, loneliness, peer pressure, school work, sibling rivalry, and spiritual doubt. Unfortunately, parents do not receive a great deal of useful information from scientific literature or even from the experiences of other parents. This book attempts to help bridge that gap.

However, parents with even the noblest of intentions must understand that many specific problems must be treated by trained professionals. Adolescents who struggle with abuse, severe depression, suicide, eating disorders, panic attacks, phobias, schizophrenia, and sleep disorders need professional help. While some helping techniques for these problems may be useful for parents to apply, effective treatment requires an objective clinician.

Parents should seek the services of trained mental health professionals in such clear cases or when little or no progress is being made in other problem areas. This chapter provides a checklist to help you decide whether professional help is needed. You will also find help in selecting a counselor or psychotherapist. In spite of the continuing stigma of psychological treatment and the belief that families should be able to solve their personal problems without outside help—especially in evangelical circles—mental health professionals can be of great value in preparing adolescents to realize in their lives the power of the Gospel and the healing comfort of the Holy Spirit.

WHEN IS PROFESSIONAL HELP NEEDED?

Nailing down what is normal in adolescence is like trying to nail gelatin to the wall. In general, the shift from "normal" to "abnormal" occurs when teens' behavior begins to interfere with their ability to carry out daily routines or sustain relationships.

The following questions may help you decide whether your teenager is going through a harmless phase or is suffering from a serious problem. If you answer yes to any of these questions, your child needs assessment and professional help as soon as possible.

- Is your teen silent for long periods and often withdrawn socially, having few friends?
- Is your teen considering dropping out or in danger of not completing high school? Failing classes?
- Is your teen obsessed with exercise and diet? Does your teen have an eating disorder?
- Does your teen practice any form of self-mutilation in the form of teeth marks, cuts, or burns? Does he wear homemade tattoos?
- Is your teen involved in any kind of illegal activity? Has she been arrested or in trouble with the law?
- Does your teen show an excessive fear of a particular family member, other relative, or family friend? Could she have been sexually abused and fears to talk about it?
- Does your teen have long periods of feeling worthless, helpless, guilty, or lethargic? Does he suffer from depression?
- Is your home life in chaos because of your teen? Is your well-being or performance at work suffering because of your teen's problems?
- Does your teen show a strong interest in the occult? Does she read about black magic or is she involved in anti-religious activities?
- Does your teen blow up with anger and get into fights a great deal? Has he been involved in vandalism? Is he a threat to someone's physical well-being?
- Are you concerned that your teen may be sexually promiscuous? Is she risking venereal disease, pregnancy, or AIDS?

- Does your teen report hearing voices that others do not hear? Does he hallucinate or is he out of touch with reality?
- Is your teen having serious problems with sleep, such as insomnia, repeated wakefulness at night, frequent nightmares, or sleeping too much?
- Does your teen have morbid thoughts, talk about death a lot? Is she suicidal?
- Does your teen run with a peer group that violates the rights of others? Do you have reason to suspect that he is involved in illegal activities or destructive acts?
- Does your teen get drunk? Does she drive while drinking? Is your teen experimenting with drugs that can kill?
- Does your teen experience relatively brief periods of intense anxiety? Does he suffer from panic attacks?

HOW TO SELECT A MENTAL HEALTH OR FAMILY PROFESSIONAL

If you answered yes to any of the above questions, you have no doubt tried many things to help your struggling child. Perhaps you have talked with a trusted friend who has gone through a similar experience with a young person. Maybe you have read a reputable book on the problem or consulted a teacher, guidance counselor, physician, or minister. These are all excellent resources, but when the problem becomes serious it is time to call a professional psychotherapist. That decision can be scary. It's not easy to tell a stranger that all is not well in your home. If you are like most parents, you're not comfortable subjecting your child-rearing skills to professional scrutiny.

The following information is designed to help you become an informed consumer of psychological services. While these suggestions may not reduce all of your fears, they may bolster your confidence and enable you to get the best help possible for your teenager.

The first item of importance in selecting a psychotherapist is to know the different kinds of qualified professionals. An old joke among practitioners asks, "What's the difference between a psychologist and a psychiatrist?" The answer: "About fifty dollars an hour." There are a number of different kinds of professionals who provide a wide variety of psychological services today, and the differences go far beyond the fees they charge.

Unfortunately, many states allow almost anyone to put out a shingle and label himself a therapist. This term, however, indicates nothing about the person's education and experience. People seeking therapy should never be shy about asking helping professionals about their credentials. Here are some of the professions genuinely qualified to help:

Clinical psychologists have received Ph.D. or Psy.D. degrees after five or six years of graduate study. They are specialists in diagnosing and treating mental illness. They also do personality and intelligence testing.

Counseling psychologists usually have degrees in education, such as an Ed.D. They frequently work in school settings and specialize in academic, vocational, marriage, and family counseling.

Psychiatrists hold M.D. degrees and have taken postgraduate training in psychiatry. They can prescribe medication for mental, emotional, and behavioral problems.

Marriage and family therapists usually hold M.A. degrees and generally specialize in overcoming relational difficulties.

Psychiatric social workers usually have earned M.S.W. (Master of Social Work) degrees or D.S.W. (Doctor of Social Work). Like counselors, many specialize in marital or family problems of adjustment.

Finding the right mental health professional cannot be done hastily, nor can the choice be made at random. And the decision should not be based solely on professional training. Making the right choice also requires careful consideration and cooperation between you and your teen. As much as possible, strive to choose a therapist *with* your teen, not *for* your teen.

The first step in choosing a therapist is to have a knowledgeable source of information. One of the best sources is people in the helping professions. Physicians, ministers, nurses, and teachers can often provide excellent referrals. Other informational sources include hospitals, community service societies, referral services, and local professional societies. Their information, however, is usually less candid and thus less helpful. Little can be told about the skills and training from a therapist's phone listing, but the yellow pages of the telephone directory do provide another source of information. If you are especially concerned that the therapist be sympathetic to Christian values and beliefs, several good referral sources can help you. Each of them has a referral base of professional men and women who are committed to Christ-centered psychotherapy:

American Association of Christian Counselors 800-526-8673
Christian Association for Psychological Studies 714-337-5117
Focus on the Family 719-531-3400
New Life Treatment Centers 800-332-8336
Rapha 800-227-2657

Once you have two or three good referrals, the next step is to find out which therapist in your area is the best match for your teen. One way of gathering information concerning a particular professional is to talk with a person who has been in treatment with that therapist. While this is desirable, it is not always possible. I recommend a preliminary phone contact with the therapist followed by an in-person interview before you and your adolescent make a final decision.

Both you and your teenager must feel comfortable before committing to therapy. Ask therapists about several issues before entrusting adolescents to their care. Here are some questions to ask.

- Are they licensed?
- Do they work with adolescents on a regular basis?
- What are their credentials?
- At what university did they earn them?
- What professional associations are they accountable to?
- How will they approach your adolescent's particular problem?
- May clients call them between sessions?
- What do they expect of you regarding their treatment?
- How long do they expect treatment to take?

In the end you will have to follow your instincts by asking yourself whether you and your child like the person. Does he seem understanding, and would your teen feel comfortable confiding in him?

Another important concern, of course, is money. How much will therapy cost? Ask the therapist about the fee structure. The average fee for treatment varies depending upon where you live and the credentials of the professional. In major metropolitan cities some psychologists charge as much as $150 an hour. In other areas the same type of therapy may be $40. You should also ask whether the therapist accepts insurance. Your insurance may or may not cover psychological services. Policies vary greatly. Many policies pay nothing at all, and others may pay the entire fee. Call your insurance company to find out what your policy covers.

How do you know whether therapy is working? By definition, "successful" therapy helps the person to achieve better adjustment. Thus, a reasonable expectation is improvement, not "cure." For example, if a teen struggles with panic attacks, the long-range goal would, of course, be the elimination of the attacks. Therapy, however, is working if frequency and intensity of attacks are decreasing. Evaluate the effectiveness of your child's therapy based on short-range goals. Therapy should end either when the goals have been completely achieved or when, over time, there has been no progress toward the achievement of goals.

One final word of advice. Growing up often hurts, but sometimes being a good parent can hurt too. Even the best of homes have children with emotional problems, drug dependencies, eating disorders, and other struggles. Do not feel guilty because your teenager needs professional help. Do not blame yourself for your adolescent's struggles, and do not neglect your own needs. Do not punish yourself for perceived inadequacies. Seek help from a professional or join a parents' support group, and your entire family will benefit.

PART TWO

The Struggles of Adolescents

ABUSE

☑ WHAT THE STRUGGLE LOOKS LIKE

A horrifying number of adolescents are abused—physically, sexually, or emotionally—by their parents, stepparents, relatives, friends of the family, or others. Each year at least 10 percent of young people are reported to have been physically abused by their parents, and another 10 percent are reported to be sexually abused. These alarming numbers are considered gross underestimates of the actual situation.[1] In addition, researchers are now finding that increasing numbers of adolescents are becoming traumatized through exposure to abusive situations that do not target them personally (whether it be in the family or in the community).[2]

Abuse may come from either parent and may be directed at one or more children, often in a repeated pattern. Physical abuse is typically accompanied by abusive language and humiliating punishment that may not be physical.[3]

Major physical injuries resulting from abuse are most frequently seen in very young children (under three years of age) and early adolescents (twelve to sixteen years old). The younger the age of child when the abuse started and the coercion by the adult to maintain secrecy is predictive of greater long-term trauma and post traumatic stress.[4] The number of male and female victims of physical abuse is about equal.[5] Sexual abuse, however, occurs more frequently with female victims.[6]

If the abuse is recent, the signs may be obvious: bruises, scars, burns, or lethargy. Most of the time, however, the damage is not so visible. No single reaction characterizes abused young people. Their reactions can manifest themselves as aggressive behavior, depression, lack of empathy toward others, inability to trust anyone, helplessness, perfectionism, overeagerness to please others, excessive involvement in school or church activities, a decline in school performance, or even prostitution.[7]

Case Description

Melody, seventeen, is an only child of divorced parents. She was referred for counseling after being in inpatient psychiatric treatment for a suicide attempt. After about six sessions of outpatient care, Melody began to feel more comfortable with her therapist and to unravel her past. She confessed that her depression and suicidal thoughts were over a fear that she would never have a happy marriage. Upon gentle inquiry from her therapist she began to cry. "I have never told anyone this. . ." she began.

For the first time Melody confessed her gruesome story. When she was eight years old she was sexually abused several times by the landlord of the apartment complex where she lived. Occasionally, when her mother was going to be working late, she asked the landlord to let Melody into the apartment. The landlord would wait behind the screen door of Melody's apartment when she arrived from school. He would tell her he had a snack for her in the kitchen. It was there he sexually abused her. Until now she had never told a soul. Melody sobbed, "I can still see him standing above me by the kitchen table."

✔ WHY THE STRUGGLE HAPPENS

It would be wonderful if abusiveness could be attributed to a genetic flaw or a wild hormone. It can't. It almost seems that the more we attempt to discover clear causes through research, the cloudier the issue becomes. Patterns of behavior and personality profiles are not consistent. Seemingly reasonable individuals, not just psychopaths or perverts, commit violent abuse. Questions still outweigh answers by a long shot when it comes to the causes of abuse.

The ultimate irony is that abuse may be the biggest cause and effect of abuse. Children who have been abused often become adults who abuse their children, a vicious cycle. Among abusing parents, 30 to 60 percent say they were abused as children. The exact manner in which this cycle is created varies from one case to another, but the child often receives messages that abuse is necessary and productive and that children are powerless possessions of parents.[8] Of course the overarching message is of their worthlessness, else they would not be treated so.

✔ HOW PARENTS CAN HELP

The following strategies for helping an adolescent struggling with abuse can be used effectively by parents; however, every parent-child relationship is unique, and some of them may be more pertinent to your situation than others. As with every significant adolescent struggle, it is best for parents to work alongside a competent counselor. With this in mind, the following is offered as a way to help you facilitate the healing process at home with your teenager.

Make Clear Philosophical Assumptions

Abuse tests the limits of our ability to be objective in helping hurting adolescents. For this reason, helping strategies designed for teens who are struggling with abuse require a solid undergirding of explicit philosophical assumptions. First, you must assume that the problem is treatable and that the young person will become a survivor. Second, assume that he or she is not responsible for the abuse (they are responsible only for their recovery). And third, assume the young person's expression and acceptance of feelings are necessary. These assumptions help insure a more effective recovery.[9]

Be Informed About False Memories

It is difficult these days to explore abuse issues and not run into "false memory syndrome." This is a pattern of memories for traumatic events, usually sexual or ritual abuse, that did not occur but are regarded as real by the person.[10] The existence of such an unofficial syndrome is highly debated and is the subject of a great deal of public, legal, and professional discussion. Proponents of the false memory syndrome assert that the retrieval of these memories is induced by therapists who have a vested interest in manipulating their clients into retrieving such memories. Opponents who doubt the existence of a false memory syndrome assert that many guilty parties will use this syndrome to hide or deny their guilt. It would take more space than is permitted here to compare and contrast arguments for both sides of this controversial issue. It is safe to say that the final answer on this issue is not clear.[11]

Be Alert to Suicidal Risk

It is not unusual for an abused adolescent to say, "I'm the cause of all these problems." The guilt and betrayal most victims experience is so intense that parents and counselors alike must assume that a high suicide risk exists in every case.[12] Statements such as "they would be better off without me" should be taken seriously. To ease their self-blame, let victims know that their feelings are acceptable and normal. Consult the section on suicide.

Give "Permission" to Feel

Abused children normally keep a tight lid on their emotions. Giving them permission to vent their feelings with intensity is critical in the healing process. Repression of feelings is common. For example, they may report an inability to feel angry. When this is the case, an important goal is to increase their affective awareness. Expressing submerged anger in the safety of a trusted relationship can be a powerful and liberating force. Take time to explore feelings that may or may not seem relevant to the abuse. Be aware that abused young people often act out their feelings through aggression or inappropriate sexual behavior. These teenagers need appropriate channels in which to express feelings, and a relationship with a professional counselor often provides this.

Facilitate Grieving

Being abused as a child and trying later to survive as a young adult is to sacrifice growing up. Most adolescents do not easily admit their losses. Grieving the loss of their childhood is a way to honor their pain. Grief work allows them to let go of their secret agony and move into the present with greater self-awareness and control. It allows them to regain some of their stolen vulnerability and prepares them for genuine intimacy with others in the future. See the section on grief for further help in this process.

Keep Your Feelings in Check

You only add to the young person's confusion if you express strong feelings—even if these feelings stem from a desire to be an advocate for the teen. You can be supportive of the child without "offender bashing." Keep your biases of disgust and anger in check. This creates a safer environment for the adolescent and invites him or her to express intense feelings. It also enables the victim to set the tone and pace of the intervention, further instilling a sense of regaining control.

Facilitate Empowerment

The imbalance of power is a key element for victims of abuse. Young persons are powerless against abusive adults. Teens may exhibit powerlessness by becoming withdrawn, isolated, and helpless. Or to regain control in response to perceived power loss, they may act out sexually or rebel at school. Effective treatment must facilitate healthful empowerment. This goal can be challenging because it requires that assertiveness not turn into aggression. Empowerment is a positive, assertive sense of control and appropriate feelings of control. Empowerment begins with the first report of the abuse.

Being believed and being able to say what really happened is the first step toward regaining control. Young people need reassurance that they did the right thing in reporting the abuse. Affirm them for their courage and acknowledge that they have taken a difficult step toward regaining command of their lives. Don't convey a sense of suspicion or doubt by asking whether he or she is "absolutely sure" events happened as reported. Young people also need to know that they have the right to say no while maintaining their place in the family.[13] Facilitating empowerment also means teaching them self-protective skills to avoid becoming victims again. Assertiveness-training exercises may empower young people with confidence. Several techniques are outlined in the section on shyness.

Set the Stage for a Survivor Mentality

Victims' distress can be eased by affirming their ability to survive their circumstances. Gently help them to begin looking toward a brighter future. Remind them that having undergone the severe trauma of abuse does not preclude their ability to function normally in the future. Tell them they are instinctively strong to have survived what they have been through. Recognize the success of their coping strategies. Praise their journey toward self-recovery. It may encourage some to know that thousands of abuse victims have become survivors. Suggest that they will feel in greater control of their lives as time goes by. Hope and realistic reassurance will instill a survivor mentality.

Explore Spirituality

A history of abuse can distort young people's concept of God. The last thing those who have been abused by their dads need is another father. They will most likely see God as an abusive parent. At the same time the one thing they need most is the Father. In time they need to see that God is love. If teens are spiritually sensitive, explore their spiritual perceptions and needs. Help them straighten out their crooked concepts and tap into God's love. This is essential to meaningful healing and peace of mind. It may mean, by the way, that they need to express their anger and disappointment toward God. "If God is so loving," they will ask, "how could he let this happen?" Accept their anger and let them know it is all right to express their true feelings to God.

Explore Forgiveness

Forgiveness of abusers cannot be forced on victims. Eventually, however— almost always a long way down the road—youths will need to assess their capacity to give up their need to hurt back. They will need to forgive others as well as themselves. Bitterness and hatred will slowly gnaw at them and cause them to carry the burden of abuse forever. If you focus on forgiveness before victims are ready, it will only stifle a healthful healing process and increase denial. Techniques and strategies that facilitate this process can be found in the section on forgiveness.

✔ HOW PROFESSIONALS CAN HELP

The following strategies for helping an adolescent struggling with abuse are commonly used by counselors. They are presented here as a way to inform you, as a parent, and help you seek the best possible professional help you can for the adolescent in your care.

Know the Limits of Confidentiality

All fifty states mandate the reporting of all types of abuse. Failure to do so is a misdemeanor if your profession is in mental health, social service, medicine, education, or ministry. Some states do exempt pastors from the reporting requirement. If a counselor is the first to learn about a specific case of abuse, he or she must report the findings to the appropriate agencies. In most states, the report must be made within a specified period of time, usually somewhere between twenty-four hours and seven days. Reports can be made by phone, in writing, or in person to a local law enforcement agency, the Department of Social and Health Services, or Child Protective Services. Those who report abuse are generally given immunity from liability and can remain anonymous, but normally confidential communication is not protected in court proceedings.

Understand Delayed Intervention

Because many children are abused in their preadolescent years and the abuse is not reported, in many situations counselors may be dealing with delayed intervention even though clients are still teenagers. Many of the strategies for delayed intervention are the same as immediate intervention. In delayed cases young people have usually built up arsenals of defenses to cope with the abuse. They may minimize the abuse ("Every dad gets mad now and then") or rationalize ("He couldn't help it; he was drunk"). The counselor must be sensitive to these barriers, which are serving as defenses. One of the most significant difficulties with this kind of defensiveness is reluctance to discover that they are actually victims of abuse.

Assess the History of Abuse

An information interview is essential for professionals who treat victims of abuse. The goal is to get an accurate picture of counselees' abuse history. Professionals will progress from general questions to a more specific focus in gathering information. They will use open-ended questions and avoid double-edged questions that might imply blame (e.g., "Don't you . . . ?"). They will put potentially embarrassing questions about sex in context (e.g., "I need to ask about . . . because . . ."). Counselors will document their observations and impressions and include counselees' nonverbal messages, facial expressions, physical appearance, and any physical signs of abuse. Notes provide a baseline on victims' behavior and may be useful if clinicians are subpoenaed for court proceedings.[14]

Consider Group Work

The use of group therapy may be a dynamic component of the healing process.[15] Groups vary but commonly provide mutual support and information that facilitate survival. Some are oriented toward young victims, others toward parents, and some toward the whole family. Groups are particularly helpful as a strategy in delayed intervention, that is, a year or more after the abuse has occurred. Effective groups reduce feelings of isolation and alienation as well as stigma, which are common in victims. Parents Anonymous for physical abuse and Parents United for sexual abuse provide national networks for support and education and may be helpful resources in locating local groups. The toll-free number of Parents Anonymous is 800–421–0353.

Understand Rape

Physical abuse and sexual abuse are not limited to family members. As adolescents begin dating, their chances of being victimized increase. The incidence of physical violence and rape during a date has become common enough to be labeled *date rape*. According to reports, a growing number of young men and teenage boys, often by using physical force, are forcing their dates to have intercourse or perform other sexual acts against their will. Each year thousands of teenage girls are victims of date rape.[16] We must be aware of and sensitive to this kind of victimization. These victims may not even recognize it as rape and will continue to be in sexual contact with abusers because of confusion.

The crisis-oriented approach to sexual-assault intervention views the counselor's role as an active one. A common obstacle to successful intervention is dealing with victims' ambivalence. Only one in ten victims will use some type of crisis intervention service such as a rape-crisis center or hospital. Once they have agreed to avail themselves of therapy, the emphasis is on assisting the victim to regain a sense of autonomy and control over her life. Treatment focus is on developing crisis-related problem-solving skills to equip girls and women for possible medical and legal procedures. A social support network for victims is also critical.[17] For more information on assisting victims of date rape, consult Robin Warshaw's *I Never Called It Rape*.

Know When to Refer

Counselors will refer adolescents who struggle with abuse to psychologically astute physicians or to psychiatrists, if physical or sexual abuse is recently inflicted. They will refer them to other competent counselors or psychologists when, over time, they become increasingly stuck in a defensive reaction to their dealing with pain or if they experience a growing sense of hopelessness or are increasingly depressed or suicidal. This requires counselors who are willing to recognize their own limitations. Even experienced abuse specialists frequently refer adolescents to achieve the therapeutic goal.

Where to Go for Additional Help

Allender, D. B. *The Wounded Heart: Hope for Adult Victims of Childhood Sexual Abuse.* Colorado Springs: NavPress, 1990.

Burgess, A. W., L. L. Holmstrom, A. N. Groth, and S. M. Sgroi. *Sexual Assault of Children and Adolescents.* Lexington, Mass.: Lexington Books, 1978.

Evans, P. *The Verbally Abusive Relationship: How to Recognize It and How to Respond.* Holbrook, Mass.: Adams Media Corporation, 1996.

Feldmeth, J. R., and M. W. Finley. *We Weep for Ourselves and Our Children: A Christian Guide for Survivors of Childhood Sexual Abuse.* San Francisco: HarperCollins, 1990.

Finklehor, D. *Child Sexual Abuse.* New York: Free Press, 1984.

Helfer, M. E., R. S. Kempe, and R. D. Krugman, eds. *The Battered Child.* Chicago: The University of Chicago Press, 1997.

Heitritter, L., and J. Vought. *Helping Victims of Sexual Abuse: A Sensitive Biblical Guide for Counselors, Victims and Families.* Minneapolis: Bethany House, 1989.

McGee, R. S., and H. Schaumburg. *Renew: Hope for Victims of Sexual Abuse.* Houston: Rapha, 1990.

Morrison, J. *A Safe Place: Beyond Sexual Abuse for Teenagers.* Wheaton, Ill.: Shaw, 1990.

Russell, D. E. H. *The Secret Trauma: Incest in the Lives of Girls and Women.* New York: Basic Books, 1986.

Warshaw, R. *I Never Called It Rape.* New York: Harper & Row, 1988.

Notes

1. R. Emery, "Family Violence," *American Psychologist* 44 (1988): 321–28.

2. A. Glodich and J. Allen, "Adolescents Exposed to Violence and Abuse: A Review of the Group Therapy Literature with an Emphasis on Preventing Trauma Reenactment," *Journal of Child and Adolescent Group Therapy* 8 (1998): 135–54.

3. B. Justice and R. Justice, *The Abusing Family* (New York: Human Sciences Press, 1976).

4. P. Ackerman, J. Newton, B. McPherson, J. Jones, and R. Dykman, "Prevalence of Post Traumatic Stress Disorder and Other Psychiatric Diagnoses in Three Groups of Abused Children," *Child Abuse and Neglect* 22 (1998): 759–74.

5. American Humane Association, *The National Study of Child Neglect and Abuse* (Denver: American Humane Association, 1981).

6. D. Finklehor, *Child Sexual Abuse* (New York: Free Press, 1984).

7. L. Brogi and C. Bagley, "Abusing Victims: Detention of Child Sexual Abuse Victims in Secure Accomodation," *Child Abuse Review* 7 (1998): 315–29.

8. D. Graybill, "Aggression in College Students Who Were Abused as Children," *Journal of College Student Personnel* 26 (1985): 492–95.

9. D. Capuzzi and D. R. Gross, *Youth at Risk* (Alexandria, Va.: American Association for Counseling and Development, 1989).

10. E. F. Loftus "The Reality of Repressed Memories," *American Psychologist* 48 (1993): 518–37.

11. B. Azar "Looking for the Roots of 'False Memories'," *APA Monitor* (October 1999): 28.

12. D. Lipschitz, R. Winegar, A. Nicolaou, E. Hartnick, M. Wolfson, and S. Southwick, "Perceived Abuse and Neglect as Risk Factors for Suicidal Behavior in Adolescent Inpatients," *Journal of Nervous and Mental Disease* 187 (1999): 32–39.

13. W. G. Wagner, "Child Sexual Abuse: A Multidisciplinary Approach to Case Management," *Journal of Counseling and Development* 65 (1987): 435–39.

14. T. L. Jackson, R. P. Quevillon, and P. A. Petretic-Jackson, "Assessment and Treatment of Sexual Assault Victims," in *Innovations in Clinical Practice: A Source Book*, vol. 4, ed. P. Keller and L. Ritt (Sarasota, Fla.: Professional Resource Exchange, 1985), 51–78.

15. A. Glodich and J. Allen, "Adolescents Exposed to Violence and Abuse: A Review of the Group Therapy Literature with an Emphasis on Preventing Trauma Reenactment," *Journal of Child and Adolescent Group Therapy* 8 (1998): 135–54.

16. E. Flax, "Panel Hears Testimony on Causes of Violent Acts by Nation's Teenagers," *Education Week* (24 May 1989): 13.

17. R. Warshaw, *I Never Called It Rape* (New York: Harper & Row, 1988).

ANGER

✔ **WHAT THE STRUGGLE LOOKS LIKE**

The body of Christ has always had trouble knowing how to express strong emotions appropriately. Especially anger. In some families it is more acceptable to be depressed than angry.[1] But anger is normal and natural. According to David Mace, we are not responsible for being angry, only for how we respond to and use anger once it appears. The apostle Paul understood this when he said, "In your anger do not sin" (Ephesians 4:26). Humans were created with a capacity to experience potent emotions, including the passion of anger.[2]

Anger is not easy to define. It occurs in varying degrees of intensity and is expressed in countless ways. In *Counseling for Anger,* Mark Cosgrove sees anger as having three components: emotional (e.g., feeling hurt), cognitive (e.g., "You need to know how much you hurt me"), and behavioral responses (e.g., yelling). These components, he says, are so intertwined that people experience the emotion of anger as one continuous surge. Some young people lose hope when they face this powerful negative emotion because they do not separate feeling and thought from behavior. They lose sight of the thinking and behaving components and focus solely on the surge of emotional arousal.[3]

Physical signs of anger include rapid talking, raised voice, shakiness, trembling, cold hands, rapid breathing, sweating, grinding of teeth, biting lips, a choked feeling, and cracking voice. Paul Eckman, a professor at the University of California, explains that narrowing of the lips is one of the earliest signs of anger. A sensitive observer may detect in a young person's face a betrayal of the deep emotion before it registers in the young person's conscious mind.[4]

Anger is so common during adolescence that many people believe its absence is a maladaptive sign. People expect adolescents to be angry and even slam doors shut now and then. Anger is a part of the important and painful process of individuation. For some quick-tempered adolescents, however, anger becomes more than a developmental phase. It becomes a chronic pattern of self-defeating hostility. In fact, an attitude of anger may become a major component in personality development.

Adolescents who struggle with anger are more isolated, less successful, less satisfied, and more impulsive than their peers.[5] Many of their relationships are marked by conflict, withdrawal, and loss. At home they fight with siblings and combat their parents.[6] They may express their anger passively by coming home late and offering phony excuses. Or they may be blatantly aggressive and break doors, walls, or furniture. They may be suspended from school or become dropouts because their teachers are hassling them.[7]

Diagnostically, according to the American Psychiatric Association, the intense behavior patterns of destructive anger may be labeled *Conduct Disorder, Oppositional Disorder, Intermittent Explosive Disorder,* or, if the adolescent is at least eighteen years of age, *Antisocial Personality Disorder.* In any case, the anger of adolescents is like a buoyant basketball forced under water: hard to sit on. When the delicate balance required to hold it down is disturbed, adolescent anger comes rushing to the surface and explodes into the environment. In children we call it a temper tantrum, but the same experience can be seen in many adolescents. When a fit of anger is provoked in adolescents, the reaction may be almost volcanic in intensity. Rage is manifested by a loss of control that erupts in screaming, cursing, breaking objects, and sometimes hitting. While tantrums are expected in young children (ages two to four years), destructive rage is out of bounds for adolescents. Often adolescents who throw tantrums have benefited from them by watching their parents raise the white flag of surrender in the face of angry fits. In this way young people learn to control the environment through outbursts of anger.

Case Description

Mark was a seventeen-year-old boy of sturdy build. He outweighed his father by twenty pounds and was in outstanding physical condition. Although he had friends at school, they had all learned from experience to let Mark have his way when he got angry. He had a reputation for being hotheaded. He came for counseling because of multiple minor delinquencies and a belligerent attitude toward parental discipline. On several occasions, his parents felt he was forcibly restraining himself from striking them. His mother admitted to extreme fear that he might eventually hurt her. She described him as "a time bomb waiting to explode." While Mark admitted to arguing with his parents, he did not see himself as having a problem with anger.

✔ WHY THE STRUGGLE HAPPENS

The list of possible causes of anger seems almost endless: frustration, betrayal, deprivation, injustice, exploitation, manipulation, criticism, violence, disapproval, humiliation, and on and on.[8] The following are just a few of the reasons some adolescents struggle with anger.

Developmental Changes

In adolescence, self-consciousness and concern with identity issues set the stage for frequent demonstrations of anger. Adolescents, more than any other age group, may be angered by an assault on their dignity and self-worth. This may include teasing, bossiness, sarcasm, rejection by others, failure, being lied to, unfairness, or criticism. Adolescents are in the serious business of building a solid personal identity, and even a minor attempt to undermine its construction might provoke retaliation. Also, during this time of continual change, the body's chemistry may interact with emotional processing. Hormone levels, for example, in adolescents have been shown to be related to anger.[9]

Continual Threat

Some adolescents have known nothing but pain and hurt all their lives. They have grown up in homes where they were put down, rejected, unjustly criticized, or even abused. Their learned response to this negative environment is to protect themselves with a heavy armor of anger and aggression. They have been burned. They have learned that relationships are painful, and they are not about to let others take advantage of them. Anger then becomes a way of life. It is adolescent insulation from psychic pain.

Social Learning

Adolescents also learn to express their anger from their parents' style of anger.[10] A comprehensive longitudinal study of grade-school children in New

York revealed that parents' aggressive behavior at home is associated with aggressiveness in children at school.[11] We hardly need a study to tell us that children model their parents. If children grow up in homes where dads fly off the handle and control their families with physical and verbal abuse, it makes sense to conclude that the children will learn to use anger in the same way.

Unrealistic Expectations

In a desire to build their identities on solid foundations of healthful self-esteem, adolescents may set unrealistic standards for themselves. In fact, they may expect perfection. For example, if they are talented in the classroom and used to receiving grades of A, they may burst into fits of anger upon receiving a B+. Young athletes who miss crucial foul shots in basketball games may experience similar surges of anger. Adolescents who expect perfection are condemned to suffer from chronic anger with themselves and others.

☑ HOW PARENTS CAN HELP

The following strategies for helping an adolescent struggling with anger can be used effectively by parents; however, every parent-child relationship is unique, and some of them may be more pertinent to your situation than others. As with every significant adolescent struggle, it is best for parents to work alongside a competent counselor. With this in mind, the following is offered as a way to help you facilitate the helping process at home with your teenager.

Avoid the Most Common Pitfalls

Daniel G. Bagby, an expert on anger in the church, points to three common misconceptions that govern an inadequate management of anger by religious people. First is the erroneous belief that God does not want us to experience any anger and that all anger is sinful. Second is the belief that angry feelings are best managed by camouflaging or ignoring them. And third is the belief that the painful feelings of anger, if ignored, will vanish and not continue to influence relationships.[12]

Understand Your Own Anger

To be human is to know anger. Even the best of us have lost our tempers and lashed out in frustration. For this reason it is imperative that you understand your own anger thoroughly. What is your attitude toward anger? What makes you angry? How do you cope with and redeem your anger? You will facilitate a healthful exploration of anger only if you have examined and understood anger in your own life.

Help Them Admit Their Anger

Buried anger may be difficult to excavate, but it is imperative for angry young people to confess their struggle. It may be especially threatening if they are directing their anger at family members or God. Helping adolescents talk honestly about their anger requires patience and empathy from caring adults. Young people are usually more comfortable projecting their bad feelings onto someone else whom they blame for their hot tempers.

If teens resist admitting to their anger, gently ask them to complete the sentence "Anger is . . ." How they define anger may help them (and you) understand their thinking. They may say, "Anger is always justified if you have been hurt;" or "Anger is always wrong, no matter how badly you've been hurt;" or they may say, "Anger is hating people." Whatever they say provides clues to their concept of anger and provides them with nonthreatening windows of opportunity to begin to admit their struggle with anger.

Be Prepared for Swearing

The issue of bad language is often part of anger in adolescence. It generally falls into three categories: (1) profanity, which is speech involving disrespect for something that is considered sacred or holy, such as the name of God; (2) cursing, which is speech reflecting the wish to harm someone (for example, "damn you"); and (3) obscenity, which is referring to sexual images in a sneering way (for example, "screw you").

Almost all adolescents use bad language sooner or later, and its use in recent years has, not surprisingly, increased.[13] Adolescents will swear to gain attention, to shock, or to rebel and assert their independence.[14] I have found that one of the best ways of dealing with it is to ignore it. If teens see that their language is not startling or upsetting to you, they will not have reason to continue using it. However, it is also important to be empathic. When they curse as a response to their frustration, try to recognize the distress and let them know you understand. At the same time, it may also be appropriate to express disapproval and set down limits for their behavior. If they continue to use profanity, for example, you may express your understanding of their feelings, but tell them that it is also upsetting for you to hear them dishonor God and that you would appreciate it if they would not use profanity. This also helps them see a constructive way of making requests without verbal emotional aggression.

Explore Anger Toward God

Angry adolescents need to know that it is okay to shout at God. God has seen anger before; he has even experienced anger. If teens are blaming God for something, allow them to say so. Allow them to talk freely about these feelings. (Counselors may have them write an honest letter to God telling him how they feel about him and their circumstances.) Once they have expressed their feelings, suggest that they also listen to God.[15]

✔ HOW PROFESSIONALS CAN HELP

The following strategies for helping an adolescent struggling with anger are commonly used by counselors. They are presented here as a way to inform you, as a parent, and help you seek the best possible professional help you can for the adolescent in your care.

Assign a "Hassle Log"

This assignment is used to heighten adolescents' awareness of where, when, why, and how often they get angry. The hassle log is a diary-like means of analyzing provocative events. They keep a record on anger, including places, happenings, persons present, what they did or said, the results, how they felt afterwards, and what they wish they had done differently. They bring their logs to each session. Counselors review the logs and use situations described in the logs as role-play examples for teaching techniques on dealing with anger.

Discover the True Source of Anger

On the surface, angry adolescents may be mad at their mothers for embarrassing them in front of their friends, at their teachers for unfair grades, at friends for not agreeing with them during lunchroom conversation, at older siblings for failing to pick them up on time. Yet all these things are only symptoms of deeper hurt. At a deeper level, they may be really angry about a close relative's untimely death or parental divorce. By pinpointing the true sources of anger, counselors can begin to deal with the real problems.

Restore Physical Well-Being

Anger creates a surge of energy and physical tension. For the chronically angry, clients may be helped by learning about socially acceptable outlets for excess tension and energy. Jogging, swimming, team sports, even screaming into a pillow and breaking pencils have been found helpful in restoring physical homeostasis within angry people. The key point in suggesting vigorous physical activity is to be sure the conscious intent of the exercise is to reduce tension, not to act out or even fantasize revenge. The aim is to restore physical well-being.[16]

Teach the "Anger Control Chain"

In 1975 Raymond Novaco designed an anger control program that has been supported by extensive research and proved highly effective. Taught incrementally over several sessions, this program centers around "the five links in the anger control chain": triggers, cues, reminders, reducers, and self-evaluation.

Triggers are the external events and internal appraisals (self-statements) that produce anger arousal. A young person's *interpretation* of a situation can become the trigger. Becoming aware of these triggers is the first step to controlling anger. The hassle log mentioned above may be helpful in identifying triggers.

Cues refer to the physiological and kinesthetic experiences that signal anger arousal. The signals include accelerated heartbeat, flushed cheeks, tightening of the muscles, butterflies in the stomach, and rapid shallow breathing. It is analogous to the response a boxer feels to the cue "and in this corner." Giving attention to cues is important because chronically aggressive adolescents are often impulsive. Becoming aware of their cues helps them slow down the process. It also helps adolescents discriminate among other affective states; it helps them see the difference between fear and anger, for example. Once adolescents can identify through these cues when an increase in anger arousal is actually taking place, they are ready for the next link.

Reminders are self-instructional means for lowering the level of anger arousal. Reminders are the opposite of triggers. They are self-statements designed to reduce anger in any situation. Examples include "chill out," "calm down," "cool out," or "I can't win by getting angry."

Reducers continue the effort begun by reminders. They arm young people with an array of means for reducing their anger arousal in provocative, real-life situations. Reducers can be relatively simple: counting backward from ten or a hundred, deep breathing, or imagining a peaceful scene.

Self-evaluation is the final link taught in this anger control chain. Reflecting on their progress enables the young people to appraise how well the links were used, and then to make changes to control anger more effectively.

This is the core of the Anger Control Training program. Contracting, assertiveness training, problem-solving techniques, and relaxation training are also sometimes incorporated into the program.

Teach Rational Alternatives to Enraging Beliefs

Angry adolescents need help to understand that anger is often a symptom of feeling hurt, fearful, or frustrated and that it is the thinking behind these feelings that gives anger the combustion to ignite. Irrational thinking provides the kindling that sparks anger to a full flame. Adolescents may benefit from seeing how this combustion works. Here are three common examples:

Labeling. "You are a total jerk!" "You're a slouch, a loser." Labeling helps young people feel morally superior to those with whom they are angry. Once labeled, people are polarized and represent only the things the angry folks despise. Counselors confront with reality. They ask angry adolescents whether they truly believe that those they are angry with are *total* jerks or just unfair in particular instances. Counselors help teens understand how labeling only intensifies their own frustration and results in more intense anger.

Mind Reading. In this distortion counselees invent explanations for actions of other persons. They do not simply hold their personal explanations as hypotheses to be confirmed; they believe them as fact. This generates and intensifies anger by allowing them to get worked up over false premises. Counselors may ask clients to articulate causes of their anger in particular situations, what they believe other persons were feeling, and why they acted the way they did. Or, counselors may reverse roles and "mind read" their clients' actions and feelings to let them know how inaccurate this distortion can be.

Magnification. In this anger-creating distortion a negative event is blown out of proportion. For example, if teens missed points on an exam because they didn't understand the instructions, they may be momentarily frustrated but realize that it can't make any difference in their final grade. However, they may choose to magnify their frustration out of proportion until they become hot with anger. They may make a catastrophe of the situation by giving one moment more importance than it is worth and therefore erupting with disproportionate anger. Counselors help clients see this process with objectivity in order to reduce its occurrence in the future.[17]

Practice Imagery Exercises

In *Self-Talk, Imagery, and Prayer in Counseling,* H. Norman Wright reports success with imagery exercises to control and reduce anger. He suggests that counselors lead their clients through the following process: Counselees indicate the five most anger-creating situations they are currently experiencing and then close their eyes and use their imaginations to recreate one of these situations. They hear their self-statements and watch how they usually react with anger. Next, they relax. Then, they imagine the same situation but with rational self-statements that slow down the process of anger. This would fulfill the biblical admonition to be slow to anger. They visualize themselves responding to the provocation in a calm and relaxed manner. Wright suggests that counselees practice this new version of the experience in their minds many times outside of counseling sessions. With practice, they will change responses the next time they confront real situations.[18]

Teach Forgiveness

Angry clients who are filled with bitterness and hatred ultimately need the healing of forgiveness. They need to learn how to forgive others as well as themselves. Forgiveness holds more promise for aiding an effective resolution to the problem of chronic anger than any other therapeutic intervention. Anger exists only in the present. Contrary to what many claim, anger does not accumulate or build up in an inner reservoir. We do not have anger left over from yesterday like an athlete with a sore muscle. We may have painful memories of yesterday that cause us to recreate feelings of anger, but anger itself is in the present. The *memories* of the hurtful events are what keep anger alive. The solution, in these cases, lies not in forgetting or even in anger-management techniques, but in breaking the power of clients' memories to re-create the feelings of hurt. The solution is forgiveness.[19] For techniques and strategies that facilitate this process, see the section on forgiveness.

Know When to Refer

Counselors refer angry adolescents to psychologically astute physicians or to psychiatrists when physical symptoms are present. Possible physical consequences of chronic anger include skin rashes, ulcers, muscle-tension aches, high blood pressure, grinding teeth, and clenched jaws.[20]

They refer youthful clients struggling with anger to other competent counselors or psychologists when, over time, the clients are feeling more out of control and angry. Counselors may also refer when they recognize that their own unresolved anger issues are interfering with treatment (for example, if their client's situation or personality is generating strong negative feelings in them).

Where to Go for Additional Help

Augsburger, D. *Caring Enough to Confront*. Ventura, Calif.: Regal, 1981.
Bry, A. *How to Get Angry without Feeling Guilty*. New York: New American Library, 1976.
Carter, L. *Getting the Best of Your Anger*. Grand Rapids: Spire, 1997.
Gentry, W. D. *Anger-Free: Ten Basic Steps to Managing Your Anger*. New York: William Morrow, 1999.
Hart, A. *Unlocking the Mystery of Your Emotions*. Waco, Tex.: Word, 1989.
Meyer, J. *Be Anxious for Nothing: The Art of Casting Your Cares and Resting in God*. Tulsa, Okla.: Harrison House, 1998.

Oliver, G. *Making Anger Work for You*. Siloam Springs, Ark.: John Brown University Press, 1998.

Oliver, G. *"More" Making Anger Work for You*. Siloam Springs, Ark.: John Brown University Press, 1998.

Oliver, G. *Good Women Get Angry: A Woman's Guide to Handling Her Anger, Depression, Anxiety, and Stress*. Ann Arbor, Mich.: Vine Books/Servant Publications, 1995.

Rubin, T. I. *The Angry Book*. New York: Collier, 1970.

Tavris, C. *Anger, The Misunderstood Emotion*. New York: Simon & Schuster, 1982.

Taylor, G., and R. Wilson. *Exploring Your Anger*. Grand Rapids: Baker, 1997.

Walters, R. P. *Anger: Yours and Mine and What to Do About It*. Grand Rapids: Zondervan, 1981.

Warren, N. C. *Make Anger Your Ally: Harnessing Our Most Baffling Emotion*. Garden City, N.Y.: Doubleday, 1983.

Wilde, J. *Hot Stuff to Help Kids Chill Out: The Anger Management Book*. East Troy, Wis.: LGR Publishing, 1997.

Notes

1. D. G. Bagby, "Anger," in *Dictionary of Pastoral Care and Counseling*, ed. R. J. Hunter (Nashville: Abingdon, 1990).

2. For a discussion of the issue of when anger becomes sinful, see Frank B. Minirth and Paul D. Meier's book *Happiness Is a Choice*, chap. 13 (Grand Rapids: Baker, 1978).

3. M. P. Cosgrove, *Counseling for Anger* (Waco, Tex.: Word, 1988).

4. D. Mace, *Love and Anger in Marriage* (Grand Rapids: Zondervan, 1982).

5. C. R. Colder and E. Stice, "A Longitudinal Study of the Interactive Effects of Impulsivity and Anger on Adolescent Problem Behavior," *Journal of Youth and Adolescence* 27 (1998): 255–74.

6. D. Cornell, C. S. Peterson, and H. Richards, "Anger as a Predictor of Aggression among Incarcerated Adolescents," *Journal of Counseling and Clinical Psychology* 67 (1999): 108–15.

7. P. York et al., *Toughlove* (Garden City, N.Y.: Doubleday, 1982).

8. For a more thorough discussion of the etiology of chronic anger, see Cosgrove's *Counseling for Anger*.

9. E. J. Susman et al., "Hormones, Emotional Dispositions, and Aggressive Attributes in Young Adolescents," *Child Development* 58, (1987): 1114–34.

10. P. Hastings and J. E. Grusec, "Conflict Outcome as a Function of Parental Accuracy in Perceiving Child Cognitions and Affect," *Social Development* 6 (1997): 76–90.

11. L. R. Huesmann et al., "Stability of Aggression Over Time and Generations," *Developmental Psychology* 20 (1984): 1120–34.

12. Bagby, "Anger."

13. R. B. Bloom, "Therapeutic Management of Children's Profanity," *Behavioral Disorders* 2 (1977): 205–77.

14. A. Montague, *The Anatomy of Swearing* (New York: Macmillan, 1967).

15. Scriptures that address anger include Ephesians 4:26, Psalm 4, Colossians 3:8, and James 1:19.

16. C. F. Alschuler and A. S. Alschuler, "Developing Healthy Responses to Anger: The Counselor's Role," *Journal of Counseling and Development* 63 (1984): 26–29.

17. H. N. Wright, *Self-Talk, Imagery, and Prayer in Counseling* (Waco, Tex.: Word, 1986).

18. Ibid.

19. A. Hart, *Unlocking the Mystery of Your Emotions* (Waco, Tex.: Word, 1989).

20. F. Stearns, *Anger* (Springfield, Ill.: Charles C. Thomas, 1972).

ANXIETY

✔ WHAT THE STRUGGLE LOOKS LIKE

We are living in the Age of Anxiety. Many see stress and anxiety as the most pervasive psychological phenomenon of our time.[1] In defining this common struggle, it is helpful to differentiate the shades of meaning in the cluster of words we often use interchangeably to describe this prevailing emotion.

Worry. This is perhaps our most common form of human suffering. It is a chain of negative and relatively uncontrollable thoughts and images. Worrying is like a rocking chair; it will give you something to do but it won't get you anywhere. Perhaps the definition that captures its essence best is that "worry is interest paid in advance on a debt you may never owe." About 15 percent of the population of the United States are chronic worriers.[2]

Fear. Even the bravest people among us have experienced fear in some form at some time, such as a sudden scare at the sight of a harmless snake, a dry mouth before beginning a speech, or sweaty palms on a flight through bumpy air. Fears are different from phobias. The critical distinction between a common fear and a phobia is the degree to which it interferes with everyday life. This difference is explained further in the section on phobia.

Stress. This is the alarm reaction that activates the body to prepare for "the fight or flight response." It mobilizes us to cope with an emergency. In stress our heart rate, breathing, and perspiration increase. Our pupils dilate and our adrenaline kicks into overdrive.[3]

Concern. This refers to mental activity that focuses on a problem with a view toward taking action to resolve the problem. Concern springs naturally from caring and is directed toward a constructive end.

While worry, fear, phobia, stress, and concern are all related to the struggle that is the focus in this section, they are different from anxiety. Anxiety is all of these emotional factors rolled up together and gone too far.

The *Diagnostic and Statistical Manual of Mental Disorders* (4th ed.) of the American Psychiatric Association (DSM-IV) discusses generalized anxiety as a disorder characterized by chronic diffuse anxiety and apprehensiveness. ("Chronic" is defined by APA as anxiety of at least one month's duration.) The most prominent emotional component is an unpleasant sense of apprehensiveness and impending calamity. Because this type of anxiety may not seem to stem from any particular threat, it is said to be free-floating.

Clinical anxiety is almost always accompanied by several physical symptoms. The list of symptoms is long, but a quick review is helpful as we highlight some of the most important ones. The person with generalized anxiety experiences varying combinations of these physical symptoms:

✓ Rapid, pounding heart rate   ✓ Shortness of breath
✓ Diarrhea   ✓ Loss of appetite
✓ Fainting   ✓ Dizziness
✓ Profuse sweating   ✓ Sleeplessness
✓ Frequent urination   ✓ Tremors and shaking

Adolescents who struggle with anxiety experience some of these symptoms on a day-to-day basis. They are more or less in a constant state of tension, worry, and diffuse uneasiness. Those suffering from anxiety can be overly sensitive to interpersonal relationships and socially uneasy most of the time. They usually have difficulty concentrating and making decisions for fear of making a mistake. They may exhibit strained and tense posture and movements. They often complain of muscular tension, sleep disturbances, and cold hands.[4] Anxious adolescents feel as though they have no control over what is happening to them. They feel terrified. If you ask them what they are frightened of, they will say, "I don't know." They feel an impending sense of doom, but they don't know why.

To be clinically diagnosed with an anxiety disorder, adolescents must exhibit excessive or unrealistic anxiety for a period of six months or longer, as indicated by the frequent occurrence of at least four of the following:

• Excessive or unrealistic worry about future events
• Excessive or unrealistic concern about the appropriateness of past behavior

- Excessive or unrealistic concern about competence in one or more skills, e.g., athletic, academic, social
- Somatic complaints, such as headaches or stomachaches, for which no physical basis can be established
- Marked self-consciousness
- Excessive need for reassurance about a variety of concerns
- Marked feelings of tension or inability to relax[5]

One further clarification is in order. A panic attack is an intense burst of anxiety accompanied by physiological uproar and many strange changes in bodily feelings. The attack lasts from a few minutes to a few hours, and each attack will leave the victim feeling shaken and exhausted. The treatment strategy with panic attacks requires a different approach from a general struggle with anxiety. For further help, refer to the section on panic attacks.

Case Description

Teresa is seventeen. She is popular at school, conscientious, and attractive. She also suffers from an almost unbearable amount of anxiety and stress. She worries about driving on the freeway, about saying something "stupid" in front of her peers, about embarrassing her parents, about failing in the classroom, and just about anything else that pops into her head. This is nothing new for Teresa. She has struggled with anxiety for at least a year and it seems to be getting worse. She sometimes gets stomachaches as a result of the worry, and of course that makes her worry all the more. She simply cannot relax.

Adolescence is a crucial period for learning how to deal with anxiety and stress. The coping style developed then will influence the rest of life.

✓ WHY THE STRUGGLE HAPPENS

Among the adolescent population anxiety is a widespread condition with numerous causes. Here are some of the major reasons for its occurrence.

Negative Self-Talk

Teenagers' self-talk, that is, their evaluation of an event, can produce anxiety. When a young person is faced with a stressful situation, he or she interprets it in terms of pairs of declarative sentences. For example, a male adolescent who fears rejection and humiliation might react to meeting an attractive young woman with the following two sentences: "She may not like me enough to go out on a date. That would mean that I am hopeless and no good." Albert Ellis, the founder of Rational Emotive Therapy, suggests that youths struggling with anxiety create their own anxiety through negative self-talk as seen in the second sentence in the example.[6]

Insecurity

The major cause of anxiety for most young people is a lack of inner security. A pattern of chronic worry is set up when adolescents feel unsafe and are awash in self-doubts. Feelings of rejection may come in greater force because they are sensitized for signs of rejection. When they look for rejection they usually find it, which in turn reinforces their insecurity. The cycle starts all over again. Insecurity breeds anxiety.

Inconsistency

Adolescents who have little stability in their lives will probably suffer from anxiety. Parents and teachers who are inconsistent in their relations with adolescents promote anxiety. Typically, one parent expects one thing and the other expects the opposite. Adolescents are caught in the middle. A teacher can add still another element of unpredictability. If students are affirmed one day for creativity on an assignment and marked down the next on a similar project for not following directions, the inconsistency creates anxiety over not knowing what is desired.

Legalistic Criticism

A steady diet of intense legalism and criticism from adults or even peers can lead to anxiety. Adolescents are already swimming in a pool of self-criticism. To be continually evaluated, judged, and exposed unjustly to additional criticism will bring about intense worry. Legalism and a bombardment of criticism make adolescents feel as if they are constantly being tested. They receive enough examination in the classroom.

Permissiveness

Some adolescents may feel anxious when there are no clearly defined boundaries. Without guidelines of behavior that will please others, teens must rely on themselves to discover the real limits. Some teenagers are almost seeking to be punished just to know that some things are off-limits.

Perfectionism

Adults' expectations of perfection directly lead to anxious reactions in a significant number of adolescents. Very high achieving, uncaring, or easygoing adolescents escape the anxiety of not fulfilling adults' expectations. But others develop tension and worry about not doing well enough. The standards are too high and the teachers, pastors, or parents never seem satisfied.

Neurology

Some anxiety is caused by disturbances in the brain's chemistry.[7] Neurochemicals, the normal tranquilizers of the brain, can be dislodged, causing anxious thoughts and states of mind. Ignorance of this component can produce a great deal of misunderstanding about some anxiety.[8]

Physical Disorders

Anxiety symptoms can be caused by physical disorders that mimic anxiety reactions. Here are some examples: cocaine abuse, alcohol withdrawal, diabetes, hypoglycemia, psychomotor epilepsy, and hyperthyroidism. There are numerous others. For this reason, a complete medical examination by a physician is necessary when treating an anxiety disorder.

Meaninglessness

Existentialist Viktor Frankl holds that our main motivation is to find meaning in our existence. Without this meaning we suffer from an "existential vacuum" and anxiety. According to Frankl, each of us needs to find his or her own meaning, and we do this through working for the benefit of others, experiencing and appreciating the things of life, and taking an uplifting attitude toward life. Existentialists believe that if we have a *why* to live for, we can bear almost any *how*.[9]

✔ HOW PARENTS CAN HELP

The following strategies for helping an adolescent struggling with anxiety can be used effectively by parents; however, every parent-child relationship is unique, and some of them may be more pertinent to your situation than others. As with every significant adolescent struggle, it is best for parents to work alongside a competent counselor. With this in mind, the following is offered as a way to help you facilitate the helping process at home with your teenager.

Help Adolescents Face Their Anxiety

Young people, like most people, will do almost anything to avoid a direct confrontation with their anxiety. Like a person terrified of going to the dentist, the anxious teenager will ignore the problem while it festers and causes further psychic decay. Our society is ashamed to admit anxiety. We want to be heroes who bravely withstand the unexpected jolts and worries of daily life just as Rambo singlehandedly defeats an entire army. However, adolescents who acknowledge their anxiety turn out to be stronger than those who equate anxiety with cowardice. A young person told me he was being tempted by his friends to drag race on a busy highway. He said he played the macho game for a minute and then confessed he was chicken. He said he could immediately feel the anxiety roll away. True courage seems to begin with the admission of anxiety. Paul Tillich spoke of the basic need for "courage to be." This courage includes the willingness to accept and face personal anxiety.

Avoid Pat Answers

It is both callous and misleading to say to a young person struggling with anxiety, "Your problem is normal. All you have to do is pray and trust God more and everything will be all right." In teaching great numbers of students in counseling courses, I have heard responses like the above over and over again in practice role plays. Anxiety is assumed, unfortunately, to be a sign of spiritual and psychological weakness, which is far from the truth. Pat answers to anxiety problems isolate troubled adolescents and push them down into deeper pain.

Recognize the Strengths of Anxiety

Franklin Roosevelt became famous for telling a frightened nation that our greatest fear is of fear itself. Well spoken! To become free of anxiety it is necessary, first, to stop fearing it and to recognize that anxiety can even work in a person's favor. Anxiety, for example, is the emotional force behind much learning activity. An anxious student under the pressure of a final exam in algebra may be motivated to pick up the book, burn the midnight oil, and cram. A more carefree classmate, not anxious enough to study, may flunk. Anxiety can also be a sign that a moral code has been violated. Furthermore, it can help prepare a young person for a future stressful situation. The adolescent who is to give an oral presentation, for example, may be goaded by anxiety to rehearse the speech until the anxiety lessens in intensity. Anxiety that motivates a young person to take corrective action is healthful. Not all anxiety is bad.

Recognize Anxiety as an Agent of Growth

Some developmental periods are almost always accompanied by anxiety. A young person who leaves home for an extended time expects to experience anxiety. I talked with a young woman who was recently graduated from high school. She was obviously tense and very anxious. She said that her coming to college was the first time she had ever been away from her family. She was determined to become independent, but she would have to do it in the face of anxiety. She described how she had always been overprotected by her mother and three older brothers; leaving home was the hardest thing she had ever done. She could have stayed near home in Illinois and gone to college there, but she decided it would be better for her to travel to a distant city, Seattle, and learn to develop into an independent and mentally healthy young woman. I have seen other students who could not face the anxiety of separation, decide to remain home, tied to their mom and dad, and never achieve individuation and full maturity. Anxiety can be a means of personal growth.

Explore Spiritual Issues

If the adolescent is receptive to Christian values, you may try to incorporate a biblical approach. Gary Collins, in his book Christian Counseling, outlines the Bible's formula for overcoming anxiety. It involves five actions: (1) Rejoice. With the knowledge of God's promises we can celebrate the security of his peace and not let our minds be wracked with anxiety; (2) Forbear. A negative condemning outlook on life supports anxiety, while a gracious forbearing attitude reduces it; (3) Pray. Philippians 4 gives several instructions about prayer in times of anxiety. Such prayer should be specific, include thanksgiving, and be accompanied by the expectation that supernatural peace will be forthcoming;[10] (4) Think. Philippians 4 also instructs us to let our minds dwell on positive things; (5) Act. The Christian's task is to do what the Bible teaches and not simply sit listening.[11] Of course, exploring spiritual issues in this way must be done with understanding and sensitivity.

✔ HOW PROFESSIONALS CAN HELP

The following strategies for helping an adolescent struggling with anxiety are commonly used by counselors. They are presented here as a way to inform you, as a parent, and help you seek the best possible professional help you can for the adolescent in your care.

Pinpoint the Severity

Anxiety is a frequently missed diagnosis in adolescence.[12] For this reason counselors will assess the intensity of the adolescent's anxiety at the beginning of treatment. A careful assessment can serve as a point from which to measure therapeutic progress.

Require a Physical Examination

A careful history and a physical examination with particular attention to anxiety symptoms is essential. Prior to embarking on a psychological treatment approach, organic disorders must be adequately ruled out.

Neutralize Some of the Anxiety

Sometimes therapy cannot proceed until some anxiety is dissipated. Various methods can be used to aid relaxation. First, counselors will speak in a soft voice, slowing down their own verbal pace. This helps set the tempo and create a climate that allows teens to move unconsciously at a slower pace. Second, they will universalize the young person's experiences, and tell them about the thousands who experience similar feelings. Counselors will reassure clients that there are successful techniques for dealing with the problem. Generally, in this setting, young people take courage and grasp hope and become perceptively more relaxed. Once the anxiety is more manageable, counseling can proceed.

Focus on Thought Patterns

One of the best ways to alleviate chronic anxiety is to exercise mental willpower.[13] A study at Oxford University found cognitive therapy superior to other forms of treatment in helping patients identify the exaggerated thoughts that made them anxious and helping them develop more realistic ways of thinking that would generate positive influences on their feelings and behavior. Six months after treatment ended, patients who had been taught to use their minds to help control their emotional state continued to show signs of marked relief from anxiety. Their ability to identify and assess anxiety-provoking thoughts improved.[14] Adolescents who can learn to control their thought patterns can change the way they feel. A great deal of undue anxiety in adolescents is related to school performance. Academic anxiety is often caused, at least partially, by unrealistic thought patterns. See the section on school for a discussion of ways to cope with this specific kind of anxiety.

Practice Positive Self-Talk

Self-talk strategies may be used alone or with other relaxation strategies. Many adolescents have not learned to stop saying negative or anxiety-producing comments to themselves. The first step is to stop self-statements such as "I'll never fall asleep;" "I know something terrible is going to happen;" "No one would ever want to go out with me." The next step is to suggest positive self-talk. Counselors will ask adolescents to practice positive statements aloud in their office. "I'm upset now but things will get better soon. When I start to worry, I am going to relax. Nobody is perfect. Worry doesn't help; action does." The goal is to help them say things to themselves that enhance relaxation. When they are confronted by problems at school, for example, they will be able to say to themselves, "Calm down and relax."

Teach Deep Muscle Relaxation

Anxious adolescents need to gain mastery over their overwhelming emotions and uncontrolled physiological state. Deep muscle relaxation techniques can help them do this. A person cannot be in a state of anxiety and relaxation at the same time. The body and the mind will not allow contradictory actions simultaneously. Progressive muscular relaxation teaches us to be aware of varying degrees of muscle tension throughout the body.

A deep state of relaxation can be produced through a series of exercises alternately tensing and relaxing various muscle groups. Particular emphasis must be placed on perceiving and feeling the transition from the state of the muscular tension to the state of relaxation. The process may be repeated with successive muscle groups throughout the body until deep muscular relaxation is achieved.

Practice Biofeedback

Biofeedback techniques traditionally require equipment and specialized training. It provides electronic signals of physiological variables such as muscle tension, skin temperature, and skin moisture. These signals are amplified and displayed to the adolescent usually as auditory or visual information. Through this feedback the young person can learn to alter any physiological activity.

Skin temperature biofeedback is commonly used to train people to warm their hands. Since blood flow to the skin of the hand is predominantly a function of the sympathetic nervous system, vigorous efforts to influence the skin temperature are usually unsuccessful. It is only when one achieves a relaxed passive state that the desired warming occurs. While specificity of biofeedback training is debatable,[15] it can be used to augment other relaxation training. The procedure has also been shown to be attractive to adolescents who may be less receptive to simple relaxation or imagery techniques.[16] In addition, the feeling of mastery and control frequently is reinforced with successful biofeedback training.

Know When to Refer

Counselors will refer adolescents suffering from intense anxiety to psychologically astute physicians or psychiatrists when physical symptoms are present or when the anxiety is severe enough to warrant medication for temporary relief.

They will also refer anxious adolescents to other competent counselors or psychologists when, over time, their clients feel more out of control and increasingly stressed and anxious. They will refer if their clients have been unable to establish some awareness of the feelings that threaten to overwhelm them, or if their anxiety initially subsided, only to return and continue at a higher level of intensity.

Where to Go for Additional Help

Agras, S. *Panic: Facing Fears, Phobias, and Anxiety.* New York: W. H. Freeman, 1985.

Beckfield, D. F. *Master Your Panic and Take Back Your Life: Twelve Treatment Sessions to Overcome High Anxiety.* San Luis Obispo, Calif.: Impact Publisher, 1994.

Benson, H. *The Relaxation Response.* New York: Morrow, 1975.

Bourne, E. *Healing Fear: New Approaches to Overcoming Anxiety.* Oakland, Calif.: New Harbinger Publications, 1998.

Charlesworth, E. A., and R. G. Nathan. *Stress Management: A Comprehensive Guide to Wellness.* New York: Ballantine, 1984.

Colten, M. E., and S. Gore. *Adolescent Stress: Causes and Consequences.* Hawthorne, N.Y.: Aldine de Gruyter, 1991.

Davis, M., M. McKay, and E. R. Eshelman. *The Relaxation and Stress Reduction Workbook.* Richmond, Calif.: New Harbinger, 1980.

DuPont, R. L., E. Spencer, and C. M. DuPont. *The Anxiety Cure: An Eight-Step Program for Getting Well.* New York: John Wiley & Sons, 1998.

Hart, A. D. *Adrenaline and Stress.* Waco, Tex.: Word, 1986.

_____. *Overcoming Anxiety.* Waco, Tex.: Word, 1989.

Wemhoff, R., ed. *Anxiety and Depression: The Best Resources to Help You Cope.* Issaquah, Wash.: Resource Pathways, 1998.

Notes

1. E. A. Charlesworth and R. G. Nathan, *Stress Management: A Comprehensive Guide to Wellness* (New York: Ballantine, 1984).

2. A. D. Hart, *Overcoming Anxiety* (Waco, Tex.: Word, 1989).

3. H. Selye, *Stress without Distress* (New York: Signet, 1974).

4. *Diagnostic and Statistical Manual of Mental Disorders, 4th ed.* (Washington, D.C.: American Psychiatric Association, 1994).

5. Ibid.

6. A. Ellis, *A Guide to Rational Living* (North Hollywood, Calif.: Wilshire Books, 1961).

7. Y. Figuero, D. R. Rosenberg, B. Birmaher, and M. S. Keshavan, "Combination Treatment with Clomipramine and Selective Serotonin Reuptake Inhibitors for Obsessive-Compulsive Disorder in Children and Adolescents," *Journal of Child & Adolescent Psychopharmacology* 8 (1998): 61–67.

8. A. Hart, *Adrenalin and Stress* (Waco, Tex.: Word, 1986).

9. V. Frankl, *Man's Search for Meaning: An Introduction to Logotherapy* (New York: Simon & Schuster, 1962).

10. Archibald Hart, however, makes a helpful observation concerning prayer and the person suffering from anxiety: One may use prayer as a way of worrying without feeling guilty.

11. G. Collins, *Christian Counseling: A Comprehensive Guide* (Waco, Tex.: Word, 1988).

12. C. K. Berenson, "Frequently Missed Diagnoses in Adolescent Psychiatry," *Psychiatric Clinics of North America* 21 (1998): 917–26.

13. J. C. Haggerty, J. S. Nevid, and J. L. Moulton, "Anxiety and Cognitive Performance in Adolescent Women with Disruptive Behavior Disorders," *Journal of Clinical Psychology* 54 (1998): 1017–27.

14. L. Emanuel, "Thinking Away Anxiety," *Health* (June 1991): 59.

15. B. V. Silver and E. B. Blanchard, "Biofeedback and Relaxation Training, the Treatment of Psychophysiological Disorders: Or Are the Machines Really Necessary?" *Journal of Behavioral Medicine* 1 (1978): 217–39.

16. Smith and Womack, "Stress Management Techniques," 581–85.

COHABITATION

✔ WHAT THE STRUGGLE LOOKS LIKE

Marriage rates have plummeted to a forty-year low. Couples are having a harder time achieving long-term wedded bliss. Young women are increasingly pessimistic about their chances for successful marriage. Americans are now less likely to marry than ever before, and those who do marry seem to be less happy than in previous decades. And 50 percent of all marriages are projected to end in divorce or permanent separation.

One of the saddest findings of those who study marriage these days is the decline in teen confidence in marriage. David Popenoe and Barbara Dafoe Whitehead, codirectors of the National Marriage Project at Rutgers University, report that young people today want successful marriages, but they are increasingly anxious and pessimistic about their chances for achieving that goal.[1] To make matters worse, researchers are finding teens to be notably more accepting of alternatives to marriage, such as unwed parenthood and cohabitation. Teens haven't given up on marriage as a cherished ideal or as a personal life goal, but the quest for a "good" marriage seems far more difficult and uncertain to them than in previous generations.

Forty percent of girls and 56 percent of boys approve of living together before marriage.[2] It is safe to say that cohabitation—living together and regularly engaging in sexual intercourse without being legally married—is on the rise for adolescents. Even for church kids! Some young couples in the church choose to cohabit, though strong prohibitions against cohabitation in most churches make it difficult to estimate how often this occurs.[3]

At one time in America, cohabitation would have been scandalous. Unmarried couples who lived together were said to be "living in sin" or "shacking up." Cohabiting was illegal throughout the country until about 1970. It remains illegal in twelve states, although the laws are rarely, if ever, enforced.

✔ WHY THE STRUGGLE HAPPENS

The reasons some kids consider cohabitation are many. Every couple in this situation will give you their own specific motivations that make theirs a "different" case. However, the following are some of the most common causes of cohabitation.

Discouraging Divorce Rates

With half of all marriages ending in divorce, many kids no longer feel that marriage is a viable option. The conclusion many kids make is that if so many people can't seem to make it work, why try? They give up before they even begin, believing they can live together without making it binding. Without the lifetime commitment, they reason, we won't set ourselves up for failure like so many other people have.[4]

Unhealthy Marriage at Home

Many kids today have grown up in homes where they observed a poor model for marriage.[5] In fact, kids who grow up with both biological parents still married and living in the same house are now a minority. Also, the share of people in first marriages who say the relationship is "very happy" was 37 percent in 1996, down from 53 percent in the early 1970s. How does this hit home with teenagers? The statistics speak for themselves: 63 percent of girls and 53 percent of boys don't want a marriage like their parents' marriage.[6]

"Everybody's Doing It"

The number of unwed couples living together is at an all-time high, with more than four million doing so. That's a quantum leap from the 430,000 cohabiting couples in 1960. And because of the high incidence of cohabitation, more and more kids are viewing it as normal. If so many people are living together without being married, the reasoning goes, it must be a pretty good thing to do. So they join the growing crowd of cohabitants.

Hedonism

Marriage expert Everett Worthington has pointed out that a teenager's moral development operates on a hedonistic level. At this stage, some kids justify cohabitation because it "feels right." A young person might say, for example, "We are in love. It feels so right to be together. But neither of us feels that we are mature enough for a lifetime commitment of marriage, so we are living together."[7]

Hollywood and Media Influence

Watch MTV for only ten minutes and you quickly learn that living together is not only common, but cool. Watch shows specifically targeted to teens and young adults, and you will see countless examples of premarital sex and shacking up—all in the absence of any moral concern. Cohabiting has been portrayed with careful neutrality in the media, and Hollywood celebrities who move in and out with each other are treated as if their behavior is normal.[8] Few would dispute that these "role models" are sending a clear message that justifies cohabitation for some kids.

Diminished Rite of Passage

For decades, marriage was the natural course for a couple who had dated and reached a certain maturity level. It was a significant sign of adulthood. Typically, couples would often marry soon after graduating from high school or college. Not so these days. As a rite of passage, marriage is losing much of its social importance and ritual significance. It is no longer the standard pathway from adolescence to adulthood for young adults today.

The "Lifestyle Option"

How adolescents define a decision to live together is crucial in predicting whether they may choose that path. Cohabitation is often seen as involving both religious issues as well as lifestyle issues. But if a kid sees it primarily as a lifestyle choice and disregards the religious and moral implications, he is far more likely to cohabit. The point is that some kids simply see this as a way to live and nothing more. Morals don't factor into the decision for them.

Postponement of Marriage

People are putting off marriage. The average age for marriage has risen considerably. It is a clear sign that some young people are postponing the big decision by giving the relationship a test drive. It is viewed as a kind of farm league for marriage, where people can determine whether they are ready to play ball in the big leagues. To use another analogy, some view cohabitation as a dress rehearsal, a dry run before the real show. If the trial run proves successful, they move on to the real thing and enjoy the fruits of a "well-tested" relationship culminating in eventual marriage.

Case Description

Ron and Cindy, seniors in high school, have been dating each other off and on since junior high school. As they are thinking about their future they are becoming more and more serious as a couple. Not feeling that they are ready for marriage, Ron is urging Cindy to rent an apartment with him and live together. He's told her how beneficial it will be for their finances and how it would be a good way to prepare for their future marriage. When Cindy, raised in a conservative churchgoing family, talks about her desire to get married after graduation, Rod "flips out." His emotional tirades scare Cindy into thinking he might leave her if she doesn't move in with him. The more she thinks about it, the more convinced she becomes that living together may be a pretty good way to prepare for marriage. Still, her ambivalence is obvious, and she knows it is not the best choice to make.

☑ HOW PARENTS CAN HELP

The following strategies for helping an adolescent struggling with cohabitation issues can be used effectively by parents; however, every parent-child relationship is unique, and some of them may be more pertinent to your situation than others. As with every significant adolescent struggle, it is best for parents to work alongside a competent counselor. With this in mind, the following is offered as a way to help you facilitate the helping process at home with your teenager.

Reveal How Cohabiting Weakens Marriage

When couples choose to live together outside of wedlock, their relationship is something quite different from and significantly weaker than marriage. Researchers have found specifically that most cohabitations end within two years and that cohabitations are not informal marriages, but relationships formed by a looser bond. Research has shown that men and women looking for someone with whom to cohabit look for characteristics such as dependency, which can reflect a short-term ability to contribute to the relationship (by making the other person feel needed). This is called a Linus Relationship. Or they may want to establish an Emancipation Relationship, to prove to parents and peers that they are free to make their own decisions and are not bound by any constraints. Or they may want a Convenience Relationship—for economic reasons. They intend on splitting everything 50/50 though the woman contributes seventy percent of the income in the relationship. This turns into the traditional role pattern: male dominant, female submissive. Other couples want a Testing Relationship—committed or thinking they are committed to getting married. But most cohabiting couples are not living together after two years.[9]

In contrast, men and women looking for a spouse pay more attention to ascribed characteristics (such as age and religion) that reflect long-term considerations. Researchers concluded, "While cohabitors anticipate time together, married persons anticipate a lifetime."[10] The bottom line is that cohabiting weakens marriage. Moving in doesn't lead to "happily ever after": Forty percent of cohabiting couples never make it to the altar. And of the 60 percent who do marry, more than half divorce.

Warn Women of Most Men's Motives

Studies have clearly found that men typically cohabit because of the "convenience" of the relationship, whereas women cohabit with the expectation that cohabitation will lead to marriage—thus creating a relationship in which men are likely to hold a position of power over women who expect much more from the relationship than they do. No wonder that cohabiting couples report greater tension in the relationship than do married couples.[11]

Show How Cohabiting Increases Cheating

Sometimes the best deterrent to a certain behavior can be to show the negative consequences of it. And there is an ever-growing collection of data that sheds an unfavorable light on the living arrangement called cohabiting. For example, if a woman lives with a man before marriage, she is more likely to cheat on him after marriage. In a study of more than 1,000 people, it was discovered that women who have cohabited before marriage are 3.3 times more likely to have a secondary sex partner after marriage. The same study also found that married women are five times less likely to have a secondary sex partner than cohabiting women and that cohabiting relationships appear to be more similar to dating relationships than to marriage.[12]

Point to Other Important Facts

Many people think living together before marriage is like a trial run, that it makes you more prepared for crossing the proverbial threshold of marriage. They assume that if they live together first, they can avoid a costly and painful mistake later. But research shows us this simply is not true. There is now little question among researchers and marriage experts that cohabitation is a good predictor of divorce, regardless of whether individuals marry the person they lived with. Why is this so? Several reasons, but one is that cohabitation gives a false sense of security to a couple that they have already experienced what marriage will be like, leaving them shocked and disappointed when further difficulties emerge.[13] Another interesting fact is that those who have cohabited are less sexually satisfied on average compared to those who have never lived with someone before marriage. In fact, 44 percent of non-cohabitors rate their sexual satisfaction a nine or ten compared to 34 percent of those who have cohabited.[14]

Speak the Truth About Sin

Many couples may need to be sensitively confronted with the biblical basis for not cohabiting. Sex outside of marriage is against the design and law of God. The task we have in working with a couple in this situation is to speak the truth in love (Ephesians 4:15). Then, only the Holy Spirit can convince the couple to change. There is no single right way to tell a couple that their cohabitation is sin. While some require a more direct and blunt approach, others need to have their positive motives affirmed while they are shown that cohabitation is still not in line with God's Word. Specific verses of Scripture that may be helpful in this process include Matthew 15:19; 1 Corinthians 6:13, 18; Colossians 3:5; and 1 Thessalonians 4:3.

Help the Church Provide a Prevention Plan

The best way to solve nearly any problem is before it starts. And when it comes to stemming the rising tide of cohabitation, there is much the church can do. Everett Worthington suggests that the church do the following to accomplish this: (a) give a clear message from the pulpit about cohabitation as being against God's law, (b) hold Sunday school and other study classes on contemporary issues in Christian living that include this issue, (c) be clear about the joys and benefits of Christian marriage, and about the benefits of chastity until marriage.[15]

☑ HOW PROFESSIONALS CAN HELP

The following strategies for helping an adolescent struggling with cohabitation issues are commonly used by counselors. They are presented here as a way to inform you, as a parent, and help you seek the best possible professional help you can for the adolescent in your care.

Teach Mate Selection Skills

One common reason single people live together is that they are trying to find a partner and don't know a better way to do it. For the most part, nowhere does any institution in society—schools, churches, even family—help you pick a mate. For this reason, teaching mate selection skills is essential. And one of the most effective tools for doing so comes in Dr. Neil Warren's excellent book *Finding the Love of Your Life*. He points out ten principles for smart dating: (1) eliminate the causes of faulty mate selection, (2) develop a clear mental image of your ideal spouse, (3) find a person to love who is a lot like you, (4) get yourself healthy before you get yourself married, (5) find a love you can feel deep in your heart, (6) let passionate love mature before you decide to marry, (7) master the art of intimacy, (8) learn how to clear conflict from the road of love, (9) refuse to proceed until you can genuinely pledge your lifelong commitment, and (10) celebrate your marriage with the full support of family and friends. The goal here is to show that dating, not living together, is the best way to go about learning about and discerning a prospective mate.[16]

Teach Marital Skills

Research clearly shows that couples who master certain skills—like conflict resolution and active listening—are less likely to split up. My wife and I wrote *Saving Your Marriage Before It Starts* to help couples learn these essential skills. In the book and the accompanying workbooks (one for males, one for females), we explore seven questions couples need to be asking before they marry: (1) Have you faced the myths of marriage with honesty? (2) Can you identify your love style? (3) Have you developed the habit of happiness? (4) Can you say what you mean and understand what you hear? (5) Have you bridged the gender gap? (6) Do you know how to fight a good fight? (7) Are you and your partner soul mates? Each of these questions targets a specific skill set that will help couples prepare for lifelong love.[17]

Where to Go for Additional Help

Aranza, J. *Making a Love That Lasts: How to Find Love Without Settling for Sex.* Ann Arbor, Mich.: Servant Publications, 1996.

Balswick, J., and J. Balswick. *Raging Hormones: What to Do When You Suspect Your Teen May Be Sexually Active.* Grand Rapids: Zondervan, 1994.

Bastian, D. N. *Counterfeit: The Lie of Living Together Unmarried.* Mississauga, Ontario: Light and Life Press Canada, 1988.

Laaser, M. *Faithful and True: Sexual Integrity in a Fallen World.* Grand Rapids: Zondervan, 1996.

Parrott, L., and L. Parrott. *Getting Ready for the Wedding.* Grand Rapids: Zondervan, 1995.

_____. *Questions Couples Ask.* Grand Rapids: Zondervan, 1996.

_____. *Relationships: Making Bad Relationships Better and Good Relationships Great.* Grand Rapids: Zondervan, 1998.

_____. *Saving Your Marriage Before It Starts: Seven Questions to Ask Before and After You Marry.* Grand Rapids: Zondervan, 1995.

Popenoe, D. *Should We Live Together?: What Young Adults Need to Know About Cohabitation Before Marriage, A Comprehensive Review of Recent Research.* New Brunswick, N.J.: National Marriage Project, 1999.

Rinehart, S., and P. Rinehart. *Choices: Finding God's Way in Dating, Sex, Singleness, and Marriage.* Colorado Springs, Colo.: NavPress, 1996.

Sexuality, Health & Relationship Education, 15935 NE 8th Suite B200, Bellevue, Wash. 98008; www.share-program.com.

Smith, M. B. *Should I Get Married?* Downers Grove, Ill.: InterVarsity Press, 1990.

Stanton, G. T. *Why Marriage Matters: Reasons to Believe in Marriage in Postmodern Society.* Colorado Springs, Colo.: Pinion Press.

Warren, N. C. *Finding the Love of Your Life.* Colorado Springs, Colo.: Focus on the Family, 1992.

Notes

1. www.marriage.rutgers.edu.

2. N. Hellmich, "Teens: Marriage Will Last Lifetime?" *USA Today* (July 10, 1999):3.

3. E. L. Worthington, *Counseling for Unplanned Pregnancy and Infertility* (Dallas, Tex.: Word Publishing, 1988).

4. D. N. Lye and I. Waldron, "Attitudes Toward Cohabitation, Family, and Gender Roles: Relationships to Values and Political Ideology," *Sociological Perspectives* 40 (1997): 199–225.

5. W. D. Manning and D. T. Lichter, "Parental Cohabitation and Children's Economic Well-Being," *Journal of Marriage and the Family* 58 (1996): 998–1010.

6. Hellmich, "Teens: Marriage Will Last Lifetime?", 3.

7. Worthington, *Counseling for Unplanned Pregnancy and Infertility,*

8. S. Wu, "The Stability of Cohabitation Relationship," *Journal of Marriage and the Family* 57 (1995): 231–36.

9. http://members.aol.com/cohabiting/types.htm. Copyrighted 1999.

10. R. Schoen and R. M. Weinick, "Partner Choice in Marriages and Cohabitations," *Journal of Marriage and the Family* 55 (1993): 408–14.

11. T. Huffman, "Gender Differences and Factors Related to the Disposition Toward Cohabitation," *Family Therapy* 21, (1994): 171–84.

12. R. Forest and K. Tanfer, "Sexual Exclusivity Among Dating, Cohabiting, and Married Women," *Journal of Marriage and the Family* 58 (1996): 33–47.

13. S. L. Nock, A Comparison of Marriages and Cohabiting Relationships," *Journal of Family Issues* 16 (1995): 53–76.

14. Forest and Tanfer, *Sexual Exclusivity,* 33–47.

15. Worthington, *Counseling for Unplanned Pregnancy and Infertility,*

16. N. C. Warren, *Finding the Love of Your Life* (Colorado Springs, Colo.: Focus on the Family, 1992).

17. L. Parrott and L. Parrott, *Saving Your Marriage Before It Starts: Seven Questions to Ask Before and After You Marry* (Grand Rapids: Zondervan, 1995).

DEPRESSION

✔ WHAT THE STRUGGLE LOOKS LIKE

Depression, the "common cold of psychopathology," touches everyone's life. Whether it be as a temporary mood or as a suicidal psychosis, no one is exempt—especially adolescents.

As young people travel the rugged road that leads to adulthood, it should come as no surprise that symptoms of depression often hover overhead like a black cloud. When adolescents leave the less demanding life of childhood and struggle for identity, many experience a sad sense of loss. Saying good-bye to the security of having their decisions made for them, they slowly accept responsibility, dragging their heels and echoing the words of Peter Pan: "I don't want to grow up." And understandably so. Failing to make the junior high basketball team, sitting alone in a crowded cafeteria, not having the right answer when a teacher calls on them in class, or not having a date on the weekend can strike a powerful blow to the wobbly underpinnings that guard against adolescent depression.

Case Description

Cindy is a seventeen-year-old in high school. She is overweight, her facial expression is sad and pained, and her eyes are lifeless. Her hair is limp and oily. She came for counseling because her life had lost the joy and energy it once had.

> As a child she loved school and church and looked forward to the days when she could go out with boys as her older sisters did.
>
> Cindy's depression seemed to be the consequence of her inability to deal with herself and her external circumstances. She views the world in negative terms and blames her former boyfriend for her negative internal state. If she had a date every weekend, however, she would find another reason to be unhappy. In other words, the source of her depression is her attitude. Listening to Cindy, I felt that if only someone would ask her out she would no longer be depressed. The truth is she needs to restructure her outlook and take responsibility for her feelings. For some reason she has made her feelings solely dependent upon other people's responses to her.

Some depression in adolescence is normal and is probably better thought of as feeling down or blue. However, a point comes at which feelings of discouragement take on the debilitating characteristics of depression. The early signs include a sad facial expression, a loss of interest in school, church, or leisure-time activities, being easily agitated and irritated, feelings of inferiority, worthlessness, helplessness, or guilt. As depression worsens, the loss of energy is accompanied by insomnia or hypersomnia, loss of appetite or excessive eating, social withdrawal, pessimism, difficulties in concentration, and an inability to enjoy pleasurable events. The most important symptoms to watch for occur together: a sad mood and a loss of interest in one's environment.[1]

Depressions come in various types. Archibald Hart, in *Depression: Coping and Caring*, outlines the three major categories of depression. *Endogenous* depression comes from a biochemical disturbance in the hormonal system, the nervous system, or even from an infection in the body. It seems to rise spontaneously, is usually found in the elderly or in psychotic disorders, and requires medical intervention.

Reactive (or exogenous) depression occurs as a result of a real, imagined, or threatened loss and usually lasts no longer than a few months. This is the typical depression found in adolescence, and counseling is the usual treatment. *Neurotic* depression is a lifestyle response to stress and anxiety. It is used to escape from other emotions and develops over a long period of time. Another type of depression noted by some professionals is *masked* depression. This depression is hidden by other symptoms. For example, teenagers who have lost parents may cover their depression by acting out sexually or by drug abuse.

✅ WHY THE STRUGGLE HAPPENS

Researchers have isolated several possible causes for depression during the teen years. Although it is difficult to label a specific source, it is safe to say that depression is probably a combination of several causes.

Biochemical Causes

Although it is not believed that people inherit depression, some evidence suggests that people can inherit a predisposition to depression.[2] Some researchers also believe that in certain cases changes in hormone levels contribute to depressed feelings.[3] While physical causes can be complicated (e.g., glandular disorders, brain tumors, etc.), they can also be as simple as medication side effects, improper diet, and lack of sleep.

Life Experience

Although life experiences do not have to lead to depression, they do increase the probability of its occurrence. When adolescents, for example, have grown up with parents who set their expectations and standards beyond the ability of their children, failure becomes inevitable and teens will eventually become depressed. Even a short life of perceived failure or rejection can increase the likelihood of depression.

Social Rewards

Some assert that people become and remain depressed because of the rewards they obtain, usually in special attention, when they appear sad in front of others.[4] The sympathy and concern they receive reinforces their depression. Well-meaning people who comfort a depressed adolescent girl, for example, can potentially be sustaining her symptoms. She may not want to risk loss of their attention by getting well.

Learned Helplessness

People can also become depressed when they think they have no control.[5] If teens believe that there is nothing they can do to cause change—to help parents understand them, for example—or that their actions are futile no matter how hard they try, they will eventually give up and be depressed.

Faulty Logic

Negative thinking can result in depression. High school students who think they are total failures because they didn't say the right thing at the lunch table is an example. They selectively concentrate on a single mistake to convince themselves they are worthless. When teens feel inadequate or view life as a burden or see their future as going nowhere, they are likely to trigger a downward spiral of depression that reinforces their negative expectations.

To assume that depression is the result of only one cause, biochemical for instance, is too simplistic. Several factors contribute to depression, including the physiological, sociological, and psychological. In other words, the causes of depression are not mutually exclusive.

✔ HOW PARENTS CAN HELP

The following strategies for helping an adolescent struggling with depression can be used effectively by parents; however, every parent-child relationship is unique, and some of them may be more pertinent to your situation than others. As with every significant adolescent struggle, it is best for parents to work alongside a competent counselor. With this in mind, the following is offered as a way to help you facilitate the helping process at home with your teenager.

Challenge Irrational Thinking

Many depressed adolescents define their life situations in global terms like "*everything* is hopeless," "*nothing* is going right," "I'm a *total* jerk." As long as they continue to see themselves or the world in bleak, generalized terms, they will remain depressed.[6] When challenged they will often answer affirmatively to questions like the following: "Is *everything* hopeless or basically only the chances of you and Dan getting back together?" "Is *nothing* going right or only the way things are going on the basketball court?" "Are you really a *total* jerk or did you act like a jerk only during lunch?" As you help them to chip away slowly at their irrational thinking, they can decrease their overwhelming feeling of depression and begin to see themselves and the world more realistically.[7]

Evaluate the Secondary Gains

Through reflective listening, clarification, and sensitive questioning, seek out any potential social rewards. For example, if you suspect that your sixteen-year-old daughter is depressed in part because she receives extraneous attention from her boyfriend, gently probe. "I wonder," you might say, "whether there are any benefits, any good things, to feeling down." Though none may be acknowledged, it will at least begin the internal process of self-questioning and eventual heightened awareness.

Encourage Physical Activity

While little can sometimes be done to change depression-producing circumstances, it is possible for depressed adolescents to change their actions; and actions influence feelings. Depression seems to put people into slow motion. In fact, depressed teenagers find it easy to stay in bed, passively pondering their misery. Gently pushing depressed people into activity and exercise can have effective results. Aerobic exercise and long-distance running have been found to increase a sense of control and to elevate the body's chemicals, which are depleted by depression.[8] A moderate but specific exercise (one at which teens are likely to succeed) can be very helpful to depressed adolescents.

Watch for Kids At-Risk for Depression

Until recently teenage depression has been easy to predict but hard to prevent. Children who suffer depression in their teenage years often have parents who are depressed. These at-risk kids are unusually moody. They have few friends. Their grades are poor. And females are statistically five times more likely to suffer depression than males. However, having depressed parents, bad grades, poor social skills, shifting moods, and being female doesn't have to doom a child to later depression. Recent research has shown that we can protect such teenagers from developing debilitating depression. Clinicians at Oregon Health Sciences University have prevented 75 percent of predicted clinical teenage depression. Through an eight-week group program, experts focus on changing students' thoughts to be more realistic. The peer group works on solving negative thought patterns for one another. They also help kids to focus on success. If a teen is failing at peer relationships, for example, the focus needs to be on relieving depression before focusing on changing how he or she interacts with peers. Too often we put the cart before the horse.[9] The point is that counselors who work with adolescents will treat the early onset of depression—especially in kids who are at-risk.

✔ HOW PROFESSIONALS CAN HELP

The following strategies for helping an adolescent struggling with depression are commonly used by counselors. They are presented here as a way to inform you, as a parent, and help you seek the best possible professional help you can for the adolescent in your care.

Pinpoint the Severity

At the beginning of treatment it is helpful to assess the intensity of the depression. A careful assessment can serve as a point from which to measure therapeutic progress. There are several reliable scales counselors will use to do this.

Provide Community

Adolescents struggling with depression often feel that they are the only ones who have ever suffered as they have. It is a feeling of being alone—even in the midst of a loving family.[10] Effective counselors not only attempt to provide a sense of empathic community within the counseling session, but when possible, outside of it as well. A concerned group in their church or other social institution (peers or adults) can do much to melt the ice of loneliness and instill hope. In fact, when people without support and other resources experience a loss, they are more likely to see their situations as hopeless.[11] Adolescents who are not alone are better equipped to conquer depression. A note of caution, however, is in order. Teenagers in this lonely and depressed state often reject what they want and need. And they will certainly bristle at overly expressive warmth or support. Tread softly.

Evaluate the Risk for Suicide

Since depressed people often contemplate suicide, counselors are alert to its signals: self-injurious talk, feelings of hopelessness, sudden and unexplainable shifts to a cheerful mood, knowledge about the most effective suicide methods, a history of prior suicide attempts, and so on.[12] The issue of suicide is addressed directly with any adolescent who is depressed. Counselors will ask, "Do you ever have thoughts of harming yourself? Have you ever attempted suicide?" Direct questioning forces the counselee to confront the issue in a rational setting. If the answer is unclear, they will ask, "Do you think about killing yourself?" If the answer is affirmative they will then ask, "Do you have a plan?" A more thorough discussion of helping suicidal adolescents is found in the section on suicide.

Know When to Refer

Counselors will refer depressed adolescents to psychologically astute physicians or psychiatrists when physical symptoms are present or when the depression is severe enough to warrant medication for temporary relief.

They will also refer depressed adolescents to other competent counselors or psychologists when, over time, counselees feel more out of control and increasingly depressed, hopeless, or suicidal.

Where to Go for Additional Help

Fassler, D. G., and L. S. Dumas. *"Help Me, I'm Sad": Recognizing, Treating, and Preventing Childhood and Adolescent Depression.* New York: Viking Penguin, 1997.

Hart, A. D. *Depression: Coping and Caring.* Arcadia, Calif.: Cope Publications, 1981.

Lloyd-Jones, D. M. *Spiritual Depression: Its Causes and Cure.* Grand Rapids: Eerdmans, 1965.

Minirth, F. B., and P. D. Meier. *Happiness Is a Choice: A Manual on the Symptoms, Causes, and Cures of Depression.* Grand Rapids: Baker Book House, 1978.

Ryan, D. and J. Ryan. *Recovery from Depression.* Downers Grove, Ill.: InterVarsity Press, 1992.

Tan, S–Y., and J. Ortberg. *Coping with Depression: The Common Cold of the Emotional Life.* Grand Rapids: Baker Book House, 1995.

Wemhoff, R., ed. *Anxiety and Depression: The Best Resources to Help You Cope.* Issaquah, Wash: Resource Pathways, 1998.

Notes

1. A. D. Hart, *Depression: Coping and Caring* (Arcadia, Calif.: Cope Publications, 1981).

2. J. D. Barchas et al., "Neuropharmacological Aspects of Affective Disorders," in *Depression: Clinical Biological and Psychological Perspectives*, ed. G. Usdin (New York: Brunner/Mazel, 1977).

3. M. M. Weissman and G. L. Klerman, "Sex Differences and the Epidemiology of Depression," *Archives of General Psychiatry* 34 (1977): 98–111.

4. R. P. Liberman and D. E. Raskin, "Depression: A Behavioral Formulation," *Archives of General Psychiatry* 24, no. 6 (1971): 515–23.

5. M. E. Seligman, *Helplessness: On Depression, Development, and Death* (San Francisco: W. H. Freeman, 1975).

6. G. N. Clarke, P. Rohde, P. M. Lewinsohn, H. Hops, and J. R. Seeley, "Cognitive-Behavioral Treatment of Adolescent Depression: Efficacy of Acute Group Treatment and Booster Sessions," *Journal of the American Academy of Child and Adolescent Psychiatry* 38 (1999): 272–79.

7. P. M. Lewinsohn and G. N. Clarke, "Psychosocial Treatments for Adolescent Depression," *Clinical Psychology Review* 19 (1999): 329–42.

8. K. E. Callen, "Mental and Emotional Aspects of Long-distance Running," *Psychosomatics* 24 (1983): 133–51.

9. G. Dana, "Catching Teenagers Before Depression Hits," *Portland Downtowner* (December 13, 1993): 13–14.

10. G. Olson, M. Nordstroem, and A. von Knorring, "Adolescent Depression: Social Network and Family Climate," *Journal of Child Psychology and Psychiatry and Allied Disciplines* 40 (1999): 227–37.

11. G. W. Brown, T. Harris, and J. R. Copeland, "Depression and Loss," *British Journal of Psychiatry* 130 (1977): 1–18.

12. A. J. Flisher, "Mood Disorder in Suicidal Children and Adolescents: Recent Developments," *Journal of Child Psychology and Psychiatry and Allied Disciplines* 40 (1999): 315–24.

DRUGS AND ALCOHOL

✔ WHAT THE STRUGGLE LOOKS LIKE

One of the most challenging problems facing society today is the use and abuse of chemical substances by teenagers.[1] The numbers of seniors in high school who report using drugs "at some time in their lives" are startling:

Alcohol—93%
Stimulants—27%
Cocaine—16%
Hallucinogens—15%
Sedatives or barbiturates—14%[2]

Inhalants—14%
Tranquilizers—13%
Opiates—10%
LSD—9%

The number-one drug problem, without a doubt, is alcoholism. About three hundred thousand Americans are addicted to heroin, but about nine million are addicted to alcohol. When alcohol abusers are added to the number of hard-core alcoholics, the number is estimated to be over fifteen million. Each day Americans consume 15.7 million gallons of beer and 1.2 million gallons of hard liquor. Another statistic paints a graphic picture of the problem: every twenty-seven minutes a person dies in an alcohol-related automobile crash.[3]

Alcohol is clearly the substance with which adolescents have the most experience. Statistics vary but the best estimates indicate that there could be more than four million American alcoholics under the age of eighteen. And the age of experimentation is getting younger. Today's junior highers are facing decisions about drugs that were once reserved only for older youth. Trying alcohol today is already more common among current fifth graders than it was among current eighth graders when they were in the fifth grade. The percentage of youth who drank alcohol "ten or more times in the last twelve months" doubles between the eighth and ninth grades. Substance use among adolescents is a problem the size of Goliath. Each weekend 30 to 40 percent of the youth in America use alcohol and drugs.[4]

Even the best of adolescents become addicts and their parents often have no idea. Stephen Arterburn and Jim Burns, in their insightful book *Drug-Proof Your Kids*, quote a sixteen-year-old who is an active church youth group member: "I don't think it even entered my parents' minds that I was a teenage alcoholic. . . . They didn't suspect that almost every day for the past two years, I was getting high." Parents today do not have the luxury of not worrying about their families being threatened by drugs. Almost every young person experiments with drugs or alcohol, and the statistics for heavy drug use for churched and unchurched kids are almost identical.[5]

The warning signs of teenage alcohol and drug abuse include social withdrawal, deterioration in school performance, resistance to authority, behavior problems, high-risk behavior such as stealing, extreme mood swings (which include signs of depression), sexual promiscuity, physical complaints, changes in relationships, changes in eating habits, and the more observable signs such as alcohol on the breath, slurred speech, staggering, appearing "spaced out," dilated pupils, the presence of drug paraphernalia (pipes, pill boxes, straws, spoons), and clothing depicting drug themes.

The *Diagnostic and Statistical Manual* (4th ed.) makes a helpful distinction in understanding pathological use of substances. It defines two categories: psychoactive substance abuse and psychoactive substance dependence. Together they constitute Psychoactive Substance Use Disorders. Substance dependence can be thought of as an addiction. It is the abuse of a drug accompanied by impairment in social and occupational functioning and by psychological dependence upon it. Substance abuse is a less severe version of dependence. It is diagnosed when the use of a substance is maladaptive but not severe enough to meet the criteria for dependence.

The DSM-IV defines psychoactive substance *dependence* as the presence of at least three of the following symptoms for at least one month.

1. The person uses more of the substance or uses it for a longer time than intended.
2. The person recognizes excessive use of the substance and may have tried to reduce it but has been unable to do so.

3. Much of the person's time is spent in efforts to obtain the substance or recover from its effects.
4. The person is intoxicated or suffering from withdrawal symptoms at times when responsibilities need to be fulfilled, such as at school or work.
5. Many activities are given up or reduced in frequency because of the use of the substance.
6. Problems in health, social relationships, and psychological functioning occur.
7. Tolerance develops, requiring larger doses (at least a 50 percent increase) of the substance to produce the desired effect.
8. Withdrawal symptoms develop when the person stops ingesting substances or reduces the amount.
9. The person uses the substance to relieve withdrawal symptoms. For example, one may drink alcohol early in the morning because one feels withdrawal symptoms coming on.[6]

The DSM-IV defines psychoactive substance *abuse* as the presence of at least one of the following:

1. Continued use despite knowledge of having a persistent or recurrent social, occupational, psychological, or physical problem that is caused or exacerbated by use of the psychoactive substance.
2. Recurrent use in situations in which use is physically hazardous. For example, driving while intoxicated.[7]

The counselor's task is to distinguish the adolescents who use drugs primarily for sociocultural reasons from those youngsters who use drugs in a desperate effort to hide or correct a perceived personal deficiency. Drug and alcohol use varies considerably from one adolescent to another. Rich Van Pelt, in his helpful book *Intensive Care*, lists five stages in adolescents' progression toward alcohol addiction. He credits Larry Silver of the National Institute of Mental Health for their development.

Stage 0.   Curiosity in a world where alcohol is readily available.

Stage 1.   Learning the mood swing. Adolescents learn how easy it is to feel good with few, if any, consequences, except perhaps mild guilt.

Stage 2.   Seeking the mood swing. Rather than using alcohol as an accompaniment to social events, the youngster decides to get drunk as a goal and arranges to have his or her own supply.

Stage 3.   Preoccupation with the mood swing. Being drunk is
            the main goal of life. Students who drink daily may
            plan their days around trips to euphoria.

Stage 4.   Drinking to feel okay (addiction). The euphoria
            becomes harder to achieve; larger amounts are
            needed.[8]

I also find it helpful to distinguish four possible and common types of adolescent drug users.

1.   *The Experimenter.* This adolescent experiments with drug use up to four or five times in order to gain acceptance and be "in the know." Their use is short-term and low in frequency.
2.   *The Recreationist.* This young person uses drugs to share pleasurable experiences with friends, not to achieve a mood or mental effect from the substance.
3.   *The Seeker.* This adolescent seeks an altered state and uses drugs and/or alcohol regularly to achieve a sedative or intoxicant effect.
4.   *The Drug Head.* This is a "sick" adolescent who has moved to regular use of hard drugs like cocaine or heroin. He or she is addicted.

John E. Meeks, in his book *The Fragile Alliance: An Orientation to the Outpatient Psychotherapy of the Adolescent,* says the "Drug Head" or "sick" users may often be identified by observing more than a high frequency of drug use. They show serious deficiencies in interpersonal relationships. They compensate for these deficiencies through group membership in a drug subculture, where the only thing members have in common is their drug experience. They simply prefer drug intoxication over pleasures derived from relationships.[9]

Case Description

Matt is sixteen. He was brought into counseling by his mom who was tired of dealing with his drug-abuse problems. Matt's school was also threatening him with expulsion unless he secured immediate treatment. He was caught drinking alcohol in the morning on school property two months ago, and more recently school officials discovered marijuana in his locker. He denied having a problem with drinking or drugs ("It's as if I committed murder or something"), but did report smoking marijuana "now and then."

As a young boy Matt was pleasant and never seemed to cause much trouble. In junior high, however, he began to hang out with young people his mom and dad did not like. "He started listening to loud music," his mom reported, "and he begged and begged to go to a Pink Floyd concert with his friends until I just had to let him go." Four years ago Matt's parents were divorced, but they live in the same town and still see each other. In the first session Matt's father joined his former wife in the intervention. He described discovering that Matt and his friends use an old rusted-out van that is up on blocks in a neighbor's back yard as their "drug club." As he described how it was sealed up to keep the smoke contained and thus increase its effect, Matt began to roll his eyes.

Before discussing the causes of this struggle, it is helpful to review the kinds of drugs that are often abused. It is perhaps most useful to define them by how they affect the body. When classified this way, four major types of drugs evolve.

1. *Depressants.* These slow down the activity of the nervous system. They include alcohol, inhalants (including glue, nail polish remover, cleaning fluid, lighter fluid, antifreeze, and gasoline), minor tranquilizers (including valium), and sedatives (including barbiturates, Quaaludes, and PCP). All depressants except PCP can be obtained legally.
2. *Stimulants.* These stimulate activity, suppress the appetite, and ameliorate emotional depression. They include the legal drugs caffeine and nicotine as well as the legal and illegal amphetamines and the illegal methadrine and cocaine.
3. *Hallucinogens.* These are mind-distorters. They have little medical use and create altered perceptions. They include marijuana, LSD, and mescaline. All hallucinogens are illegal.
4. *Narcotics.* These have an analgesic effect. They relieve physical pain and make surgery possible, but they are highly addictive. They include morphine, codeine, and heroin.

☑ WHY THE STRUGGLE HAPPENS

Drugs are readily available in our society, and most teens will experiment with some of them—usually alcohol, tobacco, and marijuana. Experimenters should not be considered in the same category as those who regularly use or abuse drugs. The following is a list of some of the reasons for regularly using drugs. As is often the case, research is not consistently clear on causes, but most experts agree that drug use entails a variety of risk factors.

Media Influence

Movies, television, and advertisements often glamorize drinking. There is an average of ten to eleven "drinking acts" (defined as ingestion of alcohol or preparation to drink) per hour of prime-time television. For many TV viewers this means witnessing about twenty drinking scenes almost every evening. Of course, marketing alcohol is serious business. By the time the average teen is eighteen years old, he or she has seen 100,000 TV beer commercials. The goal of advertisers is to increase the percentage of those who drink and increase the number of times people drink.

In *It's Killing Our Kids*, Jerry Johnston points out that Michelob Beer's ad campaign began a decade ago with the catchy slogan "Weekends are made for Michelob." Soon the ad evolved into "Put a little weekend in your week." Then the sales pitch became "The night belongs to Michelob." In about one decade, Michelob moved from advocating drinking as a way to unwind on the weekend to promoting drinking as a habitual nightly activity.[10]

Despite the legal drinking age of twenty-one in most states, adolescents are becoming a major target group for advertising campaigns featuring alcohol. These companies know that winning the brand loyalty of a young person may result in loyalty for several years. The alcohol industry also knows that the largest portion of beer drinkers is between eighteen and twenty-four, with college students spending two billion dollars annually on beer.[11]

Peer Pressure

Half of all seventh graders have been pressured to try marijuana, and by the twelfth grade, more than half of them have given in.[12] "It's cool to get drunk," according to many teens. Peer pressure in social environments of heavy party drinking is inescapable for virtually all students. Drinking at a party can even become a sign of prestige and respect. You might hear adolescents praise a classmate by saying, "What a man! Bill is still on his feet after a whole fifth. Bill can really hold his liquor." During a typical two-week period, 40 percent of high school seniors participate in binge drinking of five or more drinks in a row.

Family Factors

The literature is replete with studies citing the parent-child relationship as the primary factor in adolescent drug use. Parents who themselves use alcohol, tobacco, and prescription drugs (especially amphetamines, barbiturates, and tranquilizers) are more likely to have children who use drugs.[13] The Children of Alcoholics Foundation states that children of alcoholics are at greater risk by four times of developing alcoholism than children of nonalcoholics. There are 28.6 million children of alcoholics in the United States today; 6.6 million of them are under the age of eighteen.[14] As you may guess, parental warmth and positive control are correlated with absence of drug abuse.

Inheritance

Inherited addictive predispositions might be a factor in abuse. The research is not even close to conclusive in this area, but by studying adopted children whose biological parents were alcoholics, researchers have found them more likely to be alcoholics themselves, regardless of whether their adoptive parents abuse alcohol. Still, it must be noted that over one-third of all alcoholics have no family history of alcoholism.[15]

Personality Factors

Research has shown that a certain kind of adolescent is more vulnerable to drug use. This young person typically struggles with low self-esteem, has low expectations for personal achievement, lacks impulse control, is highly adventuresome and independent, and is seeking inclusion in a social group. Basically, the adolescent who is low on inner resources is most vulnerable. Drugs, for this young person, sometimes make unbearable feelings bearable.

In addition to these general guidelines, the following techniques have been helpful in treating adolescent drug and alcohol abuse.

✅ HOW PARENTS CAN HELP

The following strategies for helping an adolescent struggling with drugs or alcohol can be used effectively by parents; however, every parent-child relationship is unique, and some of them may be more pertinent to your situation than others. As with every significant adolescent struggle, it is best for parents to work alongside a competent counselor. With this in mind, the following is offered as a way to help you facilitate the helping process at home with your teenager.

Know the Language

It can be very difficult for parents or counselors to communicate with adolescents who are deeply into the world of drugs if terminology is not clarified. Here are some of the more common drug-related terms that have a specialized meaning:

Trip refers to the feelings, thoughts, and perceptions one experiences while under the influence of a hallucinogenic. A "bad trip" results in panic and terror.

Pot, reefer, spliff, weed, nickel, joint, roach, dime, bone, bong, hit, hooch, doobie, grass, shake, and *smoke* are used to refer to marijuana.

Burnout is the disorientation, confusion, and possible memory loss resulting from long-term and heavy use of hallucinogens or amphetamines.

Skin popping refers to injecting drugs under the skin. *Mainlining* is injecting drugs directly into the vein. *Slamming* is injecting speed, cocaine, or heroin.

Crash or *crashing* refers to coming down from a speed or cocaine high.

Bag or *baggie* refers to an amount of marijuana in a plastic bag. A *dime bag* is a ten-dollar bag of marijuana.

Blitzed, lit, ripped, wasted, freaked, blasted, buzzed, and *cooked* are used to refer to getting or being high.

These are just a few of a number of terms that adolescents who are into drugs frequently use. Beth Polson and Miller Newton in *Not My Kid* provide a more extensive slang glossary of drug terms. Counselors, however, need not learn a new language. They should be honest and ask for clarification of any terminology used by young people that is confusing. Most adolescents enjoy educating their counselors in this way.

Plug into the Support of a Church

Research has clearly shown that parental disapproval of drug and alcohol use serves as direct control against youth substance abuse. In other words, early parental disapproval becomes an internalized control in a young person's life that is one of the greatest deterrents to this negative behavior.[16] Research has also shown that many churches serve as extended families for adolescents and can play a parental role of insulating the child from negative influences. The implication of these findings underscores the importance of developing youth groups and activities that offer teens a sense of belonging, purpose, and status. In addition to promoting non-substance abusing beliefs and values, church activities provide alternatives to alcohol and drug use.[17]

Prepare for Follow-up Care

The likelihood of a relapse must be addressed. Progress and change do not always go as planned. For the adolescent recovering from drug abuse, each day is filled with land mines of setbacks and relapses. To insure their safety and to avoid these dangers, it is necessary to plan ahead. Joseph White recommends three things:[18]

1. The plan should first of all incorporate maintenance of a solid support system. Adolescents need to be around encouraging peers who reinforce drug-free living. AA organizations, youth centers, teen hot lines, and drug-abuse programs can usually connect teens to long-term support groups. Overcomers Outreach is a Christian twelve-step support group for teens with hundreds of programs in forty-two states. For more information contact Overcomers Outreach, Inc., 520 N. Brookhurst, Suite 121, Anaheim, CA 92801; 714-491-3000.

2. The plan should also recognize relapse warning signs. These include being dishonest with one's self, justifying or rationalizing how one can resume using drugs without abuse, drifting back to old drug-abusing peers, expecting life to be perfect and becoming depressed or angry when it isn't, and denying that one has to worry about drug abuse anymore.

3. Finally, the plan should incorporate a relationship with a primary resource person. This is typically the counselor or therapist they have been meeting with. There should be an open invitation to youths to meet periodically to discuss the concerns of growing up. This should not be a flip invitation. It must be backed up with specific dates and a promise to be accessible if an emergency arises.

✔ HOW PROFESSIONALS CAN HELP

The following strategies for helping an adolescent struggling with drugs or alcohol are commonly used by counselors. They are presented here as a way to inform you, as a parent, and help you seek the best possible professional help you can for the adolescent in your care.

Consider Confidentiality and Safety Issues

Counselors will assure adolescents that their counseling is a private matter held in the strictest confidence. But they will also let them also know the limits of that confidentiality. Adolescents will be told that confidentiality will be broken if counselors feel the drugs are dangerous to health or if the sale of drugs is potentially dangerous to other youngsters. Counselors must clearly explain that they will do whatever is possible to interrupt these destructive activities. A reasonable therapeutic alliance cannot exist when counselors permit behavior that is clearly self-destructive.

Consider Inpatient Treatment

Teenage drug abuse and addiction is a serious problem that may require intensive treatment by a professionally trained staff in a hospital setting.

Hospital-based programs generally last six to eight weeks with several months of follow-up.

Hospitalization should be considered in these cases:

1. Adolescents have unsuccessfully tried to quit or stop abusing drugs several times on their own.
2. They have been unsuccessful in outpatient treatment programs.
3. There has been an overdose, or the potential for one is strong. For example, they are mixing street drugs and alcohol.
4. Medical attention is necessary to control severe withdrawal symptoms.
5. Suicidal thoughts, bad trips, and flashbacks are occurring.
6. Adolescents' behavior is out of control. They are truant, failing school, stealing to obtain drugs, or in denial when confronted with evidence of drug abuse.
7. Family members are emotionally drained from the roller coaster ride of mood swings, social problems, and arguments that accompany drug abuse.[19]

A competency counselor or your local telephone directory or directory assistance is an immediate means of accessing an inpatient service. To find agencies in your area, look up the following listings in your directory: adolescent clinics, county department of health, mental health clinics, general hospitals, or psychiatric hospitals.

Century HealthCare Corporation offers a variety of programs to help young people fighting addictions. It has programs in more than seventeen cities that provide preventative education services, evaluation, outpatient services, crisis intervention, and residential treatment. You can obtain more information about HealthCare at 800-782-8336.

When psychiatric treatment within an explicitly Christian context is desired, two programs are worth investigating: New Life Treatment Centers and Rapha Hospitals. Each offers professional treatment in hospitals staffed by men and women who are committed to Christ-centered treatment. The programs have several locations across the United States where treatment is immediately available. For information about New Life Treatment Centers, call 800–NEW–LIFE. For information about Rapha, call 800–227–2657 (in Texas call 800–445–2657).

Use Psychoeducational Programs

A psychoeducational approach is designed to clarify values; improve communication, coping, and problem-solving skills; establish goals and a sense of direction; increase awareness of cues that trigger drug use; build support systems;

and explore nonchemical highs. In these programs young people have an opportunity to commit themselves publicly to nondrug use and to hear testimony from others struggling to resist peer pressure and personal desires. Their successes are also strengthened and reinforced. Many of these programs incorporate the twelve steps made popular through Alcoholics Anonymous, the largest and most widely known self-help group in the world. It currently has thirty thousand chapters and a membership of more than a million.

The twelve steps, which are the guiding principles of AA's "one-day-at-a-time" philosophy, have been adapted for young people by the authors of the helpful little book *Young Winners' Way: A Twelve Step Guide for Teenagers*:[20]

1. We admitted we were powerless over alcohol—that our lives had become unmanageable.
2. We came to believe that a Power greater than ourselves could restore us to sanity.
3. We made a decision to turn our wills and our lives over to the care of God, as we understood Him.
4. We made a searching and fearless moral inventory of ourselves.
5. We admitted to God, to ourselves, and to another human being the exact nature of our wrongs.
6. We were entirely ready to have God remove all these defects of character.
7. We humbly asked Him to remove our shortcomings.
8. We made a list of all persons we had harmed and became willing to make amends to them all.
9. We made direct amends to such people wherever possible, except when to do so would injure them or others.
10. We continued to take personal inventory and when we were wrong, promptly admitted it.
11. We sought through prayer and meditation to improve our conscious contact with God, as we understood Him, praying only for knowledge of His will for us and the power to carry that out.
12. Having had a spiritual awakening as the result of these steps, we tried to carry this message to alcoholics and to practice these principles in all our affairs.

Explore Cognitive Distortions

Adolescents' distorted self-talk surrounding drug use is usually so automatic and subtle that they are not aware of its effect. Once this self-talk is mirrored back to the struggling young person and clarified, he or she will move toward reality. Old beliefs about the necessity of using drugs to create excitement and adventure, to feel good, and to suppress unpleasant feelings can be replaced with new self-statements and beliefs that eliminate the necessity for drugs as part of the lifestyle. Here are three commonly used distortions by young drug users:

1. *Selective Abstraction.* This tunnel vision is revealed in self-statements like "The only way I can have fun is to get high."
2. *Overgeneralization.* Examples include "I stopped drinking for two days once, so I know I can stop anytime" or "I didn't have a single friend before I began to drink."
3. *Superstitious Thinking.* This is often an excuse to avoid anxiety. For example they may do drugs just before exams because "When I take this stuff I have powers I never dreamed of" and "I do my most creative work with a few drags from a joint."[21]

Teach Stress Management

Many adolescents turn to drugs as a way of escaping stress. Therapy can show better ways of coping with the pressures of life. Stress in general can be discussed, but actual stress reduction techniques can be taught and practiced. Refer to the sections on anxiety and panic attack for descriptions of a variety of stress-management techniques. Related to this aspect of treatment, of course, is the student's spirituality. Depending on the teen's maturity in faith, this can be utilized as an excellent foundation for recovery (see Spiritual Doubt chapter).[22]

Know When to Refer

Counselors will refer adolescents struggling with substance dependence and abuse to physicians for medical examination if they have long histories of alcohol and/or drug use. They will typically require a comprehensive medical examination early on in treatment. Young people who are high-frequency and high-intensity drug users may be suffering physical side effects and nutritional deficits caused by poor eating habits and lack of physical exercise.

In extreme cases, young people may need an alcohol-free and drug-free environment and an external structure, such as hospitalization, for detoxification. This should be done immediately if they are a danger to themselves (through physical problems or accidents) or to others (through accidents).

Referral to Alcoholics Anonymous or similar group meetings is also a necessary step in helping teens with addiction. These groups provide needed support and constructive options for dealing with dysfunctional patterns.

Where to Go for Additional Help

Arterburn, S., and J. Burns. *Drug-Proof Your Kids.* Ventura, Calif.: Regal Books, 1995.

Clancy, J. *Anger and Relapse: Breaking the Cycle.* Madison, Conn.: Psychosocial Press, 1997.

Johnston, J. *It's Killing Our Kids: The Growing Epidemic of Teenage Alcohol Abuse and Addiction.* Waco, Tex.: Word, 1991.

McGee, R. S., P. Springle, and S. Joiner. *Overcoming Chemical Dependency.* Dallas: Word, 1991.

The National Association of Parents for Drug-Free Youth has established a tollfree line, 800-554-KIDS, that can assist you in treatment strategies.

Nelson, D. D., and J. T. Nolan. *Young Winners' Way: A Twelve Step Guide for Teenagers.* Minneapolis: Comp Care Publications, 1983.

Polson, B., and N. Miller. *Not My Kid: A Parent's Guide to Kids and Drugs.* New York: Avon, 1983.

Schuckit, M. A., and D. L. Schuckit. *Educating Yourself About Alcohol and Drugs: A People's Primer.* New York: Plenum Press, 1998.

Somdahl, G. L. *Drugs and Kids.* Salem, Ore.: Dimi Press, 1996.

Strack, J. *Drugs and Drinking: What Every Teenager and Parent Should Know.* Nashville: Nelson, 1985.

The Will Rogers Institute has a series of booklets on the effects, composition, motives, treatment, and consequences of psychoactive drugs. These free booklets are available from the Will Rogers Institute, 785 Mamaroneck Avenue, White Plains, NY 10605. The telephone number is 914-761-5550.

The following organizations can also be helpful in providing information on adolescents struggling with substance use:

Alcoholics Anonymous
P.O. Box 459
Grand Central Station
New York, NY 10163

Alateen
P.O. Box 182
Madison Square Garden
New York, NY 10159–0182
212-254-7230

National Institute of Drug Abuse
5600 Fishers Lane
Rockville, MD 20857

Notes

1. I. Sutherland and P. Willner, "Patterns of Alcohol, Cigarette, and Illicit Drug Use in English Adolescents," *Addiction* 93 (1998): 1199–1208.

2. G. Beschner, "Understanding Teenage Drug Use," in *Teen Drug Use*, ed. G. Beschner and S. Friedman (Lexington, Mass.: Health, 1986).

3. J. Johnston, *It's Killing Our Kids: The Growing Epidemic of Teenage Alcohol Abuse and Addiction* (Waco, Tex.: Word, 1991).

4. P. Benson, D. Williams, and A. Johnson, *The Quicksilver Years: The Hopes and Fears of Early Adolescence* (New York: Harper & Row, 1987).

5. S. Arterburn and J. Burns, *Drug-Proof Your Kids* (Ventura, Calif.: Regal Books, 1995), 1.

6. *Diagnostic and Statistical Manual of Mental Disorders, 4th ed.* (Washington, D.C.: American Psychiatric Association, 1994).

7. Ibid.

8. R. Van Pelt, *Intensive Care: Helping Teenagers in Crisis* (Grand Rapids: Zondervan, 1988).

9. J. E. Meeks, *The Fragile Alliance: An Orientation to the Outpatient Psychotherapy of the Adolescent* (Baltimore: Williams and Wilkins, 1971).

10. Johnston, *It's Killing Our Kids.*

11. Ibid.

12. L. Johnston, P. O'Malley, and J. Bauchman, *Highlights from Drugs and American High School Students, 1975–1983* (Rockville, Md.: U.S. Institute on Drug Abuse, 1984).

13. M. A. Sheppard, "Peer or Parents: Who Has the Most Influence on Cannabis Use?" *Journal of Drug Education* 17 (1987): 123–28.

14. Johnston, *It's Killing Our Kids.*

15. D. W. Goodwin, "Alcoholism and Heredity: A Review and Hypothesis," *Archives of General Psychiatry* 36 (1979): 57–61.

16. L. Fritzlan, "Raising the Bottom: Setting Limits for Teenage Substance Abusers," *Networker* (July/August 1999): 61–70.

17. M. W. Brand, C. H. Mindel, and D. K. Lewis, "Alcohol and Drug Use Among Religious Adolescents," *Marriage and Family: A Christian Journal* 8 (1999): 77–91.

18. White, *The Troubled Adolescent.*

19. J. L. White, *The Troubled Adolescent* (New York: Pergamon, 1989).

20. D. D. Nelson and J. T. Nolan, *Young Winners' Way: A Twelve Step Guide for Teenagers* (Minneapolis: Comp Care Publications, 1983).

21. G. W. Rowatt, *Pastoral Care with Adolescents in Crisis* (Louisville: Westminster/John Knox, 1989).

22. A. E. Hackerman and P. King, "Adolescent Spirituality: A Foundation for Recovery from Drug Dependency," *Alcoholism Treatment Quarterly* 16 (1998): 89–99.

EATING DISORDERS

✔ WHAT THE STRUGGLE LOOKS LIKE

"Thin is in!" Our nation is obsessed with slimness. Exercise programs, diet centers, weight-loss groups, and figure salons cannot meet the demand. Dieting is one of the fastest-growing businesses in the United States. Some estimate that over twenty million Americans are seriously dieting and that we spend more than ten billion dollars yearly to do so. The media do their part to preach the slim and thin message. Slinky models smile at us from magazines, billboards, and television. Their message is clear: "If you want to be happy and succeed, you cannot be too thin."

Most people are not overly convicted by the "thin is in" idea. They may see it as desirable to lose weight, but that's about as far as it goes. However, this message deeply disturbs two groups of people. Their passion for thinness is overwhelming and out of control. It is pathological. Thinness takes priority over everything else and becomes a dangerous obstruction to well-being. The two groups are anorexics (those who starve themselves) and bulimics (those who binge-eat and purge).[1]

Anorexia nervosa literally means "nervous loss of appetite." In actuality the anorexic generally suffers extreme hunger pains but refrains from eating in order to achieve thinness. The American Anorexia Nervosa Association defines anorexia as a "serious illness of deliberate self-starvation with profound psychiatric and physical components."[2] Anorexia is a life-threatening, self-induced starvation syndrome characterized by the relentless pursuit of thinness and a

117

morbid, near-phobic fear of being fat. It can impair biochemical functions such as hormonal balance, pulse and heart rate, body temperature, and the menstrual cycle.[3] Expressions of concern from others cannot penetrate the distorted image the young person has of her body. Even when weight has been reduced by more than 25 percent of the original body weight, an anorexic adolescent cannot see her emaciated state.

Two million Americans suffer from eating disorders, and most of these are women. One in 150 women fall victim to anorexia.[4] And between .5 percent and 1 percent of women during adolescence and early adulthood are thought to be affected by anorexia.[5] However, recent research is showing an increase in eating disorders among boys.[6] It is most frequently seen in early adolescence, and it usually peaks between the ages of fourteen and eighteen. The natural course of anorexia usually extends over a period of three to four years, but it can last much longer. Pop singer Karen Carpenter died in 1983 of unexplained heart failure at the age of thirty-two. After her death, her family revealed that she had been suffering from anorexia *for twelve years.* Cherry Boone O'Neill, Pat Boone's oldest daughter, described her ten-year struggle with anorexia in *Starving for Attention.* Anorexia is not a problem that will simply go away. Without serious intervention, it can be fatal. Some studies report a death rate from anorexia nervosa as high as 20 percent. The risk of death is significant when weight is less than 60 percent of normal. Suicide has been estimated to comprise half the deaths in anorexia.[7]

The primary characteristics of anorexia include the following:

1. Intense fear of becoming obese, which does not diminish as weight loss progresses.
2. Disturbance of body image. For example, victims may claim to "feel fat" even when emaciated, or believe that one area of the body is "too fat" even when they are obviously underweight.
3. Refusal to maintain body weight over a minimal normal weight for age and height, and failure to make expected weight gain during a period of growth.
4. In females, the absence of at least three consecutive menstrual cycles when they are otherwise expected to occur.
5. No known physical cause of weight loss.[8]

Bulimia nervosa literally means "ox hunger" or "insatiable hunger." It is characterized by repeated cycles of binge eating and compensation for food intake by self-induced vomiting, laxative abuse, diuretic abuse, and/or fasting and excessive exercise. Bulimic individuals are usually within the normal weight range, with frequent weight fluctuations due to their binge-purge episodes. During the binge phase, most people consume enormous amounts of high calorie, energy-rich, fattening foods like ice cream, candy, and junk foods. The binge phase, usually about two hours or less, is terminated by physical exhaustion, exhaustion of food supply, self-induced vomiting, sleep, abdominal pain, exercise, laxative use, or interruptions by visitors. To restore a sense of control, relieve painful fullness, and reduce anxieties about weight gain, the bulimic engages in self-induced vomiting, laxatives, diuretics, fasting, exercise, or severe diets. Between these binge phases, the adolescent is likely to maintain a strict diet and avoid energy-rich foods.

Case Description

Jennifer is fourteen years old, in the eighth grade, and on the honor roll. Her dad is a banker and her mom is an administrator for a successful retail chain. A school counselor referred Jennifer to a psychologist. She is five feet, four inches tall and has lost about thirty pounds in the past year. She originally weighed 110 pounds, but now weighs 80 pounds and wants to lose more. Jennifer is "grossed out" by fat women. She wants to be "athletic looking without flabby curves." She originally started dieting because some of her friends were losing weight. For lunch Jennifer usually eats plain yogurt with fruit. For breakfast she has a stick of sugarless gum. If she eats dinner at all, it is usually carrot sticks or a salad. Despite her skin-and-bones appearance, Jennifer exercises almost two hours daily and denies that she has or might have any physical symptoms. She says her only problem is arguments with her mom about her diet. She says her mom is "jealous because she would like to lose weight too."

In bulimia, the weight loss is not so extreme or so life-threatening as in anorexia. The major consequences of repeated cycles of binge-eating, purging, and fasting are potassium depletion, deterioration of tooth enamel (from the gastric acid vomiting creates), abdominal pains, kidney problems, dehydration, and electrolyte imbalances (which can cause heart irregularities).[9] Also, in bulimia, unlike anorexia, the adolescent is aware that her eating pattern is abnormal, and she is likely to suffer depression and self-criticism about her eating behavior.

Peak risk for onset of binge eating occurs at age sixteen, whereas peak risk for onset of purging occurs at age eighteen.[10] It occurs primarily in middle-class late adolescence and in young adult white females of average weight who are beginning college. Research indicates that 90 percent of bulimic young people are females.[11] Research also suggests that about 4 percent of college-aged women have bulimia. About 50 percent of people who have been anorexic develop bulimia or bulimic patterns. Experts advise ten to twelve weeks for full nutritional recovery. However, recovery from bulimia usually takes a long time, on average six years of slow progress that includes starts, stops, slides backwards, and ultimately movement in the direction of mental and physical health.[12]

The most frequently mentioned precipitating factors for a bulimic episode are stress, loneliness, interpersonal conflict, depression, boredom, developmental transitions, and tensions built up from continual attempts at strict dieting.[13] Most bulimics prefer to binge at home, alone, or in secret. However, in recent years, the binge-purge cycle has become more of a shared experience. Most young women now know someone who binges and purges. Adolescents teach others how to binge and purge in mutual enforcing interactions.[14]

Primary characteristics of bulimia nervosa include the following:

1. Recurrent episodes of binge eating in which large amounts of food are consumed rapidly in a discrete period of time.
2. A feeling of lack of control over eating behavior during the eating binges.
3. Regular self-induced vomiting, use of laxatives or diuretics, strict dieting or fasting, or vigorous exercise to prevent weight gain.
4. A minimum average of two binge-eating episodes a week for at least three months.
5. A persistent overconcern with body shape and weight.

It is critical that counselors and parents distinguish between these two groups of struggling adolescents, the anorexic and the bulimic. In the book *Walking a Thin Line: Anorexia and Bulimia*, P. Vredevelt and J. Whitman make helpful distinctions in the symptoms of each problem, as shown on the chart on page 121.[15]

Eating disorders are a staggering problem among adolescents today. Parents must be aware of how these disorders can affect their children. Reports by Anorexia and Related Eating Disorders, Inc. indicate that anorexia and bulimia affect as many as 20 percent of today's adolescent population.[16]

Anorexia	Bulimia
Voluntary starvation often leading to emaciation and sometimes death.	Secretive binge eating can occur regularly and may follow a pattern. Caloric intake per binge can range from 1,000 to 20,000 calories.
Occasional binges, followed by fasting, laxative abuse, or self-induced starvation.	Binges are followed by fasting, laxative abuse, self-induced vomiting, or other forms of purging. Person may chew food but spit it out before swallowing.
Menstrual period ceases. May not begin if anorexia occurs before puberty.	Menstrual period may be regular, irregular, or absent.
Excessive exercise. Hands, feet, and other parts of the body are always cold.	Swollen glands in neck beneath jaw.
Dry skin. Head hair may thin, but downy fuzz may appear on other parts of the body.	Dental cavities and loss of tooth enamel.
Depression, irritability, deceitfulness, guilt, and self-loathing.	Broken blood vessels in face. Bags under eyes.
Attitude: "I'm much too fat," even when emaciated.	Fainting spells. Rapid or irregular heartbeat.
Obsessive interest in food, recipes, and cooking.	Miscellaneous stomach and intestinal discomforts and problems.
Rituals involving food, exercise, and other aspects of life.	Weight fluctuation due to alternating periods of binges and fasts.
Perfectionism.	Desire for relationships and approval of others.
Introverted and withdrawn. Avoids people.	Loses control and fears she cannot stop once she begins eating.

✔ WHY THE STRUGGLE HAPPENS

Eating disorders are the result of a complex web of factors that include at least the following matters.

Stressful Situations

Stressful life situations for which adolescents do not possess adequate coping skills often play a role in the development of eating disorders. Such a situation may be a rejection or perceived rejection, a sexual encounter, or any number of other events. The peak age of onset for anorexia coincides with the transition from junior high to high school; bulimia most often occurs during the transition from high school to college. The rigid and perfectionistic attitude that characterizes anorexics is exacerbated in even the smallest changes or transitions. The one thing, however, they believe they can control is their quest to lose weight.[17]

Developmental Change

Adolescence is a period of great vulnerability to all kinds of struggles. For this reason, eating disorders are often seen as reactions to the stresses of puberty.[18] The hallmark of puberty for females is physical changes in shape and the onset of menstruation. Some therapists theorize that anorexia is a rejection of female sexuality and an attempt to remain a "little girl." Intimacy issues and responsibility may also be avoided to some degree through maintenance of an eating disorder. Anorexics are characterized by extraordinary skill at following clear-cut rules. They are the model children who have mastered good behavior. Pre-anorexics are almost too good to be true. The familiar territory of rules governing their success, however, changes and becomes enigmatic as they mature into women. Societal expectations and women's roles have changed dramatically in recent years. Being overly compliant may cause difficulty in their becoming autonomous and forming personal identity.[19]

Biology

Studies have clearly established that disturbances in hypothalamic function exist in eating disorders. However, it is unclear whether an eating disorder produces the physiological changes or vice versa. Some researchers suggest that women may be biologically susceptible to eating disorders since they are far more likely than males to experience appetite fluctuation in response to stress.[20]

Case Description

Carla is an eighteen-year-old college freshman. She broke up with her high school boyfriend about six months ago. At that time she found herself overeating as a way of coping with feelings of loss and loneliness. At the same time she was trying to diet. Her former boyfriend is now dating a girl who is "prettier and a lot skinnier." Carla thought that by losing weight she could keep her next boyfriend. She was about five pounds above the average for her age and height. A friend of Carla told her that she wouldn't have to worry about weight gain if she would binge and purge. At the time Carla came into counseling, she had been binge-eating and purging by self-induced vomiting about twice a week for the previous four months. A typical binge would start with a large bowl of peanut M & Ms, eight or nine candy bars, a dozen cookies, a large bowl of popcorn, and a huge serving of ice cream. She would eat until she was exhausted or until she ran out of food. Her binge-purge episodes were followed by renewed efforts to diet, but that would last only three or four days before she would start again. Carla is ashamed and concerned that others will learn of her struggle.

Society

Two potent societal influences affect the increasing incidence of eating disorders. The first is the heightened consciousness of nutrition and physical fitness. In the last two or three decades, health and fitness have become major concerns. Health food and vitamin sales are soaring. Many people religiously read nutritional labels and steer away from additives and preservatives. The second factor is our national obsession with slimness. In fact we are willing to compromise the first factor, health, to achieve slimness. When the Food and Drug Administration banned cyclamates and artificial sweeteners because the agency thought them to be carcinogenic, a public outcry ensued. People didn't want to give up low-calorie Coke, even if it did supposedly cause cancer. A thin body is more important than a healthy one.

Family Issues

Many agree that the family plays a leading role in the etiology of eating disorders—especially anorexia. First, anorexic adolescents tend to come from families concerned about food. Perhaps the concern results from special dietary needs of a family member, or simply from an emphasis on nutrition. Food may be used as a sign of love and caring or as the center for family gatherings. Mothers of adolescents who struggle with eating disorders are often dominant and intrusive and frequently have episodes of depression. Fathers are described as aloof or passive, yet with high expectations. However, no single set of parental personality traits has definitely been shown to exist universally.

Peer Relationships

Most people have between six and ten close friends and another thirty acquaintances with whom they interact regularly.[21] During adolescence, peer groups are vital in easing the transition from childhood to adulthood. An absence of close friends is considered to be one feature in the onset of an eating disorder. Anorexics have a pattern of developing only one relationship at a time, and those relationships are repeatedly short-lived. Often, anorexics are overly involved with and dependent upon family to the exclusion of outside relationships. They cheat themselves out of the aid of peers to help them through the process of individuation.

✔ HOW PARENTS CAN HELP

The following strategies for helping an adolescent struggling with an eating disorder can be used effectively by parents; however, every parent-child relationship is unique, and some of them may be more pertinent to your situation than others. As with every significant adolescent struggle, it is best for parents to work alongside a competent counselor. With this in mind, the following is offered as a way to help you facilitate the helping process at home with your teenager.

Consider Inpatient Treatment

If the adolescent is already emaciated, a counselor will help you decide at once whether she should initially be treated on an outpatient basis or immediately hospitalized. If her weight is 25 percent below what it should be, hospitalization is imperative. In the marginal ranges, therapists will use their clinical judgment in consultation with physicians.

In spite of the prevalence of bulimia, in one study only thirty percent of family physicians had ever diagnosed bulimia. A physician should make a diagnosis of bulimia if there are at least two bulimic episodes per week for three months. Generally an observation of physical symptoms and a personal history will quickly confirm the diagnosis of anorexia. The standard criteria for diagnosing anorexia nervosa are: refusal to maintain a body weight normal for age and height; intense fear of becoming fat even though underweight; a distorted self-image that results in diminished self-confidence; denial of the seriousness of emaciation and starvation; and in women, the loss of menstrual function for at least three months. The physician then categorizes the anorexia as being either restricting (anorexia brought on by severe diet alone) or binge-purge. Once a diagnosis is made, physicians should immediately check for any serious complications of starvation. They should also rule out medical disorders that might be the cause of anorexia, including chronic fatigue syndrome, Crohn's disease, hyperthyroidism, Addison's disease, cancer, tuberculosis, anemia, and celiac disease. In all cases, tests should include a complete blood count, tests for electrolyte imbalances and protein levels, an electrocardiogram and a chest x-ray, and tests of liver, kidney, and thyroid problems. Low potassium levels indicate that the disorder is more likely to be accompanied by the binge-purge syndrome. Depending on the severity of the anorexia, other tests may be needed, such as a bone-density test or other types of x-rays and imaging techniques.

Most moderately to severely ill anorexic patients are admitted to the hospital for initial treatment, particularly under the following circumstances: if weight loss continues even under outpatient treatment; if weight is thirty percent below the minimum needed to maintain health; if disturbed heart rhythms occur; if depression is severe or the patient is suicidal; if potassium loss is severe or blood pressure is extremely low.[22]

Hospitalization provides, at the very least, separation from anxiety-producing stressors in the patient's life. It also insures adequate nutritional intake. Outpatient treatment is almost always necessary upon discharge. Hospitals differ in their treatment programs. For hospitalization that incorporates a Christ-centered approach to therapy, consider Rapha. Rapha has several locations across the United States where treatment is immediately available; for additional information call toll free 800-227-2657 (in Texas, 800-445-2657). A Christian treatment center that specializes in eating disorders among women is Remuda Ranch in Wickenburg, Arizona; the toll-free number is 800-445-1900.

Explore Cognitive Distortions

Correcting faulty thinking and beliefs is a major task in treating the person with an eating disorder. While a counselor will do this, it is helpful for parents to be informed of its value. The anorexic and the bulimic adolescent must learn to think differently. This requires gentle challenges. On the one hand, affirm the young person's experience as real. On the other hand, present alternative ways of seeing the world and herself. This takes patience. A major distortion, of course, involves misperceptions about the physical body. But at the root of much of her faulty thinking is perfectionism.[23]

Anorexics see total failure as their future unless *everything* is done perfectly. Yet the harder they try for perfection, the worse the ensuing disappointment. The young person with an eating disorder must be gently challenged on this style of black-and-white thinking. She must realize that if she fails a test, it does not mean she is an idiot, and that if she gains weight, it does not mean she is fat. A counselor will help her to identify the thoughts that lead to a binge or a period of starving. Simply writing out these thoughts or saying them aloud often lessens their intensity. Once she is conscious of her irrational thoughts, she can begin to refute them by replacing them with more constructive ones. You may find the section on guilt helpful in exploring how to gently refute these kinds of cognitive distortions.

Explore Feelings

Another primary therapeutic goal in treating eating disorders is the genuine and appropriate expression of feelings. Anxiety and anger are two emotions that are likely to be particularly troublesome.[24] Counselors will help her explore these frightening feelings and allow her to discover what is going on within. She needs to know that these feelings are normal and acceptable. Once these feelings are identified and acknowledged, adolescents can learn healthful options and responsible choices to help them cope more effectively with their once-unconscious emotions. Ultimately, this self-awareness leads to greater self-confidence and self-esteem. You may find the section on inferiority helpful in exploring feelings.

Consider Family Issues

Developing autonomy is hard enough for a healthy adolescent. The task is magnified for the eating-disordered adolescent who is trying to separate from her family. In many cases, the counselor's work with the family is helpful. In fact, several researchers believe that family therapy is a necessary part of all treatment of eating disorders unless the family is extremely hostile or intrusive.[25] The goals of family counseling are to help each member deal with concerns about the eating-disorder problem, become more autonomous, resolve conflict, and encourage appropriate coalitions among family subsystems. Specific goals in therapy may depend on the stage of the family-life cycle, but counselors will operate under the following general principles in working with families of eating-disordered victims:[26]

1. Approach families in a nonblaming way.
2. Assume that families have done their best.
3. Recognize that families are tired from stress.
4. Assume that families want to help.

Consider Some Do's and Don'ts

The American Anorexia Nervosa Aid Society recommends several do's and don'ts for parents:[27]

DON'T

1. Do not urge your child to eat, and do not watch her eat. Do not even discuss food intake or weight with her. Leave the room if necessary. Your involvement with her eating is her tool for manipulating you. Take this tool out of her hands by letting her alone.
2. Do not allow yourself to feel guilty. Most parents ask, "What have I done wrong?" Perfect parents do not exist. Once you have checked out her physical condition with a physician and made it possible for her to begin counseling, getting well is her responsibility. It is her problem, not yours.
3. Do not neglect your marriage partner or other children. Focusing on the sick child can perpetuate her illness and destroy the family. She needs to know that she is important to you, but no more important than any other member of the family.
4. Do not be afraid to remove the child from the home if it becomes obvious that her continued presence is undermining the emotional health of the family.
5. Do not put the child down by comparing her to her more "successful" siblings or friends. Her self-esteem is a reflection of your esteem for her. Do not ask, "How are you feeling?" or "How is your social life?" These questions only aggravate her feelings of inadequacy.

DO

1. Love your child. Love makes anyone feel worthwhile.
2. Trust your child to find her own values, ideals, and standards rather than insisting on yours.

3. Do everything to encourage her initiative, independence, and autonomy. Be aware, though, that anorexics tend to be perfectionistic. Thus, they are never satisfied with themselves.

4. Be aware of the long-term nature of the illness. Anorexics do get better; many get completely well; very few die. But be prepared for months and sometimes years of treatment and anxiety. A support group such as a parents' self-help group may make a significant difference to your family's survival.

✔ HOW PROFESSIONALS CAN HELP

The following strategies for helping an adolescent struggling with an eating disorder are commonly used by counselors. They are presented here as a way to inform you, as a parent, and help you seek the best possible professional help you can for the adolescent in your care.

Require a Medical Examination

Medical assessments of adolescents' status are essential because of the severe medical problems related to starvation and malnutrition. Adolescents' vital signs are often lowered, including blood pressure, heart rate, body temperature, and respiration rate. A physical evaluation is necessary to confirm that no other illness has caused the weight loss and to assess the severity of malnutrition. This is true for both anorexia and bulimia. The most predominant danger in bulimia is electrolyte imbalance due to purging by vomiting or abusing laxatives and diuretics. Because electrolyte imbalances may be fatal, it is imperative that medical doctors assess adolescents prior to counseling.[28]

Focus on Nutrition

Nutritional rehabilitation is the first step in any treatment program.[29] Although the restoration of body weight may seem intrusive to adolescents, it is necessary for the preservation of thinking and to increase abstract thought. Starvation greatly affects cognitive and affective functioning. Only after an appropriate weight is reestablished and a full range of food is restored will bulimic and anorexic adolescents be able to focus on psychological reasons for their problem.

Of course the method of weight restoration used depends on the severity of the illness. If the illness is in its early stages and hospitalization is not needed, consultation with a dietitian is helpful. Often the initial goal is weight maintenance; then after a week a weight gain of one or two pounds per week is advised.[30] The young person should be invited to participate in all decisions regarding her treatment. This obviously requires enormous delicacy on the part of the therapist, who essentially has the awkward role of "enforcer" even while advocating choice. The process of relearning how to eat in a normal way is time-consuming but important to overcoming the fear of food. The young person must be reassured that she will not get fat and that weight gain will not be excessive or rapid. A gradual return to a target weight will be emphasized.

Establish Trust

The most pivotal element in achieving success is the establishment of a relationship of trust between the counselor and the client. While this may seem obvious because it is a basic ingredient to all effective therapy, it is exceptionally challenging to achieve trust with anorexic or bulimic clients. They are noted for their resistance to therapy and their ability to sabotage the process. Unlike many other struggling adolescents, a young person with an eating disorder does not want to give up her symptoms, and she will regard the counselor as one with whom to do battle, as another one of the many who are trying to "fatten her up." A therapeutic alliance is crucial. [31]

Gather a Detailed History

Effective work is based on accurate and detailed information. One of the best ways to gather historical information about the young person's food intake, weight changes, exercise patterns, and so on is through a questionnaire.

Assign a Diary

Counselors will often ask the adolescent to keep a daily diary of the type and amount of food she eats, the time and place it is eaten, and the feelings and thoughts she has before, during, and after eating. The purpose of this exercise is fourfold. First, it heightens the adolescent's awareness of her feelings. Second, it helps identify the kinds of thoughts that lead to trouble so that appropriate refuting statements may be developed. Third, it provides a relatively objective record of changes that do or do not occur. And it is helpful in discovering behavioral patterns.[32]

Explore the Meaning of the Weight Loss

After some degree of trust has been built and information has been gathered, a discussion of the meaning of weight loss becomes possible. Counselors may ask what her original target weight was when she first began to diet. How did she think she would feel upon reaching that weight? How did she actually feel upon reaching it? Does she realize that the weight loss will never be good enough because that is the nature of the illness? The dieting that began as a lift and a thrill with an accompanying sense of accomplishment becomes a terrifying burden because losing weight becomes harder and harder to do. Does she see that the promises of losing weight are not being realized? Exploring these issues may help her realize that the very thing that was supposed to liberate her has entrapped her and made her increasingly unhappy. This simple realization may be an important step in allowing the adolescent to join with the counselor in fighting the problem. [33]

Consider Group Treatment

Group therapy can be an important adjunct to individual and family therapy for anorexic individuals. It provides an opportunity to work on peer relationships, to explore feelings about family, and to increase self-awareness and self-expression. Reestablishment of close peer relationships is especially important in the treatment of anorexia. Groups are also helpful in correcting perceptual and cognitive distortions. Group treatment, however, is not for everyone. If adolescents are still in denial of the illness and need medical management because of starvation symptoms, they are not good candidates for group work.[34]

Know When to Refer

Competent counselors will refer adolescents struggling with eating disorders to specialists in eating disorders if they are not thoroughly trained to work with anorexia or bulimia.

They will also refer to psychologically astute physicians or psychiatrists when unusual physical symptoms are present or when eating disorders are severe enough to warrant medication and/or hospitalization. They will refer adolescents to other competent counselors or psychologists when, over time, they are not making noticeable progress in weight rehabilitation.

Where to Go for Additional Help

Agras, W. S. *Eating Disorders.* New York: Pergamon, 1987.
Costin, C. *Your Dieting Daughter: Is She Dying for Attention?* New York: Brunner/Mazel, 1997.
Crisp, A. H. *Anorexia Nervosa: Let Me Be.* New York: Grune and Stratton, 1980.
Palazzoli, M. *Self Starvation.* New York: Jason Aronson, 1978.
Vredevelt, P., and J. Whitman. *Walking a Thin Line: Anorexia and Bulimia.* Portland, Ore.: Multnomah, 1985.

Wilkinson, H. *Beyond Chaotic Eating: A Way Out of Anorexia, Bulimia, and Compulsive Eating.* New York: HarperCollins, 1993.

The following organizations are also excellent resources.

Anorexia Nervosa and Related Eating Disorders, Inc.
P.O. Box 5102
Eugene, OR 97405
503-344-1144

The Center for the Study of Anorexia and Bulimia
Institute for Contemporary Psychotherapy
1841 Broadway, 4th Floor
New York, NY 10023
212-333-3444

American Dietetic Association
216 W. Jackson Boulevard
Chicago, Illinois 60606
800-366-1655 or 312-899-0040
http://www.eatright.org
The organization offers a hotline that allows people to speak to a licensed dietitian and also provides names of licensed dietitians for specific locations. Its Web site is excellent and highly recommended.

National Association of Anorexia Nervosa and Associated Disorders (ANAD)
Box 7
Highland Park, IL 60035
847-831-3438
http://www.injersey.com/Living/Health/anad.index.html
This is the oldest organization for eating disorders. They offer free information and help in finding or forming support groups in local areas. For an annual contribution of $25, members receive a quarterly newsletter.

Eating Disorders Awareness and Prevention
603 Stewart Street, Suite 803
Seattle, WA 98101
206-382-3587
http://members.aol.com/edapinc/home.html

American Anorexia/Bulimia Association, Inc. (AABA)
293 Central Park West, Suite 1R
New York, NY 10024
212-501-8351
http://members.aol.com/amanbu/index.html
Offers a basic information package. Send self-addressed stamped envelope with a check for $3.00.

National Eating Disorders Organization
6655 South Yale Ave.
Tulsa, OK 74136
918-481-4044
Offers information and referral service.

Notes

1. P. Charpentier, "Eating Disorders Among Adolescents: An Overview," *Psychiatria Fennica* 29 (1999): 65–77.

2. P. A. Neuman and P. A. Halvorson, *Anorexia Nervosa and Bulimia: A Handbook for Counselors and Therapists* (New York: Van Nostrand Reinhold, 1983), 2.

3. D. M. Garner and P. E. Garfinkel, eds., *Handbook of Psychotherapy for Anorexia Nervosa and Bulimia* (New York: Guilford Press, 1985).

4. "Disappearing Act," *Time* 152 (November 10, 1998): 110.

5. "Eating Disorders: Perilous Compulsions," *Consumers' Research Magazine* 80 (September 1997): 10.

6. M. Sanzone, "Eating Disorders: Girls, Boys and Bodies," *Psychology Today* (July/August 1999): 12.

7. National Association of Anorexia Nervosa and Associated Disorders (ANAD), www.injersey.com/Living/Health/anad.index.html. 1999.

8. Adapted from *Diagnostic and Statistical Manual of Mental Disorders*, 4th rev. ed. (Washington, D.C.: American Psychological Association, 1994).

9. J. E. Mitchell, "Bulimia: Medical and Physiological Aspects," in *Handbook of Eating Disorders: Physiology, Psychology, and Treatment of Eating Disorders*, ed. K. D. Brownell and J. P. Foreyt (New York: Basic Books, 1986).

10. E. Stice, J. D. Killen, C. Hayward, and C. B. Taylor, "Age of Onset of Binge Eating and Purging During Late Adolescence: A Four-Year Survival Analysis," *Journal of Abnormal Psychology* 107 (1998): 671–75.

11. A. E. Bayer, "Eating Out of Control," *Children Today* (December 1984): 7–11.

12. *International Journal of Eating Disorders* 4 (December 22, 1997): 361–84.

13. R. Geist, R. Davis, and M. Heinmaa, "Binge-purge Symptoms and Comorbidity in Adolescents with Eating Disorders," *Canadian Journal of Psychiatry* 43 (1998): 507–12.

14. R. H. Striegel-Moore, L. R. Silberstein, and J. Rodin, "Toward an Understanding of Risk Factors for Bulimia," *American Psychologist* 41 (1986): 246–63.

15. P. Vredevelt and J. Whitman, *Walking a Thin Line, Anorexia and Bulimia* (Portland, Oreg.: Multnomah, 1985), 29–31.

16. www.anred.com/stats.html. Anorexia Nervosa and Related Eating Disorders, 1999.

17. Neuman and Halvorson, *Anorexia Nervosa and Bulimia: A Handbook for Counselors and Therapists.*

18. T. Pryor and M. W. Wiederman, "Personality Features and Expressed Concerns of Adolescents with Eating Disorders," *Adolescence* 33 (1998): 291–300.

19. W. S. Agras, *Eating Disorders: Management of Obesity, Bulimia, and Anorexia Nervosa* (New York: Pergamon, 1987).

20. D. Jones, "Structural Discontinuity and the Development of Anorexia Nervosa," *Sociological Focus* 14 (1981): 233–45.

21. Ibid.

22. www.anred.com. Anorexia Nervosa and Related Eating Disorders, 1999.

23. C. M. Shisslak, M. Crago, R. Renger, and A. Clark, "Self-Esteem and the Prevention of Eating Disorders," *Eating Disorders: The Journal of Treatment and Prevention* 6 (1998): 105–18.

24. Ibid.

25. A. E. Anderson, *Practical Comprehensive Treatment of Anorexia Nervosa and Bulimia* (Baltimore: Johns Hopkins University Press, 1985).

26. J. E. Hedblom, F. A. Hubbard, and A. A. Andersen, "Anorexia Nervosa: A Multidisciplinary Treatment Program for Patient and Family," *Social Work in Health Care* 7 (1981): 67–86.

27. American Anorexia Nervosa Aid Society, *AANAS Newsletter* (January/February 1981).

28. C. Gillberg and M. Rastam, "Do Drugs Have a Place in the Treatment of Eating Disorders in Adolescence?" *International Journal of Psychiatry in Clinical Practice* 2 (1998): 79–82.

29. P. Hartley, "Eating Disorders and Health Education," *Psychology, Health, and Medicine* 3 (1998): 133–40.

30. M. Strober and J. Yager, "A Developmental Perspective on the Treatment of Anorexia Nervosa in Adolescents," in *Handbook of Psychotherapy for Anorexia and Bulimia*, ed. D. M. Garner and P. E. Garfinkel (New York: Guilford Press, 1985).

31. A. L. Robin, M. Gilroy, and A. Dennis, "Treatment of Eating Disorders in Children and Adolescents," *Clinical Psychology Review* 18 (1998): 421–46.

32. Neuman and Halvorson, *Anorexia Nervosa and Bulimia: A Handbook for Counselors and Therapists.*

33. K. A. Gabel and K. Kearney, "Promoting Reasonable Perspectives of Body Weight: Issues for School Counselors," *Professional School Counseling* 1 (1998): 32–35.

34. A. Hall, "Group Psychotherapy for Anorexia Nervosa," in *Handbook of Psychotherapy for Anorexia Nervosa and Bulimia*, ed. D.M. Garner and P.E. Garfinkel (New York: Gulford Press, 1985).

FORGIVENESS

☑ WHAT THE STRUGGLE LOOKS LIKE

While forgiveness has been a continuing struggle for millions of people throughout history, psychology has been relatively quiet on the topic until recently. In the past decade or so dozens of researchers have devoted their skills to helping us understand what forgiveness is and how it heals the human soul. Numerous professional articles and books on forgiveness have now been published, giving counselors more therapeutic tools than ever to assist individuals, including adolescents, in finding a clear path toward forgiveness.[1]

A struggle with forgiveness occurs when a person experiences a violation that causes emotional or physical pain. The wronged person experiences both frustration and loss.[2] The loss may be concrete (such as physical possessions), or abstract (such as a dream or a sense of dignity). Almost instantaneously, hurt people feel angry toward violators and want revenge. In the heat of the moment they may even vow to "get even, if it is the last thing they do." This typically leads to vindictiveness and unfocused hostility. In general, the younger the person, the more insidious and pervasive are the effects of failing to forgive.[3]

Adolescents who struggle to forgive those who have harmed them nurture their anger in order to pay back the offenders with even greater pain than they received. In a more general sense, they become rigid in other relationships, and their trust in others decreases. They develop a pattern of not giving until they are sure they will receive something in return. In short, they become bitter and resentful. That is, unless they experience forgiveness.

Archibald Hart says it straight out: *Forgiveness is surrendering our need to hurt back.* The apostle Paul laid down the essence of forgiveness: "Do not repay anyone evil for evil. . . . If it is possible, as far as it depends on you, live at peace with everyone. Do not take revenge, my friends, but leave room for God's wrath" (Romans 12:17–19).

In the Sermon on the Mount, Jesus sums up the principle of forgiveness by saying, "Turn the other cheek." The old law had called for "eye for eye and tooth for tooth" (Matthew 5:38). But the problem with the old law is that we can't stop at just one eye or one tooth. We feel that we only even the score when our offender has suffered more than we have. So Jesus says to give up our need to hurt back. Forgive. Ironically, forgiveness does not give our offender the advantage; it protects us from further offense, from outdoing our offender's harm again and again. Forgiveness is for our own protection.[4]

Case Description

April, seventeen, came to counseling because, as she put it, she was being "sabotaged by her best friend." About four months ago her friend Julie started dating one of April's former boyfriends. April was madly in love with this boy at the time of their breakup. They had dated for almost a year. April never understood why he broke up with her—until two months ago. The pieces fell into place when her former boyfriend started dating Julie. As it turned out, April learned that Julie had instigated the breakup by giving the boy the false information that April wanted to dump him. The boy, in an attempt to save face, decided to break up with her before she called it off. That's when Julie began flirting with him. April was understandably furious. She could not stand even to see Julie at school. She spent most of her time thinking about how to hurt and embarrass Julie. It became an obsession. Julie's dating relationship with the boy was short-lived, but April still cannot bring herself to forgive Julie for the wrong she did her.

Helping adolescents learn the principles of forgiveness is a significant gift and may be very rewarding. For the rest of their days they will bump up against even well-meaning people who hurt them. Knowing the power of forgiveness will empower them to heal untold numbers of relationships.

☑ WHY THE STRUGGLE HAPPENS

In short, the reason people struggle with forgiveness is that they can't or won't give up their right to hurt back. The following characteristics increase the power of this struggle.

Legalism

Some sincere teenagers have a legalistic mentality that results in a continuing need to seek revenge against anyone who hurts them. In Jesus' day, the Pharisees were religious purists who emphasized rules over relationships. Such views are still with us and keep some from experiencing the joy and freedom of surrendering their legalistic belief of "an eye for an eye."

Pride

An attitude of swollen pride keeps forgiveness at bay. Proud people get satisfaction from contemplating their superior position; thus, they are unable to empathize with others. The self-focus of pride makes troubled adolescents determined to retaliate. They have a driving need to even the score by somehow harming offenders.

Bitterness

Anger over offenses naturally fuels the fires of resentment and the desire to retaliate. If forgiveness does not do its healing work at that point, the blaze will become the white heat of bitterness. When this occurs, all of life turns sour. Offended people project their anger on everything and everybody. They become experts in fault-finding. In a word, they become bitter. This entrenched disposition makes the struggle to forgive doubly difficult.

Modeling

Parents who struggle with forgiveness are often emulated by their children. Children may come to believe that refusal to forgive offenses is proper. They hear their parents scheme about how to repay injustices done against them, so teenagers believe they are to do the same. In addition, children may bear the brunt of parental lack of forgiveness. This, of course, makes it all the more difficult for young people to forgive others.

False Forgiveness

Some people struggle with genuine forgiveness because they "forgive" too much. They forgive even the worst of mistakes at the drop of a hat. Because forgiveness has been trivialized, it loses its power and meaning. Young people who forgive too easily will struggle with genuine forgiveness because they are avoiding their real pain by repressing traumatic offenses.

Faulty Theology

Some adolescents struggle with forgiving others because they believe God can never forgive them. They may even believe that God wants them to be punished. While their beliefs may be sincere, they are obviously wrong. God does forgive them: "Whoever believes in him is not condemned" (John 3:18). The quality of young people's relationships with God has a major bearing on their capacity to forgive.

✔ HOW PARENTS CAN HELP

The following strategies for helping an adolescent struggling with forgiveness can be used effectively by parents; however, every parent-child relationship is unique, and some of them may be more pertinent to your situation than others. As with every significant adolescent struggle, it is best for parents to work alongside a competent counselor. With this in mind, the following is offered as a way to help you facilitate the helping process at home with your teenager.

Move Slowly

No one can be forced to forgive. You cannot wheedle teenagers into forgiving their enemies. Coerced "forgiveness" facilitates a kind of trigger-happy forgiver who fires off forgiveness at the least offense.[5] Be alert to sensitive adolescents who may be especially quick to forgive. These youngsters are probably forgiving out of a sense of duty. This, of course, is not forgiveness at all. It comes closer to excusing than forgiving. You must not be hasty in concluding that such cases are "cured." Learning to forgive is typically a relatively long process and requires patience.

Clarify the Goal

Forgiveness is not the same as reconciliation. One may forgive the violations of another person yet not continue a relationship with the offender. This may be the case, for example, when the offense is physical or sexual abuse. While forgiveness is an indispensable prelude to reconciliation, it does not require a continuing relationship with the violator. Even if young people are able to give up their anger and its distilled bitterness, they may judge the probability of the violator's change in a positive direction to be so slight that they decide to avoid reconciliation. In this case, the goal of therapy is to achieve an emotional position in which the offended are willing not to seek retribution from offenders.[6]

Help Them Own the Need

If we didn't want anything from people, they could not hurt us, we would not get angry, and there would be no need for forgiveness. Help adolescents reexamine the hurt caused by violators.[7] Help them see violators' unmet needs, those wounds to the spirit inflicted by other offenders. The violators' deep need may be to be trusted, loved, or respected. Labeling offenders' needs is the first step toward stirring up the personal resources that will help those who have been offended eventually to forgive. When adolescents own their need, they are not so quick to lay all the blame on offenders, no matter how despicable the offense.[8] Owning the need requires a humbling of self, and the process often takes time. Move slowly and gently in uncovering this sensitive area.[9]

Recognize a Common Misconception

Many adolescents believe that to forgive others is to condone their actions. This may cause them to hold onto their anger and keep them from experiencing the freedom of forgiveness. Clarify this point to insure that it does not slow down the process. Help them realize that their forgiveness of offenders must not depend upon any change in the offender's behavior. Nor should those who have been hurt anticipate any guarantee that offenders will not hurt them again. Forgiveness is for the forgiver's own protection, not the offender's.[10]

Explore the Disguises of Forgiveness

It is not uncommon for people to believe that as long as they don't think about the pain caused by others' offenses, they have achieved forgiveness. They equate forgiveness with a denial of their pain. Suppression is not forgiveness. Forgetting is not even a test of genuine forgiveness. The test lies in the healing of the lingering pain of the past. It is also a mistake to confuse forgiveness with excusing. Excusing is letting a person off the hook. Forgiveness keeps people accountable for their behavior. Nor is forgiveness tolerance. We do not have to tolerate what people do just because we have forgiven them for doing it.[11]

✔ HOW PROFESSIONALS CAN HELP

The following strategies for helping an adolescent struggling with forgiveness are commonly used by counselors. They are presented here as a way to inform you, as a parent, and help you seek the best possible professional help you can for the adolescent in your care.

Help Them Move Beyond the Need

Once adolescents have identified what they want from their offenders, they need to move beyond seeing the persons only in terms of their own needs. To achieve forgiveness they must come to an understanding of the others' needs and motives for acting the way they did. Perhaps the best example is Jesus' endurance of the pain of the cross: "Father, forgive them, for they do not know what they are doing" (Luke 23:34). The goal is to empathize with offenders and understand, in even a small way, that the violators were trying to protect or enhance their own interests, albeit in a misguided way.[12]

If adolescents struggle to forgive their parents for not letting them use the car, they must enter the world of their parents as much as possible to see that they are trying to be the best parents they can. Adolescents don't have to agree with parental actions, just view them from their parents' perspective. Again, this perspective requires putting aside angry defensiveness. Counselors don't expect adolescents to quickly become vulnerable to this degree. The journey may be so gradual that they will pass over the line of empathy without realizing it.

Consider Inner Healing

Intervention may have positive results for religious persons who struggle to forgive others of specific and traumatic offenses. Sometimes people cannot forgive because the memories are too painful. They may be afraid of falling apart if they forgive. Inner healing is a prayerful process whereby the counselor symbolically introduces the presence of Jesus into painful memories. As hurting people, with the aid of the counselor, relive painful memories, they are encouraged to see Jesus with them, perhaps holding them and protecting them. This procedure may not bring about instant results, but it may begin a process of healing that will empower young people to forgive. Counselors approach inner healing cautiously, and never force the experience upon clients. The decision to use this technique would be mutually agreed upon.[13]

One of the most helpful approaches to healing memories and damaged emotions is espoused by David Seamands. He suggests several general biblical principles to facilitate this process:[14]

1. *Face the problem squarely.* With ruthless honesty, the hidden memory must be confronted.
2. *Accept responsibility in the matter.* The blame must be taken off others and ownership for the situation must be embraced.

3. *Ask yourself whether you really want to be healed.* Healing the memory means it will no longer be there as a crutch to help gather sympathy from others.

4. *Practice forgiveness.* Healing cannot begin until genuine forgiveness has been accomplished.

5. *Forgive yourself.* A lack of self-acceptance and forgiveness can short-circuit healing.

6. *Ask the Holy Spirit to show you how to pray.* God can help point to the real need.

For a more thorough description of this healing process, see David Seamands's books *Healing for Damaged Emotions* and *Healing of Memories*.

Rely on God's Forgiveness

Leslie Weatherhead said, "The forgiveness of God is the most powerful therapeutic idea in the world. If a person can believe that God has forgiven him, he can be saved from neuroticism." All human forgiveness is predicated on the grace and forgiveness of God. It is central to the Gospel and our salvation. Ideally, Christian counselors help young people who are in the process of forgiving others to participate in God's forgiveness for themselves. What people cannot accomplish through psychological techniques and principles can still be achieved with the help of the Holy Spirit. Obviously, counselors would be sensitive to adolescents' expressed spiritual beliefs and values.

Know When to Refer

Counselors refer adolescents who struggle with forgiveness to other competent counselors or psychologists when, over time, their clients are feeling increasingly resentful, frustrated, depressed, hopeless, or suicidal. They are also trained to refer clients if they recognize that they have personal unfinished business involving forgiveness, so as not to allow personal issues to contaminate counseling.

Where to Go for Additional Help

Augsburger, D. *Caring Enough to Forgive.* Ventura, Calif.: Regal, 1982.

Ensor, J. *Experiencing God's Forgiveness.* Colorado Springs, Colo.: Navpress, 1997.

Grosskopf, B. *Forgive Your Parents, Heal Yourself: How Understanding Your Painful Family Legacy Can Transform Your Life.* New York: The Free Press, 1999.

Hosier, H. *It Feels Good to Forgive.* Eugene, Ore.: Harvest House, 1980.

Jeffress, R. *When Forgiveness Doesn't Make Sense.* Colorado Springs, Colo.: WaterBrook Press, 2000.

McCullough, M. E., S. J. Sandage, and E. L. Worthington. *To Forgive Is Human.* Downers Grove, Ill.: InterVarsity Press, 1997.

Safer, J. *Forgiving and Not Forgiving: A New Approach to Resolving Intimate Betrayal.* New York: Avon Books, 1999.

Seamands, D. *Healing for Damaged Emotions.* Wheaton, Ill.: Victor, 1982.

_____. *Healing of Memories.* Wheaton, Ill.: Victor, 1985.

Smedes, L. B. *Forgive and Forget: Healing the Hurts We Don't Deserve.* San Francisco: Harper & Row, 1984.

_____. *The Art of Forgiving.* Nashville: Moorings, 1996.

Stanley, C. *The Gift of Forgiveness.* Nashville: Thomas Nelson, 1991.

Notes

1. E. L. Worthington, L. Parrott, and S. Gramling, "Unforgiveness and Trait Unforgiveness: Theory and Measurement. Symposium on Forgiveness" (Division 8). Annual Convention of the American Psychological Association, Washington, D.C. (August 1999).

E. L. Worthington, J.W. Berry, and L. Parrott, "Unforgiveness, Forgiveness, Religion, and Health," in *Faith and Heatlh,* ed. T. G. Plante and A. C. Sherman, (New York: Guilford Publications, 2000).

2. R. T. Denton and M. W. Martin, "Defining Forgiveness: An Empirical Exploration of Process and Role," *American Journal of Family Therapy* 26 (1998): 281–92.

3. J. M. Brandsma, "Forgiveness," in *Baker Encyclopedia of Psychology,* ed. D. G. Benner (Grand Rapids: Baker, 1985).

4. A. D. Hart, *Feeling Free: Effective Ways To Make Your Emotions Work for You* (Old Tappan, N.J.: Revell, 1979).

5. L. B. Smedes, *Forgive and Forget: Healing the Hurts We Don't Deserve* (San Francisco: Harper & Row, 1984).

6. S. R. Ferch, "Intentional Forgiving as a Counseling Intervention," *Journal of Counseling and Development* 76 (1998): 261–70.

7. E. L. Worthington, "An Empathy-Humility-Commitment Model of Forgiveness Applied Within Family Dyads," *Journal of Family Therapy* 20 (1998): 59–76.

8. D. Seamands, *Healing for Damaged Emotions* (Wheaton, Ill.: Victor, 1982).

9. F. A. DiBlasio, "The Use of Decision-Based Forgiveness Intervention within Intergenerational Family Therapy," *Journal of Family Therapy* 20 (1998): 77–94.

10. Hart, *Feeling Free: Effective Ways to Make Your Emotions Work for You.*

11. Smedes, *Forgive and Forget.*

12. D. Augsburger, *Caring Enough To Forgive* (Ventura, Calif.: Regal, 1982).

13. J. M. Alsdurf and H. N. Malony, "A Critique of Ruth Carter Stapleton's Ministry of 'Inner Healing,'" *Journal of Psychology and Theology* 8 (1980): 173–84.

14. Seamands, *Healing for Damaged Emotions.*

GOD'S WILL

☑ WHAT THE STRUGGLE LOOKS LIKE

Invariably, the spiritually sensitive adolescent will ask, "How can I know God's will for my life?"—or some variation of that theme.

While young people of previous generations usually found major choices in life to be culturally or parentally determined, typical Christian teenagers today are faced with an incredible diversity of opportunity and choice. Their decisions are complex and often lead to confusion about the matter of knowing God's will for them.

The concern is generally not over God's sovereign or moral will, but more often over his individual will—his ideal life plan, uniquely designed for each believer. Henri Nouwen defines God's individual will as the unique way in which God's love becomes manifest in one's life: "It is an active claiming of an intimate relationship with God," says Nouwen, "in the context of which we discover our deepest vocation and the desire to live that vocation to the fullest."[1] The will of God, according to Lloyd Ogilvie, is a relationship with God in which he discloses his purpose, power, and plan for our lives.[2]

Of course, God's ultimate will is that we know him, love him, and glorify him. Difficulties arise in trying to decide, in specific terms, how best to do that. Occupational choice, for instance, can be miserable for some sincere young people seeking to serve God. Adolescents feel under pressure to choose a vocation. Most of their lives they have been asked, "What do you want to be when you grow up?" Some teens become frustrated in the decision process by their perception of God's aloofness. Some become frozen in fear that they will miss out on God's will if they make the wrong decision. And still others believe that God will want them to do something they will hate. So they stall.

Case Description

Walt is eighteen and anxious about his future. He is a model student and deeply sincere about his faith. Walt is also a gifted adolescent and considering a career in graphic design. His SAT scores are above average, and his chances of getting into a very prestigious art school look promising. His teachers and others whom he respects have encouraged him, but he still feels uneasy about making the decision to apply. Walt is afraid God may not want him to go into this field. He struggles with the thought that he may miss out on what God has planned for him if he goes to art school. Walt has a strong compassion for the homeless, and sometimes feels that God is calling him to devote his life to meeting their needs. While parts of this social work attract Walt, other parts repel him. He is tormented by trying to know what God really wants.

☑ WHY THE STRUGGLE HAPPENS

Several factors contribute to adolescent frustration regarding assurance of God's will. The following are just a few of the reasons some teens get hung up.

The Myth of a Standard Formula

Different decisions require different approaches to God's will. Sometimes teenagers do not understand the variance in the import and meaning of decisions. They seek to know God's will in very specific terms on every decision they make. They believe they must approach simple decisions in the same way they would approach complex ones. Searching for a standard formula for finding God's will in everything, they deliberate over questions that are straightforward or simply a matter of preference.

Confusion Over What "God's Will" Means

Many adolescents seek the will of God before intelligently understanding what the concept means. Some equate God's will with a detailed map for their lives. God does have a "wonderful plan" for each of us that is worthy of emphasis, as the famous Campus Crusade evangelistic tract, "The Four Spiritual Laws," tells us. But God does not outline a personalized plan that settles every future decision. That would be determinism, a philosophy that contradicts free will. In fact, the Bible nowhere teaches that knowledge of the future is necessary or even helpful for effective decision making.

Overconcern with the Future

Some young people get hung up on the matter of God's will for them because they are focused more on the future than the present. Though a tentative outline of what God is planning for our lives is not to be avoided, an obsession with knowing everything about one's future years can deter a person from discovering God's will for today.

Unrealistic Expectations of the Bible

Some sincere young people are frustrated by their failure to discern God's will because they expect to find specific answers to every conceivable question delineated in God's Word. They may feel compelled inadvertently to distort passages of Scripture that are irrelevant to their decisions. They may become superstitious about the Bible and attempt to treat it like a crystal ball. An example is the absurd story of the man who married a woman named Grace because he read the verse that says, "My grace is sufficient for thee." Some teens struggle with God's will because of the futility of this approach.

☑ HOW PARENTS CAN HELP

The following strategies for helping an adolescent struggling to discern God's will can be used effectively by parents; however, every parent-child relationship is unique, and some of them may be more pertinent to your situation than others. The following is offered as a way to help you facilitate the helping process at home with your teenager.

Reframe the Attitude

Many adolescents struggle with confusion over God's will because they approach it as if it were a perplexing puzzle to be arduously and mysteriously solved. These young people need to see that God's guidance is ultimately up to him. They can rest assured that God will make his desires known to them. Psalm 32:8 states, "I will instruct you and teach you in the way you should go." God wants to reveal his will even more than we may want to receive it. Help teens achieve a sense of security in believing that in his own good time God will reveal his will to those who are open to his direction. Some teens are afraid they will miss it if they are not obsessed with ascertaining God's will. They superstitiously look for signals that will reveal his will. This sort of anxiety is not necessary. God has promised to guide his followers, just as a shepherd guides his sheep. While this does not mean that people are to shirk all responsibility in the guidance process, it does mean they are to give God more credit for making his desires known. Gary Friesen proposes that a person should not even ask, "How do I find the will of God?" Instead, a better question to pursue is, "How do I make good decisions?"[3] This shift in attitude can do much to help the struggling young person.

Clarify the Assignment

While adolescents can rest in the assurance that God will initiate his guidance for them, they can also be helped by understanding their assignment to hear his direction clearly. Blaine Smith, in his helpful book *Knowing God's Will*, outlines four basic aspects of the quest to embrace God's will:[4]

1. Adolescents must be willing to hear God's will. Are they determined to understand that God will enable them to be effective in his kingdom? If openness and willingness are not present, it is doubtful that a genuine understanding of God's will can occur.
2. Christians need to ask God for guidance as they pray. In the New Testament the most explicit command to pray for knowledge of God's will is given in James 1:5–6: "If any of you lacks wisdom, he should ask God, who gives generously to all without finding fault, and it will be given to him. But when he asks, he must believe and not doubt." Through prayer young people may begin to glimpse God's perspective on their lives, and ask for the strength to do his will.
3. Young people need to study Scripture, not to find final answers to specific complex decisions, but to understand God and his principles for fulfilled living. This comes through regular and frequent study of the Bible.
4. Teens must use their God-given reason to make intelligent choices. Paul is a biblical example of a person who used his rational faculties to make decisions. For him, discerning God's will was primarily a matter of making logical judgments based upon that which would bring the greatest glory to God. Eventually, a person must trust that God, in his providence, will give all the information needed to follow his will.

Clarify the Types of Decisions

Some sincere teens are overwhelmed with finding God's specific will for almost every decision regardless of its importance. They wonder about whether they are to wear the blue or red sweater, for example. For these young people it is helpful to explain the degree of importance among decisions. Blaine Smith notes several types of decisions that can be delineated. *Moral decisions* are straightforward. They include such matters as stealing or premarital sex. For Christians there is a clear moral principle that simply needs to be understood and applied.

Nonmoral decisions are also straightforward. They deal with choices about actions that have no moral implications. They are simple decisions, such as whether to eat an apple or an orange. *Complex decisions* concern important personal decisions like what college to attend, whether or not to marry, how to spend money, and so on. These decisions require more than simply applying straightforward moral principles. On this level of decision making, one finds a great deal of flexibility and choice. But these are the decisions that commonly cause adolescents to wrestle with knowing God's specific will. Help young people realize that every decision does not call for an equal amount of time and thoughtfulness.

Explore the Use of Intuition

Feelings are like a compass for most adolescents. An emotional surge is more powerful for most than a rational deliberation. Sometimes hunches (intuition) or feelings are regarded as inward signs of God's leading. Some view intuition as the direct voice of the Holy Spirit. While God may certainly influence our feelings in order to tell us something, we must be cautious about putting too great an emphasis on intuition.

Nowhere does the Bible tell us that we should attempt to discern God's will merely through inner feelings. Intuition is helpful in providing insight into one's unconscious. It reveals some of our deepest desires and may tell us something about what God desires for us. However, we cannot conclude that every desire is directly from God. Desires are influenced by further information and experiences. Feelings are important in discovering God's will, but they are not the infallible voice of God.[5]

Facilitate Sound Decision Making

A struggle with knowing God's will almost always results from knowing how to make competent decisions. Blaine Smith presents a helpful fourfold process that should be considered by young people making complex decisions.[6]

1. Consider one's personal desires. Many sincere adolescents believe that a Spirit-led decision will always lead to suffering. They may, for

example, believe they should marry out of sympathy or a sense of duty. I know one young man who thought that, in order to be sure he was doing God's will, he should go into an occupation he would not enjoy. This twisted logic ignores the biblical evidence that God creates desires within the sanctified heart that draw us into his plan. Self-denial and sacrifice may be part of the decision, but they are a subset of the overarching enthusiasm for reaching one's goals. Personal desires must be affirmed to recognize and energize God's will. Sometimes it is helpful to ask teens how they would advise others who are faced with their situation. Their answers may give insight into their deepest feelings. One final note on personal desires: Desires should be given, as Smith says, time to "season." It is important, especially during adolescence, to put desires to a time test, to check whether they are worthy of a commitment.

2. Assess competence and abilities for handling the responsibilities of a particular decision. Young people must examine their skills or potentials before choosing vocations. While this seems obvious, a surprising number of young people do not consider this matter or they may regard it as irrelevant. They are walking "in faith" without considering whether they are suited to such a "call." Encourage them to experiment with it. If, for example, they want to be missionary doctors, they should enroll in some of the hard sciences to see whether they are cut out for that difficult program. Help adolescents take into account everything they can about their personalities and abilities. For some this may mean consulting career counselors or psychologists who can administer a personality assessment.

3. Young people should examine their circumstances to see what opportunities are available to them. What things prevent them from taking certain actions? What options are simply out of the question because the door has been closed? What alternatives are wide open? Circumstances should not play a predominant role in discerning God's will, but they often suggest new avenues to explore and sometimes confirm leanings.

4. There is the matter of counsel. When adolescents desire to move in directions for which they are equipped and for which they have opportunity, they should seek counsel from people they respect. Determining God's will is not the place to exercise rugged individualism. Encourage young people to share their decision process openly with a select group of knowledgeable people who are concerned about their best interests. They should avoid advisers who have their own agenda for the adolescents. The book of Proverbs is packed with wisdom on this theme; for instance, "Plans fail for lack of counsel, but with many advisers they succeed" (15:22). Encourage teenagers who wrestle with important decisions to find several sources of wise guidance.

For a more detailed description of this decision process see *Knowing God's Will* by Blaine Smith. You may also wish to consult *Living God's Will* by Dwight Carlson. Employing a ten-step procedure for knowing God's will, Carlson discusses the four actions noted above:

1. Be obedient to God's already-revealed will.
2. Be open to any means or results.
3. Examine God's Word for principles of guidance.
4. Utilize prayer.
5. Acknowledge the work of the Holy Spirit.
6. Utilize the counsel of others.
7. Consider providential circumstances.
8. Evaluate yourself and your environment.
9. Make the decision.
10. Ask whether you have God's peace about the decision.

Carlson also provides an organized checklist of "things to consider before making any major decision in your life." This may be helpful to use with some adolescents who need more structure to contain their anxiety about uncovering God's will.

Distinguish God's Plan for the Future from God's Desire for Now

God's plans for people's future are different from his wishes for their present circumstances. Predicting their specific future is not the concern of Christians. God normally reveals his specific plans for people in portions.[7] Undue anxiety is caused by thinking that one needs to know the future to understand God's will for the present. Struggling young people should be encouraged to focus more on God's desires for them right now and not jump to conclusions about tomorrow. Their future cannot be indisputably determined. For example, a young person may feel led to go on a date with a certain person, but that does not necessarily mean that God intends them to become engaged. Help the young person avoid the need to "know" what God plans for them years from now.

The highest will of God is revealed when people are doing, right now, what pleases God most.[8] They may feel led, for example, to study for the pastoral ministry, but that does not mean they will ever become pastors. At the same time, of course, young people should never be deterred from an enthusiastic vision of their future and from moving toward specific goals. Making a distinction between God's plan for the future and God's wish for the present helps youth whose anxiety renders them unable to make any decisions.[9]

Know When to Refer

You should refer adolescents who struggle with determining God's will to a competent counselor or pastor when, over time, they feel more confused and uncertain. Referral may be necessary for career counseling or personality assessment that can inform their decisions. You should also refer them to a competent psychologist if they begin to show signs of depression or hopelessness. Refer them if for any reason you are uncomfortable with assisting them in spiritual counsel.

Where to Go for Additional Help

Bence, E. *Knowing God's Will*. Grand Rapids: Zondervan, 1998.

Bright, B. *Five Steps to Knowing God's Will*. Orlando, Fla.: New Life Publications, 1998.

Carlson, D. L. *Living God's Will*. Old Tappan, N.J.: Revell, 1976.

Dollar, T. L. *A Woman After God's Own Heart: Fulfilling the Will of God for Your Life and Empowering Those Around You*. Nashville: Thomas Nelson, 1999.

Friesen, G. *Decision Making and the Will of God*. Portland, Ore.: Multnomah, 1980.

Johnson, B. C. *Discerning God's Will*. Louisville: Westminster/John Knox, 1990.

Nappa, M., A. Nappa, and M. D. Warden. *Get Real: Making Core Christian Beliefs Relevant to Teenagers*. Loveland, Colo.: Group, 1996.

Ogilvie, L. J. *God's Will in Your Life*. Eugene, Ore.: Harvest House, 1982.

Smith, M. B. *Knowing God's Will: Biblical Principles of Guidance*. Downers Grove, Ill.: InterVarsity Press, 1979.

Sproul, R. C. *Can I Know God's Will?* Orlando, Fla.: Ligonier Ministries, 1999.

Water, M. *Knowing God's Will Made Easier*. Peabody, Mass.: Hendrickson Publishers, 1998.

Worthington, E. L., and K. Worthington. *Helping Parents Make Disciples*. Grand Rapids: Baker, 1995.

Wright, H. N., and G. J. Oliver. *Raising Kids to Love Jesus*. Ventura, Calif.: Regal, 1999.

Notes

1. H. J. M. Nouwen and J. Imbach, "God's Will," in *Dictionary of Pastoral Care and Counseling*, ed. R. J. Hunter (Nashville: Abingdon, 1990), 466.

2. L. J. Ogilvie, *God's Will in Your Life* (Eugene, Ore.: Harvest House, 1982).

3. G. Friesen, *Decision Making and the Will of God: A Biblical Alternative to the Traditional View* (Portland, Ore.: Multnomah, 1980).

4. M. B. Smith, *Knowing God's Will: Biblical Principles of Guidance* (Downers Grove, Ill.: InterVarsity Press, 1979).

5. B. C. Johnson, *Discerning God's Will* (Louisville: Westminster/John Knox, 1990).

6. Smith, *Knowing God's Will*.

7. D. L. Carlson, *Living God's Will* (Old Tappan, N.J.: Revell, 1976).

8. Ibid.

9. Smith, *Knowing God's Will*.

GRIEF

✔ WHAT THE STRUGGLE LOOKS LIKE

Grief is a natural and normal response to the loss of something or someone cherished or loved. Doug Manning, in his book *Don't Take My Grief Away*, writes, "Grieving is as natural as crying when you are hurt, sleeping when you are tired, eating when you are hungry, or sneezing when your nose itches. It is nature's way of healing a broken heart."[1]

Grief is succinctly defined by Elisabeth Kübler-Ross in *On Death and Dying* as the "process of separation."[2] Grief is not limited to death. The process of adolescence is separation from childhood and movement toward becoming an adult. Adolescence is fraught with grieving. Grief is a natural response to the breaking of attachments through the loss of a person, thing, activity, status, romantic relationship, or anything that has become significant. Grief has the power to disrupt and disorganize one's total life. It is preoccupying and depleting. Generally, grief is a process, not a state. Bereaved people move through various stages of grief that allow them to reorganize life in positive ways.

According to Kübler-Ross, grief is a gift. "When it is unfiltered, it is right and good and healthy," she writes. "It needs no work or change or therapy. It heals itself. But when we begin to filter our grief through sieves of guilt, anger, resentment, bitterness, or self-pity, then we need more help."[3]

Clinically, the signs and symptoms of grief have been noted for decades: somatic distress, preoccupation with the image of the deceased, guilt, regret, fear, hostile reactions resulting from unresolved anger, and loss of conduct patterns previously influenced by the deceased.[4] The *Diagnostic and Statistical Manual* (4th ed.) describes a category of uncomplicated bereavement. In this, a depressive syndrome is frequently normal. After a death, guilt, if present, is largely about things done or not done by the survivor at the time of the death. Thoughts of death, according to *DSM-IV*, are usually limited to one's thinking that one would be better off dead, or that one should have died with the deceased. The reaction to the loss may not be immediate but rarely occurs beyond the first two or three months.[5]

Teenagers who suffer significant loss experience more stress than other teens.[6] Research has shown, however, that they often emerge as healthier people when their grieving process continues to a resolution and acceptance. For example, they are more reflective, have better relationships with parents and peers, improve school work (after temporary difficulties), have a sense of increased maturity relative to other adolescents, and have heightened moral values.[7]

Adolescents grapple with death better than do some adults. The American poet William Cullen Bryant, best known for his poem "Thanatopsis," expresses Erik Erikson's goal of ego integrity and trust. Bryant wrote:

> *So live, that when thy summons comes . . .*
> *Thou go not, like the quarry-slave at night,*
> *Scourged to his dungeon, but, sustained and soothed*
> *By an unfaltering trust. . . .*

Bryant wrote this poem when he was eighteen—an adolescent!

From her work with terminally ill patients, Kübler-Ross found common responses to news of impending death. She identified five stages of dying: denial, anger, bargaining, depression, and acceptance. While these stages are similar to the stages of grief, there are differences. Her theory is directed specifically to the dying patient. To force her stages of dying on a person who is struggling with grief, according to David Switzer, is distorting and misleading.[8]

Pastoral theologian Wayne Oates has proposed a helpful theory of grief that outlines a progression of stages: the shocking blow of the loss in itself, the numbing effect of the shock, the struggle between fantasy and reality, the breakthrough in a flood of grief, selected memory and stabbing pain, the acceptance of the loss, and the affirmation of life itself.[9]

John Bowlby suggests three basic stages of grief teens go through: protest and denial, despair and disorganization, and finally reorganization.[10] A more complete picture of the process is provided by Yorick Spiegel.[11] In this model the bereaved person moves through four stages:

1. *The Shock Stage.* Adolescents in this stage will be characterized by dis-belief, emotional numbness, occasional outbreaks of pain and tears, a frequent lack of awareness of external events and conversations, and difficulty in thinking clearly.
2. *The Control Stage.* This is characterized by a stoic self-control on the part of grieving adolescents (as well as a control on the demands by other persons around them). Here young people may be passive, feel depersonalized, have difficulty in carrying out decisions, experience distance between themselves and the external world, feel a sense of the unreality of it all, feel empty or dead inside, and try to act as if the loss had not occurred.
3. *The Regression Stage.* Here adolescents can no longer be sustained under the impact of the reality of the loss. Earlier forms of feeling and react-ing begin to dominate and are often independent of the realities of their present environment. Once again grieving teenagers experience pain, uncertainty, fragmentation, heightened emotion of all kinds, weeping, anger, complaining, often becoming exhausted and withdrawing, hav-ing a seeming apathy, self-centeredness, preoccupation with and often idealization of the deceased, a grasping at overly simplistic explanations, a pervasive sense of helplessness, and a variety of defense mechanisms directed against the pain and the fear of loss of control.
4. *The Adaptation Stage.* In this final stage, a step-by-step giving up of regressive behaviors occurs. In their place more adaptive responses arise as the loss is recognized to its full and final extent. This makes neces-sary the very painful giving up of expectations of life being again as it was, accompanied by a restoration of the deceased within one's own individual personality. In so doing, reconnecting with the present external world takes place.

Since grief is a process with stages, it is essential for adolescents to go through each one of the stages completely in order to reach a positive resolu-tion of the whole grief reaction. To repress and suppress the feelings involved in grief, to go about as if nothing had been lost, to attempt to skip stages of the grieving process, indicate that the process of resolution and reorganization has been thwarted. Pathological or unresolved grief occurs when the usual movement through recognized stages of grief is blocked, although it is not uncommon to go through the stages a bit out of order or to be in more than one stage at the same time.

Signs of pathological grief in adolescents include starting to use alcohol or drugs to "ease the pain," intense feelings of guilt, hurting others because they have been hurt, dropping activities or relationships that once were important and meaningful, experimenting with sex to get close to someone, not talking to people they are close to about what troubles them, causing trouble, behaving recklessly or trying to hurt themselves (although suicidal thoughts are often a natural part of grieving), and playing the role of the "scapegoat" or "bad guy" so as to appear tough.

Everyone's grief, like a physical wound, is on a unique timetable. Some wounds are uncomplicated and heal easily and quickly. But other wounds are more complicated and require professional intervention. So it is with grief. Some losses are grieved over and resolved quietly and alone. Others are complicated and need more help. If, after six to eight months, an adolescent has not made significant progress in the grief process, it is a good indicator that professional intervention may be necessary.

Case Description

Dorothy, a sixteen-year-old, came to counseling two months after losing her father in an automobile accident. He died upon impact. Dorothy had not expressed any feelings of grief about her father's death, but she could talk at length about it in a factual manner. Her mother reported that Dorothy had not been sleeping well and seemed rarely to be hungry since the accident. But Dorothy said she was fine. She had not confessed her pain to anyone, even her closest friend or older sister. In the second session of counseling Dorothy began to express her sorrow. It started in the latter half of the session when she said she was angry at her father for leaving. He had promised her a trip for her upcoming birthday, and she was angry that it would never happen. More powerful than her anger, however, was her guilt about feeling angry. For twenty minutes, tears streamed down her cheeks as she buried her face in her hands and sobbed.

Facilitating the grieving process for bereaved adolescents involves helping them to express feelings, remember, accept the reality of physical death, experience their own value as persons, and discover meaning in their lives in the midst of the events. Grief work can be a rewarding challenge and provide adolescents with some of life's most meaningful experiences.

✔ WHY THE STRUGGLE HAPPENS

The cause of grief, in one sense, is simply loss. A struggle with pathological grief, however, is more complicated. The question is how to identify those young people who are most at risk. In brief, those most at risk include young people with parents who have themselves been depressed, with a history of serious illnesses requiring hospitalization, and with a genetic inheritance pattern for affective disorders.[12] Gary Collins, in his book *Christian Counseling*, outlines several additional influences of pathological grief.

The Griever's Beliefs

Most young people are taught from their earliest years how to acquire things, not how to lose them. Even when a youngster loses a pet to an accident, it is often replaced on the next Saturday. Most children are not taught how to think about long-term loss, and there are some who are also taught to bury any sorrow that surrounds loss. They come to believe that showing any signs of grief or seeking comfort and help in dealing with their loss is a personal weakness. They believe they should not be affected even by the loss of a loved one through death. Also, teens who have no religious support or belief in hope for the future and who cannot find comfort in supernatural peace in times of mourning have a greater potential for suffering pathological grief.

Personal History

Grieving is always difficult, but for some adolescents it seems to hit harder than for others. This is especially true if they have had difficulty in other personal separations and losses. Adolescents with personal histories of previously unmastered losses—for example, parents' divorce or a romantic breakup—are more likely to suffer from complicated and dysfunctional grief. In other words, if adolescents have learned to deny earlier losses rather than work them through, they may not be prepared to respond to severe losses. They have no experience on which to draw.[13]

Social Environment

Adolescents who grow up in social environments that try to deny the reality of death are provided little warmth or in-depth social support. They have no intimate or continual relationships to facilitate the grieving process. Because of their environment they learn to bury their feelings and grieve alone, if at all. These adolescents are likely to get stuck in the grieving process and suffer from pathological grief.

Circumstances Surrounding the Loss

A sudden and tragic loss is generally the most difficult for young people to assimilate in healthful ways.[14] If a loss was anticipated, such as the death of an elderly or sick grandparent, the grief is less likely to be pathological. When a sibling dies, there is often a strong sense of guilt ("It should have been me"), especially if one had ambivalent feelings toward a brother or sister, and a stronger feeling of personal mortality ("There but for the grace of God go I").[15] Essentially, the greater the loss, the greater the intensity of the grief.

✔ HOW PARENTS CAN HELP

The following strategies for helping an adolescent struggling with grief can be used effectively by parents; however, every parent-child relationship is unique, and some of them may be more pertinent to your situation than others. As with every significant adolescent struggle, it is best for parents to work alongside a competent counselor. With this in mind, the following is offered as a way to help you facilitate the helping process at home with your teenager.

Know What to Avoid

Even the most experienced counselors, let alone parents, sometimes need to be reminded of the importance of reflective listening while working through grief issues. It is particularly painful to watch young people suffer heartbreaking grief. We may be tempted to solve problems for them as a means to our own comfort. Effective parents must avoid rushing the grieving process simply to help adolescents avoid more pain. Comforting grieving youth is more like comforting a teething baby than like keeping a child away from a hot stove. The core of the work is listening to their pain and suffering, not keeping them from it. Bereaved adolescents do not need advice, and they certainly do not need to be told how or what to feel. They don't need to hear statements such as "I know what you're going through," or "God is going to teach you something wonderful through this," or "It just takes time to grieve," or "Don't be so down; things could be a lot worse." Avoid all pat answers.

Examine Your Own Unresolved Grief

Parents often confront their own mortality when a child is grieving. Awareness of death is always tempered by a degree of denial, which helps us to function effectively. As Duc François de La Rochefoucauld said, "Neither the sun nor death can be looked at steadily." You, therefore, need to review and examine your own attitudes toward loss, experiences with death and grieving, and your degree of comfort with emotions that surround these issues. Failure to do so can block a healthful grieving process for adolescents and lead to undesirable consequences. You cannot substitute your knowledge about grief for personal processing of your own grief issues. Those who have learned what it means to experience the complete grieving process are tremendous help to others who are just learning how to grieve.

Prepare for Anniversary Dates

Even after grief work has been resolved, times will come that will sadden adolescents. These times are predictable. Any date that had significant meaning for survivors and the deceased is considered an anniversary date. Survivors need to prepare for these by having a safe place to talk about their feelings. During the first year of grieving, they should make a list of the upcoming dates that have potential to bring sadness—the birthday of the deceased, the date of death, holidays, and so on. It makes no difference what the day or occasion is; the grieving person should have a place to express pain and sorrow. This may be with counselors or trusted friends. The same considerations should be given to places or events that have the potential for sadness. Again, those who are grieving should not experience these alone.[16]

Incorporate Meaningful Activity

Grieving adolescents who have difficulty expressing their feelings may benefit from activities that express their grief. For example, they may plant a tree or a rose bush in memory of the deceased. Its growth will be enjoyed as a symbol of life and hope for the future. Providing fresh flowers on special days in the church may be cathartic. Wearing a special piece of jewelry in memory of the deceased may be a symbol of their love. Donating books or clothes of the deceased may be therapeutic. Making and enjoying memories may sooth adolescents who struggle with grief.

Utilize the Power of Prayer

If your son or daughter is open to prayer, consider doing this together. Having an example to model in spiritual strength is helpful to adolescents battling grief. Suggest that they also pray on their own. Suggest they ask God to comfort them. Encourage them to tell God all of their feelings, to see the deceased with Jesus, and, when they are ready, to thank God for his care. For those who need to say good-bye or express something to the deceased, this quiet moment of prayer provides a wonderful healing moment. Psalm 23 continues to be one of adolescents' favorite Bible passages. This may be a helpful resource for them in helping them to pray during their grief.

Know When to Refer

Parents should help their bereaved adolescent to see a competent counselor or psychologist when, over several weeks of time, they are stuck in the grieving process or suffering more grief and becoming increasingly depressed, hopeless, or suicidal. Refer if you recognize that your own grief issues are interfering with and complicating your relationship or if you find that you are becoming impatient with their pain and want to "fix" them.

✔ HOW PROFESSIONALS CAN HELP

The following strategies for helping an adolescent struggling with grief are commonly used by counselors. They are presented here as a way to inform you, as a parent, and help you seek the best possible professional help you can for the adolescent in your care.

Understand Their True Needs

It is imperative for parents and counselors who work with the bereaved to understand accurately what the grieving client needs. David K. Switzer has described eight needs that must be fulfilled for effective resolution of the grieving process, especially when it is the result of death:[17]

1. To accept the reality and finality of physical death (or loss).
2. To become aware of and express all the feelings they have about the loss or toward the deceased. Sometimes this concerns the way the deceased died (e.g., suicide, accident, etc.).
3. To break the emotional ties with the deceased. In other words, they need to refrain from investing emotionally in the deceased and behaving toward the deceased as if he or she were still physically present.
4. To break habitual patterns of speech and other behaviors that assume the deceased person is physically present.
5. To affirm that they themselves are worthwhile apart from interaction and connection with the deceased.
6. To reaffirm and therefore allow to come back to life those characteristics and behaviors that contribute to the ongoing and growing life of the grieving adolescent.
7. To cultivate both old and new relationships.
8. To rediscover meaning in one's own life.

Help Them Admit Their Grief

Some adolescents will come for counseling to work on their grief, but will act "recovered." They will say that they're okay and force themselves to smile. They seem put together and may even say they want to help the family deal more effectively with grief. John James and Frank Cherry call this "Academy Award Recovery."[18] These young people want the approval of others in their time of sorrow. They want to be praised for the way they have overcome the loss. Effective counselors will help this kind of young person gently discover their unresolved mourning. Counselors will ask how they have changed since the loss. Has their sleeping or eating changed? Do they have difficulties concentrating? Do they express emotions differently? Do they talk with their friends just as they always have? Counselors may even have the teen write letters to the deceased to express what they never had a chance to say. These kinds of questions and exercises help young people to see and eventually admit that they are suffering from unresolved grief. Sometimes all they need is permission and time to grieve.

Include the Family

When death has occurred in an adolescent's family, it often helps to work with all of the family members (sometimes in addition to individual therapy with the adolescent). Mary Elizabeth Taylor Warmbrod, professor of psychology at the University of Manitoba, has devised a three-stage process of working with bereaved young people and their families. In each of the three stages, the focus is on a different aspect of the family's life. The first stage is the focus on the death and the funeral of the loved one; next, the consideration of what the dead person was like, what the family did together, and so on; finally, a focus on the present with reference to adjustments and sources of comfort.[19]

1. *The Beginning: The Death and Funeral.* This stage of counseling begins with asking the family strictly factual questions: When did the person die? Of what? How were you each told that he or she was dead? What was it like going to the hospital? Where was everyone at the time of death? Questions about the funeral or memorial naturally follow: Who came to the funeral? Where was it held? What did you think of the funeral or memorial service? Where is the person buried? Have you been to the grave? In this stage the counselor will appreciate what each family member went through. This stage may take more than one or two sessions.

2. *The Middle: The Past and Memories.* Having reviewed the death and funeral, the next stage takes the family back to the time before the person died. It is important to hear what each one's memories are. Counselors may begin with questions about appearance: What did the person

look like? Do you have any pictures to show me? What did you enjoy doing together?

3. *The End: The Present and Future.* The final stage involves attention to the present and plans for the future. The kinds of questions to be discussed are: When do you miss him or her the most, in the morning or evening? To whom do you talk when you think of him or her? Where do you cry? What do you do when you see someone else cry? What would you like from others when you start to cry? How is it at school? Do people at school know? Questions like these give family members opportunity to tell one another how they are grieving together. Interwoven with the focus on support is a concern about plans for the future.

Over the course of these sessions, pain may subside. What ideally results is a satisfaction with having known the deceased, a willingness to think about him or her at special times, and confidence that the future offers hope and that the memory of the deceased will continue to influence the family in positive ways.

Consider Social Support

Social support has been shown to affect adaptation of adolescents to the deaths of family members.[20] In one study, teenagers who scored higher on a measure of social support were significantly less depressed than were those who scored lower on the same measure. Adolescents who do not find support from the surviving parent are helped the most by social support. Bereaved teenagers report that the most helpful persons are peers. Teenagers in social support groups also report great emotional support from their counselors.[21]

Typically, in the first group session, participants tell the group the details of who has died and how. The leader encourages all members to take their turn but does not pressure them. After the first meeting, the content of group discussion is generally determined by participants. Topics typically include feelings of guilt and anger, difficulties with surviving family members, memories about the deceased, school problems, and problems with fears of others dying. These groups typically range from eight to twelve weeks, and the ideal group size is from five to nine.[22]

Where to Go for Additional Help

Boss, P. *Ambiguous Loss: Learning to Live with Unresolved Grief.* Cambridge, Mass.: Harvard University Press, 1999.

Collins, G. *Christian Counseling,* rev. ed. Dallas: Word, 1988.

Hutton, L. (ed.). *Talking with Your Teen: Conversations for Life.* Nashville: Abingdon Press, 2000.

James, J. W., and F. Cherry. *The Grief Recovery Handbook: A Step-by-Step Program for Moving Beyond Loss.* New York: Harper & Row, 1988.

Kennedy, A. *Losing a Parent.* San Francisco: Harper & Row, 1991.

Kolf, J. C. *Teenagers Talk About Grief.* Grand Rapids: Baker, 1990.

Kuenning, D. *Helping People Through Grief.* Minneapolis: Bethany, 1987.

Nolen-Hoeksema, S., and J. Larson. *Coping with Loss.* Mahwah, N.J.: Lawrence Erlbaum Associates, 1999.

Switzer, D. K. *The Dynamics of Grief.* Nashville: Abingdon, 1970.

Tatelbaum, J. *The Courage To Grieve: Creative Living, Recovery, and Growth Through Grief.* San Francisco: Harper & Row, 1984.

White, M. A. *Harsh Grief, Gentle Hope.* Colorado Springs, Colo.: Navpress, 1995.

Woodson, M. *The Toughest Days of Grief,* Grand Rapids: Zondervan, 1994.

Yancey, P. *Where Is God When It Hurts?* Grand Rapids: Zondervan, 1977.

_____. *Disappointment with God.* Grand Rapids: Zondervan, 1988.

Notes

1. D. Manning, *Don't Take My Grief Away* (New York: Harper & Row, 1979).

2. E. Kübler-Ross, *On Death and Dying* (New York: Macmillan, 1974).

3. Ibid.

4. E. Lindman, "Symptomatology and Management of Acute Grief," *American Journal of Psychiatry* 101 (1944): 141–48.

5. American Psychiatric Association, *Diagnostic and Statistical Manual of Mental Disorders,* 4th ed., rev. (Washington, D.C.: American Psychiatric Association, 1994).

6. J. Jarolmen, "A Comparison of the Grief Reaction of Children and Adults," *Omega: Journal of Death and Dying* 37 (1998): 133–50.

7. D. Balk, "Effects of Sibling Death on Teenagers," *Journal of School Health* (January 1983): 14–18.

8. D. K. Switzer, "Grief and Loss," in *Dictionary of Pastoral Care and Counseling,* ed. R. J. Hunter (Nashville: Abingdon, 1990).

9. W. Oates, "Anxiety in Christian Experience Bereavement," *Psychiatry* 33 (1970): 444–67.

10. J. Bowlby, *Attachment and Loss,* vol. 3 of *Loss, Sadness and Depression* (Markham, Ont.: Penguin, 1980).

11. Y. Spiegel, *The Grief Process: Analysis and Counseling* (Nashville: Abingdon, 1977).

12. B. J. McConvill, "Assessment, Crisis Intervention, and Time-Limited Cognitive Therapy with Children and Adolescents Grieving the Loss of a Loved One," *Crisis Intervention Handbook,* ed. A. R. Roberts (Belmont, Calif.: Wadsworth, 1990).

13. F. Canziani, "Possible Children's Reactions to Their Parents' Divorce," *Giornale di Neuropsichiatria dell'Eta Evolutiva* 16 (1996): 255–82.

14. H. Vande Kemp, "Grieving the Death of a Sibling or the Death of a Friend," *Journal of Psychology and Christianity* 18 (1999): 354–66.

15. R. A. Kalish, *Death, Grief, and Caring Relationships,* 2d ed. (Monterey, Calif.: Brooks-Cole, 1985).

16. M. Woodson, *The Toughest Days of Grief* (Grand Rapids: Zondervan, 1994).

17. Switzer, "Grief and Loss."

18. J. W. James and F. Cherry, *The Grief Recovery Handbook: A Step-by-Step Program for Moving Beyond Loss* (New York: Harper & Row, 1988).

19. M. E. T. Warmbrod, "Counseling Bereaved Children: Stages in the Process," *Social Casework: The Journal of Contemporary Social Work* (June 1986): 351–58.

20. S. J. Marwit and S. S. Carusa, "Communicated Support Following Loss: Examining the Experiences of Parental Death and Parental Divorce in Adolescence," *Death Studies* 22 (1998): 237–55.

21. B. W. MacLennan, "Mourning Groups for Children Suffering from Expected or Sudden Death of Family or Friends," *Journal of Child and Adolescent Group Therapy* 8 (1998): 13–22.

22. R. E. Gray, "The Role of School Counselors with Bereaved Teenagers: With and Without Peer Support Groups," *School Counselor* (January 1988): 185–93.

GUILT

✔ WHAT THE STRUGGLE LOOKS LIKE

Almost no one is exempt from guilt. It strikes in unaccountable ways among all ages in all circumstances. I have heard scores of guilt stories in my work as a psychologist. Working mothers, sincere pastors, competent counselors, dedicated teachers, successful business executives—nearly everyone experiences guilt now and then. But I know of no group more prone to suffer the ravages of guilt than adolescents.

Everyone who works with adolescents works with guilt. Talk with young people who struggle with depression, loneliness, inferiority, alcoholism, drugs, critical attitudes, premarital sex, eating disorders, anxiety, spiritual doubt, God's will, masturbation, grief, or almost any other problem and you will find adolescents who struggle with guilt as well.

Guilt is the thud-in-the-gut feeling that occurs when a great gulf separates who we are and who we think we ought to be. According to Bruce Narramore, this emotion is experienced in three typical forms:

1. Self-punishment—"I deserve a good swift kick."
2. Self-rejection—"Nobody could love me, especially God."
3. Self-shame—"I feel worthless."

Adolescents will vary greatly in their experience of guilt, but generally they will experience one of these three forms or a combination of them.[1]

Guilt is so prevalent that several types have been identified. Social scientists and other scholars talk about *objective* or *legal* guilt where a violation of the laws of society has occurred, regardless of whether the person feels any remorse; *social* guilt when a person breaks unwritten but socially expected rules; *personal* guilt when a person breaks personal standards or resists the urgings of conscience; and *theological* guilt, which involves a violation of the laws of God.

The most troubling form of guilt, however, is *irrational* or *false* guilt. Paradoxically, guilt often hits hardest those who have very little or no real reason to be affected by it. I remember one teen who came to see me because of her struggle with guilt. In the third grade she had lost five dollars she was to turn in from selling school raffle tickets. She reported the circumstances and no questions were asked. That night she cried herself to sleep. She wrestled with false accusations from her conscience, which demanded that she be perfect. She finally made a promise to herself: She would put all of her allowance into the church collection plate the next Sunday as a form of restitution for her negligence. Only the coldest of hearts would say that this little girl needed to feel guilty. Yet she carried the residue of guilt feelings from this incident into her teen years. As an adolescent she was still suffering from nightmares about it. Was she guilty? Obviously not. The feelings were irrational.

Case Description

Jenny is seventeen, attractive, energetic, a cheerleader at her high school, and a top student. Jenny is also wracked with guilt feelings. Not a minute goes by that she doesn't blame herself for something. If she's not thinking about how she is doing something wrong in the present, she will dredge up something from her past. It is not that a specific event seems to fuel her guilty conscience; Jenny just has a general compulsion to hit herself over the head with a sense of guilt. She feels guilty about not being a better daughter, the B she got in French, the negative thoughts she has about one of the other girls on the cheer squad, the ice cream she ate at lunch, and on and on. Jenny believes she is never good enough at home, school, church, or anywhere else. She almost always feels guilty.

Irrational guilt is particularly dangerous in adolescence because it can become a personality trait, a predisposition, or a prevailing mood. When this happens young people live in a maze of condemnation and a prison of "oughts" and "shoulds." Carrying guilt feelings may become a way of life that must be challenged if adolescents are to reach their potential.

✔ WHY THE STRUGGLE HAPPENS

While causes of guilt feelings are as numerous as the adolescents who experience them, there are several clusters of reasons that explain why young people generally suffer from these feelings.

Unrealistic Expectations

Perfectionism is a major cause of obsessional guilt. Perfectionists measure their self-worth in terms of unachievable goals or accomplishments and productivity. Any deviation from the perfectionistic goal is likely to be accompanied by self-criticism and feelings of guilt.[2] Perfectionists have only a thin thread of fulfillment, which snaps quickly with the heavy weight of unrealistic expectations. Some examples of these expectations include: "I should always be at the top of my class;" "I should never disappoint anyone;" "I should always succeed at whatever I attempt to do;" "I should like everyone and everyone should always like me." Unrealistic expectations like these increase the stranglehold of obsessional guilt around the necks of adolescents prone to hold unrealistic expectations of themselves.[3]

Legalism

I once heard of a woman who chastised her neighbor for cutting his grass on a Sunday afternoon. "Don't you know this is the Sabbath day of rest?" she hollered. "You shouldn't be cutting your lawn." The man replied, "God made the Sabbath for man, not man for the Sabbath." To which she said, "Two wrongs don't make a right!"

Legalism is another cause of irrational guilt. Though it is only a substitute for responsible human behavior and understanding, it pulls many young people into its corner. It finds rules for everything and thus mathematically increases the likelihood of fault and error. Legalism takes policies to an extreme and seeks absolute consistency. It reduces the spirit of law to specific, rigid rules. Legalism obscures and distorts guidelines and is blind to options and possibilities. The absoluteness of legalism is a strong temptation for many struggling adolescents. They can be attracted to its simplicity.

Social Pressure

The sense of feeling on-stage is common in adolescents. They feel exposed, as though others can see inside them, see their faults and defects, know their fears and imaginings. Every day adolescents are immersed in an ocean of social evaluation. They are soaked in mutual criticism. And every day that pressure may move them closer to falling into the clutches of irrational guilt. Every day adolescents are bombarded with statements like "You should have asked her to go out while you had the chance;" "I can't believe you missed that shot;" "Can't you ever get it right?" "You are so conceited;" "We could have won if it weren't for you;" "You promised you would always stand up for me;" "You were such a jerk at the lunch table today." For a conscience already tender, statements like these will most certainly strengthen the grip of guilt feelings in youthful lives.

A Faulty Conscience

I often ask people, "Who said, 'Let your conscience be your guide?'" Some want to credit the apostle Paul. It was actually Jiminy Cricket in Walt Disney's film *Pinocchio*. If you let your conscience be your guide, you may get into trouble. This popular maxim fails to recognize that consciences differ greatly from person to person. One's conscience is homegrown. It does not come pre-packaged with the Ten Commandments, the Sermon on the Mount, the special rules of your church, or the laws passed by Congress. We were not born with internal emotional thermostats to determine the heat and cold of right from wrong.

Parents are the primary molders of conscience. To avoid punishment, gain rewards, or simply maintain love, children accept their parents' standards of behavior. As children, we were conditioned by "stop that," "no, no," or "naughty, naughty." The more we heard these words, the meaning of right and wrong came into focus. We felt good when we did the right thing and guilty when we did wrong. Developmental psychologist Jean Piaget has shown that the moral judgments of young children are attributed to a kind of magical divine authority given to adults. In other words, children are influenced by the consciences of their parents. Our consciences are cultivated through teaching, and sometimes that teaching is faulty.

In the New Testament Paul makes a distinction between a strong and a weak conscience (see 1 Corinthians 8). For Paul a weak conscience is focused rigidly on the letter of the law. The weak conscience, for example, insists upon refraining from meat dedicated to idols, even though idols have no divine reality. The strong conscience, on the other hand, is not bound by the falseness of idolatry. It can bend like a palm tree and adjust to an awareness of circumstances and to the environment. It lives in consideration of principles and in a commitment to ideals. The strong conscience is discerning. It brings all of the elements to bear in a process of moral evaluation. The strong conscience balances a concern for rules with a concern for relationships.

In and of itself, the conscience, contrary to popular opinion, is not ordained of God. While the capacity for a conscience is a divine endowment built into the fabric of personality, it is often informed by distortions that should in no way be regarded as reliable moral guides. The conscience is unreliable unless transformed by Christ.

Evil

Before the Fall, Adam and Eve had no need for conscience. They had no knowledge of good or evil and thus no sense of guilt (see Genesis 2 and 3). However, after their disobedience they realized their wrongdoing and tried to hide from God. At that point, according to Gary Collins, "objective theological guilt and subjective guilt feelings entered God's creation."[4] We fool ourselves if we believe that we are without sin (see 1 John 1:8). Awareness of our guilt comes from the Holy Spirit (see John 16:8–11), and Jesus offers us forgiveness.

Our struggle with guilt, however, comes in realizing that Satan can create guilt feelings. The Bible states that Satan accuses God's followers day and night (see Revelation 12:10). We see him accusing God's people both in Job and Zechariah (see Job 1:6–11 and Zechariah 3:1–2). The false experience of guilt is one of the ways he causes us to stumble. Ephesians 6:11 says, "Take your stand against the devil's schemes." Satan certainly causes sincere believers to feel guilty and unforgiven, even when they have done nothing wrong.

✔ HOW PARENTS CAN HELP

The following strategies for helping an adolescent struggling with guilt can be used effectively by parents; however, every parent-child relationship is unique, and some of them may be more pertinent to your situation than others. As with every significant adolescent struggle, it is best for parents to work alongside a competent counselor. With this in mind, the following is offered as a way to help you facilitate the helping process at home with your teenager.

Differentiate Between True and False Guilt

Most adolescents who suffer guilt, suffer in silence. When they do talk about it, a parent's first step is to discover whether the sense of guilt is rational or irrational. True guilt is the result of wrong or sinful behavior. In other words, adolescents with true guilt feel guilty because they are guilty. Where there is true guilt, the course of action is clear. Confession, forgiveness, and, in some cases, restitution are needed. Remind youth who struggle with true guilt that God is ready and willing to forgive them. Earl Wilson, Christian psychologist, suggests several questions to ask to determine whether a person is dealing with true or false guilt:[5]

1. Is what you feel guilty about a result of real sin?
2. If you had to ask forgiveness for some thought or action, what would it be?
3. If you had to ask forgiveness of a person, who would it be?

If your child cannot clearly answer these questions, Wilson suggests that the struggle is probably with false guilt. The following questions may unearth adolescents' false guilt:

1. What expectation that you are not meeting do you have of yourself?
2. Do you feel that you have let down your parents or other people?
3. Are you putting demands upon yourself that you cannot meet?
4. What action might you take now to move closer to where you would like to be?

These questions will help reveal the impossibilities of adolescent perfectionistic thinking and help young people turn off the false alarm.

Examine Unrealistic Expectations

The false guilt alarm is often set off by unrealistic expectations. I know a high school student who was nearly destroyed by her self-imposed, false guilt. She grew up in a family that had great expectations of high academic performance. This girl always seemed to be at the top of her class. When she entered college, she found herself in competition with students who were also at the top of their classes. For the first time she was not the best. She believed she had let her parents down. She punished herself by getting depressed, not sleeping much, and studying all weekend without taking a single break for fun. I helped this young woman see that not being at the top was not a sin. She learned that no reason existed for her to punish herself as she had been doing. She saw that her expectations were irrational.

Adolescents who battle false guilt confuse realistic with unrealistic expectations. The distortion probably stems from a long list of unspoken "shoulds," ironclad rules that are not to be transgressed. These teens feel compelled to be or do something, but they never bother to ask objectively whether particular achievement goals are worth the pressures upon them that the goals create. They suffer from the tyranny of "shoulds."

Here is a list of some of the most common and unreasonable "shoulds" that struggling adolescents hold dear:

- I should be the epitome of generosity, courage, and unselfishness.
- I should never feel hurt.
- I should be the perfect friend, sibling, son/daughter, and so on.
- I should be able to find a quick solution to every problem.
- I should be able to endure any hardship and difficulty without complaining.
- I should always feel loved and accepted by everyone all the time.
- I should understand and know everything.
- I should never feel emotions like anger or jealousy.
- I should never make mistakes.
- I should never get sick or even be tired.

Parents may ask adolescents to write their own lists of unreasonable shoulds to heighten their awareness of unrealistic expectations about academic abilities, spiritual dedication, relational devotion, athletic skill, and so on.

Explore the Misuse of Confession

I spent a Friday evening in an unmarked car with a detective friend to observe his work firsthand. A tour of the homicide unit confirmed something I had suspected. Every notorious murder provokes many innocent people to "confess" to the crime. I lived in Los Angeles during the reign of the "Night Stalker." Before the true criminal was caught, at least five people confessed to being that murderer. People with a great amount of guilt are looking for any way they can to assuage their consciences, even confessing to crimes they didn't commit in order to receive punishment they are convinced they deserve.

Some people find freedom from guilt through confession, while others are propelled further into the guilt trap by this same act. The endless "guilt-confession cycle" looks like this:

> **Guilt feelings** ... which lead to ... **confession in order to feel better** ... which leads to ... **temporary relief** ... which leads to ... **falling into the same behavior or attitude** ... which leads to ... **more guilt feelings** ... which lead to ... **confession in order to feel better** ... and on and on.

Confession may be an attempt to manipulate God and avoid the consequence of sin. That is, confession may serve as a temporary way of getting God off our backs, rather than a means to true change of behavior and attitude.

Sincere confession that makes a lasting difference involves a deep repentance, admission of one's inability to meet God's holy standards without his help, and recognition of the futility of trying to earn God's acceptance. Only this level of repentance and change can break up the self-glorifying function of confession.

Genuine confession is painful and frightening. It may also be humiliating. But sincere confession has its rewards. Once a truth is spoken aloud, it is much harder to hide from that truth again. Confession brings a sense of responsibility for behavior and attitudes. It may steer adolescents away from self-blame and from blaming others for difficulties. Confession may help young people avoid what I call the "chain of blame." We rarely enjoy accepting responsibility for something bad, and everyone is an expert at shifting responsibility and blame to somebody or something else. Adam blamed Eve, Eve blamed the serpent, and away we went. However, heartfelt confession may break that chain.

There is another risk to confession that is worth mentioning. Confession may be used as a further means of self-punishment. When one's problem is fear of punishment or self-inflicted punishment, confession tends to lessen the need for punishment and thus releases a sense of guilt. But if the problem is more of a feeling of inadequacy and low self-esteem, confession may actually magnify one's sense of inferiority.[6] This is why some Christians find that confession reinforces their feelings of inadequacy and failure rather than providing reassurance of forgiveness.

Encourage Assertiveness

Ask adolescents what they would do in a circumstance like this: "You have saved money to deposit in CDs, and a friend asks for a loan to help buy new Nike shoes. Can you say no and not feel guilty?" Some young people believe that passive agreeableness is the same thing as virtue, decency, and honor. It is not. This has more in common with wimpishness than civility or good manners. Affirm the natural desire to help others, but let your teen know that it is okay to disagree and it is also okay to say no if they want to. Let them know that they can take care of themselves without feeling guilty.

Focus on "Being" Rather Than "Doing"

Trying to look good will make the strongest adolescents weary. It is much less exhausting to focus on trying to be good. Help adolescents turn their spotlight away from doing the right thing and help them work instead on being the right persons. It will help spiritually sensitive teens to know that God does not want them to perform so that he will accept them; he has accepted them, so now they can perform. Ask them to think about being with close friends who accept them in spite of their mistakes. They know they don't have to perform perfectly to receive love and acceptance from this kind of friend. On the other hand, the company of friends who withhold their acceptance until your child measures up to group expectations will be deflating. When the focus is on *doing* rather than *being*, adolescents are more likely to lose control and slide down the slippery slope of guilt.

Know When to Refer

You should refer adolescents who struggle with guilt to psychologically astute physicians or psychiatrists when physical symptoms (e.g., rashes) are present. Refer "guilty" adolescents to other competent counselors or psychologists when, over time, they feel more guilty and increasingly depressed, hopeless, or suicidal. This may be due to your temptation to preach or teach "down" to the adolescent struggling with guilt feelings. Another pitfall parents may encounter is the effort to relieve young people with injunctions such as "all you have to do is trust God." Be careful not to create another layer of guilt by implying that solutions are so apparent that they should already know of them. If you find yourself displaying this kind of attitude, consider a referral to a professional.

✔ HOW PROFESSIONALS CAN HELP

The following strategies for helping an adolescent struggling with guilt are commonly used by counselors. They are presented here as a way to inform you, as a parent, and help you seek the best possible professional help you can for the adolescent in your care.

Explore Secondary Gains

Counselors who do guilt work quickly become aware of the vigorous desire many have to hold on to their guilt feelings. Clients have made restitution, they have been forgiven by those whom they wronged, they are assured of God's forgiveness, and relationships are restored. But the guilty continue to hold onto their guilt. Usually this is a sign of powerful payoffs or secondary gains. The person is receiving something that makes the suffering of guilt bearable. If the guilt were gone, they would lose the payoff.

One common secondary gain for guilty adolescents is control. They can turn guilt feelings on and off as needed to manipulate those around them. If they don't want to do something, they have a guilt attack. Sometimes they can immobilize their parents by donning their sense of guilt. Sometimes guilt helps them become the center of attention. Counselors will ask adolescents what good things they would lose or be forced to give up if they were released from their guilt feelings. For the healing of guilt fixation, counselors explore and expose the secondary benefits that guilt-ridden people cherish.

Examine the Attitude of Perfectionism

Certain jobs require near perfection, such as those of an airline pilot, a surgeon, an architect, or an accountant. But when this trait overflows into relationships and everyday life, it leads directly to guilt feelings. Perfection is the ultimate illusion. It simply does not exist. Everything can be improved, from the space shuttle to peanut butter. In a hit song by Huey Lewis, the chorus says, "There ain't no livin' in a perfect world."

Ask adolescents struggling with a sense of guilt whether they have ever done anything perfectly. Ask whether the benefits of trying to be perfect outweigh the downside. Give them permission to make mistakes! This may seem humorous, but it will probably lead them to feel as if a giant weight has been lifted from their shoulders.

Where to Go for Additional Help

Carlson, D. *From Guilt to Grace.* Eugene, Ore.: Harvest House, 1983.
Counts, W., and B. Narramore. *Freedom from Guilt.* Santa Ana, Calif.: Harvest House, 1974.
Jeffress, R. *Say Goodbye to Regret.* Sisters, Ore.: Multnomah, 1998.
_____. *When Forgiveness Doesn't Make Sense.* Colorado Springs, Colo.: WaterBrook Press, 2000.
Justice, W. G. *Guilt and Forgiveness.* Grand Rapids: Baker, 1980.
Matsakis, A. *Survivor Guilt: A Self-Help Guide.* Oakland, Calif.: New Harbinger Publications, 1999.
Narramore, B. *No Condemnation: Rethinking Guilt Motivation in Counseling, Preaching, and Parenting.* Waco, Tex.: Word, 1984.
Oden, T. C. *Guilt Free.* Nashville: Abingdon, 1980.
Parrott, L. *Love's Unseen Enemy: How to Overcome Guilt to Build Healthy Relationships.* Grand Rapids: Zondervan, 1994.
Rutledge, T. *The Self-Forgiveness Handbook: A Practical and Empowering Guide.* Oakland, Calif.: New Harbinger Publications, 1997.
Tournier, P. *Guilt and Grace.* New York: Harper & Row, 1962.

Notes

1. B. Narramore, *No Condemnation* (Grand Rapids: Zondervan, 1984).
2. B. Sorotzkin, "The Quest for Perfection: Avoiding Guilt or Avoiding Shame?" *Psychotherapy* 22, no. 3 (1985): 564–71.
3. B. Sorotzkin, "Understanding and Treating Perfectionism in Religious Adolescents," *Psychotherapy: Theory, Research, and Practice* 35 (1998): 87–95.
4. G. Collins, *Christian Counseling* (Waco, Tex.: Word, 1980), 122.
5. E. D. Wilson, *Counseling and Guilt* (Waco, Tex.: Word, 1987).

6. Narramore, *No Condemnation*. Narramore provides a thorough discussion of the use and misuse of confession in this excellent book.

HOMOSEXUALITY

☑ WHAT THE STRUGGLE LOOKS LIKE

Few topics trigger more emotional reaction and controversy today than homosexuality. The issue ignites heated debates in virtually every aspect of society: schools, local elections, the military, the courts, sports, science, professional societies, the entertainment world, business and industry, the media, and especially the church. All are caught in the crossfire. On one end of the continuum are gay bashers who are bent on condemning and harassing homosexuals. At the other extreme are the gay liberationists who are intent on making homosexuality an approved way of life, nothing more than an alternative lifestyle.[1] Most of those between these extremes make up an uneasy spectrum of individuals who grapple with the issues and try to make sense of the still-evolving realities and our understanding of causes of homosexuality. Some lean more toward tolerance, others toward condemnation. But they want to do it with thorough understanding rather than bumper-sticker philosophies.

I do not aim in this section to convert you to any one theory or to generate debate. While it is impossible to write on this topic without offending some people, my goal here is to equip you with practical helping techniques that are grounded in compassion rather than condemnation. Debating the issue has its place, but the concern here is to help struggling adolescents.

It is impossible to know how many young people, including Christians, struggle with homosexual urges. Most are understandably afraid to admit their thoughts and feelings (sometimes even to themselves) because of potential rejection or misunderstanding. Somewhere between 5 and 10 percent of the population is homosexual, while some estimate that a larger percentage engage in bisexual activity.[2]

Part of the confusion over homosexuality arises because it is not easily defined. The emphasis should be on behavior rather than on disposition. Christian psychiatrist John White endorses this emphasis in *Eros Defiled*. He writes, "A homosexual act is one designed to produce sexual orgasm between members of the same sex. A homosexual is a man or woman who engages in homosexual acts."[3] Others, who may be motivated by a desire to broaden the base of the homosexual community by including greater numbers, define it as erotic attraction toward persons of the same gender.[4]

Difficulty arises with this definition when one recognizes that gender orientation is not straightforward. It varies in degree. The 1948 Kinsey report suggested a scale with seven points in which zero represents a person who is exclusively heterosexual, three is midpoint, and six represents a person with exclusively homosexual tendencies and actions. Kinsey researchers concluded that few people are at the zero and six points on the scale. However, the plainest definition of homosexuality emphasizes the practice of homosexual acts. This is the sin evangelical Bible scholars identify in Genesis 19.

Homosexuality is not merely one stereotyped behavior pattern. There are many variants of homosexual arousal. Mansell Pattison outlines several types of homosexuality.[5] Any one of the following may show up in a counseling office where Christian professionals must find ways to be redemptive within the context of moral purity and Christian theology:

Experimental homosexuality usually refers to adolescent experimentation with degrees of sexual interaction with both genders. At a minimal level some adolescents engage in "homoerotic" activity, such as arousal as the result of comparing sexual organs. At the extreme end is adolescent experimentation in sexual intercourse with both sexes. Usually this experimentation leads to an exclusive heterosexuality.

Homosexual panic is a phenomenon seen often in young people. An adolescent may encounter nude persons in a shower room after a gym class and suddenly experience sexual arousal. Usually this does not represent homosexual urges, but merely generic sexual arousal from seeing nude bodies.

Situational homosexuality involves homosexual behavior when heterosexual relations are not available. Prisons are the most common example. Sexual release is the primary motivation with affection or intimacy being absent.

Reactive homosexuality involves fear of heterosexual encounters. Although heterosexuality is preferred, homosexual behavior is chosen as less threatening and dangerous.

Social-role homosexuality represents the adoption of homosexual behavior as part of a required social role. Pattison cites as one of the clearest examples a New Guinea tribe in which all males from eight to sixteen are required to play a passive homosexual role and from sixteen to twenty-two an active homosexual role. They are required to marry and remain heterosexual thereafter. More than 95 percent of tribal males successfully follow these socially prescribed sexual role behaviors.

Obligatory homosexuality refers to the sense of sexual orientation that some people experience as an internal necessity. They feel no heterosexual arousal but instead sense a homosexual response. Often they find little pleasure in typical adolescent dating, although they may have excellent social relationships with the opposite gender. They simply feel no attraction. When they begin to experience homosexual arousal, usually in later adolescence, they are surprised, as if against their will. They feel obliged by their own feelings to respond to the same gender. Pattison suggests that this pattern describes the majority of homosexual persons.

Preferential homosexuality occurs in those with bisexual arousal. Many homosexual persons experience heterosexual impulses and perform heterosexual acts with satisfaction. They may simply choose homosexual experiences over heterosexual ones.

Experimental homosexuality and homosexual panic are probably the most common types of adolescent homosexual struggles. Many adolescents who are troubled with their homosexuality enter counseling for other problems. These may include anxiety, depression, compulsive masturbation, grief over a dissolved relationship, or family conflict regarding sexuality. On occasion young people will come to counseling specifically with the presenting issue of clarifying or changing their sexual orientation.[6]

Case Description

Todd, seventeen, managed to convince his parents to arrange for him to go to counseling by telling them that he was worried about possible academic failure. He soon told the counselor that his real concern was related to homosexual fears. Todd remembers trying to "do it" with his younger sister, but he was really too young to know what "it" was. Nevertheless, his father caught them in an undressed state and told Todd how bad he was for what he was doing. Todd attributes his fear of sex with women to that incident. He has never acted out his fear that he is gay, but he is convinced that his early years have "caused" him to be homosexual.

☑ WHY THE STRUGGLE HAPPENS

Space does not permit a full discussion of the causes of homosexuality. A debate on the diversity of its causes will be left to others. Suffice it to say at this point that no one can accurately pinpoint why a person has such an orientation. The following are some of the most frequently espoused reasons. None of these reasons can be declared as causal, but they are often viewed as factors that increase the likelihood of homosexual predisposition.

Psychological Influence

Adolescence is the period during which emerging sexual identity is tested. Homosexuality, according to many, is due to a profound disturbance in parent-child relationships.[7] A boy, for example, may have a father who is distant, detached, and hostile and a mother who is overly warm, possessive, and controlling. As a result of the rejection of the father, the boy's desire to identify with the father is frustrated, and the seeds of fear and a longing for closeness to a male are planted. The mother's smothering ways further decrease the likelihood of the boy's establishing a complete male identity.[8] Research on this theory has not proved it to be causal, but it is still a commonly espoused view.[9]

Social Influence

Social interaction provides some information on the acceptability of sexual self-expression. Learning principles such as association, reinforcement, and avoidance conditioning are often used to explain a great variety of heterosexual as well as homosexual practices and preferences. According to some, young people, in part, *learn* their sexual behavior through social influence. Aversive conditioning of the sexual response toward the opposite sex and positive conditioning toward the same sex, for example, will tend to produce an inclination toward a gay orientation.[10] One researcher concludes after years of study that while homosexuality may develop without operative genetic or hormonal factors, it generally does not develop without the influence of learning and socialization.[11]

Early Seduction

Some experts theorize that homosexual seduction may play a significant role in creating homosexual desires, especially at an early age. During the early years when sexual choice is still relatively undifferentiated, seduction may have a profound impact. A child is not old enough to understand what is happening, and the homosexual experience may become a reinforcer of sexual expression. In these cases, homosexual patterns may develop before heterosexual habits have an opportunity to be explored. Homosexual seduction certainly does not always result in a gay lifestyle, but in some cases it may be a causal factor.[12]

✔ HOW PARENTS CAN HELP

The following strategies for helping an adolescent struggling with homosexual feelings can be used effectively by parents; however, every parent-child relationship is unique, and some of them may be more pertinent to your situation than others. As with every significant adolescent struggle, it is best for parents to work alongside a competent counselor. With this in mind, the following is offered as a way to help you facilitate the helping process at home with your teenager.

Avoid Shock and Express Acceptance

When an adolescent announces, "I think I'm gay," what is your reaction? First of all, do your best not register any visible shock. Effective help can be offered only if you express an unflappable sense of genuine care. Stay calm. Expressing shock at his or her sexual proclivities will greatly hamper healthful exploration that may lead to healing. This is especially true when a teen confesses a struggle with homosexuality.[13] Create an atmosphere of warm acceptance. Check your attitude as objectively as possible, and work to achieve a genuine sense of acceptance for them as a person even if you are not approving of their sexual orientation. You should refer your child to a competent counselor who can.

Reinforce Change

Verbal reinforcers may be effective with young people caught in the trap of feeling bound by same-sex attractions. If the young person tells you about talking with opposite-sex students during lunch hours, say, "That's terrific." If they recount their feelings of being attracted to someone of the opposite sex, say, "Good for you." These seemingly small comments may be a real boost to insecure teenagers.

Insure Social Support

Young people fighting a same-sex preference should be involved in an active social support group. Through social support, a number of Christian ministry groups help homosexuals change. Many are represented by Exodus International and Homosexuals Anonymous. These groups offer a variety of approaches, but generally agree that change is a difficult and painful process of renouncing their practices and attitudes and relying on God for help. You may receive literature and counseling referrals for local social support by contacting

> Exodus International
> P.O. Box 77652
> Seattle, WA 98177
> 888-264-0877 or local 206-784-7799

✔ HOW PROFESSIONALS CAN HELP

The following strategies for helping an adolescent struggling with homosexual feelings are commonly used by counselors. They are presented here as a way to inform you, as a parent, and help you seek the best possible professional help you can for the adolescent in your care.

Obtain an Accurate History

While I know of no valid and reliable measure that can be used to assess the intensity of homosexuality accurately, a good assessment interview by a counselor will take a great deal of guessing out of the therapeutic process. A thorough interview usually takes a couple of hours. Counselors will prepare clients by saying, "I need to understand as much as possible about your circumstances. This means that I must ask you a lot of questions. I'll try not to be obnoxious, but I am going to want details. If you can't come up with verbal answers, you may want to write them down and give them to me later."

Address Client Fears Directly

Counselors do not cause adolescents to become homosexual by allowing them to explore their anxieties in an open and accepting way. If young people are simply questioning the possibility that they may become gay, it is probably not the best time to "process" the concern in a lengthy manner. Christian counselors will calm their anxieties as much as possible. They will reassure them that their fears are not uncommon in this culture and that they are not homosexual. Most "homosexual" feelings during the teen years actually resemble pseudo-homosexuality. They occur when teens are simply in the process of constructing their sexual identity.

Clarify and Assess the Therapeutic Goal

An obvious concern of treatment is the outcome. While some secularists argue that homosexual orientation should be affirmed in therapy, many Christians believe that homosexuality should be eradicated through counsel and the power of God. Clients will ultimately determine the goal they desire.[14] The Christian's therapeutic responsibility is to provide the environment and information that will most likely aid clients both to choose and to be able to follow the most healthful course of action, one that is also consistent with God's will. This would include refraining from homosexual behavior.

Competent Christian counselors will ask adolescents what they expect, and make a distinction between *ego dystonic* homosexuality, in which people experience inner conflict over their sexual desires and what they want them to be, and *ego syntonic* homosexuality, where they are satisfied with their gay orientation and behavior. If they sincerely want to enrich their gay lifestyle through therapeutic intervention and this desire conflicts with the counselor's values, little will be achieved through debating the proper goal of therapy. Counselors can offer only as much help as clients will receive. An old joke asks, "How many psychologists does it take to change a light bulb?" The answer: "Only one. But the light bulb has to want to change." It is impossible to work with adolescents who are genuinely satisfied with their homosexual lifestyle regardless of how upset their families and others may be. As long as people have come to terms with any particular sin and are nonrepentant, little chance of change exists.

Counselors will encourage adolescents who come to counseling with the hope of changing their sexual orientation, but will also warn them that it is not always an easy journey. It may be a wrenching and long process. Sometimes clients may not change to a heterosexual orientation, but they can be helped to live a victorious, meaningful life, free of homosexual behavior. Their desire to change is one of the best predictors of whether they will become heterosexual. Research has also found other predictors of positive change: clients with fewer traits of the opposite gender, under age thirty-five, the first homosexual experience occurring after age sixteen, and evidence of some heterosexual arousal.[15] The presence of sexual ideals and values along with moral attitudes toward homosexuality also increases the likelihood of change.[16]

Correct Misinformation

Much confusion surrounds the topic of homosexuality. Young people may, for example, labor under the misinformation that homosexuality is a mental disorder or that the condition is always irreversible. Perhaps they believe they have committed the unpardonable sin and will never be acceptable to God. Maybe they blame their parents for "making" them this way. Correcting misunderstandings is appropriate. An enlightened attitude can change attitudes and therefore empower teens to overcome their difficulties.

According to James Mallory, chairman of Rapha's Medical and Clinical Advisory Board, homosexuality is best understood by utilizing an addiction model. Addictive behaviors share in common a predispositional vulnerability. Variables such as relationships with parents; learned attitudes of masculinity and femininity; biological, psychological, and social ability to manifest masculine/feminine traits; early sex abuse; quality of relationships with both genders during developmental phases—all may contribute to vulnerability to homosexual behavior, but none is causal. At some point, however, individuals decide to engage in the behavior that is destined to become addictive. Temporarily, according to Mallory, people receive reinforcement and possibly relief from emotional pain and thus conclude, "This must simply be the way I am." They feel trapped or fatalistic about their situation. Counselors have the opportunity and responsibility to correct erroneous conclusions that adolescents may have drawn about their sexual orientation.[17]

Teach Effective Social Skills

Heterosexuality, for many young people, is buried under a mountain of fear. Effective therapy will include active encouragement of appropriate heterosexual behaviors. A lack of success in dating perpetuates the vicious cycle of heterosexual failures. Learning basic dating and conversational skills may boost confidence. The boy who is wracked with fear about being gay may find it difficult to approach girls with the necessary degree of self-assertion, masculine pride, and self-confidence to attract them. In the process he may also need to learn that men can be self-respecting, assertive, and competent without being cruel, overbearing, or domineering. The section on shyness provides several strategies for teaching social skills.

It should also be noted that girls place a higher priority on personal relationships than on group activities, whereas boys' social priorities are just the opposite.[18] This difference in priorities also tends to distinguish homosexual from heterosexual males. Many adolescent males who have homosexual leanings experience difficulty in developing friendships with heterosexual males. While gay males may want to "share feelings," straight males are more likely to want to relate through shared activities like sports.

Some adolescent males who struggle with this can be helped by focusing on skills and interests that will help them develop friendships with other males who are not gay. Joseph Nicolosi, in *Reparative Therapy of Male Homosexuality*, recommends that some male clients can be encouraged to become athletic to help them discover their masculine strength. He reports that typically the pre-homosexual boy misses out on physical play. Masculinity is inherently connected with the body, and when an adolescent boy has little or no physical activity, his sense of masculinity diminishes.[19]

Teach Thought Control

Many adolescents who fear that they are homosexual or are practicing a gay lifestyle are preoccupied with sexual thoughts. They may have difficulty thinking about anything else. Words or images repeatedly invade their mind. Counselors will help them prepare a list of alternative thoughts they can focus upon. Quoting Scripture or imagining a relaxing walk through a meadow are possibilities. Certain verses of great hymns or inspirational songs may be memorized and used as needed. The key is to substitute another thought for the obsession. Relaxation training is also effective in helping people stop their obsessions. Several relaxation exercises counselors use may be found in the sections on panic attack and anxiety. If young people practice these strategies, they will find that before long the obsessions are dead.

Consider Co-Counseling

G. Keith Olson suggests that a male-female counseling team may be especially effective in working with teens who struggle with homosexuality. At initial sessions, the same-sex counselor, alone with the counselee, gathers information. Only after this is done and the two have established a therapeutic alliance does the teen begin meeting with the male-female counseling team. This approach enables adolescents to interact with both male and female role models. The method facilitates a quicker resolution of pain and anger toward both sexes. It also helps teens learn to interact with both men and women. The team approach may be a powerful strategy with adolescents.[20]

Beware of Suicidal Thoughts

Suicide rates among homosexuals are higher than those among heterosexuals. Homosexual youth are even more likely to have thoughts of harming themselves.[21] For this reason it is imperative that a counselor working with teens struggling with homosexuality be on the lookout for danger signs that may indicate the danger of suicide: depression, irrational outbursts, change in eating or sleeping habits, lack of hope, talk of self-harm, and so on. Refer to the chapter in this book on suicide for a detailed description of these warning signs.

Expect Fatigue

Counseling youth who struggle with homosexuality is an emotionally draining task. One reason is that counselors will experience a plethora of feelings directed toward them from clients. Counselors may sense suspicion, anger, fear, admiration, ambivalence, love, mistrust, or a yearning for friendship. To make matters more intense, many of these contradictory feelings will be experienced during the same hour.[22] One way that counselors may fight this fatigue is to expect it, to prepare for intense emotions when working with young people who are attracted to the same sex.

Know When to Refer

Counselors should refer adolescents who struggle with homosexuality to other competent counselors or psychologists if they are not genuinely compassionate and comfortable with their issues or if they are not fully aware of and comfortable with their own sexuality. Referral is also in order if their therapeutic goals conflict with your values.

Where to Go for Additional Help

Atkinson, D. *Homosexuals in the Christian Fellowship.* Grand Rapids: Eerdmans, 1979.

Bergner, M. *Setting Love in Order: Hope and Healing for the Homosexual.* Grand Rapids: Baker, 1995.

Comeskey, A. *Pursuing Sexual Wholeness: How Jesus Heals the Homosexual.* Altamonte Springs, Fla.: Creation House, 1989.

Davies, B., and L. Rentzel. *Coming Out of Homosexuality: New Freedom for Men and Women.* Downers Grove, Ill.: InterVarsity, 1994.

Paulk, J. *Not Afraid to Change: The Remarkable Story of How One Man Overcame Homosexuality.* Seattle: Wine Press, 1998.

Payne, L. *The Broken Image: Restoring Personal Wholeness Through Healing Prayer.* Westchester, Ill.: Crossway Books, 1981.

Van den Aardweg, G. *Homosexuality and Hope.* Ann Arbor, Mich.: Servant Books, 1985.

Worthen, A., and B. Davies. *Someone I Love Is Gay: How Family and Friends Can Respond.* Downers Grove, Ill.: InterVarsity, 1996.

Other Contacts:

Exodus International
P.O. Box 77652
Seattle, WA 98177
206-784-7799
http://exodus.base.org

Mastering Life Ministries
P.O. Box 351149
Jacksonville, FL 32235
904-220-7474
www.MasteringLife.org

New Hope Residential Program
P.O. Box 10246
San Rafael, CA 94912-0246
415-455-9758

Notes

1. *Homosexual* describes only one aspect of a person. In this section I am using the word only as shorthand for "a homosexual person" whose homosexuality is but one aspect of a diverse life. In the same vein, *gay* is used merely for convenience.

2. C. Tripp, *The Homosexual Matrix* (New York: Meridian, 1987).

3. J. White, *Eros Defiled* (Downers Grove, Ill.: InterVarsity Press, 1977).

4. E. M. Pattison, "Homosexuality: Classification, Etiology, and Treatment," in *Baker Encyclopedia of Psychology*, ed. D. G. Benner (Grand Rapids: Baker, 1985).

5. Ibid.

6. E. Coleman and G. Remafedi, "Gay, Lesbian, and Bisexual Adolescents: A Critical Challenge to Counselors," *Journal of Counseling and Development* 68 (1989): 36–40.

7. M. G. Henderson, "Disclosure of Sexual Orientation: Comments from a Parental Perspective," *American Journal of Orthopsychiatry* 68 (1998): 372–75.

8. I. Bieber, "A Discussion of Homosexuality: The Ethical Challenge," *Journal of Consulting and Clinical Psychology* 44 (1976): 163–66.

9. S. L. Jones and D. E. Workman, "Homosexuality: The Behavioral Sciences and the Church," *Journal of Psychology and Theology* 17 (1989): 213–25.

10. Ibid.

11. J. Money, *Gay, Straight and In-Between* (New York: Oxford University Press, 1988).

12. G. K. Olson, *Counseling Teenagers: The Complete Christian Guide to Understanding and Helping Adolescents* (Loveland, Colo.: Group Books, 1984).

13. J. G. Baker and H. D. Fishbein, "The Development of Prejudice Towards Gays and Lesbians by Adolescents," *Journal of Homosexuality* 36 (1998): 89–100.

14. M. Meehan, "The Homosexual Condition: Can It Be Changed?" *New Oxford Review* 66 (1999): 13–23.

15. J. Bancroft, *Deviant Sexual Behavior: Modification and Assessment* (Oxford, Eng.: Clarendon, 1974).

16. E. M. Pattison and M. L. Pattison, "'Ex-Gays:' Religiously Mediated Change in Homosexuals," *American Journal of Psychiatry* 137 (1980): 1553–62.

17. Personal conversation with James Mallory (Northwest Medical Center, Atlanta, Ga.).

18. J. Sanford and G. Lough, *What Men Are Like* (Mahwah, N.Y.: Paulist, 1988).

19. J. Nicolosi, *Reparative Therapy of Male Homosexuality: A New Clinical Approach* (Northvale, N.J.: Aronson, 1991).

20. Olson, *Counseling Teenagers.*

21. A. Ben-Ari, "Perceptions of Life and Death Among Suicidal Gay Adolescents," *Omega: Journal of Death and Dying* 37 (1998): 107–19.

22. Wilson, *Counseling and Homosexuality.*

INFERIORITY

☑ WHAT THE STRUGGLE LOOKS LIKE

Maxwell Maltz estimated that 95 percent of all people in our society feel inferior.[1] I believe the percentage is even higher among adolescents. Millions of young people suffer from a strong sense of inadequacy.

Inferiority and self-esteem receive more attention than any other topics in adolescent psychology—and with good reason. Healthful self-esteem is like a vaccine against other common teenage problems.[2] Feelings of inferiority have been found to be a factor in anxiety disorders, poor social adjustment, compulsive overeating, poor academic performance, expulsion from school, vocational aspirations, cheating, depression, delinquency, drug abuse, and unwed pregnancy, to name a few.[3] In addition, youth who struggle with a sense of inferiority upon entering adolescence are very likely to enter adulthood with the same negative feelings, if they do not receive help.[4]

Teenage years are particularly critical for cultivating positive self-esteem. With a new capacity to become self-conscious and introspective (i.e., from a formal operations stage of cognitive development), adolescents gather evidence to help them evaluate themselves: Am I intelligent? Am I competent? Am I attractive? They compare themselves with their own ideals and those of others, an experience that is often painful. The ideal self is built on aspirations that are either realistic, too low, or, for the adolescent struggling with inferiority, too high. Ideal selves that are realistic lead to self-acceptance. Those that are too low impede accomplishment. Those aspirations which are too high lead to frustration, self-depreciation, and inferiority.

Self-esteem is the subjective evaluation of one's worth. It expresses approval or disapproval. It has been referred to as the single most significant key to behavior and the mainspring that launches every child for success or failure in living. Another helpful way of defining self-esteem is SE = RS - IS. *Self-Esteem equals Real Self minus Ideal Self.* All adolescents have images of the persons they would like to be. Not a frivolous wish (I'd like to be a rock star), but a sincere desire to possess certain "ideal" attributes. When the real and ideal selves are fairly close together, young people's self-esteem will be positive. When they are quite different, inferiority emerges.

There are several indicators of low self-esteem or inferiority in adolescence. One is *locus of control.* This refers to whether adolescents believe their success or failure is due to their own actions and internal ability or to external influences such as luck or chance. Adolescents struggling with inferiority will invariably ascribe their failures to internal causes and all successes to external causes.[5] If they flunk a test, it's because they are stupid. If they pass a test, it's because it wasn't as difficult as usual.

Another indicator of inferiority is a lack of confidence, or more accurately, *self-efficacy.* This refers to the conviction one has about successfully executing behavior required to produce a desired outcome. It refers to whether adolescents believe they can make a difference in their situation. Those who believe they can make a difference exhibit more endurance and purpose. Those who don't will withdraw and drop out. Adolescents struggling with inferiority are more likely to exhibit feelings of helplessness or powerlessness. They are more likely to suffer from a lack of self-efficacy.[6]

Defensiveness is another common indicator of inferiority. Adolescents with low self-esteem feel hurt. To protect themselves from further pain they erect barriers. They may exhibit a disproportionate amount of hostility, criticism, bragging, suspiciousness, or denial. It is too risky for these struggling adolescents to be exposed to additional hurt, so they wear psychic armor. Perhaps the most common defense for these young people is apathy. It is as if they have been injected with emotional novocaine that leaves them with a lethargic I-don't-care kind of attitude.

Adolescents with low self-esteem may be distractible, shy, withdrawn, inhibited, or anxious. They are more likely to daydream and want to be in situations with minimal competition. They have few, if any, expectations of success. They often lack a sense of belongingness and fear new experiences. They usually have a poor physical appearance and a low energy level.[7]

Case Description

Ron is fifteen years old. He is withdrawn and not doing well in school. He grew up in a home where Mom and Dad held extremely high expectations for him. His father rarely gave compliments—even when Ron used to bring home sterling report cards. Today, Ron cannot remember a single time his dad affirmed him for an accomplishment. He readily admits that he "gave up" school, but he claims that his dad had nothing to do with it. Ron believes he just does not have what it takes to succeed. He feels guilty, not because he sees his behavior as bad; he believes that he, himself, is bad, defective. Ron is also highly sensitive to criticism. Any attempt to correct, encourage, or suggest is heard as a put-down. When asked about his future, he expresses a lack of concern and aloofness. He came to counseling because he thought he was depressed. However, Ron showed few serious signs of depression. He felt frustrated and accepted his situation as fate, believing he could not change. His struggle was with feeling inferior.

It is easy to become confused when thinking about self-esteem. The vocabulary becomes unclear and is often used interchangeably. Here are some important related terms:

Self-concept: The constellation of things we use to describe ourselves.

Self-esteem: The evaluation of the information contained in our self-concept.

Self-love: The affection and care we express to ourselves.

Self-efficacy: The confidence to make a difference in a situation.

Self-confidence: The trust, security, and belief we have in ourselves.

Self-acceptance: The respect, dignity, and approval of our personhood.

Self-ideal: The image of the person we would like to be.

One other issue deserves attention before we explore etiology and treatment issues. A great deal of confusion reigns over the biblical view of self-esteem.[8] Charles Ridley has pointed out that true humility, not pride, is the biblical counterpart of positive self-esteem. *Humility* is based upon self-love, not self-negation, and owes its affirmation to God's unconditional regard for humankind. *Pride* is connected with achievement and attempts to take glory due to God for one's self. *False humility,* the counterpart of negative self-esteem, is a reverse form of pride in one's badness.[9]

✔ WHY THE STRUGGLE HAPPENS

Many factors contribute to feelings of inferiority. Many of them relate to parental influences. These "causes" may persist through life to keep self-esteem low unless someone intervenes.

Perfectionistic Expectations

Some parents fall into the trap of having overly high expectations for their children. While no one has ever achieved a state of perfection, these parents believe their children somehow have a chance and they tell them so in no uncertain terms. They permit no error or weakness. They are constantly frustrated, critical, and impatient with their children. These adolescents try harder and harder to be what they are not and eventually learn they will never satisfy Mom or Dad. They will always be inadequate. This heavy burden alone almost guarantees feelings of inferiority.[10]

Overprotectiveness

Children who are smothered with protection never have a chance to learn to cope for themselves. They never have opportunities to trust their own judgment. They grow up to become timid and afraid of making mistakes. As they struggle to achieve independence they feel vulnerable and become easily hurt and incapable of fending for themselves. They have no track record to construct a sense of confidence, efficacy, and an internal locus of control.

Inconsistency

To establish a sense of well-being, adolescents need consistency from their parents. They need to know what to expect from their mom and dad. Consistency and known limits provide security and structure. If something is permissible one day and the next day they are punished for the same thing, they obviously experience confusion that instills inferiority. When predictability in relationships is missing, the result is insecurity and low self-esteem.

Modeling

Parents who, themselves, suffer from inferiority are often emulated by their children. In addition, they may treat their children with the same lack of respect they feel for themselves. Their children come to believe that not thinking much of themselves is natural. They hear their parents' comments on the way others are always more successful than themselves, so the children believe that they are not meant to succeed.

Physical Influences

Inherited physical characteristics such as physique, appearance, and handicaps also influence developing self-concepts and inferiority. These physical attributes may influence others' perceptions and behavior toward young people. Others may, for example, respond negatively to struggling adolescents' handicapping conditions or physical appearance and thus affect the adolescents' self-esteem. Adolescents who mature later than others are also more likely to be treated like children while most of their peers are progressing more quickly into the adult world. This can invoke low self-esteem as well.

Faulty Thinking

Sometimes adolescents make up self-statements that have little or no basis in reality. With little evidence they conclude, "We're not good-looking enough," "We're not smart enough," "We're not outgoing enough." They live these lies as if they are truth and suffer from inferiority as a result. Unrealistic expectations also develop low self-esteem. Bruce Narramore points to three common expectations that are enemies of self-acceptance: (1) I must meet other people's expectations if I am to be accepted and loved; (2) whenever I fail to reach my goals I need to be punished; and (3) I must master my world.[11] Each of these beliefs is irrational and undermines self-esteem.

Faulty Theology

Some adolescents struggle with low self-esteem because they assume God does not see them as significant. Other sincere Christian young people believe God wants them to feel inferior. They believe that humility is the same as self-condemnation and that self-love is sinful. While their beliefs may be heartfelt, they are wrong. God does not want us to feel inferior. The Bible continually affirms that human beings are valuable to God and urges us to love ourselves as God loves us.

✔ HOW PARENTS CAN HELP

The following strategies for helping an adolescent struggling with feelings of inferiority can be used effectively by parents; however, every parent-child relationship is unique, and some of them may be more pertinent to your situation than others. As with every significant adolescent struggle, it is best for parents to work alongside a competent counselor. With this in mind, the following is offered as a way to help you facilitate the helping process at home with your teenager.

Focus on Being Genuine

Adolescents who struggle with inferiority have an internal and highly sensitive radar system for detecting phoniness. Research has shown that these young people respond negatively to expressions of affirmation that are not genuine.[12] Parents should be cautious about dispensing praise and affirmation that is not warranted and real. According to Gary Collins, it is more helpful to give acceptance, continuing support, gentle encouragement, and mild but sincere approval for achievements that can be clearly evaluated as good.[13] False platitudes not only do nothing to strengthen adolescent self-esteem; they undermine its development.

Localize Inferiority Feelings

It is often useful to look at adolescents' feelings of inferiority in localized areas of their lives.[14] Here is a list of questions to ask yourself as you attempt to discover whether teenagers struggle with pervasive low self-esteem or only primarily in certain areas.

- *Social:* How do they feel about themselves as friends of others? Do they possess social skills that are needed to achieve relationships? Are they satisfied with the quantity and quality of their peer relationships?
- *Academic:* Do they feel good enough? Are they satisfied with their academic performance? Do they set reasonable standards for their performance so that they regularly experience success?
- *Body Image:* Are they satisfied with their appearance? Do peers accept their physical appearance and abilities?
- *Pervasive:* Do they approach new situations with confidence? Do they generally avoid self-critical statements?

Low self-esteem arises from a discrepancy between the perceived self and the real self in each of these areas. It obviously saves time to zero in on a particular area if it is the one causing most of the frustration.

Modify Unrealistic Standards

When adolescents experience success or failure, they are measuring their performance against inner standards. Sometimes these standards are explicit and conscious, while some are less clear-cut and do not even enter awareness. When this happens, the potential for dissatisfaction and self-condemnation increases.

Help your teen become aware of their standards by asking about times they have been successful and times they have failed. Ask to what extent they feel they can modify their goals and standards so that they are more or less strict than they are. Use concrete examples provided by the teen, and discuss whether their standards are reasonable or unrealistic. Now you may present the steps involved in modifying standards.[15]

1. Make concrete, explicit statements about what equals a success and what equals a failure in a particular experience. Is there a middle ground?
2. How often does your performance fall into each of these categories?
3. Decide whether you are feeling as though you fail more than you need to. In other words, are you feeling bad about yourself too often?
4. If you are feeling bad too often, think about ways you could modify your standards. Could you lower your standard for success? Could you lower your standard for failure? Could you do both and make your middle ground larger?
5. Examine your self-statement after performances that fall into success, middle ground, or failure categories. Your thoughts should be helping you feel good about success, neutral about middle ground, and disappointed but not destroyed about failure.

You can use these steps to work through several standards in major areas of adolescents' lives. The point is to help them establish standards at a level that brings them fulfillment.

Explore Their Theology

Young people who struggle with low self-esteem and are sensitive to biblical values may have distorted theological views. Little work can be done if teenagers believe that inferiority is the same as humility and that self-esteem is equivalent to sinful pride. They must be helped—gently—to see the biblical teachings about human worth and self-esteem. They must be reminded that they are made in the image of God and that self-condemnation is both destructive and wrong in the sight of God. While this information may take a while to sink in, they must shed their faulty theology before true work can be accomplished in developing a healthful self-esteem. You may find the section on guilt helpful in working with young people who see self-condemnation as a mark of true spirituality.

Help Set Reachable Personal Goals

Adolescents need to decide for themselves how they want to be different. I ask nearly all of my clients, young and old, "If you could press a magic button, how would your life be different?"This can help them to think about their goals and what they are doing to achieve them. For the young person struggling with feelings of inferiority, an exercise may be used to help them set into operation some of the behavior and attitudes they would like to change. If you have a good parental relationship with your teen, you may ask them to make a list under the heading, "Things I get down on myself about." Once they have the list, ask them to identify their level of willingness to change each behavior according to a five-point scale:

1.   "I am not ready to change this yet."
2.   "I am confused about what I want to do about this."
3.   "I want to work on this in the future."
4.   "I am working on this one step at a time."
5.   "I am working hard to change this."

Next, ask them to lift out those behavior patterns they want to change most and discuss strategies for implementing ways to improve. Help them begin to take incremental steps toward reaching their goals. For example, a teenager who has an academic C average might say, "One thing I get down on myself about is thinking I'm not smart enough." The youth may want to set a goal of getting all A's next term. Of course, this is probably going to lead to disappointment, frustration, and a deeper sense of inferiority. The teen needs incremental sub-goals that are achievable to carry one toward one's larger objectives.

A beginning goal for this student might be to separate the academic record from one's value as a person—or even one's intelligence. Another might be to complete homework before watching TV. The point is to allow teens to think creatively about ways they can become the persons they want to be. Working out their goals with adults helps them be realistic and keeps them accountable to reaching their objectives.[16]

☑ HOW PROFESSIONALS CAN HELP

The following strategies for helping an adolescent struggling with feelings of inferiority are commonly used by counselors. They are presented here as a way to inform you, as a parent, and help you seek the best possible professional help you can for the adolescent in your care.

Explore Their Understanding of Self-Esteem

Many adolescents are confused about how they should feel toward themselves. David Carlson, in his book *Counseling and Self-Esteem,* suggests that counselors ask several questions to identify the situation, people, and circumstances in which this kind of confusion occurs.[17] These questions may be given for homework but are probably more helpful if discussed and clarified during a counseling session.

- How much do I confuse humiliation with humility?
- How much do I confuse putting myself down with putting down my sinful self?
- How much do I confuse self-degradation with self-denial?
- How much do I confuse worthless with unworthy?
- How much do I confuse selfishness with self-love?
- How much do I confuse self-conceit with self-affirmation?
- How much do I confuse self-worship with self-worth?
- How much do I confuse self-absorption with self-awareness?

If, as a parent, you explore some of these, it is important to keep the questions from making the adolescent feel worse. Their purpose is to help them clarify their understanding of self-esteem.

Teach Problem Solving

For adolescents who have grown up in homes characterized by overprotection, problem solving is an essential counseling intervention. While it may seem ridiculously basic, this process should not be made light of. These are fundamental skills that overly protected adolescents have never learned. The process is broken down into several steps in the following sequence. I will illustrate the process with Jackie, a fifteen-year-old, to show you how this process might work with a counselor.

1. *Recognize a problem exists.* Jackie feels uncomfortable in a group of her friends. This is her cue that she has a problem to solve.
2. *Stop and think.* Jackie should take no further action until she identifies the problem and decides what to do. After thinking about it, she realizes that she feels she is being made fun of.
3. *Decide on a goal.* Jackie decides she wants her friends to stop teasing her.
4. *Generate possible solutions.* She now considers a number of possibilities without evaluating them. She allows herself to be farfetched and creative. She could tell them to stop. She could leave. She could tease them. She could tell them how it makes her feel. She could laugh it off.
5. *Consider consequences.* Jackie then thinks about the consequences of each of these actions. If she tells them to stop they will probably do it all the more, and so on.
6. *Choose a solution.* She decides that the best choice is a combination of two solutions. She decides to laugh it off and then tell them in

private how it makes her feel. She considers this alternative to have
the best consequences for her present situation and her future relationships with them.[18]

7. *Implement the solution*. Jackie deflects her discomfort by not taking the
teasing seriously and shrugs her shoulders. She decides to meet one
of her friends after school to tell her how the teasing makes her feel,
and she will talk with the other one on the phone that night. She
won't try to punish them (that would have negative consequences),
only to let them know how she feels.

The teen will practice these seven steps of problem solving in a counseling
session. Counselors provide guidance as necessary but allow the youth to do
most of the work. Young people who learn systematic problem-solving strategies tend to cope more effectively with stress and frustration. Their competence
is heightened and their increasing autonomy becomes a source of healthful self-
efficacy and positive self-esteem.[18]

Develop Positive Self-Statements

It is important to determine whether young people use private speech to
construct negative self-images. One way of doing this is to ask teenagers to
describe in an open-ended way what they are like. Counselors will note the
kinds of descriptors used. They will then ask what they are like in school, in
sports, and with other kids. If they determine that adolescents are undermining their self-esteem through negative self-statements, they may use an exercise
such as the following.

Counselors will first explain the concept of self-talk (how we all carry a
mental tape player that goes on automatically). Second, they will help clients
identify their self-statements. One of the easiest ways to do this is to note how
they complete the following sentences.

- When I make a mistake, I think to myself . . .
- When I look in the mirror, I think . . .
- When my parents yell at me I say to myself . . .
- Everybody should . . .
- When I don't succeed at something I am trying, I think . . .
- When I get a bad grade, I think . . .

Counselors will work to replace negative self-statements with positive alternatives. They will talk about situations that are likely to elicit self-statements
and how new ones can be substituted. They will have clients imagine being in
specific situations experiencing their old self-statements and then arguing those

statements away. Counselors may have teens keep a log of their self-statements. This process may be slow, but it may also be very powerful and rewarding.

Confront Destructive Tendencies

Maurice Wagner, in his helpful book *The Sensation of Being Somebody,* notes that the person with an inadequate self-concept usually has destructive tendencies that serve only to advance and nurture low self-esteem. These include the tendency to treat people as objects, to give up when proved wrong, to become angry if not in control of situations, to be unwilling to act when afraid, to dread problems instead of accepting them as challenges.[19] When young people exhibit destructive tendencies like these, counselors can hold a figurative mirror up to help them objectively see the destruction they create. Counselors may begin by asking teenagers what benefits they receive from these tendencies.

Know When to Refer

Remember that self-esteem often takes time to grow. Still, counselors should refer adolescents who struggle with feelings of inferiority to other competent counselors or psychologists when, over time, they feel more inadequate or if they begin to appear depressed, hopeless, or suicidal.

Where to Go for Additional Help

Clarke, J. I. *Self-Esteem: A Family Affair.* Minneapolis: Winston, 1978.
Cloud, H., and J. Townsend. *Raising Great Kids.* Grand Rapids: Zondervan, 1999.
McAllister, D., and R. S. McGee. *The Search for Significance: Youth Edition.* Dallas: Word, 1990.
McKay, M., and P. Fanning. *Self-Esteem.* New York: St. Martin's Press, 1987.
Narramore, S. B. *You're Someone Special.* Grand Rapids: Zondervan, 1978.
Osborne, C. G. *The Art of Learning To Love Yourself.* Grand Rapids: Zondervan, 1976.
_____. *Self-Esteem: Overcoming Inferiority Feelings.* Nashville: Abingdon, 1986.
Pope, A. W., S. M. McHale, and W. E. Craignead. *Self-Esteem Enhancement with Children and Adolescents.* New York: Pergamon, 1988.
Wagner, M. E. *The Sensation of Being Somebody: Building an Adequate Self-Concept.* Grand Rapids: Zondervan, 1975.
The International Alliance for Invitational Education (800-223-6872 or www.invitationaleducation.net) publishes a comprehensive newsletter on self-esteem and sponsors one national conference and several regional conferences yearly.

Notes

1. M. Maltz, *Psychocybernetics* (New York: Essandes, 1968).

2. R. Gupta, "Inferiority Feelings as a Source of Variation in Adjustment of Female Adolescents," *Journal of Personality and Clinical Studies* 12 (1996): 29–32.

3. D. L. Yanish and J. Battle, "Relationship Between Self-Esteem, Depression and Alcohol Consumption Among Adolescents," *Psychological Reports* 57 (1985): 331–34. T. M. Klein, "Adolescent Pregnancy and Loneliness," *Public Health Nursing* 15 (1998): 338–47.

4. F. P. Rice, *The Adolescent: Development, Relationships and Culture,* 6th ed. (Boston: Allyn and Bacon, 1990).

5. L. Y. Abramson, M. E. P. Seligman, and J. D. Teasdale, "Learned Helplessness in Humans: Critique and Reformulation," *Journal of Abnormal Psychology* 87 (1978): 49–74.

6. S. H. Shelton, "Developing the Construct of General Self-Efficacy," *Psychological Reports* 66 (1990): 987–94.

7. G. Domino and E. Blumberg, "An Application of Gough's Conceptual Model to a Measure of Adolescent Self-Esteem," *Journal of Youth and Adolescence* 16 (1987): 87–90.

8. Several passages of Scripture are helpful in delineating the biblical principles involved in self-esteem: Mark 12:31; Romans 12:3; Ephesians 5:1–2.

9. C. Ridley, "Self-Esteem," in *Dictionary of Pastoral Care and Counseling,* ed. R. J. Hunter (Nashville: Abingdon, 1990).

10. B. Sorotzkin, "Understanding and Treating Perfectionism in Religious Adolescents," *Psychotherapy: Theory, Research, and Practice* 35 (1998): 87–95.

11. S. B. Narramore, *You're Someone Special* (Grand Rapids: Zondervan, 1978).

12. R. M. Baron, "Social Reinforcement Effects as a Function of Social Reinforcement History," *Psychological Review* 6 (1966): 529–39.

13. G. Collins, *Christian Counseling: A Comprehensive Guide* (Waco, Tex.: Word, 1980).

14. J. J. Lau, J. E. Calamari, and M. Waraczynski, "Panic Attack Symptomatology and Anxiety Sensitivity in Adolescents," *Journal of Anxiety Disorders* 10 (1996): 355–64.

15. Ibid.

16. A helpful resource for parents wanting to instill the principle of goal setting in their children is a book by Lanson Ross, *A Kid's Goal-Setting Guide* (Wheaton: Tyndale, 1985).

17. D. E. Carlson, *Counseling and Self-Esteem.* Vol. 13, *Resources for Christian Counseling* (Waco, Tex.: Word, 1988).

18. A. W. Pope, S. M. McHale, and W. E. Craignead, *Self-Esteem Enhancement with Children and Adolescents* (New York: Pergamon, 1988).

19. M. E. Wagner, *The Sensation of Being Somebody: Building an Adequate Self-Concept* (Grand Rapids: Zondervan, 1975).

INTERNET AND COMPUTER GAME ADDICTION

☑ WHAT THE STRUGGLE LOOKS LIKE

An addict is someone who can't seem to control the desire for or dependence on something. Nothing seems to tame the "craving." When someone is addicted, the urge within is so strong and so consuming that statements such as "I can't control myself" are common. With the onslaught of technological advances and the tremendous growth of the Internet, it is not surprising that more and more parents and counselors are hearing teenagers say they are lost in cyberspace.

Online addicts and computer game addicts suffer from many of the same symptoms as alcohol and drug abusers: denial, secrecy, acting out, compulsion, lack of focus, and withdrawal from family and friends.

The electronic-games industry boasts multibillion dollar sales each year. It is the second-most popular form of home entertainment after TV. According to one survey, nine out of ten U.S. households with children have rented or owned a video or computer game.[1] What are they playing? A lot of gory stuff, apparently. Nearly a third of the top video games contain violent content.

Dr. Kimberly Young, assistant professor of psychology at the University of Pittsburgh, Bradford, and founder of the Center for Online Addiction, conducted a study of online addiction and has coined the term netaholics.[2] She has recorded hundreds of case studies about them from around the world. While Dr. Young is concerned with anyone who is addicted to the Internet, she is particularly worried about young people. And with good reason.

On a typical morning, more than fourteen million American teenagers turn off their alarm clocks, scarf down a little breakfast, brush their teeth, rush off to school, and at some point during their day up to 80 percent of them—a number that has doubled in the past two years alone—log on to the Internet. The vast majority are not looking up ways to make pipe bombs or entering chat rooms with white supremacists. Most are getting sports scores, downloading the most recent song by their favorite musician, or chatting with friends. Some even do their homework by tapping into libraries of information. No doubt about it, the Internet is a wonderful resource and communication tool. But for some compulsive adolescents it has become a tool that rules their life. Not to mention that all too many of these young people have ready access to some forty thousand pornographic Web sites (if only by accident). In fact, over 40 percent of those kids who use the Internet report having seen pornographic Web sites.[3] By the time this day is over, five thousand new Web sites will have been added to the ever increasing Web universe of an estimated 800 million to one billion pages—*one in ten are pornographic in nature.*[4]

We obviously want young people to use this technological wonder, every bit as revolutionary as the telephone. It shapes all our lives and offers countless benefits. And yet we wonder what we can do to help prevent our youth from becoming addicted to this time killer. We wonder how to protect our kids from plunging into a world of influences and values that is, most of the time, hidden from our view. Can we steer them away from the appalling filth, unspeakable hatred, and frightening prescriptions for homicidal mayhem and crime that are just a keystroke away? The answer is yes, but there are no guarantees.

☑ WHY THE STRUGGLE HAPPENS

The causes of Internet addiction and the draw of blood-soaked computer games are numerous. Here are some of the possible reasons kids may become entangled in the web of technology.

Loneliness

Web fans say that the Internet, and chats in particular, force interaction, engagement, and connection. The favored term is "community." But, in fact, the Web provides only a shadow of genuine community; the interaction with another human being that is held out as the great virtue of Web community is actually interaction with the facsimile of a human being. But it is this desire to connect with someone, to lift one out of loneliness, that pushes some teenagers into an unhealthy dependency on the Web.[5]

Pornography

The wonder and horror of the Web is not that it takes you out into the world; on the contrary, it brings the world into the privacy of your home (or bedroom). That very fact makes pornography more accessible than ever before. And for some adolescents with raging hormones, that temptation is simply too much to resist. Under the banner of privacy, Internet anonymity has become the ultimate plain brown wrapper.[6]

Being In-the-Know

Every teenager wants to be part of what everyone else is talking about or doing. When the buzz is about what's online, you can bet that it will drive some kids straight to the nearest computer—again and again and again. Whatever anyone is talking about serves as a catalyst for some teens to check it out on the Web and report back impressive findings.

Money

Some cyber-savvy kids have found ways to profit from their time on the Internet by downloading illegal software and so on, then selling it to classmates. Cybercrime is a growing concern of the FBI and other law officials, and kids seem to be one of its greatest criminals.[7]

Secrecy

A teenager can go places in cyberspace and do things that no parent would ever approve of, and no one will ever know it. The whole idea of being able to explore taboos without leaving one's home pushes many kids into harmful cyber activity.

Case Description

Randy spends as much of his time online as possible. If he wakes up early enough, he logs on before going to school. At school he gets online at one of the computers in the school computer lab during his lunch period. When Randy gets home from school he is online until his mom gets home from work. That's when he hears the garage door open and quickly logs off. That's when he usually turns to his Sony PlayStation and sits for hours blowing enemy warplanes out of the sky in Ace Combat 2. Many evenings after his mom is asleep, Randy may be back online, from 11:00 p.m. until the early hours of the morning. What's he doing with all this time in front of a computer screen? He sends and receives email, drops into the occasional chat room, visits his friends' home pages, and checks movie listings for the upcoming weekend. But he's also downloading illegally copied software (known as "warez"). And yes, he often stumbles upon pornographic sites. Randy is increasingly tired and lethargic in school and his grades are slipping.

✔ HOW PARENTS CAN HELP

The following strategies for helping an adolescent struggling with internet or computer game addiction can be used effectively by parents; however, every parent-child relationship is unique, and some of them may be more pertinent to your situation than others. As with every significant adolescent struggle, it is best for parents to work alongside a competent counselor. With this in mind, the following is offered as a way to help you facilitate the helping process at home with your teenager.

Pinpoint the Severity

One of the most effective ways to pinpoint the severity of an Internet or video game addiction is to simply track the number of hours the young person spends on the activity.

Learn Cyber-Speak

It can be very difficult for parents and counselors to communicate with adolescents who are deeply into cyberspace if terminology is not understood. Here are some of the more commonly used terms:

ASCII (pronounced "askee"): The American Standard Code for Information Interchange. The worldwide standard for the code numbers used by computers to represent all the upper- and lowercase Latin letters, numbers, and punctuation.

Attachment: A text, picture, or software program that is attached to an email or newsgroup message.

DCC: Direct client-to-client connection over the Internet. It can be used to chat, to transmit, or to receive files.

Browser: A program that retrieves information available on the World Wide Web.

Encryption: A way of making data unreadable to anyone except the receiver. An increasingly common way of sending credit card numbers over the Internet when conducting commercial transactions.

Frequently Asked Questions (FAQ): A list of questions and answers to common user questions related to a newsgroup, Internet discussions, popular software, or a Web site.

Flame: To send nasty or insulting messages, usually in response to someone's having broken the rules of Netiquette.

Freeware: Computer software that is available for free to download and use on the Internet.

Gopher: An Internet server document browsing and searching system that lets you look all over the Internet for texts of interest and helps you to retrieve them.

Java: A programming language specifically designed for writing programs that can be safely downloaded and immediately run without fear of viruses or other harm.

Netiquette: The rules of etiquette that govern online interaction on the Internet.

Server: A computer, most often Unix- or WindowsNT-based, which hosts activity or information for retrieval.

Shareware: Computer software that is available for free trial or use by the author. Payment is often based on an honor system.

Spamming: Sending unsolicited email or identical and irrelevant postings to many different UseNet newsgroups.

Zip Drive: An inexpensive, large-capacity removable disk drive.

Be Aware of Gruesome Video Games

There are certain games that put guns in the hands of kids and reward them for blasting everything that moves. Players in "Doom" and "Quake" (and a host of imitations) navigate mazes in first-person perspective, picking up ever larger and more lethal weapons. Only the victims change. In "Duke Nukem," it's pig-humans in police vests. In "Grand Theft Auto," the player gets points by stealing cars and killing police officers. Other games in this genre include "Redneck" and "Rampage." These games are off the scale on violence and have zero educational value.

Don't Rely on the Government as a Guardian

I've heard some adults argue that they aren't worried about what kids encounter online because the government is watching over it and protecting youngsters from harmful influences. Truth is that governmental action can make only minor differences. The Internet is too diffuse, too international.[8] If there is a war to be fought, the critical beachhead is in the home.

Be Wary of Your "Monitoring"

Almost every parent thinks the most effective way to protect kids online is to monitor their activity. Literally. They stand beside the computer from time to time while their son or daughter is at the keyboard, watching every mouse click. What many parents don't realize is that when a youngster starts typing numerals, they could be using the chat signal that says "parental unit nearby." The point is to avoid being duped.

Assign an Internet Time Log

By making an accurate accounting of just how much the young person spends online each day you establish objective criteria for assessing change. This kind of tracking generally requires the help of the adolescent. You may want to put the teen on the honor system to keep the log for a week or two. Be aware that if he or she balks at the idea or is clearly lying, you're likely dealing with their denial of addiction.

Don't Neglect the Obvious

It doesn't take a degree in electrical engineering to know that kids should be admonished never to reveal personal information to anyone online without parental permission. And placing the computer in the home where others can keep a watchful eye on it is crucial.[9] Many parents don't realize that a simple click on the "history" tab on a browser tool bar will produce a list of links to every site the computer has visited recently (of course most thirteen-year-olds know how to delete this kind of potentially incriminating evidence from the history files).

Make Use of Filters

There are tools that can make the task of screening out offensive or dangerous content much easier.[10] America Online, for example, has been particularly effective in helping parents give their children an online experience under the firm guidance of its editors: a "kids-only" AOL account blocks young users from all but full-time-monitored chat rooms and prescreened kid-friendly sites. Many other filtering systems work differently. They may simply block access to a list of sites ruled obscene. CyberPatrol, a piece of retail software, is a customizable system that allows parents to choose which types of sites to block based on the parents' criteria. So does Net Nanny. Cyber Snoop creates a tamperproof database so parents can examine every Web address the computer has visited since the last time they checked in. CleanWeb is a Christian-owned, nationwide, filtered Internet service provider. For more information about CleanWeb's special three-stage filtering that allows full access to the Internet while blocking offensive material, call 877-253-2693.

Check Out Credit Card Charges

Entry past the first or second level to most porn sites and other unhealthy Web operations is governed by the ability to key in a valid card number. This is reason enough to encourage parents to keep credit cards from their teenage kids. But some motivated kids will memorize necessary numbers to gain the access they desire. For this reason, it is important to keep a close eye on credit card activity. Also, be aware of statements for bills from Adult Check or customerservice@ntcor.com. Both are common porn-site clearance agencies.[11]

Help Acknowledge the Dependence

One of the first steps toward gaining control over any dependency is to simply acknowledge the dependency.[12] In Romans 7:18–19, Paul acknowledged the fact that he often participated in behavior that he didn't want to do and did not do the things that he desired to do in his life. It is this kind of acknowledgment that serves as a catalyst for change. To help young people acknowledge their dependence on the Internet or video games, help them specifically track the amount of time they spend surfing the Web or playing games. Sometimes knowing the number of hours spent online is enough of a wake-up call to help them acknowledge that they have a dependency problem.

Facilitate Acceptance of Responsibility

Getting control of personal behavior requires responsibility. As tempting as it is for all of us to shift the blame and point out other causes for our behavior, the truth is that it ultimately rests on our shoulders. This is a crucial step in helping an adolescent change addictive behavior. Paul told young Timothy to "train yourself to be godly" (1 Timothy 4:7). In other words, the discipline of change begins within at that moment when a person accepts responsibility for what he or she is doing.

Find a Source of Accountability

Once a young person makes a commitment to change unhealthy behavior, he cannot be expected to withstand alone the inevitable temptations to retreat to previous behavior. Help the young person bring into his or her life individuals who will support and challenge the commitment to stay strong. This may even involve monitory consequences or some level of censoring if necessary. In Romans 7, Paul said he had to daily reckon and yield himself to the Lord.

Keep the Internet in Perspective

Too often for the teenager who is addicted to the Internet, it has become the focal point in his life. He schedules much of his day around it and as a result pushes many other things that were once important to him off to the side. Help him recognize how his time on the Internet may be replacing family activities, friends, worship, and other activities. In other words, help the young person recognize the price he or she is paying for being online so much.[13] With a fresh perspective on how the Internet is taking over one's schedule, the teenager is more likely to want and maintain healthy change.

Know When to Refer

Refer adolescents who struggle with Internet addiction or computer game addiction to an addiction specialist when, over time, the teen is not making positive change in his or her dependency behaviors.

Where to Go for Additional Help

Baker, J. D. *Parents' Computer Companion: A Guide to Software and Online Resources.* Grand Rapids: Baker Books, 1999.

Greenfield, D. *Virtual Addiction: Help for Netheads, Cyber Freaks, and Those Who Love Them.* Oakland, Calif.: New Harbinger, 1999.

Jantz, G. L. *Hidden Dangers of the Internet: Using It Without Abusing It.* Wheaton, Ill.: Harold Shaw Publishers, 1998.

Lang, B., and B. Wilson. *A Parent's Guide to Making the Internet Family Friendly.* Nashville: Thomas Nelson, 1999.

Rice-Hughes, D. *Kids Online: Protecting Your Children in Cyberspace.* Grand Rapids: Revell, 1998.

Schultze, Q. J. *Winning Your Kids Back from the Media.* Downers Grove, Ill.: InterVarsity Press, 1994.

Turkle, S. *Life on the Screen: Identity in the Age of the Internet*. New York: Simon & Schuster, 1995.

Young, K. S. *Caught in the Net: How to Recognize the Signs of Internet Addiction*. New York: John Wiley & Sons, Inc., 1998.

The following is a sample of helpful Web sites:

"Center for Online Addiction," www.netaddiction.com

"Enough is Enough," 800-2-ENOUGH, www.enough.org

"Filtering Facts," 503-635-7048, www.filteringfacts.org

"National Coalition for the Protection of Children and Families," 513-521-6227, www.nationalcoalition.org

"CyberPatrol," 800-828-2608, www.cyberpatrol.com

"Surfwatch," 800-458-6600, www.surfwatch.com

Notes

1. J. Quittner, "Are Video Games Really So Bad?" *Time* (May 10, 1999): 50–59.

2. K. S. Young, *Caught in the Net: How to Recognize the Signs of Internet Addiction* (New York: John Wiley & Sons, 1998).

3. B. Watson, "The Internet: Potential for Great Good or Terrible Harm," *Washington Citizen* 11 (June 1999): 1–3.

4. J. Samad, Internet Safety Position Paper, National Coalition for the Protection of Children and Families (December 2, 1999).

5. M. J. Andersen, "Info Age: Teen Cyberlove Just a New Version of an Old Problem," *Providence Journal-Bulletin* 26 (1997): 1–4.

6. G. Zgourides, M. Monto, and R. Harris, "Correlates of Adolescent Male Sexual Offense: Prior Adult Sexual Contact, Sexual Attitudes and Use of Sexually Explicit Materials," *International Journal of Offender Therapy and Comparative Criminology* 41 (1997): 272–83.

7. J. R. Lingamneni, "Computer Crime," *Journal of Criminology and Social Psychology* 2 (1997): 85–95.

8. K. F. Durkin, "Misuse of the Internet by Pedophiles: Implications for Law Enforcement and Probation Practice," *Federal Probation* 61 (1997): 14–18.

9. B. Lang and B. Wilson, *A Parent's Guide to Making the Internet Family Friendly* (Nashville: Thomas Nelson, 1999).

10. Ibid.

11. A. Barak and W. A. Fisher, "Effects of Interactive Computer Erotica on Men's Attitudes and Behavior Toward Women: An Experimental Study," *Computers in Human Behavior* 13 (1997): 353–69.

12. K. S. Young, "The Relationship Between Depression and Internet Addiction," *CyberPsychology and Behavior* 1 (1987): 25–28.

13. A. Barber, "Net's Educational Value Questioned," *USA Today* (March 11, 1997): 4D.

LONELINESS

☑ WHAT THE STRUGGLE LOOKS LIKE

Feeling alone and neglected is becoming an emotional epidemic in America. Loneliness—the painful awareness that we are not meaningfully connected with others—floods the lives of millions. It is one of "the most universal sources of human suffering."[1] It knows no boundary of class, race, or age. One hit song of the Beatles asked this question: "All the lonely people, where do they all come from?" Many of them come from adolescence! Loneliness strikes everyone from time to time, but especially adolescents.

While experts consider loneliness a serious personal problem for at least 10 percent of the general adult population,[2] large-scale studies have found that 15 to 20 percent of all adolescents experience painful levels of loneliness.[3] A study that explores the severity of loneliness in all age groups shows that the loneliest people proved to be low-income, single, adolescent mothers. Alcoholics were next, followed by freshman college students and rural high school seniors.[4]

It should be no surprise that a large proportion of teenagers feel lonely. Their attempts at social connectedness are riddled with fear of rejection. Tony Campolo paints a vivid scene of the adolescent in a new group:

> At first he simply observes, attempting not to reveal any of his own thoughts or feelings. He plays it cool, trying to communicate an air of detachment. Because he is careful not to respond with either enthusiasm or contempt to what the other members

of the group are doing, his face may appear almost emotionless. He plays it cool to allow himself time to figure out what the members of the group expect him to be. Once he has the feel of the group he will gradually begin to behave in ways which he believes will earn him approval and acceptance.[5]

If an adolescent doesn't earn approval and acceptance, the trap of loneliness is sprung. Without the tools described in this section adolescents are almost certain to be snared by loneliness—in and out of the church. According to Campolo, a strong probability exists that lonely young people will never return to a church gathering if they do not gain quick acceptance. On the other hand, rejection by the "in" group at school can result in the wounded teen being tremendously dedicated to the church that offers acceptance. "The church has always attracted society's losers," says Campolo, "because they can feel like winners within its fellowship."[6]

When young people come to a gathering and sit back detached and emotionless, you can be sure they are not feeling secure. That kind of adolescent is what some call a "jellyfish in armor." They come because they want to be accepted by the group and to gain popularity in their eyes. But the needed warmth is not yet available.

It is difficult to overestimate the impact of having no one to sit with on the school-sponsored bus trip, or eating alone in the cafeteria, or staying at home on another dateless Friday evening. Loneliness is painful. Remember the haunting words of the popular song "At Seventeen"? For the struggling adolescent, loneliness is waiting for what appears will never come.

Case Description

Peter is fourteen, has red hair, and is a bit overweight. He was an only child until four years ago when his sister was born. His dad is a stockbroker and his mom works in sales. They moved to a new city a few months ago, and Peter has never felt lonelier. In a counseling session he says, "I've been alone most of my life, so this is nothing new. I come home from school and stay all alone until around six o'clock when Mom or Dad comes home from work. I watch TV, but it gets pretty boring. Maybe I'll be friends with my sister when she's older." His mother encourages him to meet friends, but Peter believes friendships "should just happen." He spends a lot of time sitting around listening to music with a Walkman.

The feeling of being alone and neglected, however, need not isolate struggling adolescents in a shadowy corner. They may be helped to move beyond its desolate darkness.[7]

Before exploring the causes and cures of loneliness, let's make sure we understand its dimensions. One research team has identified five "Cs" to define the different parts of loneliness. They are seen when the lonely adolescent is feeling a lack of (1) *congruence*—feeling out of touch with parts of the self, (2) *companionship*—the perception of self as separate from another, (3) *community*—the feeling of being ostracized by others, (4) *custom*—the feeling of separation from others because of cultural change, and (5) *communion*—the feeling of separation or alienation from God.[8] Others have identified these same dimensions in different terms: psychological, interpersonal, social, cultural, and cosmic.[9]

✔ WHY THE STRUGGLE HAPPENS

Growing up has never been easy. The road to maturity is treacherous. Maybe kids today are no lonelier than kids of a hundred years ago, but the reasons for adolescent loneliness have certainly changed.

The Spirit of Our Age

Shortly after World War II Paul Tournier wrote, "Loneliness results from the spirit of our age."[10] Today's experts agree. The push toward efficiency and convenience in our high-tech age has driven many to feel smaller and less needed. Today's adolescents do not have so much rootedness. The widespread mobility of our society tears up friendships and separates families. Even the possibility of moving may keep some adolescents from forming close friendships. Urbanization has led to a fear of strangers. Portable music headphones, handheld video games, and, of course, television may separate us from others. It seems that many adolescents interact more with screens than with people. The list could continue. The point is that our society has lost many of the traditional sources of relationships that helped adolescents of earlier generations avoid the pain of loneliness.

Developmental Separation from Parents

During adolescence the relationship to parents is realigned.[11] Young people are trying to grow out of childish ways of relating. A lapse into teens' previous mode of dependency may surprise parents who are adjusting to the new independence. Since parents often do not perceive their faltering teenagers as "dependent children," the latter may experience psychological isolation.[12] They are forced to mourn the loss of their identity as children and give up certain childhood beliefs and attachments. The role of parents in this turbulent separation is critical. Parental responses vary from the most helpful—supportive understanding—to the most destructive—premature withdrawal from the children or attempts to undermine the separation by prolonging preadolescent attachments.[13] Inevitably the progressive change in this important attachment/detachment process will be heavily invested with loneliness.

Emotional Maturation

"I want to feel the heat with somebody." Those are the words of a pop hit song by Whitney Houston, and they express the white-hot need for relatedness of the maturing adolescent. The capacity and desire for intense intimacy develops rapidly during the teen years. Such changes bring about strong needs for new emotional connectedness. Couple this with high expectations for dating activity and social popularity, and young people are bound to face deficits in desired levels of tender attachments.

Desire for Autonomy

Adolescents strive for independence in every area of life. They want autonomy in their behavior, their morals, their religion, and their ideas. To achieve this, of course, means they must depend on their own reserves. Each one must become his or her primary decision-maker. This kind of responsibility is frightening and risky. "Every time we grow more autonomous, create our own thoughts, assert our own identity," writes one expert, "we risk moving away from others and therefore risk loneliness."[14] For this reason some degree of loneliness in adolescence must be expected.

Social Comparison

Adolescents have an internal yardstick to measure how well they stack up against everyone else. Their comparisons are bound to magnify feelings of failure and rejection. They will perceive others as more popular, more successful, and less lonely. Some adolescents may even compare their experience with the imagined glamour of young musicians, media stars, and sports figures. Such unrealistic comparisons can easily drive struggling adolescents to overestimate their feelings of aloneness and neglect.

Poor Relations with Parents

Lonely adolescents often report negative relationships with parents. They don't feel supported. Mom and Dad seem to instill no vision or purpose in their future. Parents may label their teenagers as failures or simply show no interest or provide no nurture. Parents may also pressure their adolescents into membership in peer groups that do not offer them acceptance. In this case they not only do not fit in with a particular peer group, but alienation in the home also results due to failure in living up to the parents' goals.[15]

Striving for Significance

Adolescents experience a "quiet joy" when they use their newly emerging abilities for the first time.[16] Whether in the classroom, on the ball field, or on an auditorium stage, adolescents are yearning for a place to show their importance and significance. According to Rollo May, adolescents who do not find a way to demonstrate significance typically fall into boredom, aimlessness, meaninglessness, and eventually loneliness. Without the freedom to participate in activities that allow for a demonstration of significance, adolescents will stumble into the dark pit of social isolation and loneliness.

☑ HOW PARENTS CAN HELP

The following strategies for helping an adolescent struggling with loneliness can be used effectively by parents; however, every parent-child relationship is unique, and some of them may be more pertinent to your situation than others. As with every significant adolescent struggle, it is best for parents to work alongside a competent counselor. With this in mind, the following is offered as a way to help you facilitate the helping process at home with your teenager.

Affirm Their Courage and Explore the Causes

When adolescents admit to feeling lonely, you can be pretty sure they are serious about wanting help. In our society confessing loneliness is tantamount to admitting to being a misfit. Affirm them for the courage it takes to talk about this problem and comfort them by letting them know they have a lot of company—almost everyone feels lonely from time to time. Knowing they are not "freaks" can alleviate much discomfort. Also help them consider the variety of reasons they are suffering from loneliness. This allows you to work on the sources, not just the symptoms of the struggle. You may choose to refer to the causes of loneliness outlined earlier in this section.

Loneliness is one of the few struggles that begins to be alleviated simply by talking about it. Once you affirm adolescents' courage, they will feel empowered by the realization that they are doing something to overcome loneliness.

Accept the Process

Young people who struggle with loneliness often feel that it is a permanent condition—as unending as an Arctic winter. But unlike depression and other struggles, recovery from loneliness is not always long and tedious. Loneliness may melt away quickly, almost instantly, when a new relationship emerges. However, for long-lasting results that build a strong hedge against feelings of loneliness in the future, a process must begin that leads to a celebration of solitude.[17] The journey, as we shall see next, begins with helping adolescents see activity and intimacy as premature solutions.

Avoid the Myth of Activity as a Premature Solution

Almost a half-century ago David Reisman wrote a groundbreaking book, *The Lonely Crowd,* to tell us how isolated people feel even though constantly surrounded by others.[18] Since then popular magazines and best-selling books have been filled with writings lamenting our inability to be with others. They have suggested dozens of active remedies: join a club, be positive, become assertive, win friends, travel, listen to music, watch television, take up a hobby, volunteer, and so forth.

The perception of activity is misleading, however, if the heart of loneliness is not understood. Adolescents are not lonely because they lack activity and distractions. Most of them lead hectic lives in crowded schools. Adolescents are lonely, not because they are isolated from others, but because *they are alienated from themselves.* They need to make friends with solitude and embrace their sense of self. Only then will the counsel to become active prove to be genuinely helpful.

Avoid the Myth of Intimacy as a Premature Solution

Some years ago a song of Barbra Streisand's soared to the top of the charts. Its words, "People who need people are the luckiest people in the world," seemed to touch a nerve. The song made us feel good because *all* of us need people. Actually, the most fortunate people are those who need people for healthy reasons—to love and be loved in return. Some adolescents need people, however, to avoid being alone and to avoid facing themselves. Becky, a student who came for counseling, was like that. She saw the quest for intimacy as an antidote to her loneliness. She believed she could escape isolation if she could just find the right guy. She sought romance to avoid intimacy with herself.

Thomas Merton says that the person "who fears to be alone will never be anything but lonely."[19] A parent or counselor can help lonely adolescents study their drive for intimacy, which is not an escape from loneliness. Nor is intimacy a prize package that young people can hope to find or work hard enough to deserve. Intimacy is an attitude and a way of being that comes only from embracing the anxiety of being alone and working on the most basic of relationships—the one on which all others build—the one an adolescent has with his or her self.

Encourage Healthful Solitude

I learned to celebrate solitude as a junior in college. The lesson, however, didn't come from a textbook. I enrolled in a wilderness course in the Cascade Mountains of Canada. The trip was designed to help me to go beyond myself physically, mentally, and spiritually. Toward the end of the course each of us was given the challenge to go solo. Isolated on a mountainside I did not see another face or hear another voice for more than twenty-four hours. My task was to meditate, evaluate, reflect, delight in my existence, and write in my diary. The lesson behind this solo venture was to teach me I could grow from such solitude. And I did.

Adolescents don't need to be in the wilderness to learn the pleasure of solitude. It may be found in an empty football stadium or a corner of the library. Solitude presents adolescents with opportunities to take stock, pray, and simply feel the calm of quietness soak in. These are the times that help us get in tune with our deepest and most important feelings. Encourage teens in these circumstances to keep journals to process their experience. Lonely adolescents at home on a Friday evening may be empowered by understanding that being alone and feeling alone are two very different experiences. Being alone is marked by introspection and renewal. Feeling alone is marked by self-pity and feelings of abandonment. The difference is not found in circumstances but in attitude.

Encourage Social Risks

We are designed for community with God and others. Relationships are the foundation of any solutions leading to an escape from loneliness. If adolescents can avoid the compulsion to seek activity and intimacy as hasty solutions, and if they recognize that embracing solitude is the first step toward escaping the dark days of loneliness, and if they are equipped with the tools of disputation, then they are ready to consciously seek healthful activity and genuine intimacy by learning to take social risks.

Reaching out to others is essential if they are to overcome the feeling of being alone and neglected. Research has shown that about 40 percent of people suffering from loneliness never talk about it.[20] With patience and encouragement, however, the tight lid of hesitation can be loosened and a lonely adolescent may learn to muster up the courage to take social risks and venture into new relationships. If appropriate to instill optimism, you may briefly disclose an uplifting example from your own experience. Ask them to think of those to whom they can reach out and in what ways. A sense of accountability to counselors may motivate them to smile and say "Hi" to interesting-looking people. It may give them the impetus to compliment the appearance of someone they find attractive. Suggest they ask acquaintances to go to McDonald's. Genuine relationships often begin over a bite to eat.

Do not hesitate to encourage lonely adolescents to take social risks and then affirm them for their effort. Suggesting social risks is commonsense counsel found in maxims like "I went out to find a friend but could not find one there. I went out to *be* a friend, and friends were everywhere!" Proverbs 18:24 (KJV) says, "A man that hath friends must show himself friendly." The phone company puts it this way: "Reach out and touch someone." Regardless of the phrasing, the point is that loneliness does not have to paralyze a teenager.

Consider Faith Issues

If it can be done with sensitivity, exploring the adolescent's spiritual well-being is helpful in fighting loneliness. For adolescents with sincere faith, a reminder that God is very real and present instills strength and comfort. Loneliness is rarely discussed in Scripture, but it is seen repeatedly in the lives of numerous Bible characters. David, Moses, Job, Elijah, Paul, and Jesus all struggled with moments of loneliness.

Consider Shyness and Inferiority

If you suspect that self-consciousness, poor social skills, and shyness are at the root of the young person's loneliness, you will want to study the chapters in this book on shyness and inferiority and incorporate their tools into your helping strategy.

Know When to Refer

Refer lonely adolescents to psychologically astute counselors when, over time, they feel lonelier. If they are showing signs of hopelessness, I recommend serious consultation and consideration of referral because hopelessness may indicate thoughts of suicide.[21]

✔ HOW PROFESSIONALS CAN HELP

The following strategy for helping an adolescent struggling with loneliness is commonly used by counselors. It is presented here as a way to inform you, as a parent, and help you seek the best possible professional help you can for the adolescent in your care.

Dispute Irrational Thinking

Irrational beliefs and faulty perceptions may ignite like high-octane fuel in the otherwise quiet engine of loneliness. Struggling adolescents need to clean out their unrealistic self-talk. Fortunately, most adolescents catch on quickly when counselors use disputation—it requires the same skills they have mastered while arguing with others. A good disputation is built on four legs: (1) evidence, (2) alternatives, (3) implication, and (4) usefulness.

If a lonely adolescent says, for example, "I eat by myself in the cafeteria because nobody is interested in me," the first question many counselors will ask is "What *evidence* do you have for this belief? Show me the evidence that *nobody* is interested." This usually helps the young person see the absurdity of the over-reaction. Next, they will examine the *alternatives.* They will ask, "Can you think of any less destructive way to look at eating alone in the cafeteria?" This helps adolescents to avoid latching onto the most dire possible belief and to generate alternative explanations (e.g., "I never invite others to sit with me"). What if the negative beliefs adolescents hold are true? Even if the beliefs are correct, some relief may be found in unearthing the *implications.* Does the predicament imply that these teens are any less intelligent than others? Does it imply that the situation can't be changed?

The final leg that will support a platform of more rational thinking is found in questioning the *usefulness* of the belief. Perhaps believing that others should naturally eat with you without being invited is not serving a good purpose. It is like a technician doing bomb demolition and thinking, "This could go off and I might be killed." The belief itself serves no purpose. It causes his hands to shake and so on. Through role-playing and in-session practice, lonely adolescents may learn to use these strategies on their own to dispute their irrational thinking and unfounded self-accusations. Counselors will help them examine the evidence, alternatives, and usefulness of their irrational thoughts.[22]

Where to Go for Additional Help

Durham, C. *When You're Feeling Lonely: Finding a Way Out.* Downers Grove, Ill.: InterVarsity Press, 1984.

Ellison, C. W. *Loneliness: The Search for Intimacy.* Chappaqua, N.Y.: Christian Herald Books, 1980.

Gaev, D. M. *The Psychology of Loneliness.* Chicago: Adams Press, 1976.

Hymel, S. *Loneliness in Childhood and Adolescence.* Cambridge: Cambridge University Press, 1999.

Meyer, J. *Help Me, I'm Alone!* Tulsa, Okla.: Harrison House, 1998.

Olds, J., R. S. Schwartz, and H. Webster. *Overcoming Loneliness in Everyday Life.* Secaucus, N.J.: Carol Publishing Group, 1996.

Parrott, L., and L. Parrott. *Relationships: Making Bad Relationships Better and Good Relationships Great.* Grand Rapids: Zondervan, 1998.

Parrott, L. *CareNote: Feeling Alone.* Saint Meinrad, Ind.: Abbey Press, 1993.

Tournier, P. *Escape from Loneliness.* Philadelphia: Westminster, 1962.

Notes

1. H. Nouwen, *Reaching Out* (Garden City, N.Y.: Doubleday, 1975).

2. M. E. Bragg, "A Comparative Study of Loneliness and Depression" (Ph.D. diss., UCLA, 1979), *Dissertation Abstracts International* 39 (1979): 79/13710.

3. E. Ostrov and D. Offer, "Loneliness and the Adolescent," in *Adolescent Psychology*, ed. S. Feinstein (Chicago: Univ. of Chicago Press, 1978).

4. N. Medora and J. C. Woodward, "Loneliness Among Adolescent College Students at a Midwestern University," *Adolescence* 21, no. 82 (1986): 391–402.

5. T. Campolo, *The Success Fantasy* (Wheaton, Ill.: Victor, 1980).

6. Ibid.

7. N. E. Mahon, T. J. Yarcheski, and A. Yarcheski, "Loneliness and Health-Related Variables in Young Adults," *Perceptual and Motor Skills* 85 (1997): 800–802.

8. L. J. Richmond and E. D. Picken, "A Model for Working with Lonely Clients: Sadler Revisited," in *Loneliness: A Sourcebook of Current Theory, Research and Therapy*, ed. S. M. Natale (New York: Wiley, 1986), 351–78.

9. W. A. Sadler, Jr., "Dimensions in the Problem of Loneliness: A Phenomenological Approach," *Journal of Phenomenological Psychology* 9 (1978): 1–2.

10. P. Tournier, *Escape from Loneliness* (Philadelphia: Westminster, 1962).

11. L. Goosens, A. Marcoen, S. Van Hees, and O. van de Woestijne, "Attachment Style and Loneliness in Adolescence," *European Journal of Psychology of Education* 13 (1998): 529–42.

12. R. S. Weiss, *Loneliness: The Experience of Emotional and Social Isolation* (Cambridge, Mass.: MIT Press, 1973).

13. H. Stierlin, *Separating Parents and Adolescents* (New York: Norton, 1973).

14. Ostrov and Offer, "Loneliness and the Adolescent," 34.

15. S. M. Natale, *Loneliness and Spiritual Growth* (Birmingham, Ala.: Religious Education Press, 1986).

16. R. May, *Man's Search for Himself* (New York: Delta Books, 1953).

17. M. G. Davies, "Solitude and Loneliness: An Integrative Model," *Journal of Psychology and Theology* 24 (1996): 3–12.

18. D. Reisman, *The Lonely Crowd* (New Haven: Yale University Press, 1961).

19. T. Merton, *Thoughts in Solitude* (New York: Doubleday, 1968).

20. C. A. Anderson, L. J. Horowitz, and R. French, "Attributional Style of Lonely and Depressed People," *Journal of Personality and Social Psychology* 45, no. 1 (1983): 127–36.

21. J. Roergers, A. Spirito, and D. Donaldson, "Reasons for Adolescent Suicide Attempts: Associations with Psychological Functioning," *Journal of the American Academy of Child and Adolescent Psychiatry* 37 (1998): 1287–93.

22. D. Meichenbaum, *Cognitive Behavior Modification: An Integrative Approach* (New York: Plenum, 1977). This book will give you a detailed strategy for using disputation and other cognitive interventions.

MASTURBATION

✔ WHAT THE STRUGGLE LOOKS LIKE

"[Masturbation] is one of the most frequently discussed, most roughly condemned and most universally practiced forms of sexual behavior."[1] From ancient times to the present, no sexual practice seems to have been more controversial than masturbation—"the sexual self-pleasuring that involves some form of direct physical stimulation."[2]

In the 1800s abstinence from this kind of "self-abuse" was lauded as crucial to health. The Rev. Sylvester Graham, the promoter of graham crackers, wrote *Lecture to Young Men* in which he beseeched them to abstain from masturbation to avoid a reduction in health-reserving "vital fluids" and to avoid moral and physical degeneracy. John Harvey Kellogg, M.D., carried Graham's work further and developed the cornflake as an antimasturbation food and extinguisher of sexual desire.[3]

In a 1918 *Encyclopedia of Health and Home,* one could find diagnostic criteria for the adolescent "addicted to the habit":

> He is timid and bashful, the face is apt to be pale, while the eyes look dull and languid, a general slowness of growth, nervousness and unsteadiness of the hands, loss of memory, an inability to study or stupidity, he cannot look anyone steadily in the face, but will drop the eyes as if guilty of something mean. Few ever know how many of the unfortunate

inmates of our lunatic asylums have been sent there by this dreadful vice.[4]

Contemporary views reflect conflicting beliefs about masturbation, even within the church. The most frequently cited arguments against masturbation, according to *Baker Encyclopedia of Psychology*, are these:

1. Only the immature person masturbates.
2. It is condemned in Scripture.[5]
3. Masturbation is unsocial or antisocial.
4. It violates the divinely intended purpose of sex.
5. It causes fatigue and physical debilitation.
6. It is a manifestation of low self-control.
7. The fantasies associated with masturbation are emotionally unhealthy.
8. It is sexually frustrating and not as satisfying as sex relations with a marital partner.
9. It is an indication of selfishness.
10. It leads to undesirable feelings like guilt and anxiety.

Many experts see these arguments as being oversimplified and even false.[6] Still, the debate of whether masturbation is right or wrong is not settled. Ethical judgments about masturbation run all the way from viewing it as a sin more serious than fornication, adultery, or rape to placing it in the same category as head scratching.[7] Regardless of one's position on the subject,[8] it cannot be argued that masturbation among adolescents is rare.

More than 90 percent of males and 50 percent of females have masturbated to orgasm at some point in their lives. The average age for beginning to masturbate is thirteen for boys and fourteen for girls. However, some research reports that women tend to learn about masturbation over the entire life cycle. In contrast, the onset of masturbation for men appears to be an adolescent phenomenon, with 80 percent of males masturbating by about age fifteen.[9]

Not only do more young men masturbate earlier, they masturbate more frequently. A study done on college youth reports that the frequency of masturbation for men is about once per week and about once per month for women.[10]

Case Description

Tim came to counseling because he was troubled by his "thoughts." It wasn't until the third session that he confessed his real struggle, which was with masturbation. Tim was a junior in high school. He dated occasionally but had no steady girlfriend. He was not exactly the studious or the athletic type. He enjoyed carpentry. Tim, however, was finding that he could not even concentrate on his work because he was bombarded with thoughts about sex. Once a sexual image came into his mind he could not function until he found relief through masturbation. Tim masturbated as much as two or three times a day. He felt tremendous guilt and was convinced he was terribly abnormal.

Anyone who writes or speaks about masturbation is open to criticism. In the absence of clear biblical guidance on this issue, we are left with a variety of conflicting opinions. Most agree, however, that effective help and counseling may be extremely useful for adolescents struggling with masturbation.

☑ WHY THE STRUGGLE HAPPENS

While they may not be conscious of many of their motivations, adolescents masturbate for a variety of reasons. Here are some of the most widely cited.

Arousal and Orgasm

This is perhaps the most obvious reason. Adolescents enjoy masturbation. In one study, college women reported that experiencing pleasurable sensations and physical release of sexual tension were their primary motives for masturbation.[11]

Physically Ready

In adolescence, hormones increase the erogenous sensitivity of the maturing sex organs in preparation for procreation. Near the end of puberty the young are reproductively mature, with all the drives toward sexuality and sexual behavior of adults. They are physically ready to enjoy arousal and orgasm. To expect them not to have these experiences would be like expecting a family in a house with new plumbing not to open up the faucets for a few years.

Environmental Stimulation

Adolescents today live in a sex-saturated society that emphasizes immediate sexual gratification. Films, magazines, television programs, and advertisements are blatantly designed to arouse sexual urges and desires. The environment is sexually supercharged, and masturbation is a means to cope with this environmental stimulation.

Self-Exploration

Secular sex educator Eleanor Hamilton recommends masturbation to adolescents as a way of becoming "pleasantly at home with their own sexual organs."[12] Teenagers learn about their personal sexual responses through masturbation. The practice teaches them about their capacity to control their sexual urges; however, masturbation may also be misused and result in lower control of sexual desires. Adolescent boys are almost instantly at the peak level of arousal, a stimulation akin to driving a turbo-charged five-speed Porsche for the first time. Masturbation has the potential to teach an adolescent how to control unbridled sexual desires.

Escape

Masturbation may sometimes be a way to escape boredom, relieve tension, or temporarily avoid pressures of life. At least one-fourth of those people who masturbate do so when suffering from loneliness or rejection. Some adolescents, however, may use masturbation to their detriment, as a means of escape into fantasy and avoidance of meaningful interpersonal relationships.

☑ HOW PARENTS CAN HELP

The following strategies for helping an adolescent struggling with masturbation can be used effectively by parents; however, every parent-child relationship is unique, and some of them may be more pertinent to your situation than others. As with every significant adolescent struggle, it is best for parents to work alongside a competent counselor. With this in mind, the following is offered as a way to help you facilitate the helping process at home with your teenager.

Listen with Sensitivity

This, of course, should underlie all intervention strategies, but it is sometimes forgotten when helping adolescents on sexual issues. This means undergirding your discussions with the skills discussed in Part One of this book, but it also means avoiding particular pitfalls. Avoid expressing embarrassment, shock, or excessive curiosity. Monitor your discomfort with the issue to insure calm acceptance. Don't give pat answers. This may alleviate your discomfort with the subject, but it will also alienate adolescents who had the courage to talk to you about the struggle in the first place.

Alleviate Fears and Anxiety

An almost inevitable belief for young people troubled by masturbation is that their behavior is abnormal. Unaware that the practice is so prevalent, many adolescents struggle with numerous fears about their masturbatory behavior. Several sex experts, however, have written of the normalcy of masturbation, and fearful adolescents may be assured of their "okayness" with this information. It has been jokingly said that "ninety-nine percent of teenage boys admit they masturbate, and the other one percent are liars."[13] Masturbation is normal, and there is no medical evidence to indicate that the practice is harmful to the body or that it interferes physically with subsequent sexual intercourse.

Parents and counselors can alleviate any fears surrounding myths that the adolescent is carrying. Some of the most common of these myths say that masturbation causes pimples or insanity, that it indicates a dirty mind, that it may be controlled by cold showers, and so on. The teenagers who struggle with these and other myths need reassurance that these notions are false. Research, by the way, indicates that masturbation decreases when any anxiety connected with it is alleviated.[14]

For a few adolescents masturbation may be secondary to their fear of being exposed. Sometimes teens may be discovered masturbating. For example, a camp counselor, a parent, or a sibling walks in on them. An older brother may even use this discovery as a form of blackmail to manipulate his sibling. The focus, obviously, should then become the resulting fear and humiliation.

Work Through Guilt

An adolescent once told me, "Every time after I masturbate I pray and promise God that I will never do it again." Guilt over sexual matters abounds. Adolescents often worry about their particular idiosyncrasies and personal preferences. During the writing of this section an adolescent confessed to me in a counseling session that he sometimes masturbates before going to church and feels extremely guilty for doing this on Sunday. Guilt over masturbation may be one of Satan's major ways of attacking sincere Christian youth.

Mary Ann Mayo, in her book *A Christian Guide to Sexual Counseling,* says, "I have seen people invest forty-eight hours of self-wallowing condemnation and guilt as a result of four minutes of self-indulgent pleasure!"[15] On the other hand, the young person's guilt may be genuine. The apostle Paul wrote, "If anyone regards something as unclean, then for him it is unclean" (Romans 14:14). Allowing adolescents to investigate their guilt and shame is healing. You may wish to consult the section on guilt for further suggestions on how to work through guilt issues effectively.

Understand Its Developmental Context

According to Christian ethicist Lewis Smedes, moral concern about masturbation ought to focus on young people's total development toward a more wholesome heterosexual life.[16] For wholesome growth it is important for children to learn to understand their own bodies and to accept the ways in which they respond to stimulation. Adolescents are absorbed in establishing their psychosexual identity and are curious about erogenous areas, sensitive swellings, and seminal emissions. Masturbation provides a laboratory situation in which adolescents' bodily functions and pleasures may be experienced under controlled circumstances. This experience may aid them as they grow toward mature intimacy in marriage.[17]

Think Through Your Personal Theology

Masturbation may be a major source of spiritual problems for adolescents. The question they are asking is whether or not it is a sin. Scripture, of course, does not address the issue directly. Because of this, Christians have come to different conclusions concerning it. Where are you on the continuum? Do you see masturbation in general as a sin or not very serious? Masturbation is one of those areas where we must be careful not to judge others but to remain faithful to our own understanding of biblical principles.

Facilitate Personal Exploration

You might help adolescents understand masturbation in more neutral terms. Advice or ideas that suggest the practice should be resisted at all costs will likely promote the cycle of defeat and guilt. However, suggesting that masturbation may be the way to deal with sexual pressures may also add to the frustration. Lustful fantasies beget lustful fantasies, and Jesus clearly condemns this (Matthew 5:27–30). One of the most constructive approaches for parents and counselors is simply to listen without embarrassment or the need to judge. David Seamands says, "When there is open communication on masturbation it will no longer be a problem."[18] An accepting response to teens' explorations can help them "rebuild their self-esteem and propel them into more meaningful and satisfying interpersonal relationships."[19] Effective parents and counselors model the assurance of God's grace, underlining his total and unconditional acceptance.

Explore the Use of Pornography

Pornography is accessible to today's teens, and many boys and some girls at least occasionally make use of pornographic materials during masturbation. In one study only about 30 percent of the boys said they never looked at pornography while masturbating.[20] If this is a problem for your teen, you will find further suggestions in the section on pornography.

Do Not Neglect Potential Danger

Before concluding this section on how to help adolescents who struggle with masturbation, I must add a word of caution about a rare but very dangerous experiment with masturbation. It is called autoerotic asphyxia or "scarfing." It happens when a teenager (almost always a male) masturbates while constricting his throat or chest to create an altered state of consciousness by reducing the brain's oxygen supply. Some experts say this deprivation may physiologically create intensified sensations of sexual pleasure in the brain. Others say it is simply the power of the suggestion that heightens the pleasure. In either case, it is a deadly endeavor. Fatal cases are usually found hanging naked in a closet or bathroom.

The FBI reports that as many as one thousand young people die from autoerotic asphyxia each year. That means an adolescent dies every eight hours from this practice. The warning signs of autoerotic asphyxia include repeated appearance of bloodshot eyes; a fascination with ropes, chains, and leather belts; and neck abrasions or bruises.[21] If you suspect this activity, do not hesitate to ask directly: "Have you ever done anything unusual or dangerous to enhance your masturbation experience?" The inquiry could save a life.

Know When to Refer

If you are embarrassed, ill-at-ease, overly curious, or uncertain how to proceed with adolescents struggling with masturbation, referral to a counselor is necessary. It is important to let adolescents know that the referral is not a rejection of them but a way of getting them the best help possible. If you suspect autoerotic asphyxia, you should immediately initiate a professional consultation with an expert.

✔ HOW PROFESSIONALS CAN HELP

The following strategies for helping an adolescent struggling with masturbation are commonly used by counselors. They are presented here as a way to inform you, as a parent, and help you seek the best possible professional help you can for the adolescent in your care.

Pinpoint the Severity

A common concern about masturbation is "doing it too much." Even in writings where masturbation is said to be "normal," masturbation "to excess" is often presented as a problem. The question that naturally follows is what "excessive" means. Once a year, twice a week, after every meal? If adolescents masturbate so much that it interferes with certain aspects of their lives, there would be cause for concern. However, in that case masturbation would be a manifestation of the problem rather than the problem itself. For example, adolescents who experience intense emotional anxiety because of conflicts with parents may masturbate as an attempt to escape and release the anxiety. Counselors can assess the intensity of the adolescents' struggle with masturbation by asking them directly how often they masturbate.

Examine Obsessions and Compulsions

Sometimes adolescents are consumed by sexual thoughts and fantasies. Their masturbatory habits may become highly ritualized. This is a deeper problem than simply enjoying self-stimulation. In a life stage that is typically fraught with insecurity, anxiety, and turmoil, the search for the pleasures of masturbation may become compulsive. When this occurs, compulsiveness, not masturbation, is the problem that needs to be addressed. Adolescents need not be obsessed with or mastered by masturbation. Competent counselors can help tremendously when this is the case.

Assist Avoidance

For adolescents who conclude that masturbation is wrong for them and are trying to control the practice, Stephen Grunlan offers these suggestions: Avoid the time and places where masturbation has been practiced; avoid sexual stimuli in movies, television, music, or magazines; do not fight thoughts about masturbation but work at replacing them with other thoughts; take it one day at a time; commit the matter to God in prayer.[22] Remember that masturbation is rarely helped by a direct determination to quit. This seems only to magnify the issue, increase anxiety, and make failure more incriminating.

Where to Go for Additional Help

Carnes, P. *Out of the Shadows*. Minneapolis: CompCare, 1983.

Carnes, P. *Talking to Your Kids About Sex*. Colorado Springs, Colo.: Waterbrook, 1999.

Hart, A. D. *The Sexual Male*. Waco, Tx.: Word Publishing, 1993.

Jones, S., and B. Jones. *How and When to Tell Your Kids About Sex*. Colorado Springs, Colo.: NavPress, 1993.

Smedes, L. B. *Sex for Christians*. Grand Rapids: Eerdmans, 1994.

Stafford, T. *A Love Story: Questions and Answers on Sex*. Grand Rapids: Zondervan, 1977.

Notes

1. G. R. Collins, *Christian Counseling: A Comprehensive Guide* (Waco, Tex.: Word, 1988).

2. W. H. Masters, V. E. Johnson, and R. C. Kolodny, *Masters and Johnson on Sex and Human Loving* (Boston: Little, Brown, 1986), 283.

3. R. Crooks and K. Baur, *Our Sexuality*, 4th ed. (New York: Benjamin-Cummings, 1990).

4. G. Wood and E. Ruddock, *Vitalogy* (Chicago: Vitalogy Association, 1918).

5. Two passages that are most often used to condemn masturbation are Genesis 38:8–10 and 1 Corinthians 6:9. However, most scholars examining these passages do not see them addressing the issue of masturbation.

6. R. E. Butman, "Masturbation," in *Baker Encyclopedia of Psychology* (Grand Rapids: Baker, 1999).

7. R. J. Foster, *Money, Sex and Power* (San Francisco: Harper & Row, 1985).

8. Consider the variety of positions taken by Christians on this issue: Stephen Grunlan, in his book *Marriage and the Family: A Christian Perspective* (Zondervan, 1984), gives three reasons why Christians should avoid masturbation: First, there is no biological necessity for masturbation; second, masturbation is a solo act, and God created us as sexual beings to bring men and women together; third, the fantasies and thought life that accompany the act are sinful. By contrast, James Dobson, in his popular "Focus on the Family" film series, accepts masturbation as a normal part of growing up unless it becomes excessive. Charlie Shedd, in *The Stork Is Dead* (Word, 1976), speaks of masturbation as a "gift from God." David Seamands (in J. A. Petersen's *For Families Only*, Tyndale, 1977) says, "It's high time we stop making such a big deal of masturbation and give it the well-deserved unimportance it merits."

9. J. D. Atwood and J. Gagnon, "Masturbatory Behavior in College Youth," *Journal of Sex Education and Therapy* 13, no. 2 (1987): 35–42.

10. Ibid.

11. R. Clifford, "Development of Masturbation in College Women," *Archives of Sexual Behavior* 7 (1978): 559–73.

12. E. Hamilton, *Sex with Love* (Boston: Beacon Press, 1978), 33.

13. G. K. Olson, *Counseling Teenagers* (Loveland, Colo.: Group Books, 1984).

14. W. R. Johnson, *Masturbation* (New York: Sex Information and Education Council of the U.S., n.d.).

15. M. A. Mayo, *A Christian Guide to Sexual Counseling* (Grand Rapids: Zondervan, 1987), 193.

16. L. Smedes, *Sex for Christians* (Grand Rapids: Eerdmans, 1994).

17. K. Sanford, "Towards a Masturbatory Ethic," *Journal of Psychology and Theology* 22 (1994): 21–28.

18. D. A. Seamands, "Sex, Inside and Outside of Marriage," in *The Secrets of our Sexuality*, ed. G. R. Collins (Waco, Tex.: Word, 1976), 156.

19. Butman, "Masturbation," 688.

20. R. Sorenson, *Adolescent Sexuality in Contemporary America* (New York: World, 1973).

21. D. Marshall, "A Deadly Shame," *Parents of Teenagers* (August/September 1990).

22. S. A. Grunlan, *Marriage and the Family: A Christian Perspective* (Grand Rapids: Zondervan, 1984), 122.

OBESITY

✔ WHAT THE STRUGGLE LOOKS LIKE

The fastest-growing medical specialty today is plastic surgery. The number of people undergoing cosmetic surgery increases nearly 10 percent each year. And with some female teen-celebrities today making the news with their cosmetic alterations, it is not surprising to find that a growing number of those opting for aesthetic surgery are girls still in puberty.[1]

Adolescents are obsessed with the question, "How do I look?" They may be wondering about their new haircut, whether their clothes are wrinkled, or whether food is caught between their teeth. But what they really want to know is whether others see them as physically attractive.[2]

The overwhelming majority of adolescent girls aren't satisfied with what they see in the mirror. A 1999 Gallup Poll found that 67 percent of women say they weigh more than they should and 43 percent consider themselves overweight. It is no wonder that high school girls are twice as likely as boys to suffer from depression.

Interestingly, women who are unhappy with their bodies don't necessarily suffer from low self-esteem. This may be because they're in good company. It helps a young woman who wants to lose ten pounds to know that most of her friends feel the same about themselves.

There is one group of male and female young people, however, that suffers a disproportionate amount of pain and humiliation because of their body image—obese adolescents. Adolescents who are not obese and struggling with body image are more likely to be suffering from an eating disorder (refer to the section on eating disorders).

Ten to 15 percent of all adolescents are truly obese, girls more than boys.[3] Obesity among adolescents is a serious health problem. Longitudinal studies show higher levels of risk factors for cardiovascular disease, joint disease, and gynecological disorders in obese adolescents. The National Institutes of Health recommends that weight reduction be considered for anyone with one of the following medical conditions: family history of diabetes, high blood pressure, coronary disease, or history of obesity in childhood.[4]

Being overweight, however, not only represents a health hazard, it also affects adolescent social relationships, self-esteem, ego-identity development, and emotional adjustment.[5] Furthermore, if an obese teenager has a history of weight problems and does not reduce as an adolescent, the odds are twenty-eight to one that she or he will become and remain an obese adult.[6] People who hope that an obese adolescent will grow out of it are awaiting an unlikely event.

Some may indeed grow out of it, but the pain and suffering that heavy adolescents endure should not be minimized. This quote depicts the hurt: "My name is Marcy Lewis. I'm thirteen years old and in the ninth grade. All my life I've thought I looked like a baby blimp with wire-frame glasses and mousy brown hair. Everyone said that I'd grow out of it, but I was convinced that I'd become an adolescent blimp with wire-frame glasses, mousy brown hair, and acne."[7]

Case Description

Peter is an extremely overweight fourteen-year-old boy. He has above-average intelligence and does reasonably well in school when he wants to. His eating is out of control. More than once he has eaten a half-gallon of ice cream at one sitting. He stands in front of the mirror each morning and tries various combinations of shirts and pants somehow to "reduce" his size. Some mornings he has even ditched school because he is ashamed of his weight. When he is at school, his general mode is to withdraw and avoid much social contact. Peter's heaviness haunts him every minute, but he has never forced himself to throw up nor exhibited other signs of having an eating disorder. Peter has been called every "fat" name in the book, and his self-esteem is just about shot. Peter would give anything to look "normal."

Many factors determining obesity status are simply arbitrary judgments of variable criteria, for example, the "large size of skinfolds" measured by skin calipers (most often applied to the triceps). However, the best criterion, generally, is measured against a weight index (normed for age, sex, and height). Most experts consider anything above the ninetieth percentile to be an adequate indicator to diagnose obesity.[8] Experts, however, also classify the degree of the adolescent's obesity. *Mild* obesity ranges from 15 percent overweight to an upper limit of about 35 percent. *Moderate* obesity ranges from 35 to 100 percent overweight. *Severe* obesity is defined as being more than a 100 percent overweight. This severe degree may carry a dangerous risk to life, and a surgical approach to treatment (gastroplasty) should be considered if behavioral treatments have failed.[9]

✔ WHY THE STRUGGLE HAPPENS

Why does obesity develop in the first place? What makes obesity aggravatingly resistant to change? The causes of obesity are not simple. Most experts agree that it is a multidetermined problem. Genetic, biological, behavioral, familial, cultural, and even economic factors interact in complex ways to affect the development and maintenance of this struggle. Here is what some of today's researchers are telling us about its etiology.

Genes

It seems that some adolescents are born to be overweight. Selective breeding experiments and twin studies have shown a strong genetic contribution to obesity. In one investigation, researchers analyzed weight and height records. Their study of identical and fraternal pairs of twins found that siblings reach and maintain similar body weights whether or not they are reared in different families (and that they are much more likely to grow up looking like their natural parents than their adoptive ones). Their conclusion? If both biologic parents are overweight, an 80 percent chance exists that their kids are going to be overweight.[10]

Biology

Biological barriers have also been shown to work to maintain or increase weight in the obese. Studies of adipose cells and of metabolic adaptations to weight reduction make it clear that biology plays a major role in obesity. Positive biological energy must exist for obesity to occur. That is, for obesity to develop, the amount of energy consumed must be greater than the amount of energy expended. Further support of the biological view is attributed by some to studies that show adolescents of parents who are obese are much more likely to be obese than adolescents whose parents are lean.[11]

External Causes

Considerable evidence shows that less biologically oriented factors contribute to the problem. For example, significant correlations are found between the weights of spouses and measures of obesity as well as the weights of obese foster parents and their children.[12] Studies have even correlated the weights of pet owners with their dogs to show the influence of less biologically oriented factors.[13]

Eating Style and Behavior Patterns

Obese adolescents typically show a "high-density" eating style. This eating style includes excessive eating, with more gulping and less chewing than in their leaner peers.[14] An obese adolescent I once worked with would buy a box of Twinkies and eat one after the other—whole! Some evidence, not surprisingly, also shows obese adolescents to be less active than their leaner counterparts.[15] And if activity level is low, of course, fat accumulates because metabolism declines. Some, out of ignorance, are quick to label the inactivity as lazy. More often, it is probably avoided out of embarrassment. David Elkind, in his book *All Grown Up and No Place to Go*, quotes the following passage from Paula Danzinger's *The Cat Ate My Gymsuit*. It poignantly illustrates the embarrassment felt by every obese adolescent. It is a picture of a sensitive overweight girl avoiding gym class.

> I just sat there. Trying to change into a gymsuit while hiding my mini bra and fat body would have been a gymnastic feat in itself. Once the class started, I walked up to the gym teacher, Schmidt. "All right, Lewis, what is it this time?" "The cat ate my gymsuit." She shook her head, frowned, and wrote another zero in her marking book. I sat down to watch my eighty millionth volleyball game.[16]

Food Preference

Obese adolescents do not necessarily eat more food overall, but they almost always prefer foods that are calorically dense and highly flavored.[17] Furthermore, their physiological responses tend to encourage this consumption and do not become inhibited after the food is consumed. After eating foods high in carbohydrates or sugars, their insulin levels are elevated, which increases hunger and food consumption. In fact, just the sight and smell of foods can elevate the insulin level in obese people.[18]

Family Factors

The beginnings of obesity may be found in the early relationships between parents and their children. Childhood for many obese adolescents was characterized by intense parental involvement, overprotectiveness, and rigidity. The parents may have an unusually high concern for their children's welfare. For example, in an interview with the family, parents frequently speak for their obese children or correct them when they attempt to speak for themselves. In extreme cases, they may not want their obese children to be put on a diet because they don't want to deprive them of anything.[19]

Psychological Factors

Eating is often a greater positive reinforcement for obese people because they find it to be a more pleasurable activity than do people of normal weight. On the flip side, eating can also be used as a means of self-punishment.[20] With a poor self-image, weight gain becomes a way of reinforcing negative self-conceptions and proving their self-perceptions. Adolescents who are obese, already feeling ineffective, may become more inactive and withdrawn and turn to eating as a form of comfort and security.[21]

☑ HOW PARENTS CAN HELP

The following strategies for helping an adolescent struggling with obesity can be used effectively by parents; however, every parent-child relationship is unique, and some of them may be more pertinent to your situation than others. As with every significant adolescent struggle, it is best for parents to work alongside a competent counselor. With this in mind, the following is offered as a way to help you facilitate the helping process at home with your teenager.

Plan for the Long Run

Adolescents vary a great deal in their response to treatments for obesity. One thing is certain, however. There are no quick cures for obesity. Counselors and parents should plan on long-term treatment. If all other factors are equal, it is desirable for obese adolescents to meet with a counselor at least once a week for eight to twelve months, longer if needed. Research has shown that sustained, weekly therapist contact can facilitate maintenance of key strategies and improve weight loss. Even after goal-weights are achieved, weekly contact should be sustained for several months to promote generalization of behavior changes.[22]

Boost Confidence

Obese adolescents are rejected by their peers more than any other minority-type person.[23] The damage to their self-esteem can be horrendous. Many believe obese people are simply lazy, stupid, and weak. This stereotype leads to overweight people being treated as second-class citizens, especially among adolescents. It is not at all uncommon for obese adolescents to grow up hearing names like "Crisco" or "fatso." Overweight adolescents need to hear that the problem is with their bodies, not themselves. As persons they are not defective; they simply have the special challenge of managing their bodies. Without self-confidence and a sense that they can learn to control their bodies better, treatment is useless. They need to believe that change is possible and achievable. For additional help in this foundational treatment step, see the section on inferiority.

Confidence, by the way, is especially important to instill after a setback. Backsliding is inevitable in a weight-control program. The adolescent may eat too much pizza on a Friday night, for example, or not follow through on an exercise goal because the weather was bad. Catastrophic thinking by the young people in these circumstances is not unusual. Without acceptance and encouragement they may give up altogether.

Consider Intensive Treatment Centers

One method that has been devised for overweight adolescents is to send them to a residential weight-management camp. One group of researchers studying the success of these camps chose a Tacoma, Washington, camp that emphasizes three aspects: (1) nutrition education, (2) behavior modeling, and (3) physical activity. Participants attend for only five days, but follow-up studies six months after camp revealed permanent weight loss, leading researchers to conclude that this is a useful approach to adolescent weight-management therapy.[24] Similar intensive treatments include hospital settings. The Oaks Treatment Center in Austin, Texas, has a twelve-week program for teenagers that consists of nutrition classes, exercise classes, monitored diets, and so on. Before recommending a specific camp, counselors must be fully informed of its validity and effectiveness.

Examine Your Expectations

These strategies are some of the best available for treatment of this painful problem. There is, of course, much more to treating obesity effectively. This chapter is simply a springboard into other excellent resources that describe in greater detail therapeutic interventions for obese adolescents. Some of them are noted at the end of this chapter. Be aware of the difficulty of this assignment. Examine your expectations for treatment. Are they unrealistic? Remember that small weight loss or simply stopping the inevitable rise in weight with increasing age can enhance health.

Work with a Counselor

Since eating plays a central role in family life, it is helpful to be involved in the treatment strategy. If adolescents agree with the idea, the counselor may ask to meet with you. The counselor may help you decide to be more sensitive to buying or making calorie-dense foods, serving meals that are excessively high in fat, and keeping the refrigerator stocked with foods that are high in calories. Along these lines, the following may be useful: *American Heart Association Cookbook* (New York: Ballantine Books, 1994) and *The New Living Heart Diet* by Michael DeBakey, Antonio M. Gotto, Lynne W. Scott, and John P. Foreyt, (New York: Raven Press, 1996). You may also be urged to model routine physical exercise.

If frequent conflict occurs in the home, the counselor may help you with child-management skills to reduce the turmoil. Studies have shown that families who experience patterns of relational chaos have less adequate dietary habits than other families.[25]

☑ HOW PROFESSIONALS CAN HELP

The following strategies for helping an adolescent struggling with obesity are commonly used by counselors. They are presented here as a way to inform you, as a parent, and help you seek the best possible professional help you can for the adolescent in your care.

Assess the Conditions

Several measures are available to assess the severity of the adolescent struggling with body image and obesity. One preliminary measure that is often helpful assesses adolescents' belief in their ability to control weight loss. The Internal Versus External Control of Weight Scale will give the counselor some idea of whether the adolescent is optimistic about change. The Compulsive Eating Scale can be used to measure the adolescent's tendency to eat uncontrollably (especially during times when they are not necessarily hungry). It is one of the few assessments on eating that was developed specifically for adolescents. Many counselors will use these or other assessments.

Require a Physical Exam by a Physician

The most successful approaches to treating obesity recognize that it is a multicausal problem encompassing genetic, metabolic, environmental, familial, and emotional factors. Counselors cannot effectively treat this problem without incorporating the expert assistance of medical consultation to provide them with a complete picture of the struggle. Physical complications may be present, which a physician, not a therapist or counselor, should be treating. If an unusually low-calorie diet is prescribed, it is especially essential that medical assessment and follow-up be built into the treatment program.

Assess the Goals

At the beginning of treatment, it is important to assess the appropriateness of young people's goals for weight loss. Although improvement in physical appearance is usually a major motivation for most obese adolescents beginning counseling, such motivation may be problematic because the weight loss achievable by many may not alter physical appearance dramatically. The goals teens have in mind may be unrealistic, and the time to tackle this situation is at the beginning of treatment. Competent counselors will help them shift their therapeutic goals away from entirely cosmetic considerations.

Begin a Weight Graph and Eating Diary

Counselors assist adolescents to construct personalized charts for a record of weight changes. The Y-axis includes incremental amounts of weight. The X-axis is labeled "dates." They enter their weight about once a week and record the date. This does not have to be highly regimented, but it can serve as a helpful reinforcer to keep them accountable. Besides, the chart gives them visual access to their progress.

Adolescents are also encouraged to keep an eating diary, recording when, where, what, and with whom they eat. This exercise allows them to observe their eating habits with more objectivity. It helps answer questions like the following: Do I eat mostly when I am alone? Do I often eat between meals? Does a certain feeling precede my eating?

A sample eating diary is shown on page 236.

Modify Eating Style

As noted under the causes of obesity, heavy adolescents exhibit a high-density eating style. They eat rapidly, with big spoonfuls, gulping food by chewing

EATING DIARY

DATE	TIME	FOOD EATEN Quantity	Type	SOCIAL STATE Alone	With Whom	WHERE	EVENT BEFORE	MOOD
1/4	7 a.m.	2	Bagels	✓		Kitchen	Woke up	Tired
	9:15 a.m.	1	Milky Way		Jim	Locker	Math	Bored

relatively little for the amount of food consumed. This eating style can increase the body's propensity to store excess nutrients as fat. Effective treatment must emphasize the change in eating styles through a sustained self-monitoring of their eating behavior.[26] Counselors often give an assignment to adolescents to help them modify these habits. They are encouraged to take time to appreciate their food—its color, aroma, texture, and so on. They are required to take a two-minute time-out during each meal. If they cannot remember to do this, counselors may suggest they set an alarm to go off in the middle of each meal. Or they are taught to divide their meal and rest before eating the second half. To slow down eating further, the young person may pause briefly after each bite and put down their utensils before taking another bite. This allows them to become more aware of stomach fullness and eventually change their high-density eating style.[27]

Implement an Exercise Routine

It is becoming clearer that weight-control interventions must focus on increasing physical exercise in addition to the traditional goal of changing eating patterns. Evidence suggests that exercise can even decrease appetite. One study found that including a ten-minute exercise period before lunch reduced the caloric intake of obese adolescents just as effectively as nutritional education.[28] The problem with trying to increase the exercise activity of sedentary adolescents is that they often don't follow through on the plan. A variety of interventions must be considered to make this effort successful. For example, we know that people tend to maintain exercise regimens better if (1) they enjoy their exercise, (2) if the exercise is convenient to do, and (3) if the exercise includes other people (e.g., a team sport). These points will be considered by the counselor when setting up an exercise routine. In sum, research says that the best advice in this area is to encourage the use of specific weekly (not daily) planning to increase exercise in obese adolescents' lives.[29]

Use Behavioral Contracts

A behavioral contract is an explicit agreement specifying expectations and plans for the changing of behavior. The contract is written rather than verbal and includes specific target behavior and consequences. It is often desirable to have clients write out their own contracts with the counselor each week and include the week's goals, which, by the way, should be challenging yet achievable. For example, the adolescent might include in his or her contract "to record calorie intake; to play soccer three times; to enter my weight on my weight-loss graph once; to avoid ice cream or other dessert foods." The reward for achieving contracted goals can be anything that may further motivate them. For example, youths may deposit the modest sum of five dollars, which will be returned to them at the end of the week if they have kept the terms of the contract. Research has shown that the amount of reward does not usually influence the outcome.[30] Other rewards may include positive social events or special privileges at home.

A sample behavioral contract is shown below.

Contract for the Week of _____

This week I will—
1. Self-monitor my food at least six out of seven days.
2. Jog at least twice for at least thirty minutes.
3. Eat only in the kitchen for at least four days.
4. Read a chapter of my book on nutrition.
5. Walk home from school on three days.
6. Enter my weight on my weight graph.

If I meet these goals successfully, I will be refunded my deposit of five dollars.

_____

Signature, Date

Know When to Refer

Counselors will refer obese adolescents to psychologically astute physicians or psychiatrists for a complete physical examination at the beginning of counseling treatment. The purpose is to address the presence or absence of physical problems that are beyond the scope of counseling or that might interfere with treatment.

If counselors do not feel qualified to deal with problems of obesity, they should refer clients to their colleagues. If it becomes clear that adolescents' struggles with obesity signal the generalized problems and conflicts within the family, focused training in child management or more intense family therapy is in order.

Where to Go for Additional Help

Antony, M. M., and R. P. Swinson. *When Perfect Isn't Good Enough: Strategies for Coping with Perfectionism.* Oakland, Calif.: New Harbinger Publications, 1998.
Brody, J. *Jane Brody's Nutrition Book.* New York: Bantam, 1981.
Cash, T. F. *The Body Image Workbook: An 8-Step Program for Learning to Like Your Looks.* Oakland, Calif.: New Harbinger Publications, 1997.

Collipp, P. J. *Childhood Obesity.* New York: Warner Books, 1986.

Dalton, S. *Overweight and Weight Management: The Health Professional's Guide to Understanding and Practice.* Gaithersburg, Md.: Aspen Publisher, 1997.

Lipe, D., and J. Wolff. *Help for the Overweight Child: A Parent's Guide to Helping Children Lose Weight.* New York: Scarbrough, 1978.

Powers, P. S. *Obesity: The Regulation of Weight.* Baltimore: Williams and Wilkins, 1980.

Notes

1. B. Hey, "Portrait of an Obsession," *Health* (June 1991): 68–70.

2. G. D. Rosenblum and M. Lewis, "The Relations Among Body Image, Physical Attractiveness, and Body Mass in Adolescence," *Child Development* 70 (1999): 50–64.

3. United States Department of Commerce, Bureau of the Census *Statistical Abstract of the United States* (Washington, D.C.: U.S. Government Printing Office, 1987).

4. National Institutes of Health Consensus Development Conference Statement, "Health Implications of Obesity," *Annals of Internal Medicine* 103 (1985): 1073–77.

5. M. Nowak, "The Weight-Conscious Adolescent: Body Image, Food Intake, and Weight-Related Behavior," *Journal of Adolescent Health* 23 (1998): 389–98.

6. K. D. Brownell, "Obesity: Understanding and Treating a Serious, Prevalent, and Refractory Disorder," *Journal of Consulting and Clinical Psychology* 50 (1982): 820–40.

7. P. Danziger, *The Cat Ate My Gymsuit* (New York: Dell, 1973), 7.

8. D. S. Kirschenbaum, W. G. Johnson, and P. M. Stalonas, *Treating Childhood and Adolescent Obesity* (New York: Pergamon, 1987).

9. W. S. Agras, *Eating Disorders: Management of Obesity, Bulimia, and Anorexia Nervosa* (New York: Pergamon, 1988).

10. *Time* (June 4, 1990): 80.

11. S. M. Garn and D. C. Clark, "Trends in Fatness and the Origins of Obesity," *Pediatrics* 57 (1976): 443–56.

12. Ibid.

13. E. Mason, "Obesity in Pet Dogs," *Veterinary Record* 86 (1970): 612–16.

14. D. S. Kirshenbaum and A. J. Tomarken, "On Facing the Generalization Problem. The Study of Self-Regulatory Failure," in *Advances in Cognitive–Behavioral Research and Therapy*, ed. P. C. Kendall (New York: Academic, 1982), 1:121–200.

15. K. D. Browness and A. J. Stunkard, "Behavioral Treatment for Obese Children and Adolescents," in *Obesity*, ed. A. J. Stunkard (Philadelphia: W. B. Saunders, 1980).

16. D. Elkind, *All Grown Up and No Place To Go* (New York: Addison Wesley, 1984), 34.

17. P. Hoare and L. Cosgrove, "Eating Habits, Body-Esteem and Self-Esteem in Scottish Children and Adolescents," *Journal of Psychosomatic Research* 45 (1998): 425–31.

18. J. Rodin, "Obesity: Why the Losing Battle?" in *Psychological Aspects of Obesity: A Handbook*, ed. B. B. Wolman (New York: Van Nostrand Reinhold, 1982), 30–87.

19. R. J. Brone and C. B. Fischer, "Determinants of Adolescent Obesity: A Comparison with Anorexia Nervosa," *Adolescence* 23 (1988): 155–69.

20. A. Gila, J. Castro, J. Toro, and M. Salamero, "Subjective Body-Image Dimensions in Normal and Anorexic Adolescents," *British Journal of Medical Psychology* 71 (1998): 175–84.

21. J. Sobal, "Group Dieting, the Stigma of Obesity and Overweight Adolescents," *Marriage and Family Review* 7 (1984): 9–20.

22. Kirschenbaum et al., *Treating Childhood and Adolescent Obesity.*

23. M. D. Lebow, *Child Obesity: A New Frontier of Behavior Therapy* (New York: Springer, 1984).

24. G. Brandt, T. Maschhoff, and N. S. Chandler, "A Residential Camp Experience as an Approach to Adolescent Weight Management," *Adolescence* 15 (1980): 807–22.

25. A. C. Israel, L. Stolmaker, and C. A. G. Andrian, "The Effects of Training Parents in General Child Management Skills on a Behavioral Weight Loss Program for Children," *Behavior Therapy* 16 (1985): 169–80.

26. R. Dixey, "Healthy Eating in Schools: Overweight and 'Eating Disorders': Are They Connected?" *Educational Review* 50 (1998): 29–35.

27. Kirschenbaum et al., *Treating Childhood and Adolescent Obesity.*

28. L. H. Epstein, B. J. Masek, and W. R. Marshall, "A Nutritionally Based School Program for Control of Eating in Obese Children," *Behavior Therapy* 9 (1978): 766–78.

29. Kirschenbaum et al., *Treating Childhood and Adolescent Obesity.*

30. Ibid.

OBSESSIONS AND COMPULSIONS

✔ WHAT THE STRUGGLE LOOKS LIKE

It is not unusual for preschoolers to insist on certain kinds of routines. They may need a drink of water before going to bed, or they may want a particular doll with them in bed every night—and no other doll will do. They may insist that their shirt be put on before their pants. They may require that the same glass be used for their milk at every meal. The attention to regular patterns among young children is an attempt to control their environment and their own behavior. The more predictable they can make their lives, the more secure they feel.

In the same way that fears turn into phobias, these kinds of routines may turn into maladaptive rituals and preoccupations. Routines may become an *obsessive-compulsive personality style* characterized by a pervasive tendency to be preoccupied with concerns of neatness, orderliness, punctuality, control, efficiency, hard work, rigid adherence to rules, and perfection in every way.[1] Mild compulsivity or perfectionism, if handled well, may be an asset. Often, however, these traits lead to problems.

Obsessions are intrusive and recurring thoughts, ideas, fears, or doubts that certain people cannot prevent from bombarding their conscious awareness. Though they want to avoid them, they cannot keep from ruminating and worrying about them. These ruminations rarely serve any constructive purpose and often paralyze any capacity to take action.

Compulsions are repetitive, nonproductive impulses that people feel required to carry out over and over again, even against their better judgement. The compulsion may be as absurd as counting every tile on a bathroom floor or washing one's hands every fifteen minutes. I treated one young man who routinely measured his nose. Failure to carry out certain self-prescribed rituals gives compulsive people a terrible sense of impending catastrophe. Compulsions often occur with obsessions and vice versa, but not always.[2]

Obsessive-compulsive behavior is fairly common. Most of us know people who are regarded as perfectionistic worriers, who are indecisive, meticulous, or inflexible. Obsessive-compulsive symptoms are considered pathological only when at least five of the following events occur:[3]

1. Perfectionism that interferes with task completion. For example, the inability to complete a project because self-imposed strict standards are not being met.
2. Preoccupation with details, rules, lists, order, organization, or schedules to the extent that the major point of the activity is lost.
3. Unreasonable insistence that others submit to exact ways of doing things, or unreasonable reluctance to allow others to do something because of the conviction that it will not be done correctly.
4. Excessive devotion to productivity to the exclusion of leisure activities and friendships.
5. Indecisiveness due to total avoidance, postponement, or protraction of decision making. For example, those who cannot get assignments done on time because of concentration on priorities. They fear making mistakes.
6. Overconscientiousness, scrupulosity, and inflexibility about matters of morality, ethics, or values (not accounted for by cultural or religious identification).
7. Restricted expression of affection.
8. Lack of generosity in giving time, money, or gifts when no personal gain is likely to result.
9. Inability to discard worn-out or worthless objects even when they have no sentimental value.

Although obsessive-compulsive disorder is more prevalent among adults than among young people, it often has a youthful onset. Obsessive-compulsive adolescents show an average age of onset of about ten years and more than half of all cases of the problem begin before age twenty. It occurs about equally between males and females.[4]

✔ WHY THE STRUGGLE HAPPENS

In spite of much effort devoted to development of a theory of the origins of obsessive-compulsive disorder, its causes are largely unknown. Nevertheless, there are several suggested reasons for its occurrence.

Biology

To date, biological approaches to the understanding of this disorder have yielded only traces of definitive information. Genetics appears to have a weak influence that may predispose some people to develop problems with obsessions and compulsions. But no biochemical or structural deficits can explain its emergence.[5]

Case Description

Rick, fifteen, is the only child of middle-class, emotionally stable parents. He enjoyed a happy childhood free from any significant problems, but during the fourth grade his parents sought professional help because they thought he might have a learning disability. Rick was very nervous about tests, and he spent hours on homework that should have taken only minutes. An evaluation by a learning specialist revealed no significant pathology. He and his parents were counseled briefly, and the next few years passed without any major difficulties. In fact, Rick was considered a model child by his parents' friends. He was always well behaved, orderly, and "mature" for his age. His bedroom was a showroom of neatness.

About the time Rick entered high school, however, things began to worsen. Rick started doing very poorly in school. His parents realized it wasn't due to a lack of "smarts," however. Rick read his assignments over and over looking for errors. It was not unusual for him to recopy a written assignment four or five times. Regardless of how good his work was, it never seemed to be good enough for him. He developed perfectionistic rituals like keeping the inside of his locker extremely clean and organized. Three times after he locked it he would check his locker to be sure it was secure.

> Rick's waking life became governed by rituals, and he was ter-
> rorized by thoughts that if he failed to carry them out "some-
> thing terrible" would happen.

Fear Reduction

Obsessions and compulsions are attempts to master the environment and feel safe. Perfectionistic behavior enables people to avoid the anxiety and fear that accompany less than perfect performance. By doing the "right" thing people troubled in this area are certain of their behavior and thus reduce their fear of making a mistake or otherwise not being acceptable. Fear is also reduced by engaging in behavior that postpones undesirable events. By counting objects, for example, teens may delay imagined catastrophes.[6]

Self-Doubt

Unfortunately, self-doubts dominate many adolescents' feelings about themselves. This may contribute to occurrences of obsessions and compulsions in susceptible teens. Young people who repeat behavior doubt that they performed the behavior correctly. They become anxious and are compelled to repeat the act again. Orderliness and organization may also be vain attempts to help them dismantle their self-doubt. Having everything "in its place" provides psychological balance and lets them know they are okay because their things are okay.

Guilt

Compulsivity may be a counteraction to the desire to be sloppy, messy, and disorganized. The guilt of having "forbidden" wishes fuels perfectionistic behavior. Instead of being the slobs they want to be, they become models of orderliness. Instead of stealing and cheating, they become models of virtue and are horrified by the misbehavior of others. They become overly scrupulous and feel guilt over minor misdeeds. They even feel guilty for not being constructive during their leisure time.

Parental Expectations

Many children learn from their parents that things must be done in a specific and exact manner to be acceptable. Overly strict parents with high expectations, who are themselves rigid and perfectionistic, do not tolerate children's deficiencies and inconsistencies. Their home emphasizes etiquette and cleanliness. They both model and reinforce compulsive behavior. If the children do not rebel against their perfectionistic behavior along the way, they will probably react by becoming overly conscientious and perfectionistic.

✔ HOW PARENTS CAN HELP

The following strategies for helping an adolescent struggling with obsessive compulsive disorder can be used effectively by parents; however, every parent-child relationship is unique, and some of them may be more pertinent to your situation than others. As with every significant adolescent struggle, it is best for parents to work alongside a competent counselor. With this in mind, the following is offered as a way to help you facilitate the helping process at home with your teenager.

Facilitate a Slow Pace

Obsessive-compulsive individuals are very tense. They are almost continually hurried to the point where they can't relax or slow down. It is up to parents to set a slow pace. Be aware of your tone and attitude. The last thing they need are driving and pressured parents. You may eventually approach this hurriedness directly by asking them how they rest and relax. Sometimes all they need is "permission" to lighten up.[7]

Steer Clear of Superstition

Superstition promotes compulsive behavior. To ward off bad luck young people battling this problem may, for example, always sharpen their pencils at predetermined times, or they may wear certain colors on specific days. If they grew up with adults who knocked on wood for luck, never walked under ladders, and so on, they need help in seeing that they can make free choices and do not have to imitate these habits. Another means of staying clear of solidifying these rituals is to have them purposely vary their behavior. For example, ask them to dress in a different order or walk home from school along a different route, or sit in a different area of the cafeteria. This gives them permission to be flexible and creative. Of course, for hard-core obsessive compulsives, any variation in routines will be difficult and should not be forced.

Teach Constructive Behavior

Perfectionistic behavior is unnecessary and inefficient. Show the young person how he or she may use good intentions more constructively. For example, challenge a young woman to substitute different behavior or at least reduce repetition, if she takes two hours in the bathroom washing in a particular way several times, arranging her toothbrush and paste, hanging the towels perfectly, and so on. Rather than washing four times, urge her to wash only twice. Rather than washing each finger individually, suggest that she wash all fingers of one hand together. Rather than hanging the towels several times until they are perfect, tell her that she may have two tries and then she must quit. This will help cut her time in half and help her see that her rituals are unnecessary.

The idea is for the teens to recognize the positive value in their behavior and eliminate unnecessary repetition. Take the pressure off by telling them that failures are okay, and challenge them to keep trying until they succeed.

Reinforce Noncompulsiveness

Parents can praise any sign of better self-control and reduction of perfectionism. Congratulate adolescents on their progress. If they have been struggling with the need at school to hand in assignments that are not perfect, applaud them for turning in papers regardless of their quality and extent of completion. Focus on their new ability to control their rituals, not on the result of the control. You may also suggest that they reward themselves when they break compulsive habits by doing something they enjoy.

✅ HOW PROFESSIONALS CAN HELP

The following strategies for helping an adolescent struggling with obsessive-compulsive disorder are commonly used by counselors. They are presented here as a way to inform you, as a parent, and help you seek the best possible professional help you can for the adolescent in your care.

Explain the Problem

Simply labeling struggles and discussing their nature relieves anxiety and a great deal of stress in distraught adolescents. Labeling helps teens know that they are not alone in their struggles. I remember a spiritually sensitive teenager, fighting a compulsion, who was relieved to find that she was not possessed by a demon! Counselors will explain the dynamics of the struggle, and make a distinction between obsessive thoughts and compulsive behavior. They will tell them it is a means of coping with anxiety and stress and that they can learn new ways of coping with anxiety that are more constructive. Counselors, however, must use labels cautiously. If a teen grapples with mild symptoms of the disorder, it may be best to avoid anything that feels like a clinical diagnosis. A label can be self-fulfilling.

Encourage Feelings

Open expression of feelings prevents compulsive rituals and obsessive thoughts from becoming more intense. The difficulty for those who battle this problem is that they often are not aware of their feelings. For this reason they can benefit from keeping a "feeling log." It is a place for them to record what they feel, not what they *should* feel. Counselors will suggest that troubled adolescents keep track of their feelings by recording them throughout the day. They will have them note what happens, what they say to themselves, and what they feel as a result. Of course, this assignment may become a compulsion. They may become more concerned about carrying out the assignment correctly than actually becoming more aware of their emotions. They need to be assured there is no right or wrong way to do this exercise and that it needn't be done consistently.

Use Reconditioning

Perfectionism is associated with avoidance of anxiety. It is necessary to recondition young people so that compulsive behavior is no longer necessary to avoid anxiety.[8] They may behave without rituals or perfectionism and still feel good. Counselors will teach them to relax on cue. They will learn to breathe deeply, for example, just before a task in order to prevent the usual rise of anxiety. The section on anxiety outlines several relaxation strategies that may be used by counselors for this purpose.

Another avenue used by counselors is to teach relaxation and then desensitize clients by showing that their not performing compulsive rituals does not result in disaster. While they are relaxed, teens are asked to imagine themselves not following their usual perfectionistic and compulsive behavior. Each time they imagine that scene, they will become less anxious about giving up their compulsions.

For example, an adolescent may be obsessed with and compulsive about having trash in the trash can. Once they are in a state of relaxation a counselor may ask them to see themselves in their mind's eye sitting at a desk in their bedroom. They will be asked to imagine that they just threw a piece of paper into their trash can under the desk, and then be lead to imagine that they do not immediately empty the trash can into the garbage can in the garage. They will imagine that they simply keep studying while the paper lies in the bottom of the trash can. They will probably experience at least mild anxiety at this image, and be urged to relax more deeply. Then, they will imagine themselves tossing another piece of paper into the trash can, and so on. Each time they visualize the scene their anxiety lessens, and the exercise brings them closer to letting go of their compulsion.

Practice Thought-Stopping

Obsessive thoughts have been successfully treated using the thought-stopping technique developed by Joseph Wolpe.[9] It involves telling clients to focus on their obsessive thoughts for a moment, then the counselor shouting,

"Stop!" This will distract them, and they will momentarily interrupt the obsessive thoughts. The procedure is repeated several times until clients can silently give the command to themselves and thereby stop the obsession. Another variation of this strategy is to have clients wear a rubber band around the wrist and snap it whenever they sense a buildup of an obsession. It is also helpful to have a thought to substitute for the obsession once it is stopped.[10] For example, the person who is obsessed with an image of a gory accident can stop the thought and substitute a picture of an ocean scene.

Consider Medical Consultation

Some of the most successful treatments for severe obsessive-compulsive disorder have included medication. Antidepressant medications such as clomipramine and imipramine (both inhibitors of serotonin) have helped many people suffering with this problem. Unfortunately, these medications have a number of significant side effects that must be outweighed by their benefits.[11]

Know When to Refer

Counselors will refer adolescents struggling with obsessions and compulsions to psychologically astute physicians or psychiatrists if the symptoms are severe enough to warrant consideration of medication.[12] They should refer clients to other competent counselors or psychologists when, after three months of regular therapy, they show no decrease in their ritualistic behavior or if they are becoming increasingly depressed. In this case a more severe underlying disorder may be operating, and a second opinion might help therapists make this determination.

Where to Go for Additional Help

Adams, P. L. *Obsessive Children*. New York: Brunner-Mazel, 1973.
Francis, G., and R. A. Gragg. *Childhood Obsessive Compulsive Disorder*. Thousand Oaks, Calif.: Sage Publications, 1996.
Rachman, S. J., and R. J. Hodgson. *Obsessions and Compulsions*. Englewood Cliffs, N.J.: Prentice-Hall, 1980.
Rapoport, J. L. *The Boy Who Couldn't Stop Washing: The Experience and Treatment of Obsessive-Compulsive Disorder*. New York: Plume, 1990.

Notes

1. C. M. Berry, "Obsessive-Compulsive Disorder," in *Baker Encyclopedia of Psychology*, ed. D. G. Benner (Grand Rapids: Baker, 1985).
2. C. Wever and J. M. Rey, "Juvenile Obsessive-Compusive Disorder," *Australian and New Zealand Journal of Psychiatry* (1997): 31.

3. American Psychiatric Association, *Diagnostic and Statistical Manual of Mental Disorders*, 4th ed. rev. (Washington, D.C.: American Psychiatric Association, 1996).

4. C. E. Hollingsworth et al., "Long-Term Outcome of Obsessive-Compulsive Disorder in Childhood," *Journal of the American Academy of Child Psychiatry* 19 (1980): 134–44.

5. E. T. Sturgis, "Obsessional and Compulsive Disorder," in *Comprehensive Handbook of Psychopathology*, ed. H. E. Adams and P. B. Sutker (New York: Plenum, 1984).

6. M. M. Grados, M. C. Labuda, M. A. Riddle, and J. T. Walkup, "Obsessive-Compulsive Disorder in Children and Adolescents," *International Review of Psychiatry* 9 (1997): 83–98.

7. Ibid.

8. L. Salzman and F. H. Thaler, "Obsessive-Compulsive Disorders: A Review of the Literature," *American Journal of Psychiatry* 138 (1981): 286–96.

9. J. Wolpe, *Psychotherapy by Reciprocal Inhibition* (Stanford, Calif.: Stanford Univ. Press, 1958).

10. D. C. Rimm, "Thought Stopping and Covert Assertion in the Treatment of Phobias," *Journal of Consulting and Clinical Psychology* 41 (1973): 466–67.

11. E. T. Sturgis and V. Meyer, "Obsessive-Compulsive Disorder," in *Handbook of Clinical Behavior Therapy*, ed. S. M. Turnger, K. C. Calhoun, and H. E. Adams (New York: Wiley, 1980).

12. T. R. Insel, "Toward a Neuroanatomy of Obsessive-Compulsive Disorder," *Archives of General Psychiatry* 49 (1992): 739–44.

OVERACTIVITY AND WORK STRESS

☑ WHAT THE STRUGGLE LOOKS LIKE

"They go to work with no plan and no training; their jobs usually anything they can get, having nothing to do with their interests and their capacities, only with business demand. . . . What would the average middle-class parent say to such an 'educational' program for adolescent boys and girls?"

That statement was written by Katherine DuPre Lumpkin in 1937, but it could have appeared in today's *New York Times*. Kids working at jobs "having nothing to do with their interests and their capacities" are busier today than ever.

"He's not even home for dinner most nights," a mother confided in me recently. "He is on the school yearbook staff, the church youth council, he plays guitar, and works twenty hours a week at Pizza Hut!" With desperation, she added, "I'm afraid his circuits are going to explode from activity overload! We take care of his needs; I don't understand why he wants to work."

During the past decade, researchers, educators, and policymakers have been scrambling to understand the effects of widespread teenage employment. Since 1940, there has been a sevenfold increase in the number of sixteen-year-old boys who work while in school and a sixteenfold increase in the number of girls. Nearly two-thirds of all high school juniors hold jobs in the formal part-time labor force *during* the school year.[1]

Consider Jim, age sixteen, as an example. He takes orders and earns money at the Orange Julius in the shopping mall. How can his situation be worse than his friend Dave's, who presumably sits in front of the TV at home or hangs out at the very same mall where he could be working? "Why shouldn't kids be working," the question goes, "if the alternative is simply wasting time doing nothing?"

Despite the common assumption that idleness breeds laziness, or that "hanging out" is at the root of adolescent problems like drugs, alcohol, or delinquency, the evidence simply does not support the proposition that a part-time job is always better for kids than doing "nothing." The very opposite can be true.

A series of studies at the University of Wisconsin involving thousands of teens has shown that working adolescents are more, not less, likely to use drugs and alcohol; they are more, not less, involved in deviant activities than their peers who are not employed.

Besides, there is a lot more to doing "nothing" than meets the eye. Tina is unburdened from the responsibilities and time demands of a job. She has time for daydreaming, for "working through" the day's experiences, for leisure, and for building and strengthening relationships with friends. All of these activities contribute in very healthy ways to Tina's psychosocial development. To deny her these luxuries is to foreclose the process of her identity development.

Playing basketball in the schoolyard, practicing the electric guitar in the basement, or learning dance steps in front of the mirror in a bedroom helps build a sense of mastery. It develops competence in ways that repetitively selling thousands of hamburgers or Levis cannot.

Training for the typical adolescent job is quick and there is little room for future advancement. The jobs teens hold are simple, unchallenging, and irrelevant to their future. They create what sociologist David Riesman calls "adjusted blandness" at a time in life when curiosity and imagination should be fueling identity formation.

Doing "nothing"—that is, improving a jump shot, learning a new chord technique, or mastering a difficult dance routine—helps develop autonomy, self-esteem, and purposefulness. It teaches the value of self-control, the necessity of perseverance, and the pride of accomplishment. Teenagers have a strong need to realize many facets of their personalities, and they can't do this without time to do "nothing." Extensive commitment to a job interferes with the work of growing up.

☑ WHY THE STRUGGLE HAPPENS

There is one primary motivation for why adolescents work the way they do these days and it can be seen in the shallow soil of consumerism. Teens do not work out of a dire economic need. Researchers have shown that *a materialistic lifestyle is the number-one driving force behind kids getting on the payroll*. One of the few things uniting teens these days are the things they buy. A school principal recently told me his students would not be seen dead at the lunch table without a prestigious Dove Bar on their tray.

Young people once labored in the fields alongside their parents, motivated by the economic needs of the family. Today, however, most adolescent work is done in fast food chains and retail stores. It is labeled *luxury employment*—where adolescents themselves are the chief beneficiaries. Fewer than one in ten kids who hold a job during the school year contribute a portion of their paycheck to the support of their families.

But it's not the children of blue-collar or poor families who predominate the youth labor force. The earliest and most numerous entrants into the world of work are the children of the well-to-do and the well-educated. Sociologists explain this in two ways: first, they live in the economically thriving, typically suburban areas where service jobs abound; second, their parents, who are "going and getting" at a frenetic pace, see earning money as no less important for their children than gleaning knowledge.[2]

Case Description

Rachel, an eleventh grader, is always on the go. She drives a temperamental VW bug, has a steady boyfriend, tries to be active at church and school, and loves to paint. On top of it all, Rachel works most weekends and many weeknights at the Gap, a trendy clothing store. She makes about $7.50 an hour and averages $150 a week. She told me the fun in her work wore off after the first month, but she "needs" the money. Rachel also enjoys an employee discount on Gap clothes, another major incentive for keeping her job. Rachel doesn't come close to reading everything her teachers assign. Like most kids who work, she compensates for her job commitments through cutting classes when convenient, copying assignments, and even cheating. She also misses time with friends and hasn't touched her paintbrush in months. Rachel manages to show up for most youth group activities, but she is almost always visibly stressed and exhausted.

✔ HOW PARENTS CAN HELP

The following strategies for helping an adolescent struggling with overactivity or work stress can be used effectively by parents; however, every parent-child relationship is unique, and some of them may be more pertinent to your situation than others. As with every significant adolescent struggle, it is best for parents to work alongside a competent counselor. With this in mind, the following is offered as a way to help you facilitate the helping process at home with your teenager.

Assess the Stress Level

It is helpful to determine if their workload is healthy or unhealthy. The most important clue is whether or not the teenager is enjoying his job. A University of Chicago study found that adolescents' moods were most positive and their activity levels higher when participating in arts, hobbies, or sports than in any other activity, including working at a part-time job. If the job is purely a source of spending money, the work is not healthy. But don't make the mistake of thinking what is stressful and unfulfilling for one kid is the same for another.[3]

Explore the Meaning of Work

Most young people's jobs involve unskilled manual labor with no future. A meaningful job, however, promotes personal growth and autonomy. It increases cooperation and social responsibility and leads to learning and mastery of useful skills and information. It provides opportunities for experimentation and identity exploration. A meaningful job also brings young people into contact with adults who can contribute to these ends.[4]

Conduct a Time Inventory

It is often helpful for young people to discover exactly how they spend their time. This can be done by creating a time inventory where students keep track of everything they do for one day. They record their activities every hour on the hour. Teens are often surprised to see how much their job eats up their life. Explore with them what could be done in place of the time they spend at work and their freedom to make choices with their time.

Avoid Equating Work with Maturity

Job-holding by adolescents is often viewed as an important step in the direction of growing up. But performing roles typically filled by adults does not equal adulthood. Maturity is an inside job. Playing adult roles is a superficial attempt to achieve maturity and it short-circuits the development of self-understanding. Work may help kids acquire the appearance of maturity, but not its substance.

Catch Kids Dreaming Big

When a kid shares a piece of something she feels might be a little too far-fetched or unreachable, perhaps even a little foolish—dream with her. A working teen is often so busy keeping up with her immediate schedule she can't anticipate her future. When you catch them exploring their options, validate their dreams.[5]

Foster Inner Peace

The title of a classic book by Brother Lawrence captures the essence of what is needed by teens with jammed schedules: They need to "practice the presence" of God by surrendering their desires, inviting God into the details of life, and retreating from pressures to commune with him. Of course, "practicing the presence" is better seen than preached.

Talk About "Head Cruising"

Some kids feel guilty for daydreaming, especially the teens who appear harried and frazzled with "work" left undone. Let them know it's okay to allow their minds to just wander and do nothing. Give them permission to let their souls catch up with their busy pace by having them "head cruise."

Teach Money Management

Teens need to be taught to delay their gratification with money. One way of doing this is for parents to encourage them to have a portion of their earnings be tithed to church and another portion saved for longer-term goals, such as college education. You can help contribute to this end by teaching teens to budget their money and spend it wisely.

Bash Madison Avenue

There is no escaping our consumer society, especially for kids. Marketing giants spend billions of dollars trying to get teens to spend their money on CDs, movies, button-fly jeans, candy bars, Coca-Cola, styling gel, and on and on. Nevertheless, students don't have to get sucked into consumerism. Teach them to fight back against slick and sly advertising.

Know When to Refer

Refer adolescents who struggle with job stress and overactivity to a competent counselor or psychologist when, over time, the young person's lifestyle shows no sign of improved decision making and boundary setting. Consider, also, a referral to a competent career counselor for assessment and guidance if the young person is especially serious about exploring career options and future educational plans.

Where to Go for Additional Help

Cloud, H., and J. Townsend. *Boundaries with Kids: When to Say Yes, When to Say No, to Help Your Children Gain Control of Their Lives.* Grand Rapids: Zondervan, 1998.

Goleman, D. *Working with Emotional Intelligence.* New York: Bantam Books, 1998.

Hahn, D. *Teaching Your Kids the Truth About Consequences: Helping Them Make the Connection Between Choices and Results.* Minneapolis: Bethany, 1995.

Maxwell, J. C. *Developing the Leaders Around You: How to Help Others Reach Their Full Potential.* Nashville: Nelson, 1995.

Olson, K. G. *Why Teenagers Act the Way They Do.* Loveland, Colo.: Group Books, 1987.

Peel, B., and K. Peel. *Discover Your Destiny: Finding The Courage to Follow Your Dreams.* Colorado Springs, Colo.: NavPress, 1996.

Whelchel, M. *How to Thrive from 9 to 5.* Ann Arbor, Mich.: Vine Books, 1999.

Notes

1. W. Meeus, J. Dekovic, and J. Iedema, "Unemployment and Identity in Adolescence: A Social Comparison Perspective," *The Career Development Quarterly* 45 (1997): 369–80.

2. E. G. Menaghan, L. Kowaleski-Jones, and F. L. Mott, "The Intergenerational Costs of Parental Social Stressors: Academic and Social Difficulties in Early Adolescence for Children of Young Mothers," *Journal of Health and Social Behavior* 38 (1997): 72–86.

3. T. D. Dzhebrailova, "Individual Features of Resistance to Emotional Stress During Work on a Computer in Fifteen- to Sixteen-Year-Old Pupils," *Human Physiology* 21 (1995): 125–29.

4. C. S. Smith, J. Tisak, S. E. Hahn, and R. A. Schmieder, "The Measurement of Job Control," *Journal of Organizational Behavior* 18 (1997): 225–37.

5. D. J. Terry, R. Rawle, and V. J. Callan, "The Effects of Social Support on Adjustment to Stress: The Mediating Role of Coping," *Personal Relationships* 2 (1995): 97–124.

Panic Attacks

✔ WHAT THE STRUGGLE LOOKS LIKE

Fear is when you look up and see a half-ton weight about to fall on your head. In a panic attack you feel the same fright but don't know why.

It is estimated that up to 6 percent of the people in the United States have at some time in their lives been diagnosed as having problems with panic attacks. However, since anxiety reactions rarely require hospitalization, statistics on the incidence of the disorder are difficult to compile. Until recently panic attacks were believed to be confined to adults. Research is showing that this is not true.[1] About 65 percent of all cases begin between the ages of ten and twenty-nine.[2] In a survey of 338 high school students, 32 percent reported experiencing at least one panic attack that meets clinical diagnostic criteria in the *Diagnostic and Statistical Manual* (4th ed.). In addition, 5 percent of the students reported experiencing panic severely and frequently enough to fulfill the diagnostic criteria of panic disorder. Surprisingly, this researcher found that fewer than half the students surveyed with panic disorder reported any contact with mental health services.[3] In spite of this, many professionals report an increase in the incidence of panic symptoms in adolescents.[4]

A panic disorder is characterized by sudden, brief attacks of acute anxiety and extreme autonomic arousal. The individual experiences intense apprehension and terror and a sense that something dreadful is about to happen. Attacks are usually unexpected and sudden, lasting anywhere from a few seconds to an hour or more. Most commonly they last about three or four minutes. The anxiety mounts to high intensity and then subsides, all in the absence of any obvious cause.

A person's first panic attack, according to Stewart Agras at Stanford University, usually occurs in a public place. The victim of the attack suddenly feels ill, notices a fast and erratic heartbeat, experiences a tight feeling in the chest, breathes rapidly, and may feel faint. The rapid breathing leads to chemical changes that cause tingling in the hands and feet and numbness around the mouth.[5]

Adolescents struggling with panic feel that they are losing control. Physiological symptoms, together with the sense of impending death or catastrophe, make panic attacks truly terrifying. They are real experiences and must not be downplayed. To underestimate, dismiss, or laugh at the irrationality of the attacks will only make them worse.[6]

The symptoms of panic are so markedly physical that in the eighteenth century the disorder was termed "hysterical vertigo" in an attempt to describe the sensations of dizziness often reported by patients.[7] To be clinically diagnosed today with panic disorder the person must have at least four of the following symptoms during at least one of the attacks:

1. Shortness of breath or smothering sensations
2. Dizziness, unsteady feelings, or faintness
3. Palpitations or accelerated heart rate
4. Trembling or shaking
5. Sweating
6. Choking
7. Nausea or abdominal distress
8. Depersonalization or derealization
9. Numbness or tingling sensations
10. Flushes or chills
11. Chest pain or discomfort
12. Fear of dying
13. Fear of going crazy or of doing something uncontrolled[8]

Symptoms vary from one person to another, but they usually include varying combinations of the above signs. If the attack lasts more than a few minutes, the victim may frantically implore someone to summon a doctor or to be taken to a hospital emergency room. After medical treatment has been administered, usually in the form of verbal reassurance and a minor tranquilizer, one generally feels better. In fact, the patient may feel ridiculous after arriving at the hospital when the physician or nurse attempts to ascertain the presenting problem.

Attacks vary in frequency, but generally occur from several times a day to once a month or even less often. They may occur during the day, or the person may be sound asleep when awakened with a strong sense of apprehension that quickly develops into a full-blown attack. Between attacks the person may be mildly anxious or tense, but one can also be relatively unperturbed.[9]

Clinicians often misdiagnose panic disorder as agoraphobia—the fear of open places.[10] Since people who struggle with panic attacks do not know when an attack will strike; they may anticipate its disastrous occurrence and become reluctant to venture far from home. The real fear here is not going out of the house. It is a fear that the panic symptoms will occur while they are walking on the streets, while driving, or while out with friends. Once they learn how to control the attacks, they typically resume their normal lifestyle.

Case Description

Tina was a vivacious cheerleader and a senior in high school. She first came in for therapy at the request of her physician. She believed she had a physical disorder because of her attacks. Her medical examinations, however, revealed no physical problems that could account for the dramatic experience of the panic attacks. Because of the discrepancy between the intensity of her experience and the failure of her physician to find any significant disorder, she was convinced that the doctor had made a mistake and that she was suffering from a very serious but hidden physical disorder. She described her attacks as "horrendous." "I can't predict when the next one will come, but when it does I know my legs will cave in and I'll feel as if I can't breathe. It feels as though my throat is closing up, and my heart wants to jump right out of my chest!"

Tina was terrified. Since she could not predict when her "illness" was going to occur, she was constantly on the alert for symptoms to appear. She was especially fearful that one would strike while she was doing a routine on the cheer squad during a game. One time, to get out of a game when she thought she might have an attack, she even reported to her captain that she was sick. She kept a thermos of ice water and some cold face cloths handy to place on her neck whenever she started feeling weak. This seemed to make her feel better, but she was desperate to alleviate her terror permanently. At the time she came in for counseling, she had already been to several physicians, most of whom had suggested psychological

treatment. She was relieved finally to learn that she was struggling
with a common form of anxiety—panic disorder.

✔ WHY THE STRUGGLE HAPPENS

Panic disorder may have distinct diagnostic criteria, but its causes are
clouded. Certainly, its etiology has much in common with general anxiety. You
may wish to refer to the section on anxiety. Here are some of the possible reasons for the occurrence of panic attacks.

Genetics

Studies have shown that panic disorder runs in the family. Children of anx-
iety-disorder parents are more than seven times as likely as others to be victims of the same problem.[11] Another researcher found that if an identical twin
suffers from panic disorder or agoraphobia with panic attacks, the other twin
will likely also suffer from panic attacks.[12]

Physical Disorders

Anxiety symptoms may be caused by physical disorders that mimic anxiety
reactions. Here are some examples: Hyperthyroidism, cocaine abuse, alcohol
withdrawal, diabetes, hypoglycemia, psychomotor epilepsy. There are numerous others. For this reason, a complete medical examination by a physician is
necessary when treating an anxiety disorder.

Family Environment

Disabling anxiety often originates in dysfunctional families. This condition
in adolescents or young adults should prompt counselors to investigate the family's role. While external stress may be beyond the patient's control, it may be
affected for better or worse by their families. Moreover, families may cause anxiety directly through mistreatment, substance abuse, or marital problems that
disrupt family relationships.[13]

Fear of Independence

To complete the individuation process begun in adolescence, young adults
need to gain psychological and geographical independence from both home
and parents. It is during this growing apart that they are most vulnerable to
anxiety. Anticipation of leaving home has been especially difficult for many
adolescents in the current generation. Today's adolescents are not prepared to
separate from their parents and become independent. The disappearance of the

extended family support system, the loss of the economic importance of children as members of a family work force, and overly indulgent parents are some of the reasons for this phenomenon. In any case, fear of independence is a causal factor of panic cited by some.[14]

☑ HOW PARENTS CAN HELP

The following strategies for helping an adolescent struggling with panic attacks can be used effectively by parents; however, every parent-child relationship is unique, and some of them may be more pertinent to your situation than others. As with every significant adolescent struggle, it is best for parents to work alongside a competent counselor. With this in mind, the following is offered as a way to help you facilitate the helping process at home with your teenager.

Insure a Proper Diet

Just as there is a definite connection between diet and physical illness, so there is between diet and anxiety. The key is to improve adolescents' vitality by avoiding foods with added sugar, caffeine, salt, and artificial additives. Instead, urge them to eat more fresh fruit and vegetables, whole-grain breads, and lean meat and fish. This diet will help adolescents feel more energized and less susceptible to panic.

Encourage Avoidance of Caffeine

Caffeine triggers the release of adrenaline and has been linked to panic attacks. Research at the Yale University School of Medicine has shown that when people with anxiety disorders are given caffeine, they register significant increases in anxiety, nervousness, fear, nausea, palpitations, restlessness, and tremors. People struggling with panic attacks show marked signs of anxiety when using products containing caffeine. While most teens do not drink coffee, they may be drinking soft drinks that contain significant amounts of caffeine.

Encourage Laughter

"Laughter can provide immediate relief from life's daily pressures," says Joel Goodman, editor of *Laughing Matters* magazine. "But it also builds up immunity to stress for the long haul." Other experts agree. "Laughter is not only as good a method of stress relief as a massage, a hot bath, or exercise; it's essential to stress relief," says Steve Allen, Jr., M.D., son of comedian Steve Allen.

Laughing, like aerobic exercise, also diffuses physical tension directly. It triggers a sequence of actions in which muscle tension first increases, then decreases. That is why much hilarity can make us "weak with laughter." It also decreases production of adrenaline and cortisone. Adolescents are not too young to be caught up in a spinning vortex of conflicts and confusion. They need to laugh as much as possible.

Explore Adolescents' Preferences in Music

When young David played his harp for troubled King Saul, he became one of history's first-known music therapists. Today's music therapists talk about two kinds of music. The first is stimulating music that sets people to clapping their hands, tapping their toes, or dancing. The second is calming music, which has a much slower, easier rhythm (about sixty beats per minute). Calming music has been used to reduce distress and pain among people in dentists' offices, coronary-care units, and migraine-headache clinics.

The right music can take a person in a matter of minutes from a highly tense state of panic to a relaxed yet alert state. A young woman I once treated for panic disorder almost always had an attack while at a nightclub where loud rock music was played. Relaxing music triggers the release of endorphins in the brain that make us feel less anxious. Most adolescents, of course, prefer very stimulating music. Young people struggling with panic attacks, however, can usually be convinced to replace Aerosmith or the Red Hot Chili Peppers with something more calming, if it will help them avoid future attacks. While I have had little success in motivating teenagers to play *Harpsichord Concerto in F Minor* in their Walkmans, I have seen several enjoy the benefits of listening to a selection of environmental sounds or soft jazz.

✔ HOW PROFESSIONALS CAN HELP

The following strategies for helping an adolescent struggling with panic attacks are commonly used by counselors. They are presented here as a way to inform you, as a parent, and help you seek the best possible professional help you can for the adolescent in your care.

Pinpoint the Severity

While specific symptoms of panic disorder are difficult to assess through a rapid assessment instrument, therapists may quickly gain a clinical picture of the symptoms through interview. They will assess the occurrence of specific characteristics of the attacks and their frequency. Although it is designed to measure the amount, degree, or severity of generalized anxiety, the Clinical Anxiety Scale may be used in conjunction with assessing panic.

Require a Medical Examination

A careful physical examination with particular attention to panic attack symptoms cannot be overemphasized. Prior to embarking on a psychological treatment approach, organic disorders must be adequately ruled out. Certain antipanic drugs like alprazolam (Xanax), imipramine (Tofranil), and phenelzine (Nardil) may be helpful for those who suffer from extreme attacks of panic. The question, of course, is how the side effects of the medication will affect patients. Psychologically astute physicians or psychiatrists will generally prescribe the lowest dosage needed for the shortest period of time if medication is seen as necessary.[15]

Generally, once an effective drug regimen has been found, patients are kept on the medication for six months with dosages tapering off gradually over the next three months. Of course, if medication is prescribed, adolescents continue under medical supervision throughout treatment. Patients' misunderstandings about medications and their alarm concerning side effects are often the main cause of their noncompliance and their dropping out of treatment. Therefore, contact with physicians must be made whenever questions or concerns related to their medical treatment arise.

Discuss the Nature of the Struggle

Once medical examinations are over and diagnoses of panic disorder are completed, therapists will fully discuss the nature of the disorder and its treatment with the young victims. They need to hear that their problem has a name and that much is known about it. In addition to providing information and answering questions during office sessions, clinicians may refer adolescents to one of several books written about panic disorder for the lay reader. Three excellent books for this purpose are listed under "Where to Go for Additional Help" at the end of this section: *Panic: Facing Fears, Phobias, and Anxiety*, *Overcoming Anxiety*; and *The Anxiety Disease*.

Prescribe a Diary

It is helpful to have adolescents keep diaries or logs of symptoms. Counselors will ask them to record the time and setting of each attack, to rate its intensity on a zero-to-ten scale, its duration, any medication taken and side effects experienced, and an account of their experience together with any questions. These records will prove helpful in assessing their response to treatment.

Teach Breathing Exercises

When undergoing attacks, victims breathe shallow, rapid breaths from the chest. By changing their breathing patterns during attacks, they may reverse the body's panic-provoking symptoms. Counselors will urge them to breathe from the diaphragm and use the lower part of their lungs with each breath so that the stomach expands instead of the chest. While they may learn a breathing exercise in a matter of minutes and experience some immediate benefits, the profound effects of the exercise may not be fully appreciated until months of persistent practice have passed.

Practice Autogenics

Autogenic Training is a systematic program that teaches adolescents to respond quickly and effectively to their own verbal commands to relax and return to a balanced, normal state. It is one of the most effective and comprehensive reducers of stress and has been used successfully with panic disorder. The goal is to reverse the "fight-or-flight" alarm state and to get physical, mental, and emotional processes normalized when they begin to get out of balance. Essentially, the method is to relax in a comfortable position and concentrate passively on verbal formulas suggesting warmth and heaviness in one's arms and legs.[16]

Practice Guided Imaginal Coping

Our thoughts, images, and other mental activities may be harmful when they upset us. Guided imagery provides an avenue for adolescents to replace troubling thoughts with pleasant ones. The goal is to reduce and control mental anxiety. Research has shown that treatment incorporating guided imagery reduces panic attack frequency and duration.[17] By using pleasant visual images, adolescents control upsetting thoughts and enjoy a deep state of physical relaxation.

Implement a Desensitization Strategy

If counselees are particularly fearful of situations where they have had panic attacks, it is important to practice *in vivo* desensitization. Counselors will have adolescents gradually reenter the feared situation, accompanied by a trusted companion. Beneficial results are optimal if this can be done with their therapists. This exercise may be helpful in reducing anticipatory anxiety and phobic avoidance once the panic has been controlled. It allows them to resume their normal activities and regain confidence.

Know When to Refer

Counselors will refer adolescents suffering from panic disorder to psychologically astute physicians or psychiatrists when physical symptoms are present or when the anxiety is severe enough to warrant medication for temporary relief.

They should also refer them also to other competent counselors or psychologists when, over time, they feel more out of control and increasingly anxious.

Where to Go for Additional Help

Agras, S. *Panic: Facing Fears, Phobias, and Anxiety.* New York: W. H. Freeman, 1985.

Benson, H. *The Relaxation Response.* New York: Morrow, 1975.

Charlesworth, E. A., and R. G. Nathan. *Stress Management: A Comprehensive Guide to Wellness.* New York: Ballantine, 1984.

Collins, G. R. *Breathless: Transform Your Time-Starved Days into a Life Well Lived.* Wheaton, Ill.: Tyndale, 1998.

Colten, M. E., and S. Gore. *Adolescent Stress: Causes and Consequences.* Hawthorne, N.Y.: Aldine de Gruyter, 1991.

Davis, M., M. McKay, and E. R. Eshelman. *The Relaxation and Stress Reduction Workbook.* Richmond, Calif.: New Harbinger, 1980.

Freeman, L. *Panic Free: Eliminate Anxiety/Panic Attacks Without Drugs and Take Control of Your Life.* Sherman Oaks, Calif.: Arden Books, 1999.

Hart, A. D. *Adrenalin and Stress.* Waco, Tex.: Word, 1986.

_____. *Overcoming Anxiety.* Waco, Tex.: Word, 1989.

Lee, J. *Coping with Anxiety and Panic Attacks.* New York: Rosen Publishers, 1997.

Marks, I. M. *Living with Fear.* New York: McGraw-Hill, 1978.

Osborn, C. *Release from Fear and Anxiety.* Waco, Tex.: Word, 1978.

Sheehan, D. V. *The Anxiety Disease.* New York: Scribner, 1984.

Walker, E. *Learn to Relax.* Englewood Cliffs, N.J.: Prentice-Hall, 1975.

Notes

1. C. Hayward, J. D. Killen, and C. B. Taylor, "Panic Attacks in Young Adolescents," *American Journal of Psychiatry* 8 (1989): 1061–62.

2. M. R. Von Korff, W. W. Eaton, and P. M. Keyl, "The Epidemiology of Panic Attacks and Panic Disorder: Results of Three Community Surveys," *American Journal of Epidemiology* 122 (1985): 970–81. Also see M. Giesecke, "Panic Disorder in University Students: A Review," *Journal of American College Health* 36 (1987): 149–57.

3. G. D. Zgourides and R. Warren, "Prevalence of Panic in Adolescents: A Brief Report," *Psychological Reports* 3 (1988): 935–37.

4. W. K. Silverman, J. A. Cerny, W. B. Nelles, and A. E. Burke, "Behavior Problems in Children of Parents with Anxiety Disorders," *Journal of the American Academy of Child and Adolescent Psychiatry* 6 (1988): 779–84.

5. S. Argas, *Panic: Facing Fears, Phobias, and Anxiety* (New York: W. H. Freeman, 1985).

6. V. Reed and H. U. Wittchen, "DSM-IV Panic Attacks and Panic Disorder in a Community Sample of Adolescents and Young Adults: How Specific Are Panic Attacks?" *Journal of Psychiatric Research* 32 (1998): 335–45.

7. Ibid.

8. *Diagnostic and Statistical Manual,* 4th ed. (Washington, D.C.: American Psychiatric Association, 1994), 238.

9. T. H. Ollendick, "Panic Disorder in Children and Adolescents: New Developments, New Directions," *Journal of Clinical Child Psychology* 27 (1998): 234–45.

10. H. Wittchen, V. Reed, and R. C. Kessler, "The Relationship of Agoraphobia and Panic in a Community Sample of Adolescents and Young Adults," *Archives of General Psychiatry* 55 (1998): 1017–24.

11. Silverman et al., "Behavior Problems in Children of Parents with Anxiety Disorders."

12. S. Torgersen, "Genetics of Panic Disorder," *Psychiatria-Fennica: 1989 Supplement* (1988): 29–34.

13. Silverman et al., "Behavior Problems in Children of Parents with Anxiety Disorders."

14. D. E. Gredanus et al., "Anxiety in Young Adults," *Medical Aspects of Human Sexuality* 12 (1986): 76–83.

15. For an excellent review of the importance of a medical evaluation for panic-attack victims, see A. Raj and D. V. Shehan, "Medical Evaluation of Panic Attacks," *Journal of Clinical Psychiatry* 48 (1987): 309–13.

16. For a thorough understanding of this technique you may wish to consult W. Luthe, *Autogenic Therapy* (New York: Grune and Stratton, 1969).

17. P. L. Watkins and E. T. Sturgis, "Guided Imaginal Coping: An Integrative Treatment for Panic Disorder," *Journal of Behavioral Therapy and Experimental Psychiatry* 19 (1988): 147–55.

PARENTAL DIVORCE

✔ WHAT THE STRUGGLE LOOKS LIKE

The number of children affected by a parental split is staggering. Divorce is a fact of life for more than a million kids a year in the United States. About forty percent of white children and seventy-five percent of black children born to married parents will experience their parents' divorce prior to the age of sixteen.[1] Most of these youngsters will live in a single-parent home for at least five years. A small majority of those who experience a divorce eventually end up in a stepfamily, but well over a third of them will endure the extra trauma of seeing that second marriage break up.[2] What's more, children in single-parent families are six times as likely as children in two-parent families to be poor; two to three times as likely to have emotional and behavioral problems; more likely to drop out of school and to be expelled or suspended from school;[3] more likely to get pregnant as teenagers; and more likely to use drugs and to be in trouble with the law.[4] Their difficulties persist into adulthood as they have struggles in achieving intimacy in their relationships, in forming a stable marriage, even in holding a steady job.[5] As respected researcher and specialist in this area Barbara Dafoe Whitehead puts it, "Children who grow up in single-parent or stepparent families are less successful as adults, particularly in the two domains of life—love and work—that are most essential to happiness."

Children of divorce commonly react with depression, withdrawal, grieving, fear, fantasies of responsibility for the breakup and of possible reconciliation, anger, shame, decreased school performance, a sense of loss or rejection, and conflicts over which parent to express loyalty to.

Not surprisingly, many believe that the problem of young people struggling with parental divorce is at the root of a national crisis. Divorce is said to weaken our social fabric and place unbearable burdens on schools, courts, and the welfare system. There are few other modern-day problems where the call of a counselor is more needed.

☑ WHY THE STRUGGLE HAPPENS

It has been an established fact for some time that parental divorce has a long-term negative impact on children. Their development and adjustment is affected in harmful ways in both the home environment and in the school setting. When it comes to explaining why these young people have such struggles the reasons hinge on several factors.

The Rise of the "Expressive Divorce"

In the past thirty years, Americans have come to think about the family in a radically new way. Many now see the dissolution of marriage as not a tragedy that undermines the social order, but an entitlement that offers individuals the chance to remake themselves and live more emotionally satisfying lives. In the vast number of divorces, there is no gross strife or violence that could warp a youngster's childhood. The majority of marital breakups today are driven by a quest for greener grass. It is known as the "expressive divorce." And the thinking behind it is that if one or both parents are happier because of divorce, it should also enhance their children's well-being—but in these cases the children will almost always be worse off.[6] This attitude over the last several years is a major cause of so many young people growing up in single-parent and stepparent families.

Lack of Gender Role Models

In nine cases out of ten the custodial parent is the mother, and fully half of all divorce-children living with their mother have had no contact with their father for at least a full year. Only one child in ten sees his noncustodial parent as often as once a week. Overall, only about one young person in five is able to maintain a close relationship with both parents. Joint child custody receives a lot of publicity, but it remains unusual. Most children of divorce live solely with their mothers and have little opportunity for experiencing a male role model in the home. By the way, studies show that remarriage makes fathers particularly likely to reduce involvement with the children from their previous marriage. What's more, Gallup youth surveys show that three out of four teenagers age thirteen to seventeen think it is too easy for people in this country to get divorced.[7]

The Unbearable Pain of Loss

Ask most kids how they feel about their parents' divorce and they may struggle to put it into words, but you can count on it being the most painful thing they have ever experienced. In a survey of seven hundred junior high school students, asking them to rate a number of life events in terms of stressfulness, the only thing students ranked as more stressful than parental divorce was death of a parent or close family member. Parental divorce received a higher rating than the death of a friend, being "physically hit" by a parent, feeling that no one likes them, or being seriously injured.[8] The emotional trauma and pain of losing your parents through the dissolution of their marriage is, without question, one of the most significant factors contributing to the struggles teens cope with in the aftermath of parental divorce.

The Gender Factor

Divorce more seriously affects boys than girls, and older boys show more significant emotional and academic problems than younger boys. Relative to boys, girls appear to make a more satisfactory adjustment over time.

Parental Emotional Health

Another factor that may add to the struggle teens have with parental divorce is the emotional stability, or lack of it, in either parent. Parents who are less able to accomplish their parenting tasks because of the toll divorce is taking on them personally, are obviously less likely to be there for their kids. These parents may be more likely to place unrealistic maturity demands on their children, be more inconsistent with discipline approaches, and less affectionate and involved with them.

Case Description

Monica, a sophomore in high school, arrived home from a typical school day to find her father packing boxes and moving out of the house. That was the first she learned that her parents were getting a divorce. She knew that her mom and dad had a rocky marriage, but since she was small they had reassured her that they were in love and that nothing would break them apart. Monica held on to their promises and believed them. When her father told her that he was leaving her mother, Monica ran from the house and just kept running. She didn't know where to turn. Some of her friends at school had parents who were divorced, but she didn't want to talk to them. The only thing that got her to go home late that evening was remembering her little brother. She couldn't imagine him going through this on his own. So she returned home to comfort him and eventually to put the pieces of her fractured life back together.

✔ HOW PARENTS CAN HELP

The following strategies for helping an adolescent struggling with a parental divorce can be used effectively by parents; however, every parent-child relationship is unique, and some of them may be more pertinent to your situation than others. As with every significant adolescent struggle, it is best for parents to work alongside a competent counselor. With this in mind, the following is offered as a way to help you facilitate the helping process at home with your teenager.

Expect Serious Grief

Adolescents who have seen their own parents divorced will mourn the death of that marriage, just as they would mourn the death of a parent. The signs of sorrow will keep popping us as they work through denial, anger, bargaining, and depression (see the Grief chapter in this book for more information on these stages). So as you implement any of the following strategies, be sure to keep in mind that the young person's peace and acceptance—the final stage of grief—will not come quickly. In addition, it can be quite therapeutic for an adolescent to learn from a counselor what the stages of grief are and how his or her parents may be going through similar experiences.

Allow for Anger

Of all the stages of grief resulting from parental divorce, anger is the one that is most likely to linger and be expressed. And after being left in a lonely position, that the young person's resentment leads to plenty of anger is certainly understandable. They are angry because their parents broke up. Because they didn't try harder. Because they are now unhappy and miserable on account of something that they didn't cause. They may have a seemingly endless stream of angry emotions that they can't control. Give them a place where they can vent their anger and help them express it in ways that are not violent or damaging (see the Anger chapter in this book).

Expect a Guilt Trip

In addition to plenty of anger, you can expect many young people in this painful situation to carry around a great deal of guilt. In the early months after divorce, young people can become plagued by feelings of guilt. *I should have done more to keep them together*, they may say to themselves. No matter what the reasons are in reality and no matter what their parents tell them, they often feel that they are somehow responsible for their parents' split. Counselors can also help to alleviate some of this false guilt by helping them focus on rational thoughts about their mom and dad's situation. This is far easier with adolescents than with young children, but don't expect this to be easy. Some teenagers are convinced they could have done more to keep mom and dad together. So do what you can to lighten their load of guilt (see the Guilt chapter in this book).

Help Prevent School Problems

Children of divorce often struggle to maintain their normal performance in school. One study even found that they are five times more likely to be expelled or suspended. Even in Wallerstein's middle-class sample, thirteen percent of the youngsters had dropped out of school altogether.[9] Help them avoid school-related problems by ensuring that they get the academic help they need. Consider coordinating your efforts with a competent tutor or in meetings with teachers. For additional assistance in this area, you may find the Schoolwork chapter of this book helpful.

Explore School Programs

School-based interventions for young people who have experienced their parents' divorce are being implemented in an increasing number of communities. Research has found that school-based interventions help counter the adverse effects of divorce.[10] One school-based study found that "children of divorce who perceived themselves as having more overall support had lower scores on measures of post-divorce difficulties, anxiety, and worry, and higher scores on measures of openness about the divorce and positive resources."[11] The implication from this and other studies is that emotional support in the school setting is effective in helping children of divorce cope, and these programs can augment the parents' and counselor's efforts with young people. As you evaluate such programs, look for those that consider developmental stages, parent and teacher involvement, structured activities, and skill building.

Help Teenagers Avoid Triangulation

The challenge for the teenager whose parents have divorced is not to be "tri-angled" into taking sides, where one parent becomes the undisputed victim and relationships are severed. This typically occurs when young people are made to feel obligated to carry information about one parent to the other. Make it clear that this is not the case and that the child should never be a go-between. Let them know that it is legitimate to stay out of the middle by saying something to either parent like, "I don't feel comfortable talking to you about Mother/Father." You can also suggest that they say "I don't know" to questions they feel uncomfortable answering from one parent about the other. The point is that children need not carry this kind of burden and they need you to let them know it's okay.

Don't Expect the Stepfamily to Solve Problems

On the surface, the stepfamily is thought to be a reasonably good substitute for a child's natural family of both parents. It provides two adult role models and is typically at an economic advantage over single-parent households. However, it must be understood that the stepfamily does not recreate the nuclear family for the teenager. It does not put the family back together again. Surprisingly, in fact, children from stepfamilies have a behavioral profile much more like that of single-parent children than that of children from natural two-parent families. Indeed, remarriage of a parent can add to, rather than subtract from, the stress on the adolescent. As a parent, therefore, it is imperative that you understand this and not assume that the young person is going to automatically feel good about being in a blended family.

Beware of Important Dates

Christmas, Thanksgiving, Mother's Day, Father's Day—any occasion that calls for traditional celebrations and remembrances can be painful and awkward for the child whose parents have divorced. Indeed it can be difficult to know how to best handle these occasions. Divorced parents can help ease some of this inevitable difficulty by simply exploring these issues with the young person. Have them express how they hope these occasions might be and then have them imagine more realistically how they will be. While each situation is unique, you can explore possible coping strategies that fit the situation by having the adolescent come up with solutions with you.

Beware of Suicide Risk

Research makes it clear: Suicide rates for children of divorce are much higher than for children from intact families.[12] Interestingly, death of a parent does not correlate with teen suicide, but family instability or disruption is one of the leading causes of suicide among teenagers.[13] After surveying more than 750 families at random, researchers in one study divided the children into those who had never attempted suicide and those who had done so at least once. The two groups differed little in age, family income, race, and religion. But those who attempted suicide were more likely to live in nonintact family settings than were the nonattempters. More than half of the attempters lived in households with no more than one biological parent.[14] In another study, it was found that three out of four teenage suicides occur in households where a parent has been absent.[15] The bottom line is that you need to beware of signs of potential suicide. These are noted in detail in the Suicide chapter of this book.

Expect Long-term Effects

In Judith Wallerstein's landmark study on how divorce impacts children, she found that five and ten years after the divorce had occurred negative results were still quite staggering. In overview they look like this: initially, two-thirds of all the children showed symptoms of stress, and half thought their lives had been destroyed by the divorce. Five years down the road, over a third were still seriously disturbed (even more disturbed than they had been initially, in fact), and another third were having psychological difficulties. A surprisingly large number remained angry at their parents. After a decade, 45 percent of the children were doing well, 14 percent were succeeding in some areas but failing in others, and 41 percent were still doing quite poorly. This last group "were entering adulthood as worried, underachieving, self-deprecating, and sometimes angry young men and women."[16] In addition to their emotional struggles, often with depression, many felt sorrow over their childhoods and fear about their own marriage and child-rearing prospects.

Know When to Refer

Refer adolescents who are struggling with parental divorce to a counselor or psychologist when, over time, they are feeling increasingly angry or depressed.

☑ HOW PROFESSIONALS CAN HELP

The following strategy for helping an adolescent struggling with a parental divorce is commonly used by counselors. It is presented here as a way to inform you, as a parent, and help you seek the best possible professional help you can for the adolescent in your care.

Facilitate Expression of Feelings

Adolescents are often reluctant to communicate their feelings with their divorced parents since they mistakenly believe that open communication with their parents will increase the stress that is already apparent in the troubled atmosphere. However, open communication can actually reduce the anxiety that is experienced by the family members and can also aid in enhancing the young person's self-concept. A counselor can facilitate this process by having the adolescent write a letter to both parents. Even if the letter, at least for now, will not be delivered, but only used as a way to help them express their feelings.

Where to Go for Additional Help

Buchanan, C. *Adolescents After Divorce.* Cambridge, Mass.: Harvard University Press, 1996.

Emery, R. E. *Marriage, Divorce, and Children's Adjustment.* New York: Sage Publishers, 1999.

Isler, C. *Caught in the Middle: A Teen Guide to Custody.* New York: Rosen Publishing Group, 2000.

Johnston, J.R., and V. Roseby. *In the Name of the Child: A Developmental Approach to Understanding and Helping Children of Conflicted and Violent Divorce.*

Lansky, V. *Vicki Lansky's Divorce Book for Parents: Helping Your Children Cope with Divorce and Its Aftermath.* Deephaven, Minn.: Book Peddlers, 1996.

Murray, S. *Divorce Recovery for Teenagers.* Grand Rapids: Zondervan, 1990.

Rothchild, G. *Dear Mom and Dad: What Kids of Divorce Really Want to Say to Their Parents.* New York: Pocket Books, 1999.

Sommers-Flanagan, R., and C. Elander. *Don't Divorce Us: Kids' Advice to Divorcing Parents.* Washington, D.C.: American Counseling Association, 1999.

Teyber, E. *Helping Children Cope with Divorce.* San Francisco: Jossey-Bass, 1996.

Wallerstein, J. S., and S. Blakeslee. *Second Chances: Men, Women, and Children a Decade After Divorce.* New York: Ticknor & Fields, 1990.

Parents Without Partners, Inc., 401 North Michigan Avenue, Chicago, IL 60611– 4267. 312-644-6610. This nonprofit organization is devoted to the welfare and interests of single parents and their children. Single parents may join one of more than five hundred local chapters. For additional information contact the local chapter in your area.

Stepfamily Association of America, Inc., 215 Centennial Mall South, Lincoln, NE 68508. 800-735-0329. This educational association is for individuals who want to learn about stages of stepfamily development. The *Stepfamilies* quarterly newsletter includes research, book reviews, and information for professionals who work with stepfamilies.

Notes

1. *USA Today* 124 (May 1996): 8.

2. K. Zinsmeister, "Divorce's Toll on Children," *American Enterprise* 7 (May/June 1996): 39.

3. M. Gallagher, "Marriage-Saving," *National Review* 51 (November 8, 1999): 38.

4. M. Zuckerman, "Children of Divorced Parents," *U.S. News & World Report* 114 (April 12, 1993): 72.

5. H. Marano, "Divorce and Children," *Psychology Today* 31 (March/April 1998): 19.

6. B. W. Dafoe, "Family Life," *Policy Review* 85 (September/October 1997): 58.

7. K. Zinsmeister, "Divorce's Toll on Children," *American Enterprise* 7 (May/June 1996): 39.

8. Ibid.

9. J. S. Wallerstein, "Children of Divorce: Report of a Ten-Year Follow-up of Early Latency-Age Children," *American Journal of Orthopsychiatry* 57 (1987): 199–211.

10. J. L. Pedro-Carroll, L. J. Alpert-Gillis, and E. L. Cowen, "Prevention Interventions for Children of Divorce," *Journal of Primary Prevention* 18 (1997): 5–23.

11. E. L. Cowen, J. L. Pedro-Carroll, and L. J. Alpert-Gillis, "Relationships Between Support and Adjustment Among Children of Divorce," *Journal of Child Psychology and Psychiatry* 31 (1990): 727–35.

12. S. Larson and D. Larson, "Divorce: A Hazard to Your Health?" *Physician* (May/June 1990): 16.

13. F. L. Nelson, "Youth Suicide in California: A Comparative Study of Perceived Causes and Interventions," *Community Mental Health Journal* 24 (1988): 31–42.

14. C. N. Velez and P. Cohen, "Suicidal Behavior and Ideation in a Community Sample of Children: Maternal and Youth Reports," *Journal of the American Academy of Child and Adolescent Psychiatry*, 273 (1988): 349–56.

15. J. B. Eshtain, "Family Matters: The Plight of America's Children," *Christian Century* (July 1993): 14–21.

16. J. S. Wallerstein, "Children of Divorce", 199–211.

PARENTS

✓ WHAT THE STRUGGLE LOOKS LIKE

Mark Twain said, "When I was seven my father knew everything. When I was fourteen my father knew nothing. But when I was twenty-one I was amazed how much the old man had learned in just seven years."

While teenagers usually do grow out of their struggles with Mom and Dad, that doesn't offer much solace to adolescents or to their parents. The problem is almost inevitable. Accounts of stress and strain between adolescents and their elders date back virtually as far as recorded history. Despite considerable love between most teens and their parents, they can't help sparring. Increasing autonomy in adolescence almost necessitates difficult periods for adolescents and parents. Parents need to be needed. Adolescents need not to need them. Haim Ginott, in *Between Parent and Teenager*, wrote, "Teenagers are like a person needing a loan but wishing they were financially independent."[1]

Although adolescence is not a tumultuous ordeal for most families, research reveals that more than 20 percent of adolescents experience excessive argumentativeness directed at either parent (more often with their mothers than with their fathers).[2] Conflict between adolescents and their parents is different from conflict between peers. With parents the conflict is over both content, as in how late to stay out, and the process by which decisions are to be made. In other words, both the rules and the way the rules are made may become subjects of controversy. The process usually relates to a perceived lack of freedom by adolescents.

The content of parent-adolescent struggles frequently focuses on one of the following areas.[3]

- *Social life and customs.* This probably creates more discord than any other area. It includes conflict over everything from teenagers' choice of friends to the choice of clothes and hairstyles. One of the most common complaints of parents is that their teens are never home and spend no time with the family.[4] Curfew hours, dating, and certain activities are also examples of social-life conflicts.
- *Responsibility issues.* Parents want teenagers to care for their personal belongings and to be responsible in money matters and use of the telephone and the car.
- *School performance.* Grades, study habits, attendance, and general attitudes toward learning receive a great deal of attention from parents. Sometimes pressure on adolescents to succeed also contributes to the problem.
- *Family relationships.* Quarreling with siblings, relationships with relatives, and the amount of autonomy from the family is grist for the conflict mill.
- *Values and morals.* Parents are concerned especially with their children's sexual behavior, drinking, smoking, use of drugs, basic honesty, staying out of trouble, and church attendance.

The ages of young people play a role in the focus of parent-adolescent conflicts. Girls are increasingly in conflict with their parents about boyfriends from age twelve on, with the peak years being fourteen and fifteen. The same conflict for boys about girlfriends peaks at age sixteen. The gender of adolescents is another factor influencing conflict. Girls report a greater number of family problems than do boys.[5]

Socioeconomic status is another well-documented determinant of conflict. Low-income families are more often concerned about obedience and respect, whereas middle-income families are more concerned with grades and achievement. Some researchers have also found that the larger the family, the greater degree of parent-youth conflict.[6]

Case Description

The Johnson family was in a stalemate. They had waged a heated battle for several months before the parents called a truce and retreated to a counselor for help. The atmosphere in the counselor's office during the initial session was very tense and emotionally charged. The clash was over the selection of a particular group of friends by Glen, their fourteen-year-old son. He wanted to hang out with guys his parents didn't approve of. His mother called them "ruffians" and explained that they were a terrible influence on her son. They were kids Glen had met at school, and his parents wanted him to run with the group of teens at church. Glen said his school friends were "cool," while he was quick to label his parents' choice as "a group of nerds."

About a month ago, Glen's dad laid down the law and demanded that he not see his friends on the weekend. When his father saw Glen at the mall with them on a Friday evening, the battle escalated to a fierce war. In the first session, neither Glen nor his parents could finish a sentence before one of them would jump in to defend a position. Their communication strategy was predictable: "frontal attack," resulting in rage, defensiveness, or passive withdrawal. Both sides were obsessed with being right and having their way. The issue, of course, spilled into every part of their relationship, to the point that even the smallest of annoyances would evolve into a major debate.

✔ WHY THE STRUGGLE HAPPENS

No list of reasons for parent-adolescent conflict is exhaustive. The following are some of the most frequently cited sources for chronic adolescent struggles with their parents.

Marital Instability

One of the most important influences upon young people is the emotional climate of their parents' relationship.[7] Numerous research studies emphasize the positive relationship of stable marital adjustment and family cooperation.[8] When parents are not getting along with each other, teenagers feel threatened, afraid, and angry. Unstable homes are a significant cause of adolescent rebellion against parents.

Generational Differences

Personality differences between parents and adolescents are a major source of conflict.[9] While not all adults or youths fit the stereotypes, experts have noted that parents see teenagers as too inexperienced, naïve, and reckless. While adults are careful and sometimes skeptical, adolescents tend to be adventurous and idealistic. Adults value the past and are generally contented; adolescents view the past as irrelevant and want reform. Adults want to stay youthful; adolescents want to be grown-up.[10] Perennial generational differences account for a sizable portion of parent-adolescent struggles.

Poor Communication

Parents teach communication skills to their children. If they do not model and practice effective styles of communication, they may be planting seeds for discord in the teen years. Poor parent-child communications during the earlier years backfire in adolescence with hostility and rebellion. Instead of openly discussing issues and arriving at mutually agreed upon solutions, or spending time with their adolescents in leisure activities, these parents resort to snooping, interrogating, and blaming. They do this in a futile attempt to maintain control—not to have a relationship.

Lack of Trust

Some conflict occurs because adolescents use discord as a means of testing the relational waters with their parents. Teens will put out a piece of information designed to upset or irritate their parents. They do this, consciously or not, to see whether their parents can be trusted with what is really on their teenagers' minds. If the parents overreact, they lose.[11] Deciphering these kinds of hidden messages requires sensitive and empathic parents. The more self-control and calmness parents display, the more open and sharing teenagers become.

Parental Expectations

Some parents almost see adolescence as a disease, a period of transitory sickness. Bruce Narramore's helpful book *Adolescence Is Not an Illness* is an attempt to dispel that myth.[12] The point is that many parent-adolescent struggles happen because conflicts are expected. Parents, hearing of other parents' "war stories," have stereotyped images of teenagers. Parents often create attitudes, perceptions, and responses to teenagers that are built upon myths. For example, they may have heard, and consequently believe, that adolescents are "explosive" and "totally out of control." These expectations and fears may exacerbate normal human friction.[13]

Changing Roles and Rules

Much of what was acceptable for adolescents to do when they were children is no longer acceptable now that they are teenagers. As children make the transition into adolescence, both they and their parents are redefining roles and rules. For example, they are negotiating curfew and the kinds of clothes, music, and friends they will have. Deciding what is now acceptable and unacceptable behavior may cause strain in parent–child relationships.

✅ HOW PARENTS CAN HELP

The following strategies for helping an adolescent struggling with parental issues can be used effectively by parents; however, every parent–child relationship is unique, and some of them may be more pertinent to your situation than others. As with every significant adolescent struggle, it is best for parents to work alongside a competent counselor. With this in mind, the following is offered as a way to help you facilitate the helping process at home with your teenager.

Consider Training

Being parents of adolescents can be overwhelming. At times almost all parents feel discouraged or confused. If you sense that your adolescents' struggles would be alleviated if you had better parental support and training, seek the help of a counselor for yourself.[14] Tension between parents and teens may sometimes be reduced with a little objective guidance. Often the mistakes you may have made are what stand out in your mind, to the neglect of all the positive things you've done and said. Every counselor will tell you there has never been a perfect parent. A counselor can also alert you to the fundamental dangers of overprotection, overpermissiveness, overrestrictiveness, and overmeticulousness. A number of helpful books for parents of adolescents are on the market. Some are noted at the end of this section.

Learn Fair Fighting

Adolescents and parents who are in conflict often engage in "dirty fighting." For example, they resort to switching the subject, bringing up more than one accusation at a time, interrupting, attributing guilt, sarcasm, or silence. When chronic arguing of this nature is the problem, it is generally best for counselors to see both the adolescent and the parents at the same time, at least for a few sessions. Together, you can learn how to fight fairly.

The technique outlined below was developed by George Bach. It is a means to reaching a resolution, most typically after a complaint or frustration doesn't seem to simmer down after an emotional blowup. The fair fight allows parents and adolescents to express their frustrations in a more rational mode. Bach states that "the only kinds of specific issues that are not negotiable under the fair fight format are disputes over behaviors that are beyond willful control and therefore not open to change by an act of will."[15] These include alcohol, smoking, and problems of mood swings or social withdrawal. The nine steps of fair fighting emphasize how a conflict is resolved rather than the content of the dispute. The following is a brief summary of the strategy as applied to the parent-adolescent struggle. A more detailed description can be found in George Bach's book, *Creative Aggression*.

Step 1. An adolescent with a complaint asks the parent to engage in a fair fight. If the parent agrees, a time and place for the fight is set.

Step 2. Neutral people (family members) should be present at the agreed-upon time. Before beginning the fair fight, the adolescent and the parent should have a strategy session with a neutral observer to help define the complaint. The strategy session should be open so that all who are involved can listen.

Step 3. The initiator of the fight, in this case the adolescent, states the complaint.

Step 4. The parent must repeat the complaint, not word for word, but accurately reflecting its essence and the feelings of the adolescent. From this point on in the fight, each participant must repeat every statement made by the other during the fight.

Step 5. The adolescent states a "demand for change." This must be a change in behavior, not attitude.

Step 6. The parent responds to the complaint and the demand for the change.

Step 7. The fair fight alternates back and forth with direct, simple statements.

Step 8. The fight is ended when parent and adolescent agree on change, one of the two rejects a resolution, or when the two sides establish specific conditions for partial change.

Step 9. At a future meeting the success or failure of the agreement is discussed by the parent and adolescent.

✔ HOW PROFESSIONALS CAN HELP

The following strategies for helping an adolescent struggling with parental issues are commonly used by counselors. They are presented here as a way to inform you, as a parent, and help you seek the best possible professional help you can for the adolescent in your care.

Provide Comfort

Adolescents love and resent their parents at the same time. They themselves find this ambivalence difficult to accept. They understandably think that something is inherently wrong for them to feel two ways about the people who provide for them. Sensitive counselors can spare young people a great deal of unhealthful guilt by showing them how "normal" their mixed-up feelings are, that the conflict is a natural part of growing up. Counselors can give voice to adolescents' ambivalent feelings. For example, "You seem to feel two ways about your dad. You admire him, but he also makes you angry." A calm, uncritical statement like this helps youth see that their "crazy" feelings are understandable. This is far better than saying, "Make up your mind! Which way do you feel?"

Understand Family Origins

While most parents try to do their best in rearing their children, sometimes teenagers' conflicts with parents stem from sincere but unhealthy parenting. Effective counselors are aware of these styles and can empower you to break out of unhealthful ways. Keith Olson notes several patterns of damaging parenting styles that influence parent-adolescent struggles.

Perfectionistic parents don't see good as good enough. Their teenagers can never do anything right and consequently suffer from feelings of inadequacy.

Rejecting parents are perhaps the most damaging because they direct their rejection squarely at their children instead of at their performance. The most extreme form comes in physical abuse.

Overprotective parents have a difficult time letting go, and they continue to do things for the children long after such help is necessary. This creates an aching feeling of helplessness and inadequacy within adolescents.

Overindulgent parents give too many things to their children. The result is usually selfish, demanding adolescents who believe everyone else owes them.

Overpermissive parents provide a free environment with few rules and few expectations. Adolescents who are brought up in this way usually make disastrous interpersonal adjustments because they are not accustomed to adapting to others.

Severe parents are harsh and excessive in their punishment. While adolescents reared in these homes carry a huge pack of guilt, they will eventually rebel against this form of treatment (often as a way of hurting the severe parents).

Inconsistent parents shift from one pattern to another without any logical rationale. This confusion leaves adolescents with no solid moral basis to live by. They often become skilled manipulators and make others angry.

Double-binding parents trap their adolescents in no-win situations. No matter what the adolescents do, they can't feel good. Parents use double binds as a means of subtle and insidious control.

A knowledge of these parenting styles may help you and a counselor identify potential sources of conflict and work to modify them.

Explore Communication Skills

Communication is at the heart of harmony between parents and children. With developing autonomy in the teen years, adolescents deserve more egalitarian communication patterns than parents developed when their teens were children.[16] How well the family negotiates this shift may be the critical factor in how smoothly they get along. Research has revealed a number of patterns of communication in families. Unspoken rules about who can talk to whom and about what are not unusual. But in some families these rules may cause so much dysfunction that teenagers who want their dads to know something tell Mom, and Mom tells Dad. Communication styles like this obviously create parent-teen problems.[17]

Effective counselors can help families implement open, honest, democratic communication and problem-solving skills that are essential if families are to overcome conflicts. Both parents and adolescents must learn a number of communication guidelines in order to maintain open and nondefensive positions and thereby avoid blaming and interrogating.

Sven Wahlroos, in *Family Communication*, lists a number of rules to help adolescents and parents speak to one another so that genuine understanding is achieved.[18]

- Remember that actions speak louder than words.
- Define what is important and ignore what isn't.
- Be as realistic as possible.
- Be clear and specific.
- Be as positive as possible.
- Check out your assumptions.
- Recognize that it is all right for two people to view the same thing differently.
- Recognize that your family members know you well.
- Keep discussions from turning into arguments.
- Become aware of and express your true feelings.
- Accept all feelings and try to understand them.
- Be considerate and respectful.

- Do not preach or lecture; ask questions instead.
- Do not use excuses.
- Do not nag, yell, or whine.
- Know when to use humor and when to be serious.
- Above all, listen.

A list like this is much easier to talk about than it is to follow. You may wish to highlight and practice two or three of these rules in specific situations. Trying to practice the entire list at once may be overwhelming.

In a survey of adolescents, one researcher collected teenagers' advice to their parents on communication. Here it is: (1) Listen and understand; (2) be up front and honest; (3) don't cop out when tough subjects come up; (4) trust us and let us learn from our own mistakes; (5) don't live in the past; (6) discipline, don't dominate; (7) compromise; (8) show that you love, care, and will be there.[19]

While effective communication may not be a panacea, and it may seem too simple to some, research has made it abundantly clear that learning skills such as clarifying content and reflecting feeling is well worth the effort.[20]

Explore Runaway Potential

A frightening number of adolescents see running away as their only alternative to conflict with their parents. These teens survive on the streets and are often referred to as "children of the night." They turn to drugs, crime, and prostitution as the means of coping with their pain. Both runaway girls and boys are often offered a roof over their heads and the promise of protection if they sell their bodies. In a strange way, a dangerous pimp becomes their substitute parent. Some runaways eventually return home; others make it on their own or die young. Most homeless street kids are from white, middle-class, mainstream homes. However, a crisis such as divorce or physical or sexual abuse by a parent usually precipitates such drastic behavior.[21]

Counselors working with adolescents who struggle with severe conflicts with their parents consider the possibility that young people may run away. Adolescents who are thinking about running away are typically depressed, insecure, impulsive, and wrestling with seemingly unmanageable problems.[22] Arguments with parents are the number-one reason young people give for leaving home.[23] The National Runaway Youth Program promotes assistance to youths who are apt to run away and vulnerable to dangerous encounters. Aid is offered nationwide through this toll-free number: 800-999-9999. Your community social service agencies may be of assistance with this problem as well.

Know When to Refer

Refer adolescents who struggle with chronic conflict with their parents to competent counselors or psychologists when, over time, you feel more out of control and increasingly frustrated.

Where to Go for Additional Help

Bach, G. B., and H. Goldberg. *Creative Aggression: The Art of Assertive Living*. New York: Avon, 1974.

Bell, R., and L. Wildflower. *Talking with Your Teenager: A Book for Parents*. New York: Random House, 1983.

Bell, V. *Getting Out of Your Kids' Faces and into Their Hearts*. Grand Rapids: Zondervan, 1994.

Campbell, D. *How to Really Love Your Teenager*. Wheaton, Ill.: Victor, 1981.

Cloud, H., and J. Townsend. *Raising Great Kids*. Grand Rapids: Zondervan, 1999.

Davitz, L., and J. Davitz. *How to Live (Almost) Happily with a Teenager*. Minneapolis: Winston, 1982.

Elias, Z. *How Not to Embarrass Your Kids: 250 Don'ts for Parents of Teens*. New York: Warner Books, 1999.

Ginott, H. G. *Between Parent and Teenager*. New York: Avon, 1969.

Gnagey, T. D. *How to Put Up with Parents: A Guide for Teenagers*. Ottawa, Ill.: Facilitation House, 1975.

Habermas, R. *How to Have Real Conversations with Your Teen: Tips for Parents from Veteran Youth Workers—with Teens of Their Own!* Cincinnati: Standard Publishing, 1998.

Habermas, R. T. *Raising Teens While They're Still In Preschool: What Experts Advise for Successful Parenting*. Joplin, Mo.: College Press, 1998.

Habermas, R., and D. Olshine. *How to Have Real Conversation with Your Teen*. Cincinnati: Standard Publishing.

Haggard, T. *Confident Parents, Exceptional Teens: Creating a Teen-Friendly Family*. Grand Rapids: Zondervan, 1999.

Leman, K. *Becoming the Parent God Wants You to Be*. Colorado Springs, Colo.: NavPress, 1998.

Lucas, R. L. *Proactive Parenting*. Eugene, Ore.: Harvest House, 1993.

McCarty, R. J. *Tips for Raising Teens: A Primer for Parents*. New York: Paulist Press, 1998.

McIntire, R. *Losing Control of Your Teenager: Ten Rules for Raising an Adult While Keeping a Friend*. Amherst, Mass.: Human Resources Development Press, 1985.

Meier, P. D. *Christian Child-Rearing and Personality Development*. Grand Rapids: Baker, 1977.

Narramore, S. B. *Help! I'm a Parent*. Grand Rapids: Zondervan, 1995.

_____. *Parenting with Love and Limits*. Grand Rapids: Zondervan, 1979.

_____. *You Can Be a Better Parent*. Grand Rapids: Zondervan, 1979.

_____. *Adolescence Is Not an Illness*. Old Tappan, N.J.: Revell, 1980.

Patterson, G., and M. Forgatch. *Parents and Adolescents Living Together*. Eugene, Ore.: Castalia Publishing, 1987.

Ridenour, F. *What Teenagers Wish Their Parents Knew About Kids.* Waco, Tex.: Word, 1982.

Ross, L. *A Kid's Goal-Setting Guide (for Parents).* Wheaton, Ill.: Tyndale, 1985.

Scott, B. *Relief for Hurting Parents.* Nashville: Oliver-Nelson, 1989.

Stinnett, N., and M. O'Donnell. *Good Kids: How You and Your Kids Can Successfully Navigate the Teen Years.* New York: Doubleday, 1996.

Weinhause, E., and K. Friedman. *Stop Struggling with Your Teen.* New York: Penguin, 1984.

Worthington, E. L., and K. Worthington. *Helping Parents Make Disciples.* Grand Rapids: Baker, 1995.

Notes

1. H. G. Ginott, *Between Parent and Teenager* (New York: Avon, 1969).

2. J. D. Balswick and C. Macrides, "Parental Stimulus for Adolescent Rebellion," *Adolescence* 10 (1975): 253–66.

3. J. A. Hall, "Parent-Adolescent Conflict: An Empirical Review," *Adolescence* 22 (1987): 767–89.

4. M. Felson and M. Gottfredson, "Social Indicators of Adolescent Activities Near Peers and Parents," *Journal of Marriage and the Family* 46 (1984): 709–14.

5. D. R. Papini et al., "Early Adolescent Age and Gender Differences in Patterns of Emotional Self-Disclosure to Parents and Friends," *Adolescence* 25 (1990): 959–76.

6. A. Bell, "Family Structure and Parent-Adolescent Relationships: Does Family Structure Really Make a Difference?" *Journal of Marriage and Family Therapy* 47 (1985): 503–8.

7. D. Olshine, "Scanning Beneath the Surface: A Look at Family Systems," *Youthworker* (May/June 1996): 34.

8. B. Burman, R. S. John, and G. Margolin, "Effects of Marital and Parent-Child Relations on Children's Adjustment," *Journal of Family Psychology* 1 (1987): 91–108.

9. D. V. Ary, T. E. Duncan, S. C. Duncan, and H. Hops, "Adolescent Problem Behavior: The Influence of Parents and Peers," *Behaviour Research and Therapy* 37 (1999): 217–30.

10. F. P. Rice, *The Adolescent: Development, Relationships and Culture* (Boston: Allyn and Bacon, 1990).

11. L. Ross, *A Kid's Goal-Setting Guide (for Parents)* (Wheaton, Ill.: Tyndale, 1985).

12. S. B. Narramore, *Adolescence Is Not an Illness* (Old Tappan, N.J.: Revell, 1980).

13. G. K. Olson, *Counseling Teenagers: The Complete Christian Guide to Understanding and Helping Adolescents* (Loveland, Colo.: Group Books, 1984).

14. C. Pilgrim, Q. Luo, K. A. Urberg, and X. Fang, "Influence of Peers, Parents, and Individual Characteristics on Adolescent Drug Use in Two Cultures," *Merrill-Palmer Quarterly* 45 (1999): 85–107.

15. G. B. Bach and H. Goldberg, *Creative Aggression: The Art of Assertive Living* (New York: Avon, 1974).

16. S. Vogl-Bauer, P. J. Kalbfleisch, and M. Teatty, "Perceived Equity, Satisfaction, and Relational Maintenance Strategies in Parent-Adolescent Dyads," *Journal of Youth and Adolescence* 28 (1999): 27–49.

17. D. J. Burnett, "Improving Parent-Adolescent Relationships: A Structured Managed Care Treatment Model," *Marriage and Family: A Christian Journal* 2 (1999): 25–36.

18. S. Wahroos, *Family Communication* (New York: Macmillan, 1974).

19. J. Normon and M. W. Harris, *The Private Life of the American Teenager* (New York: Rawson, Wade, 1981).

20. J. Alexander and B. V. Parsons, *Functional Family Therapy* (Monterey, Calif.: Brooks-Cole, 1982).

21. J. J. Christensen, "Survival on the Streets: Homeless Teens and What You Can Do To Help," *Youth!* (March 1991): 26–31.

22. B. Benalcazar, "Study of Fifteen Runaway Patients," *Adolescence* 17 (1987): 553–66.

23. E. Spillane-Grieco, "Characteristics of a Helpful Relationship: A Study of Empathetic Understanding and Positive Appeal Between Runaways and Their Parents," *Adolescence* 19 (1984): 63–75.

PEER PRESSURE

✔ WHAT THE STRUGGLE LOOKS LIKE

In a cartoon, a boy with spiked hair is talking with his dad. The caption says, "But, Dad, I gotta be different. How else can I be like the other kids?"

All of us want to please others. We want to be liked, respected, and accepted. The people around us have a substantial influence on what we do, think, and say. And it's a good thing! Our desire to accommodate ourselves to the group norm is one of the most civilizing forces in society. But it also has the potential to create a great deal of personal conflict and loss of self-esteem. This harm is perhaps greater for adolescents than for any other group.

Young people change their speech, clothing, behavior, thinking, and even values to fit in with their cohorts. Peer pressure doesn't have to be bad, however. Joining a scout troop, playing tennis, even attending church and reading the Bible can be the result of peer pressure. Traveling between the child world they left and the adult world they have not yet reached, teens turn to each other for support; that support may lead in positive directions.

But negative consequences also result from peer pressure. Dropping out of school, experimenting with drugs, racism, and shoplifting are just a few examples. Premarital sex is another behavior that is often the result of peer pressure. In fact, love is one of the least-named reasons teens give for having sex. Peer pressure is number one.[1] Negative peer pressure occurs when young people feel forced to do something they really don't want to do—something they would not have done on their own—in order to be part of the gang.

Peer pressure is not a phenomenon that suddenly occurs in adolescence. The need to be accepted by our peers is seen in our earliest friendships. But it is during adolescence that we become more acutely aware of peer pressure because the stakes and risks are higher. The natural and healthful individuation process may explode into a tumultuous eruption of rebellion against parental values because of peer influences.

Case Description

Connie, a fifteen-year-old, came to counseling at the insistence of her mom and dad. She was doing about average in school and attended her youth group at church frequently. But Connie's recent behavior caused her parents a great deal of concern. First of all, she was part of a neighborhood party that got out of hand and had to be broken up by the police. She was brought home by the father of one of her friends, and he reported to Connie's parents that she had been drinking.

This was a surprise to her parents. They didn't suspect that Connie was involved in this kind of activity. At church and at home she seemed like a different person. She dressed differently and acted differently. Her parents later learned that Connie would take a different set of clothes to school in her gym bag and change in the restroom before classes began. At school she didn't hang out with her church friends, but was trying to break into a group of students that had very different values. Her parents were especially concerned about the older boys she was dating. After three or four counseling sessions, Connie admitted that she would do just about anything to be accepted by "the popular" students. She felt phony and hollow.

Before examining the causes and interventions for peer pressure, it may be helpful to take a quick look at the kinds of peer groups influencing today's teens. Sociologists have discovered a variety of specific high school groups:

Ravers frequent all-night parties (raves) in secret locations and are known for consuming designer drugs.

Goths are fascinated with death. They wear black clothes and paint their fingernails dark colors.

Straight Edgers look like skinheads, but these clean-living kids crusade against alcohol, drugs, and animal products—not minorities.

Jocks are usually males who are consumed by athletics. They tend to make average to above-average grades; they are clean-cut, friendly, and self-confident. More recently, Jocks are referred to as *White Caps* (mocking their well-worn baseball caps).

Motorheads are also usually male, and they are consumed by cars. They make below-average grades, are rude to teachers, and wear clothes dirtied by working on their cars.

Whiggers are white kids who adopt the hip-hop dress, music, and speech of the inner city. The term is banned as offensive in many schools.

Freaks consist of both males and females who are into drugs. (Some pot smokers these days are also known as *420s*—the term's origins are disputed.) They are unconcerned about school and frequently skip classes.[2]

Rah-rahs are the socially elite, the female equivalent of jocks.

Politicos are the governing elite who run student government. They intercede with the school administration and are generally well liked.

Intellectuals are the academic elite, known for their ability to breeze through classes with ease.

Greasers are throwbacks to the fifties and tend toward the delinquent side. They smoke marijuana, drink, and are ambivalent about school.

Grinds are a very small group of math wizards who spend most of their time in math lab.

With the exception of the politicos, all of these groups occupy specific territory on school campuses—places where they congregate when not in class.

Students who do not fit into one of these sociological categories make up the silent majority. They attend school regularly, are involved in various interest groups off and on campus, and have friends like themselves.[3]

✔ WHY THE STRUGGLE HAPPENS

Many factors influence struggles with negative peer pressure. The following are just a few of the most commonly cited "causes."

Insecurity

The more insecure young people are about their own worth, the more they tend to look to others for direction in making their decisions. In their need to belong, adolescents are susceptible to the influences of their peers. It helps keep them from "looking stupid" in their friends' eyes if they are doing just what their friends would do. Teenagers achieve a false sense of security that quickly disappears when they encounter even a small dose of rejection.

Parental Relationships

One of the strongest and most consistent findings concerning peer pressure is its relationship to family interactions. Research links high peer conformity to poor parent-child relationships.[4] Antagonism, rejection, poor communication, extreme authoritarianism, and permissiveness at home are strongly linked with adolescents' susceptibility to peer influence.[5]

Lack of Assertiveness

Learning to "just say no" isn't always that easy. Some adolescents give in to negative peer pressure because they do not have the interpersonal skills that are needed to stay their ground, express their genuine feelings, and choose their own behavior.[6] They are like a feather in the wind, blown about by any prevailing opinion and unable to influence their environment.

Faulty Thinking

Sometimes young people act on beliefs that are irrational—beliefs that have little or no basis in reality. With little evidence they conclude, "I have to do whatever anyone else wants to do in order to be his or her friend," or, "I have to dress a certain way and talk about certain things in order to be popular." They base all of their decisions on faulty thinking.

✔ HOW PARENTS CAN HELP

The following strategies for helping an adolescent struggling with peer pressure can be used effectively by parents; however, every parent-child relationship is unique, and some of them may be more pertinent to your situation than others. As with every significant adolescent struggle, it is best for parents to work alongside a competent counselor. With this in mind, the following is offered as a way to help you facilitate the helping process at home with your teenager.

Ease Your Concerns

Parents generally worry about the impact of peer pressure on their children, but most of their worries are unfounded. Most adolescents continue to live by their parents' values regarding religion, education, politics, and careers. Although adolescents spend less time with their parents and more time with their friends than they did as children, they still turn to their parents for advice and guidance on the important issues in their lives. Moreover, when asked who is most influential and most important in their lives, most adolescents name their parents, not their friends.[7]

Be sure to help them see the big picture of adolescent transition. During teen years, conflict between parents and children is at its height. Typical adolescents are overly concerned about establishing their independence, while at the same time, most parents are overly concerned with maintaining control to counteract the presumed peer pressure. Parents often worry that the first year or so of adolescence is only the tip of the iceberg, that their conflicts are going to get worse rather than better. In reality, however, the reverse usually occurs after that first year or two.

Explore Helpful Pressures

Adolescents may be empowered by examining in what ways their peers are influencing them. One of the least threatening means to heighten this awareness is to help adolescents explore how their friends influence them in positive ways. For example, friends may help them try out for a team, get better grades, get in shape, run for class office, save money, and so on. This discussion may lead to an exploration of how they are being influenced in negative ways.

Boost Self-Confidence

Many of the principles discussed in the section on inferiority (for example, developing positive self-statements, modifying unrealistic standards, confronting destructive tendencies, and exploring theology) can be used to help boost the confidence of adolescents who battle peer pressure.

Help Them Challenge the System

Teenagers often believe they must go along with the crowd to be popular. Explore with them what might happen if they were to buck the system. What if they were to walk out of a movie that offends them? Would their friends think they were wimps? How do they know? If their friends were to look down on them for standing up for their beliefs, explore the value of relationships with those people. Empower young people to question the behaviors of others and decide for themselves how they want to direct their lives.[8] Challenge teenagers to break out of the expected mold and to influence their environment. Use the illustration of a thermostat. Most young people act like thermometers. They have no control over their environment and adjust to everything around them. Thermostats, on the other hand, influence their environment. It is an old cliché, but new to most adolescents.

Know When to Refer

Refer adolescents who struggle with negative peer pressure to a competent counselor or psychologist when, over time, they feel more out of control and increasingly give in to peer influence.

☑ HOW PROFESSIONALS CAN HELP

The following strategies for helping an adolescent struggling with peer pressure are commonly used by counselors. They are presented here as a way to inform you, as a parent, and help you seek the best possible professional help you can for the adolescent in your care.

Take an Inventory of Their Experiences

Counselors will help adolescents achieve perspective by examining past decisions based on negative peer pressure. They may ask them to list how they have responded to situations in the past few months, how things turned out, and what they have learned in the process. They might ask whether they would do the same again. This helps them see who is "bad news" and to make conscious decisions about who will be their friends. The inventory can also help young people localize areas where they are especially prone to giving in to negative peer pressure.

Question Self-Talk

Adolescents who give in to peer pressure often have automatic thoughts that keep them from standing their own ground. They are irrational thoughts that perpetuate a fear of rejection. A student, for example, may think, "I look silly," whenever someone looks at him or her. The thought just pops into mind automatically. Counselors will help adolescents question the validity of these thoughts by first discovering what their self-talk is. These thoughts are usually lightning fast and difficult to catch.

To identify them, a counselor will have counselees recall the thoughts they had just prior to the start of a feeling. For example, what judgments of their experience did they make just before feeling insecure? It may be helpful to reconstruct a situation that led to giving in to something they didn't want to do. Counselors will lift out the self-talk statements and explore how changing their thinking (that is, substituting rational thoughts for faulty logic) may help them resist giving in. They may have them imagine potential situations that may be difficult, and help them prepare self-talk statements that will give them inner strength and self-respect. For example, "I can stand up for what I believe," "I am a person of integrity," or "I believe in me."[9]

Teach Assertiveness

Perhaps the most effective strategy for helping adolescents withstand negative peer influence is assertiveness training. It has been found to help youths resist drug use, negative sexual behavior, and other actions.[10] Teenagers can learn to use nonverbal skills to bolster their ability to be assertive—to express feelings, ask for what they want, or say no to something they don't want. They can be taught to look directly at others when addressing them, maintain an open rather than a closed posture, and literally "stand their ground" by not physically backing away from others. Adolescents can also learn to be assertive by expressing their feelings and desires. Struggling adolescents often evaluate their feelings for appropriateness. They ask, "What *should* I be feeling?" rather than, "What *am* I feeling?" Once they have learned to identify their feelings, counselors will encourage young people to express them in peer groups.

For more information on assertiveness training you may find *Your Perfect Right* (Alberti and Emmons) and *Asserting Yourself* (Bower) helpful. For assertiveness training within a Christian context, *Beyond Assertiveness* (Faul and Augsburger) and *The Assertive Christian* (Emmons and Richardson) are useful.

Where to Go for Additional Help

Adler, R. B. *Confidence in Communication: A Guide to Assertive and Social Skills.* New York: Holt, Rinehart, 1974.

Alberti, R. E., and M. L. Emmons. *Your Perfect Right: A Guide to Assertive Behavior.* San Luis Obispo, Calif.: Impact Publishers, 1978.

Bower, G., and S. Bower. *Asserting Yourself: A Practical Guide for Positive Change.* Reading, Mass.: Addison-Wesley, 1976.

Emmons, M., and D. Richardson. *The Assertive Christian.* Minneapolis: Winston, 1981.

Faul, J., and D. W. Augsburger. *Beyond Assertiveness.* Waco, Tex.: Word, 1983.

Hartley, F. *Dare to Be Different.* Old Tappan, N.J.: Revell, 1980.

Kaplan, L. S. *Coping with Peer Pressure.* New York: Rosen Publishers, 1999.

Sanders, B. *Tough Turf: A Teen Survival Manual.* Old Tappan, N.J.: Revell, 1986.

Scott, S. *How to Say No and Keep Your Friends.* Amherst, Mass.: Human Resource Development Press, 1986.

_____. *Peer Pressure Reversal: An Adult Guide to Developing a Responsible Child.* Amherst, Mass.: Human Resource Development Press, 1985.

Welch, E. T. *When People Are Big and God Is Small: Overcoming Peer Pressure, Codependency, and the Fear of Man.* Phillipsburg, N.J.: P & R Publishers, 1997.

Notes

1. *Psychology Today* (May 1989): 10.

2. M. H. Leona, "An Examination of Adolescent Clique Language in a Suburban Secondary School," *Adolescence* 13 (1978): 496–502.

3. R. W. Larkin, *Suburban Youth in Cultural Crisis* (New York: Oxford University Press, 1979).

4. C. Jackson, "Initial and Experimental Stages of Tobacco and Alcohol Use During Late Childhood: Relation to Peer, Parent, and Personal Risk Factors," *Addictive Behaviors* 22 (1997): 685–98.

5. J. E. Marcia, "Identity in Adolescence," in *Handbook of Adolescent Psychology*, ed. J. Adelson (New York: Wiley, 1980).

6. K. A. Urberg, S. M. Degirmencioglu, and C. Pilgrim, "Close Friend and Group Influence on Adolescent Cigarette Smoking and Alcohol Use," *Developmental Psychology* 33 (1997): 834–44.

7. J. Williamson and L. Campbell, "Parents and Their Children Comment on Adolescence," *Adolescence* 20 (1985): 745–48.

8. A. D. Farrell and K. S. White, "Peer Influences and Drug Use Among Urban Adolescents: Family Structure and Parent-Adolescent Relationship as Protective Factors," *Journal of Consulting and Clinical Psychology* 66 (1998): 248–58.

9. A. T. Beck, *Cognitive Therapy and Emotional Disorders* (New York: New American Library, 1979).

10. J. M. Williams and D. W. Hall, "Conformity to Peer Influence: The Impact of Assertion Training on College Students," *Journal of College Student Development* 29 (1988): 466–71.

PHOBIAS

☑ WHAT THE STRUGGLE LOOKS LIKE

Fear is both common and natural. Some people are afraid to walk through certain sections of town late at night. Others fear vicious dogs or tornadoes. Those are reasonable, appropriate fears that help us survive.

A phobia, however, is irrational and inappropriate. A phobia is experienced in situations that present no real threat. It is not adaptive or natural. A phobia is an intense, irrational fear that greatly interferes with a person's life. The fear revolves around some object, event, activity, or situation. As a result, phobic individuals begin to structure most, if not all, of their daily activities around that which they fear. And they will do almost anything to avoid confronting that fear.

Most people define their behavior based on prior knowledge. People with phobias, however, tend to think the worst of a situation. For example, people who are claustrophobic in a small dark room might think the ceiling will collapse on them or that they will suffocate because they will get trapped with no air.

It can be difficult to distinguish a phobic person from one who is experiencing a panic disorder, but there are distinctions. A panic attack seems to appear suddenly, with no obvious precipitating factor. A phobia, by contrast, appears to be much more directed and specific. Phobic people are overcome with anxiety only in the presence of what they fear (e.g., an elevator or a dog). The section on panic attacks may be helpful for further comparisons.

Approximately seventy-seven out of a thousand people in the general population suffer from some type of phobic disorder. The most common phobia treated by therapists is agoraphobia—fear of venturing out into open or public spaces like stores, restaurants, theaters, or public transportation. Phobias are common at all levels of society, at all ages, and in both sexes.

Phobic reactions usually have three components. The first is *cognitive*. The phobic individual may report negative thoughts like "I know I am going to make a fool of myself" or "I'm going to die." The second is *behavioral*. The phobic person will generally avoid the feared situation. And last, the person may experience a whole range of *physiological* responses in the presence of phobic stimuli.[1]

Literally hundreds of phobias have been identified. In fact, the number is indefinite because phobic reactions may occur with almost any situation or object. *Blakiston's Gould Medical Dictionary* lists 368 different phobias.[2] Some common phobias along with their uncommon names are cats (ailourophobia), thunder (asterophobia), dirt (mysophobia), snakes (ophidiophobia), and stage fright (topophobia). The most widely accepted classification system, the *Diagnostic and Statistical Manual* (4th ed.), subdivides phobias into three groups: simple phobias, social phobias, and agoraphobia.[3] Counselors working with teens should be familiar with each of these phobias.

Simple Phobias

These involve maladaptive fear and avoidance of discrete objects or situations. They are sometimes called specific phobias because the range of phobic stimuli is narrower than in other phobic disorders—everything from acrophobia (fear of high places) to zoophobia (fear of animals). Some of the most common simple phobias are fear of animals and insects such as birds, cats, dogs, bees, spiders, snakes, or moths. Others include fear of disease or illness like cancer or a heart attack.[4] These phobias rarely cause a serious problem for the phobic person, unless the feared stimulus happens to be something that is commonly or out of necessity encountered (such as a person who fears elevators but lives in a high-rise apartment). Simple phobias are experienced more by women. One researcher found that 95 percent of animal phobics are women. This figure is accepted for postpubescent individuals, but before puberty, fears of animals are found commonly in boys as well as girls.[5]

Social Phobias

This is characterized by excessive anxiety in social situations such as parties, meetings, interviews, making complaints, writing in public, interacting with the opposite sex or with teachers. These people are especially fearful of potential public scrutiny and evaluation. For fear of looking ridiculous, social phobics may refuse to sit facing another person at the lunch table. They may avoid going swimming since swimming involves exposing their bodies to the view of others. This is obviously quite maladaptive since it interferes with important areas of normal social functioning and development for adolescents. Social phobia is rarely reported before puberty and most frequently begins in the late teens.[6]

Counselors must make the important distinction between adolescents struggling with social phobia and adolescents struggling with social inadequacy. Young people may experience anxiety in social situations simply because of poor social skills. This is not the same as social phobia. This has significant implications for treatment. If young people are experiencing anxiety caused by skill deficiency, anxiety reduction procedures will not be effective. They need assertiveness and social-skills training. See the section on inferiority for a discussion of this treatment approach.

Agoraphobia

This term dates back to ancient Greece and literally means "fear of the marketplace." The most common clinical feature is a fear of leaving a familiar setting. The agoraphobic becomes anxious at the thought of leaving home or being outside, particularly when alone. Many phobic persons rarely, if ever, go out in public, but they can often function fairly well within the home. Many agoraphobics also suffer from panic attacks. Fear of having a panic attack outside the home is often cited as the reason for staying home. As with panic disorders, onset of agoraphobia is generally in adolescence, and it usually follows a course of repeated episodes of anxiety interspersed with mild, diffuse anxiety. Agoraphobia is three times more likely to occur in women than in men. More than any other phobia, agoraphobia is frequently accompanied by a variety of other problems such as depression or the abuse of alcohol.

Case Description

Laura came to counseling at the insistence of her parents. Her mom and dad were prominent and wealthy members of their community. Laura was their first child and they had high expectations for her. They brought her to counseling because, according to her father, she had "low self-esteem." As it turned out, Laura was struggling with a social phobia. She would suffer intense anxiety in a social situation that she saw as potentially awkward or embarrassing. The straw that broke the camel's back for her parents was when she retreated to her room at a recent family reunion where she was expected to be with her relatives from around the country. It was apparent that Laura was not lacking social skills; she simply feared being evaluated by others. She dreaded the thought of doing something embarrassing and having others talk about it.

☑ WHY THE STRUGGLE HAPPENS

Phobias rarely materialize out of nowhere. While it is difficult to pinpoint a single causal factor, most agree that phobias are generated out of a combination of the following reasons.

Biology

Recently, biological theories have put forth the notion of "preparedness" to explain some phobic behavior. They have noticed that symptoms do not appear at random. They argue that our biological constitutions cause us to be more "prepared" to avoid certain situations or objects. In other words, certain phobias may be indicative of some sort of biological predispositions to avoid certain dangers.[7]

Conditioning

Under some circumstances phobias may be learned from frightening experiences. For example, being bitten by a dog may lead to a persistent, unreasonable fear of something that bears little relationship to the likelihood of being bitten again. Once the fear is acquired, the phobic person may extend any such excessive fear to other stimuli, such as all four-legged animals. A classic psychological experiment by John Watson demonstrated that unreasonable fears may be learned from unpleasant experiences, not only directly but indirectly through association with a fear-provoking event. Working with "Albert" (an eleven-month-old boy), Watson made a loud banging noise every time the boy reached out toward a white rat. Over a seven-day period Albert gradually came to show fear in the presence of the white rat, without any noise being made, and his fear subsequently "generalized" to include all furry objects.[8] While ample research confirms that phobias can result from conditioning, it is usually agreed that origins of phobias are more complex.

Modeling

Many fears in childhood are acquired by observing and imitating parents who are frightened by dentists, storms, darkness, and so on. Children have even been observed in new situations to look at their parents to see how they are reacting before they will show their own reactions. Verbal as well as behavioral messages may generate fear in children. Youngsters may become terrorized by the dire warnings that "spiders can kill you" or that "strangers will kidnap you and kill you." Young people may become phobic of what they were taught to fear.[9]

Displacement

Displacement is the process by which feelings and attitudes are transferred from their real source to a previously neutral object or situation. Freud was the first to describe the origin of phobias in displacement. He wrote about his conversations with the father of "Little Hans," a five-year-old boy who was afraid of horses. Freud's analysis of the information he obtained suggested that Hans was really afraid that his father was angry at him, and he had displaced his fear onto horses to minimize his anxiety (he could more easily avoid horses than his father).[10]

G. Keith Olson illustrates this causal factor in describing an adolescent who became phobic of sharp knives. Olson explains, "A few months ago, during an angry fight with her mother while they were in the kitchen, [the adolescent] saw a sharp knife and thought of stabbing her mother with it. The thought horrified her. She felt guilty and afraid, and she repressed it as quickly and as thoroughly as she could."[11] From that experience forward, she was desperately afraid of knives.

✔ HOW PARENTS CAN HELP

The following strategy for helping an adolescent struggling with phobias can be used effectively by parents; however, every parent-child relationship is unique, and some of them may be more pertinent to your situation than others. As with every significant adolescent struggle, it is best for parents to work alongside a competent counselor. With this in mind, the following is offered as a way to help you facilitate the helping process at home with your teenager.

Inspire Optimism

As adolescents see themselves to be more effective in confronting challenging situations, their levels of anxiety diminish and so do their phobias.

Albert Bandura of Stanford University calls this self-efficacy and has shown the importance of individuals' belief in their ability to overcome their struggles. While actually behaving in successful ways is one of the best ways to instill this kind of optimism, verbal persuasion from parents and counselors has also been shown to have a positive influence.[12] Knowing that others believe they can succeed helps struggling adolescents also believe they can.

✔ HOW PROFESSIONALS CAN HELP

The following strategies for helping an adolescent struggling with phobias are commonly used by counselors. They are presented here as a way to inform you, as a parent, and help you seek the best possible professional help you can for the adolescent in your care.

Pinpoint the Severity

At the beginning of treatment it is helpful to assess the intensity of adolescents' phobias. A number of assessments that work nicely with phobic struggles are available.

Examine Secondary Gains

Some phobias enable people to feel "privileged." They may receive a great deal of attention and love for remaining fearful of birds, for example. These fringe benefits of their phobia are called *secondary gains*. Do phobic young people fear a loss of attention if they do not maintain their dysfunctional behavior? How badly do they *really* want to overcome their phobic struggles? Counselors will ask them what good things they will have to give up if they do not have their fears. Using a scale of one to ten, they may ask them to estimate how badly they want to overcome their fears.

Practice Relaxation Techniques

Phobic adolescents must acquire the basic tools of relaxation. This process usually begins in the first few sessions.[13] Several relaxation techniques are discussed in the sections on anxiety and panic attack. They include deep muscle relaxation, breathing exercises, autogenics, and biofeedback. It may take adolescents a while to learn to use these exercises, but with practice they will soon be able to relax and thereby experience a sense of control over their physiological responses to their phobias.

Teach Coping Skills

Once young people have begun to master relaxation techniques, they are ready to learn coping skills. The first step counselors use is to have them make a list of all current life situations that trigger their fear and anxiety. They should be as specific as possible and try to come up with at least twenty items (they may range from very mild discomfort to the most dreaded experiences). Counselors will have them arrange lists into a hierarchy by ranking the stressful experiences in order from the least to the most anxiety-producing. Each item represents an increase in stress over the last item, and the increases are in approximately equal increments.

The rating system is based on *Subjective Units of Distress* (suds). Total relaxation is zero suds, while the most stressful situation in the hierarchy is rated at one hundred suds. All others fall somewhere in between and are assigned suds scores based on their subjective impression of where each situation falls relative to their most relaxed or most anxious states. For example, if the most stressful item in the hierarchy, "making conversation with attractive members of the opposite sex," is ranked at one hundred suds, then "thinking about calling a member of the opposite sex" might be ranked sixty-five suds, and "seeing an attractive member of the opposite sex from across the room" might rank down around thirty-five suds. Counselors allow clients to be the experts on how they react to each situation and to decide where each stressful event fits. On a list of twenty items, each situation may be separated by increments of five suds.

Once the hierarchy is in place, counselors use it to desensitize adolescents to their strongest fears. Starting with the first scene (lowest suds), counselors build a clear picture of the situation for clients to see in their imagination. They are asked to hold the stressful image for about a half minute and to notice the beginning of any tension in their bodies. Counselors show the teens how to use the tension as a signal for deep muscle relaxation or deep breathing. They will relax away the tension as they imagine the stressful situation.

After they have imagined a particular scene without anxiety or tension, they go on to the next item in the hierarchy. They move through the entire hierarchy of stressful situations using this same procedure. With each step they will use early signs of tension as their signal to relax. Once they have mastered those items with the highest suds, they will have a much stronger degree of confidence to battle their fears in actual situations.

Work on Inner Dialogue

Counselors will teach adolescents that their thoughts do not need to inten-sify fear. Instead, how they think can act as a tranquilizer for their tension and push away their panic.[14] They can tell themselves to relax in the middle of a pho-bic reaction by beginning to repeat to themselves a series of fear-conquering statements such as "There is nothing to worry about;" "This won't last long;" "Nothing can hurt me here;" "I can relax." In the midst of fearful situations, the more attention they give to their coping monologue, the quicker they will experience physiological relief. Counselors let them make their own lists of inner dialogue statements that will help them inoculate themselves against pho-bia. Counselors will then ask them to practice these in actual situations.

Practice *In Vivo* Coping and Systematic Desensitization

For phobia treatment to be effective, adolescents must have opportunities to transfer their coping skills from the counselor's office to "real life." They must confront the feared stimuli through direct exposure (*in vivo*). A substantial body of evidence has accumulated that attests to the superiority of this technique.[15] In this strategy adolescents are actually exposed to crowded shopping malls, birds, airplanes, snakes, or whatever it is they are afraid of.

One of the most thoroughly researched *in vivo* treatments for phobic dis-orders is participant modeling developed by Albert Bandura and his colleagues.[16] Therapists accompany adolescents and assist them in any way that helps them conquer their irrational fears. Therapists may simply be there for encourage-ment and support or, even better, to model nonphobic behavior. A preliminary step in conducting this kind of modeling may include a graded hierarchy of fear-provoking situations that will allow patients systematically to desensitize themselves to the feared object.[17]

In the case of snake phobics, for example, an initial hierarchy item might include looking at or touching a picture of a snake.[18] Intermediate items might include putting hands on the glass of the cage housing a real snake. The next step is to put their faces up to the glass. Once the hierarchy has been con-structed, therapists then model for clients each of the graded tasks on the hier-archy. After the modeling of all the graded tasks of the hierarchy, therapists again model one of the first hierarchy items and instruct the adolescents to repeat the behavior. This step is repeated with each item.[19] Of course, using the skills in the face of the feared object will be more difficult than in an imagined scene. Setbacks are inevitable. This performance-based strategy is sometimes impossible, for example, in the case of fear of death or fear of injury. In these cases, imaginal exposure becomes the treatment of choice.

Create "Win" Situations

It is crucial for adolescents to accomplish something on their own. This allows them to break patterns of possible dependency. To accomplish this counselors may provide homework assignments. These will be very small at first to insure success. For example a counselor working with social phobia may give the assignment of buying a newspaper from a machine in a public place. They eventually assign clients to go into a store to buy a newspaper from a clerk. Next, into a library to check out a book, and so on. This strengthens their belief in their abilities and gives them efficacy for future situations.

Explore Other "Frightening" Emotions

Adolescents struggling with phobic disorders may be dealing with any number of unexpressed feelings. After they have faced what initially appeared to be overwhelming situational fears, they may then be ready to face other fearful emotions. With a solid platform of trust where therapists have helped clients take behavioral risks with their environment, the next step is often to take risks with feelings that seem dreadful. It may be anger, guilt, resentment, or a number of other "unsafe" feelings. In any case, therapists may help young people deal with safe dosages of feelings, working toward the goal of enabling them to manage the fears that surround them.

Know When to Refer

Counselors will refer adolescents struggling with phobias to psychiatrists for evaluation whenever drugs are involved. If during any point in treatment the phobic behavior is exacerbated or seems to be becoming entrenched, consultation or referral is necessary.

Where to Go for Additional Help

Agras, S. *Panic: Facing Fears, Phobias, and Anxiety.* New York: W. H. Freeman, 1985.

Bourne, E. J. *The Anxiety and Phobia Workbook.* Oakland, Calif.: New Harbinger, 1989.

Davis, M., M. McKay, and E. R. Eshelman. *The Relaxation and Stress Reduction Workbook.* Richmond, Calif.: New Harbinger, 1980.

Kahn, A. P. *Facing Fears: A Sourcebook for Coping with Phobias, Fears, and Anxieties.* New York: Checkmark Books, 1999.

Wanderer, Z. *Acquiring Courage,* 1990. This in an audiocassette program for the "rapid treatment of phobias." It applies the techniques of implosion therapy in a self-help style. I recommend that this be used in conjunction with a competent psychotherapist.

The Phobia Society of America lists more than one thousand phobia specialists in North America. To receive general information on phobias or the latest information in effective treatment of phobias, write to the Phobia Society of America, Department R, 133 Rollins Avenue, Suite 4B, Rockville, MD 20852–4004.

Notes

1. P. J. Lang, "Fear Reduction and Fear Behavior: Problems in Treating a Construct," in *Research in Psychotherapy,* vol. 3, ed. J. M. Shlien (Washington, D.C.: American Psychological Association, 1968).

2. A. Osol, *Blakiston's Gould Medical Dictionary*, 3d ed. (New York: McGraw-Hill, 1972).

3. *Diagnostic and Statistical Manual of Mental Disorders* 4ᵗʰ ed. (Washington, D.C.: American Psychiatric Association, 1994).

4. I. M. Marks, *Fears and Phobias* (New York: Academic Press, 1969).

5. J. W. McFarlan, L. Allen, and M. P. Hanzik, *A Developmental Study of the Behavior Problems of Normal Children Between 21 Months and 14 Years* (Los Angeles: University of California Press, 1954).

6. S. Shafer, "Aspects of Phobic Illness: A Study of 90 Personal Cases," *British Journal of Medical Psychology* 49 (1976): 221–36.

7. M. E. P. Seligman, "Phobias and Preparedness," *Behavior Therapy* 2 (1971): 307–20.

8. J. B. Watson and R. Rayner, "Conditioned Emotional Reactions," *Journal of Experimental Psychology* 3 (1920): 1–14.

9. J. L. Deverensky, "Children's Fears: A Developmental Comparison of Normal and Exceptional Children," *Journal of Genetic Psychology* 135 (1979): 11–21.

10. S. Freud, "Analysis of a Phobia in a Five-Year-Old Boy," standard ed., vol. 10 (1909; reprint, London: Hogarth, 1955).

11. G. K. Olson, *Counseling Teenagers: The Complete Christian Guide to Understanding and Helping Adolescents* (Loveland, Colo.: Group Publishing, 1984), 303.

12. A. Bandura, "Self-Efficacy Mechanism in Human Agency," *American Psychologist* 37 (1982): 122–47.

13. S. Prior, "Determining the Effectiveness of a Short-Term Anxiety Management Course," *British Journal of Occupational Therapy* 61 (1998): 207–313.

14. D. H. Meichenbaum, *Cognitive-Behavior Modification* (New York: Plenum, 1974).

15. A. Bandura, "Self-Efficacy: Toward a Unifying Theory of Behavioral Change," *Psychological Review* 84 (1977): 191–215.

16. A. Bandura, R. W. Jeffery, and C. Wright, "Efficacy of Participant Modeling As a Function of Response Induction Aids," *Journal of Abnormal Psychology* 83 (1974): 56–64.

17. The theory underlying this technique was designed by Joseph Wolpe, who believed that phobias are not explained by unconscious conflicts but through undergoing traumatic experiences. See J. Wolpe, "Experimental Neuroses As Learned Behavior," *British Journal of Psychology* 43 (1952): 243–52.

18. You can find photos of many feared objects for this purpose in a standard encyclopedia.

19. Bandura et al., "Self-Efficacy Mechanism in Human Agency."

PORNOGRAPHY

✔ WHAT THE STRUGGLE LOOKS LIKE

The reading of sexually explicit materials or looking at pictures of sexual acts has been around for a long time. Cave drawings depict sexual activity. Erotic art of ancient Greece, India, Africa, and Japan indicates the cultural universality of such interest.

Today, it is practically impossible to find a high school student in America who has not come across some form of sexually explicit material. Although "adult" bookstores and movie theaters cater to people twenty-one or older, inquisitive teenagers have ample opportunities to experience erotica and pornography. Magazines, best-selling novels, advertisements, comic books, and general-release movies guarantee that anyone remotely interested in viewing such materials has the opportunity. Chances for doing so are not limited to sneaking a look at a friend's collection of *Playboy* centerfolds. Adolescents may experience pornography on the telephone through so-called "Dial-a-Porn" services, through VCRs and the neighborhood video store, on late-night cable television, and on the Internet. Josh McDowell and Dick Day in *Why Wait?* report that experts estimate that as much as 70 percent of all pornography ends up in the possession of teenagers.[1]

With its widespread dissemination and efforts to achieve glossy respectability, pornography is safely estimated to be a multibillion-dollar business in the United States. Instead of being a fringe influence on society, its moral values pour into the mainstream.[2]

Defining pornography is not a simple matter in part because different kinds of pornography have been identified. In the view of many, *violent pornography* champions the notion that sexual violence, usually directed against women, is normal. *Degrading pornography* debases and dehumanizes women even if the material does not depict explicit violent behavior. In contrast to degrading and violent pornography, *erotica* advocates the view that nonviolent and nondegrading sexual expressions are normal and serve a useful purpose.[3] Of course, the lines of demarcation become fuzzy when using an ambiguous term like *degrading*. Some prefer the general definition of Langly Longford: "Pornography is that which exploits and dehumanizes sex, so that human beings are treated as things, and women in particular as sex objects."[4]

There are arguments over almost all definitions of pornography, but, as Richard Foster says, "That should not obscure its existence. There is a world of difference between the nude figures in the Sistine Chapel and those in a 'skin' magazine, and any reasonable person knows the difference."[5]

While almost every adolescent has been exposed to pornography, male adolescents are about three times more likely than females to report being sexually aroused by it.[6] While not all males become obsessed with it, adolescents who tell their counselors that they battle it probably feel like hostages to their preoccupation with it. They may indeed be addicted.

Dale Ryan, known to some as "the missionary to the addicted," identifies five aspects of addiction. The first is *tolerance*; the addict needs to see more to achieve the same degree of mood alteration. The second is *withdrawal*; the addict would be very uncomfortable not to continue. The third is *self-deception*; the addict denies that the behavior is really affecting oneself. The fourth part is *the loss of willpower*. Finally, the behavior process causes *real problems* in the person's life.[7]

Case Description

Before I had even said hello, Ron was confessing his problem. "I can't stop thinking about sex. I have never told anyone, but I can't stand it anymore." Ron was fighting back his tears. "I am getting scared. Last week I stole money from my mom to buy more pornography, and I think she knows what I am doing." As a senior in high school, Ron's existence seemed to be consumed by sex. He saw his first piece of pornography, a *Playboy* magazine, in a neighbor's trash can when he was nine. When he came to my office he was hooked on "the

> hard stuff"—mostly magazines, but he also used dial-a-porn services from time to time.
>
> Ron has a pattern of bingeing on pornography. He buys or steals about four magazines every couple of weeks and hides them inside his record album jackets in his bedroom. He uses them for several days as he masturbates, and then goes through great pains to destroy them. It is his ritual by which he promises himself and God that he will never do it again.

Sexual addiction has been described by Patrick Carnes as "the athlete's foot of the mind."[8] It never goes away. It continually asks to be scratched, promising relief. To scratch, however, is to cause pain and to intensify the itch.

☑ WHY THE STRUGGLE HAPPENS

Numerous reasons explain why some teenagers grapple with pornography. The following are only a few of the most commonly cited factors.

Curiosity

According to John Court, "Pornography is a significant factor in shaping the sexual mores and attitudes of teenagers."[9] While it may hinder healthful development, a young person will seek out pornography as a source of knowledge and comparative information about sexual behavior. Court also points out that while certain well-chosen sexually explicit materials may educate young people, studies have not shown that pornography has the same beneficial effects.[10]

Physiological Desires

Teenagers are physically ready for sex far sooner than they are for social intimacy and the responsibilities of marriage. Masturbation is a natural "safety valve" while nature is synchronizing growth in young people's lives. The problem for some teenagers is that the safety valve may become an all-consuming obsession. Frederick Buechner, acclaimed author and Presbyterian minister, has written, "Lust is the ape that gibbers in our loins. Tame him as we will by day, he rages all the wilder in our dreams by night. Just when we think we're safe from him, he raises up his ugly head and smirks, and there's no river in the world flows cold and strong enough to strike him down. Almighty God, why dost thou deck men out with such a loathsome toy?"[11] Agonizing adolescents are not too young too understand this plaintive query.

Availability

Magazines like *Playboy, Penthouse, Hustler,* and dozens of others are available at neighborhood stores. R-rated, NC–17-rated, and X-rated movies are everywhere. Porno shops abound. Erotic art has been legitimized. The advent of videotape and cable television has added new dimensions to availability of pornography—to say nothing of the Internet (see separate chapter). A University of Utah psychologist studied junior high customers of a New York dial-a-porn service. He found that without exception the adolescents became addicted to listening to explicit adult sex by phone. In several cases the children made more than three hundred telephone calls before parents received enormous phone bills and ended the practice.[12] Adolescents seeking access to pornography will manage to obtain it.

Faulty Thinking

Generally, adolescents who become addicted to pornography do not perceive themselves as worthwhile. They use pornography as a way of making their isolation bearable. Out of this thinking come denial and distortions that keep them from confronting their temptations.

The Addictive Cycle

Addiction to pornography follows a four-step cycle, which, according to Patrick Carnes, intensifies with each repetition:

1. *Preoccupation*—the trance or mood when the addict is completely engrossed with thoughts of sex. This mental state creates an obsessive search for sexual stimulation.
2. *Ritualization*—the addict's special routine leading up to masturbation or other sexual behavior. The ritual intensifies the preoccupation, adding arousal and excitement.
3. *Compulsive sexual behavior*—the actual sex act, which is the goal of the preoccupation and ritualization. The true addict is unable to control or stop this behavior.
4. *Despair*—the feeling of utter hopelessness about one's behavior and powerlessness in the face of it.[13]

✔ HOW PARENTS CAN HELP

The following strategies for helping an adolescent struggling with pornography can be used effectively by parents; however, every parent-child relationship is unique, and some of them may be more pertinent to your situation than others. As with every significant adolescent struggle, it is best for parents to work alongside a competent counselor. With this in mind, the following is offered as a way to help you facilitate the helping process at home with your teenager.

Instill Hope

Affirm the courage the youth have demonstrated in their asking for help with such a difficult matter. Confession of the attraction that pornography holds for them is like a healing ointment that brings immediate relief, if not the much-needed long-term cure. Knowing that they may talk about their problem in a nonjudgmental setting is a boon to the ease they seek. But adolescents also need to know that there is a permanent way out of this problem. Hope will energize optimism and fuel the steps toward complete recovery.

Understand Its Pull

Since teenagers are immoderately curious about the opposite sex, pornography reaches out and pulls them in like a magnet. Pornography draws on their need to know about the unknown. If young people talk openly with a parent or counselor about the attractiveness of pornography, they will be taking the first step toward gaining control over the power of this pernicious vice. Much of adolescent energy that would be used in devouring pornography will then be immediately directed into positive action. According to Keith Olson, "Simply talking about the desires and conflicts in a non-judgmental setting will reduce the chances of sexual acting-out."[14]

Understand Its Serious Damage

In the early 1970s it was widely publicized that pornography is benign or beneficial. Following a massive increase in its availability and the appearance of violent and child pornography, further research has shown the earlier optimism by secularists to be misplaced.[15] Several lines of evidence show that in many sex crimes pornography has been among the triggering influences—especially in cases of rape.[16]

Pornography promotes the myth that women want to be raped.[17] Victims are often depicted as secretly desiring sexual assault and deriving pleasure from violent sex. Evidence suggests that the depiction of a woman becoming aroused while being raped is strongly associated with potential violence against women. In one study 41 percent of the participants reported that after seeing such a scene they might rape if they were certain of not being caught.[18] Regardless of whether the act is actually carried out, exposure to violent pornography does reduce sensitivity to rape victims.[19] Callousness toward women is seen in such statements as "a woman doesn't mean no until she slaps you." As one researcher put it, "Pornography promotes a climate in which acts of sexual hostility directed against women are not only tolerated ideologically, but encouraged."[20]

Understand Its Relational Damage

Pornography contributes to unrealistic expectations about sexuality. Even so-called soft porn like *Playboy* magazine presents a world of sexual fantasy that distorts meaningful relationships. The staged photo sessions and dye-transfer printing cover a multitude of flaws. The glossy photos that appear on the pages of these magazines have been air brushed beyond reality.

Researchers have found that after repeated exposure to pornography, men and women become less satisfied with the physical appeal of "real" partners.[21] Pornography also perpetuates the myth that a "real man" is always ready for sex and that sex may be experienced without regard for the other person. Pornography by its nature debases sexuality and creates relational damage.[22] In pornography goodness and purity are ridiculed in favor of lust and immorality. Researchers have found that the consequences of viewing nonaggressive pornography may include increased aggressive sexual fantasies, aggressive behavior against women, and acceptance of antifemale attitudes and beliefs about sexual behavior that are not conducive to respect for the opposite sex.[23]

Understand Its Power

Pornography represents a powerful mechanism for learning because pornographic images are paired with the powerful reinforcer of sexual arousal and aggressive arousal, which by context leads to mislabeling of the experience as sexual.[24] The "forbidden fruit" hypothesis argued that liberalization of laws related to pornography would result in reduced interest and a withering of the market. Evidence for this view has obviously been found faulty. In recent years the porn market has escalated to an unprecedented degree. The violent and degrading nature of much of these materials is certainly market driven. Sales are not just to the one-time curiosity seeker. The billion-dollar business is based on repeat customers.

Know When to Refer

Refer adolescents struggling with the lure of pornography to a counselor or psychologist if you are embarrassed, ill at ease, overly curious, or uncertain how to proceed. Parents referring adolescents with this problem should go to great lengths to let the young person know that it is not a personal rejection of them. Let them know how sincerely you want them to receive the best help available.

Counselors will refer adolescents to other competent counselors or psychologists when, over time, the young people are feeling more out of control and increasingly obsessed with pornographic material.

✔ HOW PROFESSIONALS CAN HELP

The following strategies for helping an adolescent struggling with pornography are commonly used by counselors. They are presented here as a way to inform you, as a parent, and help you seek the best possible professional help you can for the adolescent in your care.

Focus on the Beliefs

In counseling, focus will not be simply on a "sexual problem." The addiction may be interpreted as symptomatic or symbolic of other needs that are not being met. These unmet needs may be seen in four core beliefs that are central to adolescents who are wrapped up in this painful conflict.

1. "I am basically a bad, unworthy person." Young people see themselves in a secret world in which only they know the whole truth. Each effort to quit adds to the sense of worthlessness. Adolescents recovering from an obsession with pornography may say, "I am a worthwhile person."
2. "No one would love me as I am." Adolescents who see themselves as unworthy add the parallel belief that no one else would love them either. Rejection and abandonment are constantly feared. Adolescents recovering from an obsession with pornography may say, "I am loved and accepted by people who know me as I am."
3. "My needs are never going to be met if I have to depend on others." Believing they are unworthy and unlovable, adolescents will conclude that they cannot depend on others. After all, who would listen or sympathize with those who are unlovable? They are convinced they are never going to have what other healthy people have. Adolescents recovering from an obsession with pornography can say, "My needs may be met by others if I let them know what I need."
4. "Sex is my most important need." Adolescents who have fallen into this line of thinking eventually substitute sexual obsession for people. Using pornography becomes their primary source of comfort. Adolescents recovering from an obsession with pornography may say, "Sex is but one expression of who I am."[25]

Interrupt the Addictive System

In his book *Out of the Shadows,* Patrick Carnes adapts the twelve steps of Alcoholics Anonymous to use with those struggling with addiction to sex. Leading young people through these steps has been shown to result in a fundamental altering of the addictive system. As with Alcoholics Anonymous, this Twelve-Step approach has been found to work best for sexual addicts in a group setting. Seeing and hearing other sexual addicts facing reality and coming to grips with their lives is one of its strong points. A professional organization that provides information on these groups is

> National Council on Sexual Addiction Problems
> 1090 Northchase Parkway, Suite 200
> South Marietta, GA 30067
> 770-989-9754
> www.ncsac.org

The greatest potential for long-lasting change is in the process of individual counseling coupled with a Twelve-Step group. The goal is to integrate the young people's addictive needs into a healthy self so that the needs are met, rather than acted out. Here are the Twelve Steps for Sexual Addicts:

1. We admitted we were powerless over our sexual addiction—that our lives had become unmanageable.
2. We came to believe that a Power greater than ourselves could restore us to sanity.
3. We made a decision to turn our will and our lives over to the care of God as we understood Him.
4. We made a searching and fearless moral inventory of ourselves.
5. We admitted to God, to ourselves, and to another human being the exact nature of our wrongs.
6. We were entirely ready to have God remove all these defects of character.
7. We humbly asked Him to remove our shortcomings.
8. We made a list of all persons we had harmed, and became willing to make amends to them all.
9. We made direct amends to such people wherever possible, except when to do so would injure them or others.
10. We continued to take personal inventory and, when we were wrong, promptly admitted it.
11. We sought through prayer and meditation to improve our conscious contact with God as we understood Him, praying only for knowledge of His will for us and the power to carry that out.

12.   Having had a spiritual awakening as the result of these steps, we tried
      to carry this message to others and to practice these principles in all
      our matters.[26]

Where to Go for Additional Help

Carnes, P. *Out of the Shadows.* Minneapolis: CompCare, 1983.

Court, J. H. *Pornography: A Christian Critique.* Downers Grove, Ill.: InterVarsity Press, 1980.

Eutsler, S. D. *Clothing the Mind: How to Overcome an Addiction to Pornography.* Springfield, Mo.: Teen Challenge, 1999.

Sexuality, Health & Relationship Education, 15935 NE 8th, Suite B200, Bellevue, WA 98008; www.share-program.com.

Smedes, L. B. *Sex for Christians.* Grand Rapids: Eerdmans, 1994.

Stafford, T. *A Love Story: Questions and Answers on Sex.* Grand Rapids: Zondervan, 1977.

Zillmann, D., and J. Bryant. *Pornography: Research Advances and Policy Considerations.* Hillsdale, N.J.: Lawrence Erlbaum Associates, 1989.

Notes

1. J. McDowell and D. Day, *Why Wait? What You Need to Know About the Teen Sexuality Crisis* (San Bernardino, Calif.: Here's Life, 1987).

2. J. H. Court, "Pornography," *Baker Encyclopedia of Psychology,* ed. D. G. Benner (Grand Rapids: Baker, 1985).

3. W. A. Fisher and A. Barak, "Sex Education As a Corrective: Immunizing Against Possible Effect of Pornography," in *Pornography: Research Advances and Policy Considerations,* ed. D. Zillman and J. Bryant (Hillsdale, N.J.: Lawrence Erlbaum Associates, 1989), 289–320.

4. L. Longford, *Pornography: The Longford Report* (London: Coronet, 1972).

5. R. J. Foster, *Money, Sex and Power* (San Francisco: Harper & Row, 1985).

6. P. Y. Miller and W. Simon, "The Development of Sexuality in Adolescence," in *Handbook of Adolescent Psychology,* ed. J. Adelson (New York: Wiley, 1980).

7. M. G. Maudlin, "Addicts in the Pew," *Christianity Today* (22 July 1991): 19–20.

8. P. Carnes, *Out of the Shadows: Understanding Sexual Addiction* (Minneapolis: CompCare, 1983), vii.

9. J. H. Court, "Pornography," *Dictionary of Pastoral Care and Counseling,* ed. R. J. Hunter (Nashville: Abingdon, 1990).

10. Court, "Pornography," *Baker Encyclopedia.*

11. F. Buechner, *Godric* (New York: Harper & Row, 1980), 153.

12. T. Minnery, "Pornography: The Human Tragedy," *Christianity Today* (7 March 1986).

13. Carnes, *Out of the Shadows,* 9.

14. G. K. Olson, *Counseling Teenagers: The Complete Christian Guide to Understanding and Helping Adolescents* (Loveland, Colo.: Group Books, 1984).

15. G. Zgourides, M. Monto, and R. Harris, "Correlates of Adolescent Male Sexual Offense: Prior Adult Sexual Contact, Sexual Attitudes, and Use of Sexually Explicit Materials," *International Journal of Offender Therapy and Comparative Criminology* 41 (1997): 272–83.

16. Court, "Pornography," *Dictionary of Pastoral Care.*

17. S. L. Caron and D. B. Carter, "The Relationships Among Sex Role Orientation, Egalitarianism, Attitudes Toward Sexuality, and Attitudes Toward Violence Against Women," *Journal of Social Psychology* 137 (1997): 568–87.

18. S. Feshbach and N. Malamuth, "Sex and Aggression: Proving the Link," *Psychology Today* (1978): 110.

19. D. Linz, "Exposure to Sexually Explicit Materials and Attitudes Toward Rape: A Comparison of Study Results," *Journal of Sex Research* 26 (1985): 50–84.

20. S. Brownmiller, *Against Our Will: Men, Women and Rape* (New York: Simon & Schuster, 1975), 395.

21. D. Zillmann and J. Bryant, "Pornography's Impact on Sexual Satisfaction," *Journal of Applied Social Psychology* 18 (1988): 438–53.

22. C. Itzin, "Pornography and the Organization of Intrafamilial and Extrafamilial Child Sexual Abuse: Developing a Conceptual Model," *Child Abuse Review* 6 (1997): 94–106.

23. D. Byrne and K. Kelley, "Introduction: Pornography and Sex Research," in *Pornography and Sexual Aggression,* ed. N. M. Malamut and E. Donnersten (Orlando, Fla.: Academic Press, 1984), 1–9.

24. R. A. Baron and D. Byrne, *Social Psychology* (Boston: Allyn & Bacon, 1977).

25. For a more thorough discussion of these beliefs and how to facilitate their change, see Carnes, *Out of the Shadows.*

26. Carnes, *Out of the Shadows,* 137. For a Christian evaluation of the Twelve-Step method see T. Stafford, "The Hidden Gospel of the 12 Steps," *Christianity Today* (22 July 1991).

PROMISCUITY AND PREMARITAL SEX

✔ WHAT THE STRUGGLE LOOKS LIKE

Every adolescent walks along the moral precipice of premarital sex. In spite of efforts to install safety rails, more and more young people are falling off the cliff. Statistics are startling. A study by the U.S. Center for Disease Control found that 54 percent of today's high school students reported having had sexual intercourse at least once in their lives, and 39 percent reported having had intercourse in the last three months.[1] By age twenty, 81 percent of today's unmarried males and 67 percent of today's unmarried females have had sexual intercourse. Most research shows that the average age for first having sex is fifteen for girls and fourteen for boys.[2] Recent research is also finding a trend in an increase of sexual activity among teenagers under fifteen years of age.[3]

✔ WHY THE STRUGGLE HAPPENS

Adolescents who are sexually active engage in intercourse for different reasons. Though their motives may appear similar on the surface, they often have diverse origins.

Curiosity

Going through puberty is like exchanging a Volkswagon bug for a red Corvette and being told you can't drive over thirty miles per hour until you are married. When it comes to sex, most adolescents' curiosity is in high gear.

When young people reach puberty, changes occur that make them physically capable of sex, and they want to experiment, not wait. They are curious about the unknown, especially when it is prohibited. They want to see for themselves if sex is as great as "everyone" says it is.

Environmental Stimulation

It has been said that the typical adolescent "faces more sexual temptation on his way to school each morning than his grandfather did on Saturday night when he was out looking for it!"[4] Only a hermit in today's society stands a chance of escaping the bombardment of provocative images used by Madison Avenue. Sex sells, and no one can avoid the hundreds of titillating images that flash before us daily. Sex is used to sell everything from deodorants to soda pop. Sexy images are described in top forty songs. They are blatantly depicted on MTV (along with explicit "advice" shows on sexuality) and network television, and in movies, books, magazines, and newspapers. Today's adolescent cannot avoid sexual stimulation from the everyday environment.

The Media's Message

Thirty years ago a teenager's behavior was influenced by peers, parents, teachers, relatives, and religious leaders. Today television, radio, and movies have replaced most of those influences. While adolescents are still shaped by peers and parents, the media rank third in influencing values. And the media value sex. It has been estimated that ten years of viewing television provides 92,000 scenes of sexual activity.[5] What is doubly disturbing is how sex is portrayed in the media. Sex on TV rarely depicts the unsettling but real consequences. Every day 33,000 Americans become infected with a sexually transmitted disease. But when was the last time you saw an actor or actress portray a character with VD, AIDS, or an unwanted pregnancy? The message from the media is that "everybody's doing it" with no guilt and no worry, just fun.

Case Description

Julie, seventeen, came into counseling depressed and plagued with guilt. After a few sessions of talking around these ambiguous emotions the real issue emerged. Through a stream of tears (with ten minutes left in the session), Julie began to tell how she was sleeping with her boyfriend. She was madly in love, but terribly burdened by her sexual activity. Three weeks ago she missed her period and was scared to death that she was pregnant. It turned out to be a false alarm, but Julie (along with her boyfriend) vowed to quit. In spite of sincere intentions, she found it to be impossible. She came to counseling, without her parents' knowing and with resistance from her boyfriend, to get help. She wanted desperately to stop but didn't know how.

Peer Pressure

A young person reared by good parents with solid morals and wholesome values will still be pushed to become sexually active. The ideals of goodness and purity in many cases are offset by the greater pressure of the "you'd do it if you loved me" argument. While girls may often be coerced by their dates, both sexes are pressured by their peers, young men to be macho, and young women to be liberated. In the locker room or at a slumber party, one's sexual "track record" is a sign of "mature" behavior, a passage to adulthood. On some high school and college campuses, the term *virgin* is used in a derogatory way, like "nerd" or "jerk."

Society also does its share to pressure teens. It portrays sex as natural and "hip." A smash single on the pop charts has the chorus "Sex is natural, sex is good, not everybody does it but everybody should." If you are a celibate teenager, you may be tempted to wonder if you're a freak. If not a freak, perhaps a nerd.

Emotional Longings

Why do so many adolescents succumb to temptation and engage in premarital sex? One reason is that they mistake sex for intimacy. Many sexual encounters, especially for girls, occur out of a desperate need to be loved. A *Seventeen* magazine survey reported that most girls opt for affection over sex. In fact, only 1.1 percent of the girls surveyed said sex is more important than affection.[6] Adolescents are not so much seeking a sexual experience as they are longing for a loving relationship. The phrases "making love" and "being intimate" are often used as synonyms for sexual intercourse. Adolescents searching for security and a sense of identity make up for the shortage of love they receive from their parents by sleeping around. They mistakenly come to believe that real emotional sharing, openness, and love come through sexual intercourse.

✔ HOW PARENTS CAN HELP

The following strategies for helping an adolescent struggling with promiscuity and premarital sex can be used effectively by parents; however, every parent-child relationship is unique, and some of them may be more pertinent to your situation than others. As with every significant adolescent struggle, it is best for parents to work alongside a competent counselor. With this in mind, the following is offered as a way to help you facilitate the helping process at home with your teenager.

Examine Your Attitudes

It is easy for parents to be drawn into subjective responses to adolescents who report sexual activity. In examining "why sex talks with adolescents go wrong," Gordon Jensen and Myra Robbins report that parents and counselors may (1) fail to listen; (2) take a condemning, moralizing attitude; (3) transmit inaccurate information; (4) show shock or excessive curiosity; (5) fail to keep confidentiality; or (6) too readily give "easy answers."[7]

To avoid these pitfalls effective parents and counselors must be aware of their own attitudes toward teenage sexuality. Are you embarrassed, shocked, angered, overly curious, etc.? If you are unable to respond with an understanding and compassionate attitude, which may still acknowledge the reality of sin, then you will want to consult a counselor to help teenagers who face this problem.

Demonstrate Forgiveness

A study at the University of Wisconsin–Madison shows that the people who come to psychologists with issues of premarital sex see their primary problem as the sense of guilt that results from it.[8] This is especially true for adolescents in the church. If they are already involved in sexual activity, they are probably plagued with guilt. They need to hear that God forgives and helps people to begin again. They need to hear that no matter what they have done, no matter how many times they have broken their own standard, Jesus Christ is ready to heal and to purify.

Young people with guilt from sexual behavior may be on the brink of losing hope of ever again living a holy lifestyle. Because of one bad experience some young people will say, "Why should I even try again to do right after what I have already done?" They assume that their past has already mortgaged their future and that they are left morally bankrupt. While sex outside of marriage is sinful (see 1 Corinthians 6:12–20), young people need to know that it is never too late for forgiveness. Parents and counselors have a beautiful opportunity to demonstrate that very fact.

Reframe the Concept of Waiting

When adolescents are in love, the frustration of waiting is hard to take. However, by discussing the ways in which waiting can help their relationship, young people may begin to change their attitude and see waiting as a challenge rather than a duty. When two people are sleeping together but not living together, sex tends to become larger than life. It becomes a consuming passion that excludes other ways of experiencing love.

When sex is put on hold, however, it frees a couple to channel their love into getting to know each other better. Also, the way two young people respond to sexual pressures tends to set the course for their responses to other pressures later in life. Do they give in, or help each other stand strong? Each time a problem or pressure arises and the couple is able to solve it together, their love will grow. Framing the wait in positive terms may do much to empower a young couple concerned about their sexual future.

Be Prepared for Rationalizations

Sooner or later adolescents who experience stress in this area will ask, "Why does it matter? We are going to get married and have sex anyway. What difference does the date of a wedding ceremony make?" The question begs for a counterpoint.

Colleen Kelly Mast, creator of *Sex Respect,* points out that premarital sex may fool a young person into marrying the wrong person: "Because sex is so powerful, it creates very strong emotional bonds between partners. These bonds can make us believe a relationship is deeper than it really is, that we know our partners much better than we actually do. Or, because we've had sex, we may be tempted to hang on to the relationship, not out of love, but just to 'save face.'"[9]

Another common rationalization for premarital sex is "I owe it to him." If a girl thinks she owes a boy sex, it is normally because he wants her to think so. A girl with this concern needs to be shown her dignity as a person. She needs objective feedback to show that respect is actually expressed through concern, not manipulation. All rationalizations, however, must be listened to at the emotional level from which they rise. Once parents and counselors have listened fully to adolescents, the possibilities of helping relationships are greatly increased.

Explore How Sex Affects Future Relationships

One study of adolescent sexuality concluded that premarital sex creates "emotional deprivation," a restricted range of feelings.[10] In other words this behavior has long-term emotional results that are generally characterized by guilt, jealousy, fear, anxiety, insecurity, anger, and depression. Few adolescents realize that premarital sex may be a great source of distrust in a later marriage. The suspicion is well founded. People who cannot control themselves before marriage may have a difficult time controlling themselves after marriage. Premarital sex does not necessarily lead to extramarital sex; it simply increases the odds that it will. This understanding will do much to motivate the adolescent who values a secure marital relationship later on.

Explore How Sex Affects Spirituality

If your adolescent values their relationship with God, it is important to discuss ways that premarital sex will impact them spiritually. In fact, for religiously committed adolescents, this will probably be of great concern. Discuss ways that the joy of relating to God fades when they begin to do the opposite of what is best for them. Prayer and worship become meaningless, and if they continue to engage in premarital sex, they will be shot through with heavy doses of guilt. Few activities do more to nag at the conscience of committed Christian young people than premarital sex.[11]

One note of caution: In exploring this issue guard against conveying the idea that sex is bad. God created human bodies capable of sexual intimacy and orgasm. As with other parts of his creation God called sexual human beings "good." Adolescents with overly active consciences can distort God's gift of sex and set themselves up for years of sexual anxiety as married adults.

Provide Helpful Literature

Generally it is not helpful to recommend a book to struggling adolescents. They simply don't read books about depression, anger, sibling rivalry, and so on. However, young people are usually eager to read anything on sexuality. In fact, a teacher has half jokingly said that many young people's first examination of the encyclopedia results from a rumor that there is detailed sexual information in it.

Reading material will help teenagers secure accurate information about questions they may be hesitant to ask. Tim Stafford's book *A Love Story* is a classic written in question-and-answer format. It covers a number of topics, including premarital sex, masturbation, dating, and several others. Another work by Stafford, *Worth the Wait,* also speaks to teens about the frustration of premarital sex. It addresses such things as why sex is so attractive, how to build healthful relationships, twenty questions for choosing the right person at the right time, finding forgiveness, and how to say no and stick with it. Both books are straightforward, filled with insight and sensitivity, and eagerly read by most teenagers. Another book that addresses issues of premarital sex and is often helpful to young people is James Dobson's *Preparing for Adolescence: Straight Talk to Teens and Parents*. In addition, two current books on sex and dating worth checking out are *I Kissed Dating Goodbye* by Joshua Harris and *Boundaries in Dating* by Henry Cloud and John Townsend.

Set Up Safeguards

The time to look for a fire escape is before the building is ablaze. Young people often find themselves in situations from which they cannot escape. Once they've let their hormones loose, they will have trouble harnessing them again. The solution is to stop the tragedy before it begins. By helping young people decide ahead of time what they may and may not do, you are helping them draw lines that they do not want to cross over. One example might be to guard against being alone as a couple in an empty house. More than half of today's teenagers first had intercourse in their own or their partner's house (usually between 3:00 and 5:00 P.M.).[12] Other suggestions might include avoidance of a certain style of provocative dress, parking in a car, and certain parties. A couple should also always have an activity planned ahead of time when going out on a date. By setting up safeguards, adolescents define specific areas they will not enter and thereby avoid potentially dangerous situations.

Respect the Value of Romance

Setting up safeguards does not mean avoiding romance. According to Erik Erikson, if by late adolescence young people have not been involved in romantic love relationships, they may settle for a series of impersonal relationships; and they may suffer from a permanent sense of depersonalization.[13] However, youth may enjoy the glory of romance and get relational needs met without having sexual intercourse. As a parent, you may help embattled adolescents become aware of their relational longings and be assertive in getting them met through nonsexual means.

Encourage Community

Adolescents often feel terribly alone in their difficult battle for sexual purity, even within the church. A sensitive and caring community offers great refuge in the midst of battle. Remind Christian teens that God is with them every moment (see Deuteronomy 31:8), and that they have power to resist even the strongest urges (see Philippians 4:13). Of course, these messages are heard best from respected peers. Knowing there are others fighting yet drawing on God's strength does much for adolescents who feel isolated in this war.[14] Relationships build convictions.

Focus on Relational Needs

The problem facing adolescents who scuffle temptation to engage in sex outside of marriage is not just a sexual one. It is a relational one as well. Teens need to learn to get their relational needs met without having to resort to sex. Intercourse is not the price they have to pay for warmth, intimacy, or romance. Helping adolescents to become aware of the particular needs that underlie sex and helping them become assertive in getting those needs met in other ways will quiet the battle. For example, some teens become sexually active to develop autonomy and assert separate identity from parental authority. The privacy of sex helps prove to adolescents that they are no longer dependent children. Once they understand the strength of their drive for autonomy, they may choose to channel it in ways that will serve them better.

Understand Sexually Transmitted Diseases

No discussion of premarital sex would be complete without emphasizing the importance of knowledge of Sexually Transmitted Diseases (STDs). It is estimated that 2.5 million teens are infected with STDs each year.[15] That means that every thirteen seconds a teen in the U.S. contracts a sexually transmitted disease. Sexually active adolescents should be questioned directly but sensitively about STDs. They may be too embarrassed to ask about their symptoms and may need encouragement to talk about it. The risk of infection with STDs increases enormously in relation to the number of different people with whom they have had sexual contact. The fewer the number of contacts, the lower the risk.[16] The most common STDs and their symptoms are these:

Gonorrhea: A woman may have no signs or symptoms or she may have burning urination, vaginal discharge, fever, or stomach pain. A man will see whitish discharge from his penis and feel itching or burning when urinating. Symptoms usually appear two to eight days after contact.

Chlamydia: This disease is twice as common as gonorrhea. Its symptoms resemble mild gonorrhea and they often appear at the same time. Chlamydia appears from one to five weeks after contact.

Syphilis: The person infected with syphilis gets a sore, sometimes painful, on the sex organs or mouth. The sore will slowly disappear even without treatment, but the disease has not gone away. Several weeks later other signs will appear, including low fever, sore throat, sores, or rashes.

Herpes: Officially, this is herpes simplex virus type 2 (HSV–2). It may be extremely painful or very mild. A man will see a small sore or cluster of blisters on his penis. A woman may have blisters in or around her vagina. She may have fever and headaches. Without treatment, symptoms disappear in a week or two, but the herpes virus doesn't leave the body.

An adolescent who is found to have an STD should be referred to a physician immediately. Serious danger results from failure to treat. The disease may cause irreparable damage to female reproductive organs, sterility in men and women, arthritis, heart disease, or even eye infection serious enough to end in blindness. Some of these effects show up years after the disease is first contracted. Medical treatment is essential. Refer adolescents to physicians even if they only wonder whether they may have been exposed to a sexually transmitted disease. And, of course, if tests are positive, they must tell anyone with whom they have had sex to go at once for a test.

Understand AIDS

More than eighteen thousand people in their twenties have been diagnosed with AIDS (acquired immunodeficiency syndrome), and most of them were probably infected with the virus while they were teenagers.[17] Research has clearly shown that far too many adolescents put themselves at risk for contracting AIDS.[18] It is a disease in which the body's immune system breaks down. It is caused by the human immunodeficiency virus (HIV). People infected with HIV may appear completely healthy, but they may also develop many health problems that signal the onset of AIDS, including extreme weight loss, severe pneumonia, a form of cancer, and damage to the nervous system. A person becomes infected when HIV is introduced into the bloodstream, most commonly through homosexual or heterosexual intercourse or by sharing drug needles or syringes with infected people.[19]

Several excellent books on understanding and counseling people with AIDS are available. Michael J. Christensen's *The Samaritan's Imperative: Compassionate Ministry to People Living with AIDS* (Abingdon, 1991) stresses a back-to-basics approach to dealing with AIDS patients that includes fresh insight on love, acceptance, and forgiveness. For a resource that is specifically written for professional practitioners in a Christian context, Gregg R. Albers's *Counseling and*

AIDS (Word, 1990) will be of interest. It includes advice on everything from counseling those who need AIDS testing to counseling the families of AIDS patients.

Know When to Refer

Refer adolescents if your attitude threatens them (evaluative, vindictive, and so on) or if you are too shocked or embarrassed to continue discussing it. Nonunderstanding may drive worried adolescents back into further immorality. As always, referrals must be made with sensitivity so as not to be misinterpreted as rejection.

☑ HOW PROFESSIONALS CAN HELP

The following strategy for helping an adolescent struggling with promiscuity and premarital sex is commonly used by counselors. It is presented here as a way to inform you, as a parent, and help you seek the best possible professional help you can for the adolescent in your care.

Assess the Facts

In assessing the intensity of adolescents' sexual activity, the goal is to have an accurate understanding of how it affects their lives and how they have been coping with the matter up to this point. While some instruments are available to help in assessing the depth of this problem, their use is too threatening for most adolescents. The severity of the strain can be assessed easily enough through direct yet sensitive questioning by the counselor.

Where to Go for Additional Help

Arterburn, S. *Addicted to "Love."* Ann Arbor, Mich.: Vine Books, 1991.

Barnes, B. *Preparing Your Child for Dating.* Grand Rapids: Zondervan, 1998.

Dobson, J. *Preparing for Adolescence: Straight Talk to Teens and Parents.* Ventura, Calif.: Vision House, 1984.

Howard, M. *How to Help Your Teenager Postpone Sexual Involvement.* New York: Cross-road-Continuum, 1991.

Johnson, T. C. *Understanding Your Child's Sexual Behavior: What's Natural and Healthy.* Oakland, Calif.: New Harbinger Publications, 1999.

Jones, S. L., and B. B. Jones. *How and When to Tell Your Kids About Sex.* Colorado Springs, Colo.: NavPress, 1993.

McDowell, J., and D. Day. *Why Wait? What You Need To Know About the Teen Sexuality Crisis.* San Bernardino, Calif.: Here's Life, 1987.

National Abstinence Clearing House, 801 E. 41st St., Sioux Falls, SD 57051, 888-577-2966.

Parrott, L., and L. Parrott. *Relationships: Making Bad Relationships Better and Good Relationships Great*. Grand Rapids: Zondervan, 1998.

Parrott, L. *7 Secrets of a Healthy Dating Relationship*. Kansas City, Mo.: Beacon Hill, 1995.

Sexuality, Health & Relationship Education, 15935 NE 8th, Suite B200, Bellevue, WA 98008; www.share-program.com.

Short, R. E. *Sex, Love, or Infatuation: How Can I Really Know?* Minneapolis: Augsburg, 1990.

Smedes, L. B. *Sex for Christians*. Grand Rapids: Eerdmans, 1976.

Stafford, T. *Worth the Wait: Love, Sex, and Keeping the Dream Alive*. Grand Rapids: Zondervan, 1990.

_____. *A Love Story: Questions and Answers on Sex*. Grand Rapids: Zondervan, 1977.

Warren, N. C. *Finding the Love of Your Life*. Colorado Springs, Colo.: Focus on the Family, 1992.

Notes

1. Morbidity and Mortality Weekly Report, vol. 40, U.S. Department of Health and Human Services, Public Health Service, Centers for Disease Control (January 2, 1992): 885–88.

2. J. McDowell and D. Day, *Why Wait? What You Need To Know About the Teen Sexuality Crisis* (San Bernardino, Calif.: Here's Life, 1987).

3. D. J. Bersharov and K. N. Gardiner, "Trends in Teen Sexual Behavior," *Children and Youth Services Review* 19 (1997): 341–67.

4. C. K. Mast, *Sex Respect: An Option of True Sexual Freedom, A Public Health Workbook for Students* (Bradley, Ill.: Respect, 1986).

5. McDowell and Day, *Why Wait?*, 40.

6. J. Gaylin, "What Girls Really Look for in Boys," *Seventeen* (March 1978): 107–13.

7. G. Jensen and M. Robbins, "Ten Reasons Why Sex Talks with Adolescents Go Wrong," *Medical Aspects of Human Sexuality* (July 1975): 7.

8. McDowell and Day, *Why Wait?*, 261.

9. Mast, *Sex Respect*.

10. G. R. Collins, *Christian Counseling; A Comprehensive Guide* (Waco, Tex.: Word, 1980).

11. L. Jensen, R. J. Newell, and T. Holman, "Sexual Behavior, Church Attendance, and Permissive Beliefs Among Unmarried Young Men and Women," *Journal for the Scientific Study of Religion* 29, no. 1 (1990): 113–17.

12. R. Coles and G. Stokes, *Sex and the American Teenager* (New York: Harper & Row, 1985).

13. E. H. Erikson, *Identity: Youth and Crisis* (New York: Norton, 1968).

14. J. P. Roche, "Premarital Sex: Attitudes and Behavior by Dating Stage," *Adolescence* 21 (1986): 107–21.

15. L. Furby, L. M. Ochs, and C. W. Thomas, "Sexually Transmitted Disease Prevention: Adolescents' Perceptions of Possible Side Effects," *Adolescence* 32 (1997): 781–809.

16. F. Wattleton, "American Teens: Sexually Active, Sexually Illiterate," *Curriculum Review* 27 (1988): 16–23.

17. Ibid.

18. K. Greene, J. L. Hale, and D. L. Rubin, "A Test of the Theory of Reasoned Action in the Context of Condom Use and AIDS," *Communication Reports* 10 (1997): 21–33.

19. L. L. Lockhart and J. S. Wodarski, "Facing the Unknown: Children and Adolescents with AIDS," *Journal of the National Association of Social Workers* 34 (1989): 215–22.

RAGE, VIOLENCE, AND GUNFIRE

☑ WHAT THE STRUGGLE LOOKS LIKE

Littleton, Colorado was the kind of place parents moved to make sure their kids would be safe, to get away from the stress and crime of the city. No one would have ever guessed that the quiet community framed by mist and mountains would one day turn into a killing field. But on a Tuesday morning, Eric Harris and Dylan Klebold, two kids in a clique known as the Trench Coat Mafia, walked into their high school with a semiautomatic pistol, carbine, and two sawed-off shotguns, laughing and hooting while they shot up the place, killing twelve students and a popular coach before turning their weapons on themselves. Before they did, however, they planted at least thirty pipe bombs and other explosives, including one that police believe was intended to destroy the school.

Thomas Solomon Jr. is no monster. He was never a member of the Trench Coat Mafia. He was literally a Boy Scout, a pleasant fifteen-year-old kid who went to church and didn't care for Marilyn Manson, Duke Nukem, Goth life, or any of the other cultural markers we have come to expect from kid killers. But that didn't prevent Solomon from starting a melee at Heritage High School in Conyears, Georgia. He came to school on a Thursday morning bearing the weight of a breakup with his girlfriend and wearing a determined stare. He maintained a dazed expression as he began randomly firing into the school's indoor commons. No one died, and thankfully only six students were injured—one of them seriously. Sophomore Stephanie Laster had just stood up from a cafeteria table where she was chatting with a teacher about a missionary trip she was planning for the next month.

Comparison can be made in these two cases (in fact, the patterns of recent school violence reveal young, white males who are tragically depressed), but what is striking to most is how different "twisted teens" can be. Just because a kid wears black clothes and likes bloody video games doesn't mean he's going to kill his classmates. And just because a kid doesn't wear a swastika on his jacket and black steel-toed boots doesn't mean he might. This is exactly what leaves most experts reeling with questions and desperately seeking answers to teenage rage and violence. Why? Why would kids with so many years before them turn to unthinkable violence? More importantly, how can we keep other kids from resorting to gunfire? Are there warning signs?

There are no simple checklists for spotting every rage-filled kid who is at risk for doing serious damage to others, but the key thing to watch for is drastic changes in behavior. Other warning signs, most experts say, indicate a kid may be crossing the line from run-of-the-mill teenage weird into a danger zone of violent destruction: difficulty maintaining relationships, slipping grades, depression, dropping school activities, loss of appetite, sleeplessness, increasing isolation, and a new gang of friends parents don't know. But one of the clearest signs is a fascination with firearms or other means of destruction, including books on bombs. The same goes for kids making serious and multiple threats to hurt or kill someone. Let's put it this way: These are troubled kids who have a history of bullying, are fascinated with guns, violence, and bombs, and have typically been teased or are outcasts. Their life's predicament combines all the ingredients for rage and violence. This chapter is dedicated to helping them find an alternative to destruction.

☑ WHY THE STRUGGLE HAPPENS

There are numerous reasons a kid might fantasize about going on a violent rampage. But trying to pinpoint why some kids actually act out their violent fantasy is tough to say. No one knows for sure, but here are a few of the most commonly cited reasons some kids try to solve their problems with rifles.

Nihilism

A few years ago, this would probably not have been among the top reasons some kids commit acts of violence. But some of today's teens are shaped by a cultural environment that nurtures a growing dissatisfaction and hardhearted nihilism. One example is the affection some kids have for the grim posturing of certain music groups. The German groups Rammstein and KMFDM, for example (the latter's name translates as "No pity for the majority"), have an industrial sound while their lyrics are laced with self-loathing and questions of life's meaning. The point is that many of these kids are open to anything that speaks to their alienation and despair. Shooting classmates at school is just a reflection of how meaningless they see life to be.[1]

Racism

For some kids, racism plays a major role in their violent acts. Skinheads, as some of them are known, are easily spotted with swastikas adorning their coats and the steel-toed combat boots (for maximum damage when kicking enemies) with red shoelaces—a symbol of blood shed for the "master race." Their dark belief system and fascination with all things German, from the language to World War II insignias, are hallmarks of a large band of racist skinheads who boast of being "soldiers of the Fourth Reich."

Disconnected Parents

Some parents have left a big vacuum in their kids' lives, and the vacuum has been filled with a second family of angry, disconnected, and confused peers who are often virtually raising themselves. When kids enter puberty and start demonstrating defiance, attitude, secretiveness, and an emotional volatility that can make even the best of parents feel helpless, some parents who are over-stressed, overworked, and otherwise preoccupied head for the hills.[2]

Media Violence

While it is by now a cliché to speak of the violence of popular culture, it is nonetheless true that teenagers today have access and exposure to a bewildering array of violent imagery. The escalation of violence in the media—on TV, videos, the Internet, and video games—is truly beyond comprehension.[3] The vast assortment of slasher and gore films on video as well as the proliferation of video games offering players the chance to engage in vicarious carnage of every sort, bring into homes depictions of graphic violence never available to children and young people in the past. According to the American Psychological Association, the average child will witness at least eight thousand murders on TV by the time he or she leaves elementary school, along with more than one hundred thousand assorted other acts of violence.[4] When asked why he thought students were resorting to gun violence again and again, Michael Woods, a student in a recent school shooting, said, "Kids are seeing it and hearing about it all the time now. It's like the new way out for them."[5]

Violent Video Games

While video games can be lumped in with "media violence," they deserve special mention among the reasons some kids act out their rage (see the chapter in this book on the Internet and Video Game Addiction). Take the popular game Doom, a favorite of the two boys who killed their classmates in Littleton, Colorado. In the game, players take on the character of a marine, walking around a maze blowing away beasts with a vast array of high-tech cannons, growing mesmerized by the thrill of staring down a digitized gun barrel, or snaking around corners in search of fire-hurling beasts, waiting for their blood to be splattered upon the walls. The research is clear: spending hours fantasizing and enacting this kind of violence can only serve to fan the flame of rage and violent behavior.

Accessibility of Guns

Even tough gun laws can be beaten. The 1994 Brady law was widely hailed for its ban on rapid-fire "assault" weapons, for instance, but recent incidents of school violence were at the hands of students packing semiautomatic handguns and Hi-Point 9-mm carbine rifles designed to comply with the Brady rules.[6]

Copycat Syndrome

After every school shooting that hits the national airwaves, there are hundreds of schools that are hit with threats of similar violence. Classes are sometimes canceled. Arrests are sometimes made. According to a Gallup poll, 37 percent of thirteen- to seventeen-year-olds nationwide have heard of threats at their own schools, and 20 percent said their schools have been evacuated because of a bomb threat.[7] The point is that some kids near the edge get an idea from another kid who has crossed over. They then model themselves after the person whom they may identify with. Sometimes copycats are just looking for pointers on how they can commit the crime or violence they are already thinking about. Some see the nation in a furor over a high school shooting and regard it as a quick way to achieve significance. It is a power trip for the powerless, those who feel they have nothing to lose.

Case Description

Aaron is a fifteen-year-old loner who despises the status quo. He wears a heavy dark jacket, even in summer—a trait that often brings ridicule from some of his classmates. At lunch, he sits with a couple of other outsiders and plays war games on a laptop computer. Last weekend, the police busted him in the park with a bottle of bourbon, something that surprised his parents, who never knew him to drink at all. In spite of Aaron's troublesome behavior, he is still concerned about his grades at school. In a recent writing assignment, Aaron wrote sympathetically about murderer Jeffrey Dahmer and how he was probably bullied by other kids when he was growing up. Once, Aaron was so riled by a grade in a social studies class that the teacher asked him to leave the classroom. As he was walking out he muttered a few derogatory remarks interspersed with something in German. That earned him a three-day suspension. During those three days Aaron contemplated how he might steal his uncle's rifle and wreak havoc the next week in his teacher's classroom.

✔ HOW PARENTS CAN HELP

The following strategies for helping an adolescent struggling with violence issues can be used effectively by parents; however, every parent-child relationship is unique, and some of them may be more pertinent to your situation than others. As with every significant adolescent struggle, it is best for parents to work alongside a competent counselor. With this in mind, the following is offered as a way to help you facilitate the helping process at home with your teenager.

Gauge the Threat

If you ask a thousand students to list the most dangerous kids in their school, you'll see the same names show up again and again. Students themselves are in the best position to sense danger signals from another student. But that's different from knowing that a kid is about to go over the edge. A classmate may be a brooder, a loner, or just plain bizarre without ever being a threat to anyone. And even students who make multiple threats often never follow up on them. The best way to weigh the threat is to look for a few specific warning signs: Does the student act out his or her anger by throwing things or punching walls? Does the student avoid reality by turning to drugs, alcohol, or computers? Does the student try to shock? Most teens will do some of these things from time to time, but the more a student behaves in these ways, the more serious the danger.

Set Up an Anonymous Tip Line

"Tell an adult." These three words of advice are fundamental to catching problems of violence before they begin. Many towns have found it extremely helpful to set up an anonymous school tip line that students can phone twenty-four hours a day to report questionable behavior of their classmates. Many kids are terrified that the dangerous student will spot them as the tattletale and come for blood. This takes care of that problem.

Watch for the Bullied Becoming Bullies

Luke Woodham of Pearl, Mississippi, was a short, fat boy who was beaten and ridiculed by his peers. Mitchel Johnson of Jonesboro, Arkansas, was a pudgy outcast. And Eric Harris and Dylan Klebold of Littleton, Colorado, were disturbed loners whom classmates taunted as often as Harris and Klebold taunted them. All four teens took revenge by killing their schoolmates. Bullied, they became bullies themselves. Because bullying is so often an underlying cause of school violence, the National School Safety Center now calls it "the most enduring and underrated problem in American schools."[8] Luke Woodham of Pearl, Mississippi, wrote a letter saying: "I killed because people like me are mistreated every day. I did this to society, 'Push us and we will push back.'"[9]

Set Up a Community Advisory Council

Since most people would like to be better parents and more engaged members of the community, it is only logical to turn toward one another. A community advisory council, composed of dozens of people from inside and outside the local schools, can meet monthly to keep students, faculty, school administrators, civic leaders, clergy, and the community at large in touch with one another. It has the potential to create an atmosphere in which more communication takes place before problems occur.

Set Up a Bully Intervention Program

Bullying is the practice of teasing, harassing, and violence inflicted by the supposedly powerful against the presumably powerless. More than three hundred schools nationwide, however, have found success in curbing this kind of bullying by initiating rules that not only take a stand against it, but against not doing anything about it. It is against the rules, for example, for a student to watch a fellow classmate being bullied without intervening or seeking help. Largely as a result of the program, misconduct reports at these schools have been cut nearly in half.[9]

Provide Options to Long-term School Suspensions

Some communities are finding success with a program that offers young-sters who are facing suspension from school a chance to cut the suspension in half by taking an individualized, multiple-hour conflict-resolution program with their parents. Sometimes a fee is charged which can be refundable after completion of the program. Using the crisis stage of suspension as one of the intervention points makes sense because that's when people are highly amenable to change. It gets troubled kids and families to therapists before catastrophes occur, and from there, they can get linked up with supportive services.

Avoid Too Much "Privacy"

Keep the family computer in some common area so the kids won't be tempted to surf to the bomb-making and Nazi Web sites. Ditto the TV and VCR. Avoid situations where the child can spend the majority of his time behind a closed door.[10] All kids need privacy, but you don't want the bulk of their time spent that way.

Stand Your Ground

A mom and dad recently told me a story about their sixteen-year-old who wanted to go to Cancun, Mexico, for spring break. They both complained about how his persistence was wearing them down. Somehow, in the ongoing discussions, the Cancun trip became a test of trust, and the parents found themselves on the defensive. The real issue here, however, was not one of trust. It was one of safety and parental authority. Too often in dealing with aggressive kids, the main issue of parental concern gets lost. So keep the main thing the main thing.

Know Their Friends

All authorities agree that the best thing parents and leaders can do to help the high school student who is filled with rage is to know and listen to their friends. Do you know who they're spending their time with? What movies and videos are they watching? What music do they listen to? Make a habit of getting to know their friends and their friends' parents. Know their role models, who they want to be like, and why.[11]

Talk to Others

It almost goes without saying that if parents or youth workers suspect trouble from a specific kid, they should immediately talk to school officials: teachers, principals, guidance counselors, and coaches. They may need to talk to other kids or other kids' parents.[12] But mostly, parents need to talk to their own children.

Listen to Them

There is surely some connection between the fact that parents spend 40 percent less time with their kids now than thirty years ago, and the violence that some children commit.[13] Needless to say, kids who are prone to violence feel a significant disconnection from their parents. And oftentimes it is shocking to discover just how little Mom and Dad know about the activities, not to mention the thoughts and feelings, of their son or daughter. So anything that facilitates genuine conversation where parents are truly listening to their child is worth more than we will ever know.[14]

Reveal God

Newsweek ran a cover with the oversized word "Why?" The subhead read, "The Science of Teen Violence." The story provided the latest research into how an adolescent's brain chemistry can increase the odds for acting out violent impulses. But if we are to prevent teenage violence, we need to see it as a disease of the soul as much as it is of the brain. The rage and anger of violent youth reveals a deep pain and hunger for something to ease their pain. These kids are looking for something: perhaps for God, for meaning. As Luther once said, we either have God in our lives or we have false gods. The point is to not neglect the spiritual side of this ugly problem.

Keep Guns Locked Up

It should go without saying, but it can't: Keep guns locked up! Easy access to weapons exacerbates the temptation to formulate a violent plan. In addition, guns depersonalize violence. They maintain distance between the aggressor and the victim and decrease a certain level of empathy that might serve to intervene before a different kind of violence would occur. Guns can be used on impulse, with little physical effort and even less thought to the consequences. Every day thirteen children die from firearms in the United States. We also know that about half the guns used by young offenders are acquired by adults who buy them from legitimate dealers.[15] Bottom line? Make guns inaccessible and lock them up.

Know When to Refer

When a student is making serious and multiple threats to hurt or kill someone, little time should be spent in wondering when to get the police involved.

If you know of a specific situation with a young person making such threats, the sooner you make the call, the better.

Where to Go for Additional Help

Branch, C. W., ed. *Adolescent Gangs: Old Issues, New Approaches.* Philadelphia: Brunner/Mazel, 1999.

de Becker, G. *Protecting the Gift: Keeping the Children and Teenagers Safe.* New York: Dial Press, 1999.

Garbarino, J. *Lost Boys: Why Our Sons Turn Violent and How We Can Save Them.* New York: Free Press, 1999.

Goldstein, A. P., ed. *School Violence Intervention: A Practical Handbook.* New York: The Guilford Press, 1997.

Gurian, M. *A Fine Young Man: What Parents, Mentors, and Educators Can Do to Shape Adolescent Boys into Exceptional Men.* New York: Jeremy P. Tarcher/Putnam, 1999.

Gurian, M. *The Wonder of Boys: What Parents, Mentors, and Educators Can Do to Shape Boys into Exceptional Men.* New York: Jeremy P. Tarcher/Putnam, 1997.

Huckabee, M., and G. Grant. *Kids Who Kill: Confronting Our Culture of Violence.* Nashville: Broadman, 1998.

Kelleher, M. D. *When Good Kids Kill.* Westport, Conn.: Praeger, 1998.

Kindlon, D., and M. Thompson. *Raising Cain: Protecting the Emotional Life of Boys.* New York: Ballantine, 1999.

Mintle, L. *Kids Killing Kids.* Altamonte, Fla.: Creation House, 1999.

Oliver, C., and G. J. Oliver. *Raising Sons and Loving It: Helping Your Boys Become Godly Men.* Grand Rapids: Zondervan, 2000.

Osofsky, J. D., ed. *Children in a Violent Society.* New York: The Guilford Press, 1997.

Pollack, W. S. *Real Boys: Rescuing Our Sons from the Myths of Boyhood.* New York: Henry Holt & Company, 1999.

Notes

1. B. Murray, "Boys to Men: Emotional Miseducation," *APA Monitor* 30 (July/August 1999): 1.

2. D. J. Flannery, M. Singer, L. Williams, and P. Castro, "Adolescent Violence Exposure and Victimization at Home: Coping with Trauma Symptoms," *International Review of Victimology* 6 (1998): 29–48.

3. J. R. Janes, *Mayhem* (New York: Soho Press, 1999).

4. B. I. Koerner, "From Way Cool to Out of Control, *U.S. News* (May 3, 1999): 20–25.

5. J. Cloud, "Just a Routine School Shooting," *Time* (May 31, 1999): 36.

6. J. Volz, "Congress Looks to APA on Violence Prevention," *APA Monitor* (July/August 1999): 32.

7. A. Cohen, "Criminals as Copycats," *Time* (May 31, 1999): 38.

8. A. Mulrine, "A Common Thread?" *U.S. News & World Report* (May 3, 1999): 24.

9. Ibid.g

10. B. Pfefferbaum and J. R. Allen, "Stress in Children Exposed to Violence: Reenactment and Rage," *Child and Adolescent Psychiatric Clinics of North America* 7 (1998): 121–35.

11. S. A. Hritz and P. A. Gabow, "A Peer Approach to High Risk Youth," *Journal of Adolescent Health* 20 (1997): 259–60.

12. C. M. Borduin, "Multisystemic Treatment of Criminality and Violence in Adolescents," *Journal of the American Academy of Child and Adolescent Psychiatry* 38, (1999): 242–49.

13. Cloud, "Just a Routine School Shooting," 34–38.

14. Murray, "Boys to Men: Emotional Miseducation,", 1.

15. "The Long Road After Littleton," *Christianity Today* (June 14, 1999): 32–33.

SCHIZOPHRENIA

✅ WHAT THE STRUGGLE LOOKS LIKE

A patient of mine once told me a joke with this punch line: The difference between schizophrenics and neurotics is that neurotics say that 1 + 1 = 2 and they can't stand it. Schizophrenics say that 1 + 1 = 11, and they love it!

Plenty of humor has been derived from this problem, but schizophrenia is not a joke. It is a painful group of diseases characterized by a loss of contact with reality. At some point in the illness several features may become prominent: hallucinations, delusions, decreased self-care, social inappropriateness, or markedly disturbed thinking. The schizophrenic's personality becomes severely disorganized, and often requires acute management and treatment in a hospital during the more active phases of the illness.

Schizophrenia is considered by many to be the leading mental health problem in the United States. At least one out of every one hundred people is likely to suffer an episode of schizophrenia during his or her life. One hundred thousand new cases are added each year. Schizophrenia requires more hospital beds than any other medical or psychiatric condition and more hospital beds than cancer, heart disease, arthritis, and diabetes combined.[1] The treatment and rehabilitation of people suffering from schizophrenia today is estimated to cost over twenty billion dollars each year. Schizophrenia may prevent young people from completing late adolescence and ruin a promising future. It is a disheartening societal and personal problem that cries out for a solution.

Schizophrenia in teenagers has been a concern since the early 1900s. It used to be called adolescent insanity. In 1911, the famous Swiss psychiatrist who coined the term *schizophrenia*, Eugene Bleuler, wrote, "The adolescent age period seems to offer a particular predisposition to this disease."[2] Subsequent research and clinical observations confirm that most forms of schizophrenic disturbance tend to first appear during or soon after adolescence.[3] In fact, it is the most common diagnosis among adolescents in mental hospitals.

The DSM Criteria for Schizophrenia[4]

A. At least two of the following symptoms:

1. Bizarre thinking and delusions: thoughts that are blatantly untrue, such as that the person's brain is being controlled by a television station or that others are broadcasting one's thoughts

2. Grandiose, religious, nihilistic, or persecutory delusions

3. Prominent hallucinations such as voices conversing with each other or one voice keeping a running commentary on the patient's thoughts and behaviors

4. Prominent hallucinations on several occasions, with the content of words having no apparent relationship to depression or elation

5. Incoherent thinking, marked loosening of associations, illogical thinking, or marked poverty of content of speech if associated with at least one of the following:

    a. Blunted, flat, or inappropriate affect

    b. Delusions or hallucinations

    c. Catatonic or other grossly disorganized behavior

B. Deterioration from previous level of functioning in areas such as school, work, social relations, self-care, or failure to achieve expected level of development

C. Duration: Continual signs of the disorder for at least six months at some time during the person's life, with some signs at present

D. During the early and the residual phases, at least two of the following present but not owing to a mood disturbance or drug abuse: social withdrawal; digressive vague speech; illogical thinking and loosening of associations; peculiar, odd behavior; grossly disorganized behavior; or blunted, flat, or inappropriate affect

The *Diagnostic and Statistical Manual of Mental Disorders* (4th ed.) recognizes five types of schizophrenia:

1. *Disorganized*. This usually begins in early adolescence and is marked by incoherence, loose associations in thought and speech, and flat, inappropriate, or silly affect. No elaborate delusional system is present. The clinician is more likely to see fragmented delusions or disorganized hallucinations. Without treatment this type will suffer chronic and extreme social impairment.

2. *Catatonic*. This type most often begins between the ages of fifteen and twenty-five following some type of emotional trauma. It is characterized by a major psychomotor disturbance that may include rigidity, excitement, or a stupor. Mutism is common. The prognosis for recovery after a single catatonic episode is more favorable than for recovery from other types.

3. *Paranoid*. This type tends to occur after adolescence around the age of thirty. Symptoms include delusions and/or hallucinations of persecution or grandiosity.

4. *Undifferentiated*. Psychotic symptoms (delusions, hallucination, incoherence, or severely disorganized behavior) are present, but the patient's clinical picture either does not meet the criteria for any of the three forms mentioned above or it meets the criteria of more than one of them.

5. *Residual*. This diagnosis is used when a history of schizophrenia exists, but the current evaluation of the patient no longer indicates significant psychotic symptoms.

Clinical studies of adolescents suffering from schizophrenia indicate that only about 35 percent initially show clear signs of a schizophrenic breakdown. The rest tend to present a masked or mixed picture in which features of schizophrenia are secondary to or even obscured by other kinds of problems or complaints. Two kinds of mixed-symptom pictures are likely to be seen—one is depressive, the other antisocial. In one picture the young person shows some signs of schizophrenia but complains primarily of depression, with a loss of interest in people or activities, feelings of hopelessness, and even suicidal thoughts. In the other picture indications of schizophrenia are present but overshadowed by an apparent antisocial personality disorder and a turbulent history of family conflict and truancy. Schizophrenia may be difficult to detect in adolescents who show signs primarily of depression or antisocial features. Still, these symptoms may alert the clinician to its presence.[5]

Three guidelines should provide the basis of diagnosis of schizophrenia in adolescents:

1. *Persistence of the Schizophrenic Features.* The longer the schizophrenic features in a mixed clinical picture persist, the more likely a diagnosis of schizophrenia becomes. Emerging schizophrenia is especially clear when these features remain after other kinds of presenting complaints have become less noticeable. For example, they may no longer complain of depression, but they are still not thinking coherently.

2. *Extent of Usual Adolescent Concerns.* Disturbed adolescents who are becoming schizophrenic show a marked inability or reluctance to grapple with usual adolescent concerns. If teens are not involved in such age-appropriate concerns as adapting to bodily changes, increasing their interest in self-care, attaining independence from parents, and gaining social skills in relating to the opposite sex, a diagnosis of schizophrenia becomes more likely. It is as though these troubled young people are skirting around adolescence through pseudomaturity or avoiding it by being overly immature.[6] Neither pattern in and of itself, of course, is conclusive evidence of schizophrenia.

3. *Prominence of Formal Manifestations of Disturbance.* Here we are concerned with how young people are saying or doing something peculiar rather than what they are actually saying or doing. Among disturbed adolescents, the likelihood of an emerging schizophrenic disorder increases in direct relation to the prominence of formal manifestations. In other words, it is not so much peculiar thought content but peculiar ways in which this content is arrived at and expressed that point to schizophrenia in teen years.

It is helpful to establish a distinctive profile of impairment in adolescent schizophrenia. A team of researchers studying hundreds of thirteen- to eighteen-year-olds diagnosed with schizophrenia found several symptomatic factors. Here are five of the highest-rated characteristics.

1. *Bizarre Cognition.* These adolescents may substitute, confuse, or misuse pronouns in conversation. For example, the adolescent may use her own name rather than "I" when referring to herself in conversation. Speech is disconnected or incoherent and one may report hearing voices or other hallucinations.[7]

2. *Bizarre Action.* Schizophrenic adolescents may display odd postures, movements, or facial expressions. They may shut out sounds by putting their fingers in their ears, and they may rock back and forth while sitting or standing.

3. *Social Withdrawal.* These adolescents may seem to be in their own lit-
    tle world. They may have a blank stare or faraway look in their eyes.
    They may walk around oblivious to others or they may simply look
    puzzled.
4. *Emotional Detachment.* They tend to keep their emotional distance and
    may even seem apathetic. These adolescents seem to lack appropriate
    feelings, and they may be unaware of how others are feeling around
    them. They have a "blunted affect."
5. *Poor Emotional Control.* These young people may become explosively
    upset if things do not go their way. They may become easily outraged
    with their peers and express their anger in an unbridled fashion.[8]

Before we discuss etiology and treatment of schizophrenia it is important
to understand a common distinction. The more severely disabled a schizophrenic disturbance is and the longer it persists, the more likely it is to be classified as *chronic*. This is also labeled as *process* or *typical* schizophrenia. Three
features are associated with chronicity. The first is *an insidious onset*, which means
that the person's functioning slowly deteriorates over a period of months or
even years in the absence of any clearly precipitating stressors. The second is
symptom tolerance, which occurs when the person displays little concern about
the schizophrenic features. And the third is *prior maladjustment*, which means
that the person was experiencing interpersonal and school difficulties even
before the insidious onset began.[9]

Case Description

Rick was a sixteen-year-old. About six months earlier he was
considered a creative, yet quiet, adolescent with a bright
future. He had many friends, was well liked, and had never
been involved in any serious disciplinary difficulty. Shortly
before beginning his sophomore year he was in a minor
automobile accident. He suffered no head injury or any
other physical distress for that matter, but after that time he
began to sleep poorly and have nightmares. More surprisingly, he would frequently lose his temper as never before.
For seemingly no reason, he would slam his bedroom door
or yell obscenities at his parents. For the first time he began
to do poorly in school. He was even apprehended by the
police for illegally attempting to enter the school building at
night. At that point his parents sought the help of the school
counselor.

> In the counselor's office Rick displayed very little emotion and mostly stared at the wall. He expressed no concern about his failing grades. The counselor knew Rick's problem was beyond his training, and he referred Rick to a clinical psychologist. A psychological examination clearly identified features of a schizophrenic disturbance. For example, Rick had poor reality testing and an impaired capacity for social judgments. He showed signs of impulsive reactions to fairly clearly defined situations. Rick was diagnosed with acute undifferentiated schizophrenia and was hospitalized for further evaluation, pharmacological treatment, and psychotherapy.

Acute schizophrenia, sometimes known as *reactive* or *atypical* schizophrenia, on the other hand, begins rapidly in response to clear stressful experiences. Acutely schizophrenic individuals tend to recognize and worry about the unusual nature of their symptoms. One may say, "I feel as if I am going crazy. I just can't seem to think straight." Typically, their families and friends are surprised at their suddenly becoming disturbed. Acute schizophrenia responds more quickly and successfully to treatment than chronic cases.[10] After five years, 80 to 90 percent of acute schizophrenics are rated recovered or improved as compared to 50 to 60 percent for chronic schizophrenics.[11]

✔ WHY THE STRUGGLE HAPPENS

The search for the causes of schizophrenia has baffled investigators for more than a hundred years. It is most commonly thought, as it is with almost all other disorders, that schizophrenia is the result of a complex interaction of several factors.

Biochemistry

In the past few decades, researchers have concentrated a great amount of effort on understanding the brain's function in schizophrenia. Many conclude that the neurotransmitter, dopamine, is the cause of some forms of schizophrenia. The basis for a biochemical theory of schizophrenia lies in the following observations: (1) schizophrenic-like reactions may be created by hallucinogenic drugs such as LSD; (2) hallucinogenic drugs affect the chemical balance of the brain's regulatory centers and are similar to chemical compounds, such as dopamine, normally found in the brain; (3) dopamine is known to be involved in the normal functioning of the brain; (4) antipsychotic medications reduce the level of dopamine in the brain; and (5) certain drugs (like amphetamines) that increase the level of dopamine may intensify symptoms in schizophrenics and produce schizophrenic-like symptoms in non-schizophrenics. While the biochemical theory is sufficiently promising to warrant further investigation, it is certainly not seen as conclusive.[12]

Genetics

The tendency of schizophrenia to run in families is offered as evidence to support the idea of a genetic transmission of biochemical abnormalities in the brain. While the rate at which schizophrenia occurs in the general population is about 1 percent, children of one schizophrenic parent have a 10 percent chance of developing schizophrenia. Children of two schizophrenic parents have about a 40 percent chance.[13] In spite of strong evidence for a genetic link to schizophrenia, this theory has its critics. Its strength, however, is that the biochemical predisposition or vulnerability to schizophrenia is inherited rather than schizophrenia itself. The question is not whether there is an influence, but rather how much influence genetic factors have.

Family Factors

A family environment characterized by excessive distortions in communication, a hostile, confused, or ambivalent emotional climate, and destructive marital interactions have been linked to the genesis of schizophrenia.[14] Interpersonal communication in the context of family life is worth highlighting as a key element in the socialization process. According to theorists in this area, communication in schizophrenogenic homes is characterized by a vague, fragmented, ambivalent, contradictory quality. The situation creates a double-bind situation where the child cannot win.

The double messages usually involve an "impossible" appeal to come closer yet stay away. Such messages occur over and over again. For example, a mother may invite a child to kiss her while assuming a cold, rejecting posture. A father may encourage self-reliance while subtly maintaining control. These parents may "push" the child away and then accuse the child of not loving them. I once observed a father picking up his teenage daughter who was recovering from a reactive schizophrenia attack at the hospital. He seemed very glad to see her, gave her a hug, then said, "Is that how you are wearing your hair these days? Wait till your mother sees you!" This kind of paradoxical communication during the important early years of development obviously creates fear and confusion. While some children learn to cope with this environment, many others imitate the vague amorphous style of sending double meanings.[15] Obviously, family factors cannot fully explain and predict schizophrenia.

Peer Relations

Friendship patterns of adolescents may be significant in determining whether young people are at risk of schizophrenia. Those who have very few friends, who see their "friends" only infrequently and have little in common with them, and who are involved in exploitative rather than mutual relationships with them are more predisposed to schizophrenia than young people who, even if they have a relatively inactive social life, carry on at least a few really close and mutual friendships.[16]

✔ HOW PARENTS CAN HELP

The following strategies for helping an adolescent struggling with schizophrenia can be used effectively by parents; however, every parent–child relationship is unique, and some of them may be more pertinent to your situation than others. As with every significant adolescent struggle, it is best for parents to work alongside a competent counselor. With this in mind, the following is offered as a way to help you facilitate the helping process at home with your teenager.

Know Your Limits

Schizophrenia is a serious illness that requires treatment by trained professionals. This generally means clinical psychologists or psychiatrists. As a parent of a young person who may suffer from schizophrenia, the greatest service you can perform is as a bridge to programs and people who are experts in meeting the needs of schizophrenics and their families. Your local telephone directory or directory assistance, as well as the Internet, are two of the most immediate means of accessing such a service. To find agencies in your area, look up the following listings in your directory: adolescent clinics, county department of health, mental health clinics, general hospitals, and psychiatric hospitals.

When psychiatric treatment within an explicitly Christian context is desired, two programs are worth investigating: Rapha hospitals and New Life Treatment Centers. Each offers professional treatment in hospitals staffed by people committed to Christ-centered psychiatric treatment. All programs have several locations across the United States where treatment is immediately available. For additional information about Rapha, call 800-227-2657 (in Texas call 800-445-2657); for New Life, call 800-NEW-LIFE.

Avoid Exotic Spiritualizing

A young woman came to see me after four unsuccessful exorcisms had been conducted on her at her church. A sincere minister and two lay counselors had been working with her for months. The damage was horrendous. They didn't know her bizarre symptoms were signs of schizophrenia. They labeled her "demon possessed." It can be very harmful to assume exotic or supernatural causes like demon possession. There is no need to give Satan free publicity. And the hopelessness such a label engenders in the victim can often do more harm than the original disease. Misdiagnosing those who suffer from schizophrenia as demon possessed places blame on the patients for what they have little or no control over. Archibald Hart has pointed to several dangers of falsely attributing psychological problems to demons: "It removes the victim from responsibility for recognizing and confessing human sinfulness. It enhances Satan's power inappropriately. But most importantly, it delays the introduction of effective therapy. And a delay in the treatment of schizophrenia can decrease the likelihood of the sufferer's return to normality."[17]

Understand the Major Phases of Treatment

Treatment for schizophrenia today involves a mixture of hospitalization, antipsychotic medication, psychosocial therapy, and family intervention. The treatment is often divided into two major phases, the acute and the aftercare. The goal of the first stage is to reduce disruptive symptoms, reestablish contact with reality, prevent harm to self, and improve psychosocial functioning. This usually takes place in a hospital setting over the course of about a month in public psychiatric hospitals. In a private psychiatric hospital, the stay may continue for six months or more, depending on need and the patient's insurance coverage. Disruptive symptoms are reduced primarily through a combination of antipsychotic drugs and psychosocial therapy.

The goal of the aftercare phase is to assist in the continuing recovery in the community. It also assists adolescents in reentry into the mainstream of school and the developmental tasks of adolescence. This is where patients' families become especially important. With proper training and counseling, families may do much to relieve the pressure of coping and aid in the recovery process. The goal of family intervention is to establish a clear, practical set of guidelines for living with patients; it is not necessarily to resolve past family conflicts, and it is certainly not to fix the blame on anyone for an adolescent's condition. Some of the resources noted at the end of this chapter may be particularly helpful in guiding family members through this difficult experience. The emotional climate of the home may have decided effects on recovery and relapse rates.[18]

Understand the Importance of Medication

Psychotropic medications decrease adolescents' confusion, stabilize emotions, and diminish social withdrawal. Medication allows the work of psychosocial therapy to take place. One researcher cites three principal uses of these medications: (1) to bring clients out of acute schizophrenic crises; (2) to facilitate management and control of clients; and (3) to prevent recurrence of schizophrenic symptoms.[19]

The most widely used group of antipsychotic drugs is classified chemically as phenothiazines, and of these the best known is marketed under the trade name Thorazine. Another commonly prescribed drug for schizophrenia is haloperidol (Haldol). While these medications may bring relief to schizophrenic symptoms, they unfortunately have unpleasant side effects that often lead patients to discontinue using them. For this reason they are sometimes called neuroleptics because, in addition to their beneficial effects, they have side effects similar to behavioral manifestations of neurological diseases.

Know When to Refer

Appropriate referral of schizophrenic adolescents is imperative, and the sooner effective treatment is begun, the better the prognosis.

If you have an adolescent and he or she is showing signs of psychotic defenses such as hallucinations or delusions or extreme anxiety, despite your efforts to help contain them, you should refer. If medication is needed or their current medication is ineffective, counselors will refer schizophrenic adolescents to a psychiatrist. They need psychiatric evaluation in order to determine whether increasing the dosage of the present medication or changing the medication is advisable.

If, despite every effort to help, adolescents are unable to maintain adequate contact with reality or to control destructive impulses, you have a psychiatric emergency on your hands. Their judgment is impaired and their delusional system adds to the feeling of being out of control. You must take action to insure the safety of patients and others. Most state hospitals and general hospitals have psychiatric emergency units in which adolescents' need for hospitalization can be evaluated.

If the family environment seems to exacerbate symptoms, referral to a day care center may be appropriate. If after time patients are able to return to stable functioning, a socialization group may be an appropriate referral. This allows them to maintain active engagement in a social environment. Many mental health centers and hospital outpatient departments provide groups for previously hospitalized clients where they may form friendships and practice social skills.

Referral to other therapists is necessary if clients see the therapist as the personification of something or someone they despise (a "bad" parent, for example).

✔ HOW PROFESSIONALS CAN HELP

The following strategies for helping an adolescent struggling with schizophrenia are commonly used by counselors. They are presented here as a way to inform you, as a parent, and help you seek the best possible professional help you can for the adolescent in your care.

Pinpoint the Severity

As with almost all psychological struggles, it is helpful to assess the severity of the problem. Psychological assessments for schizophrenia are complex and require specific training. Most psychologists who assess schizophrenia rely on a battery of instruments that include the Minnesota Multiphasic Personality Inventory, the Millon Clinical Multiaxial Inventory, the Wechsler Adult Intelligence Scale, the Thematic Apperception Test, the Rorschach Ink Blot test, and many others. In addition to these measures, an extensive clinical interview would occur that notes interview behavior (speech patterns, appearance, style of relating, and so on), and details client history.

Work at a Positive Therapeutic Alliance

The treatment of schizophrenia depends on the stage of the disorder, the depth of regression, the grasp on reality that remains, and patients' desire for therapy. In any case, however, it is necessary from the outset to work at establishing a positive working relationship. This may try the patience of even the most sensitive of therapists. Schizophrenic adolescents may view therapists' attempts to establish supportive relationships as exploitative acts. Gentle inquiries into their personal histories may be seen as hostile efforts to interrogate them. Helping them clarify the reality of a situation may lead patients to spew out vulgar accusations. Persons working with schizophrenic adolescents are prepared for a slow and difficult road to the establishment of positive therapeutic alliances.

Identify Thoughts and Feelings

Schizophrenics often hide inner experiences. Therapists know that the emotional responses of schizophrenics are appropriate to their perceptions of reality. Therapists continually seek to empathize with and understand schizophrenic patients. Symptoms may express patients' feelings. Schizophrenic clients, for example, may choose to remain silent throughout treatment time. When they finally feel safe and trusting enough to communicate with the therapist, a revelation of all that was absorbed during the silence—a prevention of rejection—may come forward. Making an accurate interpretation or clarification of what patients are thinking and feeling may make them feel secure enough to relinquish some psychotic manifestations.

Hospitalize When Necessary

Hospitalization certainly has its downside. It is a major life disruption that removes young people from their normal surroundings of home and school, threatens their self-esteem, and often produces a stigma evidenced by reactions from their friends, teachers, and others. But insufficient treatment of a serious disorder like schizophrenia is much too high a price to pay for trying to avoid these problems. At least three circumstances necessitate hospitalization of a troubled adolescent:

1. When a more thorough evaluation is required than can be accomplished on an outpatient basis
2. When the adolescent is already out of control and potentially dangerous to himself or herself or to others
3. When environmental stress has become intolerable[20]

Consider Group Therapy

Group treatment is commonly used in the hospital setting. It is also widely used in the treatment of schizophrenia following discharge from hospitals. It can be a powerful strategy because it "forces" patients into a certain amount of social interaction and helps prevent the social isolation that is so common among schizophrenics. One study, for example, found that after two years, 40 percent of individual therapy patients had to be rehospitalized, but only 24 percent of group patients had to return to the hospital.[21] Many clinicians agree that in an outpatient setting, group therapy, in conjunction with individual therapy and medication, is fairly effective in preventing further rehospitalization. However, research has also given us guidelines for knowing when it is most effective. For example, group therapy is less effective and may even be detrimental for acutely psychotic individuals.[22]

Consider a Social-Learning Approach

Rather than trying to change the whole schizophrenic syndrome, social-learning techniques usually focus on target behavior patterns that are interfering with adolescents' functioning. Such programs are often termed token economies. This strategy has been successful in increasing appropriate behavior (such as social interaction) and in eliminating or decreasing inappropriate behavior (such as noncompliance, hallucinations, and delusional speech). Most often these treatment programs are established in institutional settings where they are more easily implemented.[23] But they also may be used in some form in the home during aftercare to provide continuity and structure for the recovering adolescent.

Where to Go for Additional Help

Friedman, M. S. *Everything You Need to Know About Schizophrenia*. New York: Rosen Publishers, 1999.

Hatfield, A. *Coping with Mental Illness in the Family: The Family Guide*. Washington, D.C.: National Alliance for the Mentally Ill, 1982.

Torrey, E. F. *Surviving Schizophrenia: A Family Manual*. New York: Harper & Row, 1983.

Walsh, M. E. *Schizophrenia: Straight Talk for Families*. New York: Warner Books, 1985.

Waso, M. *Coping with Schizophrenia: A Survival Manual for Parents, Relatives and Friends*. Palo Alto, Calif.: Science and Behavior Books, 1982.

The National Alliance for the Mentally Ill is a nationwide advocacy organization with more than 25,000 members in 300 state and local chapters. It assists families with schizophrenic members by exchanging information on treatment and financial resources, hospital procedures, and common experiences.

National Alliance for the Mentally Ill
Colonial Place Three
2107 Wilson Blvd., Suite 300
Arlington, VA 22201–3042
703-524-7600

Notes

1. D. C. Kimmel and I. B. Weiner, *Adolescence: A Developmental Transition* (Hillsdale, N.J.: Lawrence Erlbaum Associates, 1985).

2. E. Bleuler, *Dementia Praecox or the Group of Schizophrenias*, tr. J. Zinkin (1911; reprint, New York: International Universities Press, 1950).

3. A. Arieti, *Interpretation of Schizophrenia*, 2d ed. (New York: Basic Books, 1974).

4. Adapted from *The Diagnostic and Statistical Manual of Mental Disorders*, 4th ed. (Washington, D.C.: American Psychiatric Association, 1994).

5. S. C. Feinstein and D. Miller, "Psychoses of Adolescence," in *Basic Handbook of Child Psychiatry*, vol. 2, ed. J. D. Noshpitz (New York: Basic Books, 1979).

6. I. B. Weiner, "Adjustment to Adolescence," in *International Encyclopedia of Neurology, Psychiatry, Psychoanalysis, and Psychology*, ed. B. B. Wolman (Princeton, N.J.: Van Nostrand Reinhold, 1977).

7. H. Chabrol, G. Peresson, and D. Bonnet, "Cognitive Deficits in Adolescents with Schizophrenia Undergoing Antipsychotic Treatment," *American Journal of Psychiatry* 156 (1999): 497–98.

8. G. Spivack, P. E. Haimes, and J. Spotts, "Adolescent Symptomatology and Its Measurement," *American Journal of Mental Deficiency* 72 (1967): 74–95.

9. Weiner, "Adjustment to Adolescence."

10. J. H. Stephens, "Long-term Prognosis and Follow-up in Schizophrenia," *Schizophrenia Bulletin* 4 (1978): 25–47.

11. R. W. White and N. F. Watt, *The Abnormal Personality*, 5th ed. (New York: Wiley, 1981).

12. R. P. Malone, R. Sheikh, and J. M. Zito, "Novel Antipsychotic Medications in the Treatment of Children and Adolescents," *Psychiatric Services* 50 (1999): 171–74.

13. J. R. Asarnow and M. J. Goldstein, "Schizophrenia During Adolescence and a Developmental Perspective on Risk Research," *Clinical Psychology Review* 9 (1986): 211–35.

14. L. C. Waynne, M. L. Toohey, and J. Doane, "Family Studies," in *Disorders of the Schizophrenic Syndrome*, ed. L. Bellak (New York: Basic Books, 1979).

15. G. Batson et al., "Toward a Theory of Schizophrenia," *Behavioral Sciences* 1 (1956): 251–64.

16. D. Kreisman, "Social Interaction and Intimacy in Preschizophrenic Adolescence," in *The Psychopathology of Adolescence*, ed. J. Zubin and A. M. Freedman (New York: Grune and Straton, 1970).

17. A. Hart, "Regeneration, Deliverance, or Therapy?" *Leadership* 12 (Summer 1991): 74.

18. C. W. McGill and E. Lee, "Family Psychoeducational Intervention in the Treatment of Schizophrenia," *Bulletin of the Menninger Clinic* 50 (1986): 269–86.

19. H. E. Lehmann, "The Somatic and Pharmacologic Treatments of Schizophrenia," *Schizophrenia Bulletin* 13 (1974): 27–45.

20. B. G. Winsberg et al., "Home vs. Hospital Care of Children With Behavioral Disorders," *Archives of General Psychiatry* 37 (1980): 413–18.

21. C. P. O'Brien, K. B. Hamm, and B. A. Ray, "Group vs. Individual Psychotherapy With Schizophrenics: A Controlled Outcome Study," *Archives of General Psychiatry* 27 (1972): 474–85.

22. Ibid.

23. R. P. Liberman et al., "Interventions With Psychotic Behaviors," in *Innovative Treatment Methods in Psychopathology*, ed. K. S. Calhoun, H. E. Adams, and K. M. Mitchell (New York: Wiley, 1974).

SCHOOLWORK

✔ WHAT THE STRUGGLE LOOKS LIKE

Sharon handed her report card to her dad. While her father stood silent and in a state of shock, Sharon asked, "Dad, do you think those grades are the result of heredity or environment?" Ron came home with a report card displaying four F's and a C. When his parents asked about the problem, he said, "I guess I've been concentrating too hard on one subject."

Both Sharon and Ron used humor to deflect the pain of their problems with schoolwork, but for parents of underachieving students, failing school is no laughing matter. The problem is grim and gargantuan. Millions of adolescents perform poorly in math and reading. It is now estimated that 30 percent of our nation's youth are failing to acquire the basic education and skills needed to obtain secure jobs.[1]

Adolescents who struggle with schoolwork do not always look the same. Some sit in the back of crowded classrooms, chewing gum or a strand of hair, hoping teachers will not call on them.[2] Some train teachers to leave them alone by maintaining a hostile silence whenever they're called upon. Some become the class clowns, blurting out irrelevant remarks whenever the class becomes quiet. Some steal homework from classmates or turn in blank test papers (on multiple-choice tests they circle all the A's). Some suffer crippling anxiety over their school performance, fainting or throwing up during major exams. Some come to class late, skip classes or even whole days of school. Some get suspended or expelled. Some drop out.

351

In spite of their different coping styles, each of these adolescents is battling with the same problem—underachievement in school. They are what some education specialists call "sleepers." They are capable young people who are not doing well in school.

While some of these students may have slipped through the screening system with learning disabilities (they are generally identified and placed in special classes),[3] many have average IQ's but fight against two common problems: (1) lack of motivation, and (2) lack of study skills.

Motivation is the engine that drives behavior. Almost all activity is initiated and continued because of motivation. When motivation is high, students are said to be high achievers. Students with high-achievement motivation set goals and are persistent in trying to meet them. Students who lack motivation are often labeled "underachievers." They are not motivated to meet academic goals and therefore do not work up to their potential. Their feelings of frustration at school do not lead to problem solving, but to a lack of motivation and an avoidance of the real problems. Estimates of underachievement range from 15 to 40 percent of all adolescents.[4]

Poor study skills also contribute to adolescents' difficulties with schoolwork. A sure sign of this problem emerges when homework becomes a major source of conflict in the family. Surveys reveal that 60 percent of seventeen-year-olds in the United States do less than five hours of homework per week. Six percent say they have no homework, and 7 percent acknowledge that they are assigned homework but they simply do not complete it. Only 6 percent do more than ten hours of homework per week.[5] Study skills are a major factor in whether students do homework at all. Knowledge of how to study efficiently and motivation to learn are the greatest needs of adolescents who have trouble with schoolwork.

Case Description

Allen, a fourteen-year-old, had done relatively well in his elementary school years. But after only four months of high school it became apparent that he was laboring to keep his head above water. Allen felt tense and inadequate, he would lose his concentration quickly, and he rarely completed all of his homework. He reported that he would read a chapter in one of his textbooks and later have no recall of its contents. In his own words, he was "dragged" into the counselor's office by his parents, who began the session by reciting a list of Allen's academic failures. The pressure Allen was feeling from his parents was horrendous. They expected him to perform at the top of his class, yet he had few of the skills needed simply to survive.

✔ WHY THE STRUGGLE HAPPENS

Many factors contribute to failure at school. Adolescents who have difficulty with schoolwork bring together a unique combination of "causes." The behavioral and attitudinal patterns that result from these influences may persist throughout young people's lives and govern their opportunities for future work if intervention is not sought.

Lack of Information

Many students simply do not know how to study. Their poor academic performance is a result of the poor study habits they developed or picked up from a variety of sources. They were never taught effective study skills. For example, they never learned how to use the library, take notes in class, organize a scheme to study for exams, or separate the important from the trivial. To criticize these students for not studying better is like complaining that an automobile is faulty when the only difficulty is an empty gas tank.

Psychological Problems

Fear of failure, dependency, inferiority, and critical attitudes may lead to teenagers not wanting to try to study or to ineffective study. Perfectionism can lead to procrastination or failure to complete assignments. Students with more severe psychological problems almost always experience difficulties with studying. For example, traumatic family conflicts may cause children to have difficulty concentrating. And battles with depression or anxiety are obviously detrimental to academic achievement. Medication or drug use may cause a lethargy that interferes with study. Psychological problems have a powerful impact on schoolwork.[6]

Parental Influence

When parents hold unreasonably high expectations, their children often develop a fear of failure and low motivation. Adolescents may "get even" with their overly controlling parents by giving up in school.[7] Since they cannot consistently be good enough to please their parents, they stop trying. The reverse may also be true and just as detrimental. That is, if parents give little encouragement, underestimate their children, and communicate very low aspirations, their children may respond accordingly.

Some parents become so absorbed in their own affairs that they express no interest in their children's schoolwork. Some parents who are overly permissive expect no compliance, and their children do not learn discipline. Therefore, they have little motivation. Children who are overly protected also have difficulty at school. They do not learn to set goals, be self-motivated, or to work under even minimal stress. Parents have a great influence on whether children succeed or fail at school.

Low Self-Esteem

Feeling worthless is a major factor in low motivation. Students who suffer from feeling inferior often see themselves as helpless. They almost appear to want to fail. Failure becomes a way to confirm their low self-regard. The result of a poor self-concept is an "I can't" attitude that leads to almost no motivation for success in the classroom. These adolescents underestimate their abilities and have low aspirations. You may find the section on inferiority helpful when dealing with these students.

Poor Environment

Just as students' home life influences their level of enthusiasm for learning, so does school environment. The learning atmosphere in a school system or in a particular class relates directly to levels of motivation. A school should have the feel of excitement and a spirit of optimism about learning. Young people develop an interest in learning when their instructors are actively interested in the success of their learning. Some adolescents fail at school simply because instructors who "go through the motions" have turned them off to the excitement of learning.

External Locus of Control

According to some researchers, the concept of locus of control encapsulates the single most important personality dynamic associated with underachievement.[8] Locus of control refers to a person's belief about who controls the future. Adolescents high in internal locus of control believe themselves responsible for their own success. If they do badly on a test, for example, such persons are likely to blame themselves for not studying enough, for not paying attention in class, or for staying up too late. Adolescents high in external locus of control believe the factors that control success are outside themselves. For example, they may blame a teacher, or bad luck, or unfair questions for their failure on an exam. Struggling students are most often very high externals. They assume little responsibility for their failure and are therefore prone to give up. They develop what Martin Seligman calls "learned helplessness."[9] The student says, "I can't do it, so why try?"

✔ HOW PARENTS CAN HELP

The following strategies for helping an adolescent struggling with school-work can be used effectively by parents; however, every parent-child relationship is unique, and some of them may be more pertinent to your situation than others. As with every significant adolescent struggle, it is best for parents to work alongside a competent counselor. With this in mind, the following is offered as a way to help you facilitate the helping process at home with your teenager.

Consider the Family Context

If tension exists between parents, if there has been a recent divorce, or even a new sibling, academic problems may serve as a diversion from the real issue. Adolescent anxiety, anger, or depression about home life drains young people emotionally and makes concentration at school next to impossible. On the other hand, youth who compete with successful siblings may opt for failure as a means to gain attention at home. In any case, the family context is an important consideration and worthy of exploration.

Focus on Encouragement

The foundation of any work with adolescents who have trouble at school must be to encourage an "I can" attitude. Adolescents must be able to sense acceptance of themselves by their parents, and parents must avoid sarcasm and teasing at all costs. Criticism of any kind will most likely squelch any opportunity for effective intervention. Effective parents work diligently to distinguish students' self-worth from their academic performance.

Examine Study Conditions

High school students should have adequate conditions to study on their own. The best setting for most should be as quiet and uncluttered as possible. A desk in a bedroom is ideal. A bright light should come from the direction opposite the writing side (to avoid shadows). Interruptions and distractions should be minimized. Students should not accept telephone calls during study time. Dictionaries and other reference books should be available and easily accessible as well as pens, pencils, and paper. Students should also create a system that fits their style to organize their various courses in a notebook. These conditions can be discussed with adolescents. The goal is to create the best study conditions, not to force them into a setup that they will resist. Some young people, for example, may find a desk in their room too isolating. They may prefer working at a kitchen table. The key is to have a regular place and time to study.

Build Self-Esteem by Assuring Successful Achievement

The old adage that "nothing succeeds like success" is not just a cliché. It is the truth. Adolescents who are failing school need hope. They need to see signs of possibilities, signs that help them believe they can succeed. This can be done by placing them in classes that are challenging but not over their heads. Students who have failed a great deal in the past should be able to succeed about 90 percent of the time in order to like what they are doing. Discuss this principle with teachers to get their suggestions of what can be done to facilitate success. With a sense of achievement they begin to feel like winners, and are eager to master new material and skills. Self-esteem is not a prerequisite for academic achievement; it is the consequence of success.

Explore How to Study

Some students have never been taught how to study. Explore with them how they prepare for exams, write papers, and do homework. If they are at all motivated to do better, you can help them by showing them more effective ways to study. One of the most straightforward, effective, and researched methods of how to study effectively is called SQ4R—survey, question, read, recite, write, review.[10]

Survey. The goal of surveying is to determine what important questions are answered in a textbook chapter. The students go first to the beginning and end of the chapter to look for any stated objectives, a list of questions, or a chapter summary. They read these first to discover the questions they should be able to answer after completing the chapter. Next is the survey. This is the process of quickly skimming the chapter to determine what important questions it answers. They are to read titles and subtitles, and examine any illustrations, pictures, or charts. This gives them a basic understanding of what the chapter is about.

Question. A part of surveying is turning titles and subtitles into questions. For example, students who keep in mind the title of this book and the subject of this section of the book would combine them and turn them into "What are the ways to help adolescents who struggle with schoolwork?" By generating questions as they survey, students keep alert to important points in the chapter. After completing their survey, they should have a list of questions. If a chapter does not have subtitles, the lead sentences of paragraphs can be used. Before reading, students may wish to attempt to answer the questions they have formulated. They can then test their answers against the book.

Read. Next, students read to find full answers to their questions. They do not need to pore over every word and minute detail. Their goal is to answer their questions. They are to read as quickly as they can, and to read selectively to find answers to questions. If they come to an answer to a question they did not anticipate, they slow down, formulate the question, and make sure they know the answer.

Recite and Write. After students have read the answers to the questions from their survey and developed new questions and answers that they hadn't anticipated, they are to recite the answers. Just because they have read the chapter doesn't mean that they really know what it is about. Having them talk out loud about the concepts they've found helps them to get a better grasp of the content of the chapter. They are also to write a summary "self-discussion."

Review. The final step in the SQ4R method is to review the chapter. This may be done at any time. For example, in preparing for an exam, students may quiz themselves on questions they generated until they know they could give accurate answers if those questions should appear on their exam. When they know they can answer correctly and make accurate summaries, students will be more confident and perform better on examinations.

With the SQ4R method students spend less time memorizing facts they will soon forget. Instead, they focus on key concepts rather than on details, and they don't waste time reading and looking for things they already know. They are also equipped for a thorough review for test preparation. High school students who have learned the SQ4R method of studying have been shown to improve their school performance significantly.[11] If you do not feel as though you can help your child with these skills, contact a learning specialist who can.

Explore Class Attendance and Note Taking

Attending class is such an obviously useful thing to do that it is almost embarrassing to have to bring it up. Unfortunately, some adolescents need encouragement in simply being there when class opens. They need to understand the important relationship between attending class and the grades they receive. Eighty-five percent of students with a B average or higher almost always attend class.[12]

Students troubled by schoolwork also need guidance in how to take notes in class. A helpful note-taking strategy is to record notes on the right-hand side of the page, leaving the left-hand side for study questions. Students should be encouraged to write down the major ideas and statements in the lecture and not every word. After the lecture, they should take a few minutes to turn their notes into questions. The main theme and subtopics may be turned into questions and recorded next to the lecture notes. The point is to go to class looking for questions and answers.

Consider Rewards

Most parents have already used positive reinforcers, such as the privilege of watching television after studying. Rewards can sometimes be useful in motivating the unmotivated. A struggling student with a new driver's license, for example, may be highly motivated by the availability of the family car, once certain conditions have been met. Threatening kids with punishment for bad grades, however, is another popular method that does not work very well. Positive rewards work better. The best motivator of all is success. Focus on increasing the positive rather than diminishing the negative.

Explore Getting a Tutor

One of the most direct ways of improving the performance of students who are troubled by schoolwork is through professional tutors. This may be an especially helpful alternative for students who resist placement in schools for special education. Students may stay in public school and parents may use the money they would have spent on tuition to hire tutors to work with their children at home. Some tutors are experts in particular academic subjects; others can be hired to teach general study skills.

Research in education reinforces the gains that may be achieved from one-on-one instruction. An area college or university education department is an excellent resource for tutors. Some high schools have tutoring programs. And an increasing number of corporations sell tutorial services. One of them, Sylvan Learning Centers, increased from two hundred franchise holders to four hundred fifty in two years. Adolescents often develop relationships with their tutors that resemble the bond between clients and therapists. And that student/tutor bond has similar therapeutic effects. Some embattled students may find it easier to form relationships with adults they identify as tutors than with adults they call parents, or shrinks or therapists. For students with emotional problems as well as academic struggles, however, the combination of tutoring and psychotherapy produces outstanding, even dramatic results.

Consider Private Schools

Some parents are frustrated by their experiences with public schools and may find a high-performance prep school or a Christian school a positive alternative. Generally, these schools are orderly, safe, wholesome, and traditional in instruction. Sometimes the challenge of a rigorous program is precisely what an unruly or unmotivated student needs. To locate a Christian school in a specific area these organizations can be helpful:

Association of Christian Schools, International
P.O. Box 4097
Whittier, CA 80607

Christian Schools International
3350 E. Paris Avenue S.E
Grand Rapids, MI 49512

National Association of Private Schools
2021 K St., N.W.
Washington, DC 20006
(For locating preparatory schools)

Know When to Refer

Refer struggling students to education specialists for evaluation if you suspect a learning disability. Most learning disabled and emotionally disturbed students have been identified and placed in special classes or assigned to resource teachers for special help. But occasionally they are missed.

Where to Go for Additional Help

Felton, G. S., and B. E. Biggs. *Up from Under-Achievement*. Springfield, Ill.: Charles C. Thomas, 1977.

Lee, P. M. *Helping Your Child with Homework*. Washington, D.C.: U.S. Department of Education, 1999.

Lillie, D. L., and P. A. Place. *Partners: A Guide to Working with Schools for Parents of Children with Special Instructional Needs*. Glenview, Ill.: Scott, Foresman, 1982.

Nemko, M., and B. Nemko. *How to Get a "Private School" Education in a Public School*. Washington, D.C: Acropolis Books, 1986.

Rich, D. *Mega Skills: How Families Can Help Children Succeed in School and Beyond*. Boston: Houghton-Mifflin, 1988.

Robinson, F. *Effective Study*. New York: Harper & Row, 1970.

Wrenn, C. G., and S. Schwaryrock. *Grades: What's So Important About Them, Anyway?* Circle Pines, Minn.: American Guidance Service, 1970.

Zifferblatt, S. M. *Improving Study and Homework Behaviors*. Champaign, Ill.: Research Press, 1970.

Notes

1. Education Commission of the States, "Securing Our Future: The Report of the National Forum for Youth At Risk" (Denver: Education Commission of the States, 1988).

2. D. T. Fenwick, "Managing Space, Energy, and Self: Junior High Teachers' Experiences of Classroom Management, Teaching, and Teacher Education," *Teaching and Teacher Education* 14 (1998): 619–31.

3. "Learning disabilities" is a generic phrase describing problems that an estimated 6 to 10 percent of otherwise normal students encounter in taking in, processing, and retrieving information. The most familiar is dyslexia, a neurological disorder that causes students to reverse letters and misread words.

4. C. A. Asbury, "Selected Factors Influencing Over- and Underachievement in Young School-age Children." *Review of Educational Research* 44 (1974): 409–28.

5. National Assessment of Educational Progress, *Newsletter* 11 (1978): 1–3.

6. W. B. Carey, "Temperament and Behavior Problems in the Classroom," *School Psychology Review* 27 (1998): 522–33.

7. K. Metcalf and E. Gaier, "Patterns of Middle-Class Parenting and Adolescent Underachievement," *Adolescence* 22 (1987): 919–28.

8. L. Nielsen, *How To Motivate Adolescents* (Englewood Cliffs, N.J.: Prentice-Hall, 1982).

9. M. Seligman, *Learned Optimism* (New York: Knopf, 1991).

10. F. P. Robinson, *Effective Study* (New York: Harper & Row, 1970).

11. J. M. Greiner and P. Karoly, "Effects of Self-Control Training on Study Activity and Academic Performance: An Analysis of Self-Monitoring, Self-Reward, and Systematic Planning Components," *Journal of Counseling Psychology* 23 (1976): 495–502.

12. H. C. Lindgren, *The Psychology of College Success* (New York: Wiley, 1969).

SHYNESS

✔ WHAT THE STRUGGLE LOOKS LIKE

Some adolescents are socially invisible. They are not noticed or selected as leaders. They do not participate much in class or other social activities. They do not stand up for their own rights, and they are too timid to express their opinions on matters that concern them. They are afraid to ask others out on dates. They feel awkward and tense in social situations. They seek quiet corners at parties. Because they want to be liked, they are easily influenced by others and lack self-confidence. These are the adolescents who struggle with shyness.

Shyness is fear to meet people and discomfort in their presence. At its core is anxiety about being evaluated by others and consequently rejected. In its extreme form, shyness becomes a social phobia (see the section on phobia). While many adolescents recognize shyness in themselves, it would probably come as a surprise to them to learn that only 7 percent of Americans claim they have never experienced attacks of shyness.[1]

Anyone who writes about shyness owes an enormous debt to Philip G. Zimbardo of Stanford University, who has studied shyness for more than two decades. Much of what I have written here was inspired by his work. His research reveals that more than 80 percent of high school and college students perceive themselves as shy at times, and 40 percent report current shyness and embarrassment around peers. Symptoms include blushing, inability to make eye contact, an avoidance of social gatherings, a tendency to speak in a voice almost too low to be heard, clammy hands, dry mouth, excessive perspiration, trembling hands and legs, pounding heart, queasy stomach, a sinking feeling, or even a sudden need to go to the bathroom.[2]

Case Description

Martha, age fifteen, came to counseling at the encouragement of her mother, who described her as "a wallflower." In the first session Martha barely said a word. She seemed cold and emotionally aloof. She was, however, visibly upset at having to be in counseling. It was almost as though she were using her silence as a weapon to preserve her sense of dignity. To talk freely with the counselor would mean that she had lost the power struggle with her mom. There was more to her silence, however, than not losing that battle.

Therapy progressed slowly at first, but after three or four sessions, Martha confessed her dread of being with people whom she did not already know. She wanted to meet other people but was terribly fearful of doing or saying something that would embarrass her. To avoid having to sit uncomfortably next to another student, she walked alone to and from school and always arrived at her classes just as they were beginning. She confessed that she had even retreated to the isolation of a bathroom stall for safety. Martha arranged much of her life so as to avoid situations where she might be put on the spot.

Shy adolescents suffer numerous disadvantages. Compared with others, shy people are more likely to be anxious, depressed, lonely, have lower self-esteem, and regard their social networks as less supportive and less satisfying. Unlike introverts, shy people are not happy to be by themselves or to participate minimally in social encounters.[3] Zimbardo likens shyness to a prison that is every bit as real and in some ways more restricting than iron bars.[4]

☑ WHY THE STRUGGLE HAPPENS

For many years researchers have attempted to make sense out of the complexities of shyness. The following is not an exhaustive list of causes.

Learned Helplessness

One of the ways adolescents learn their social style is by trying behaviors out and receiving various rewards and punishments. Over time they develop expectations concerning the likely results of their behaviors. If their behaviors achieve desired goals, they develop positive expectations. They also learn what doesn't work. They learn to expect a negative response to their behavior, and they make choices to avoid that behavior again. Helplessness is learned when expectations, either positive or negative, are not present. For example, if young people are in new social situations where they do not know what to expect, they will probably become anxious and clam up. It is almost as if they are visiting a foreign country where they do not understand the language. They feel helpless and give up trying to communicate. This may also happen if their behaviors produce inconsistent rewards (whether real or simply perceived). If they do not know what to expect they become helpless. They become shy.[5]

Formality

Formal situations can elicit shyness. Religious ceremonies, graduations, weddings, funerals, and important meetings all have a greater number of rules than other situations. People want to do the right thing. A mistake in a formal setting can be embarrassing. And the likelihood of making a mistake becomes greater where there are more spoken and unspoken rules. Formality makes teens feel exposed and vulnerable. Of course, formality often results in situational shyness, but for some teens, every interaction is "formal."

Social Attention

Adolescents do not want to be ignored. But being conspicuous or being stared at also tends to cause social anxiety. Shyness is likely to be the reaction of a girl in a group of boys. Physical handicaps frequently result in shyness. These adolescents may avoid others so as not to be stared at or talked about. Even subtle handicaps like learning disabilities or expressive language problems may lead to social withdrawal. An example is adolescents who arrive late at gatherings and find everyone stopping to look at them as they enter. While a few adolescents love the attention, many shrink away and look for a place to hide to avoid all eyes upon them. It's the middle ground of social attention that produces psychological comfort for most young people.

Novelty

Teens often deplore new social environments. For many, a new social setting is about as comfortable as a new pair of tight shoes. Adolescents have a hard enough time dealing with their changing bodies without the discomfort of a strange social context. The threatening social situation is likely to make young people inhibited and careful in their behavior. Generally, this guardedness is relaxed after they grow more accustomed to the setting. However, some teens never seem to jump over the hurdle of novelty. They maintain their role as the "new kid" and incorporate shyness into their basic social style.

Heredity

Some researchers blame genetics for shyness. They say shyness runs in families. The evidence is not conclusive, but a study conducted by psychologists at Yale and Harvard revealed that 10 to 15 percent of us are born with a propensity to become shy. This shyness is seen in infants and toddlers who turn away from strangers and hide behind parents when spoken to, even by adults they know. Jerome Kagan of Harvard reports that shy infants and toddlers develop a rapid heart rate and become wary, withdrawn, reserved, and silent when faced with unfamiliar people or new situations. Their hypersensitivity makes them uncomfortable, self-conscious, even panicky in social settings. Of course, circumstances play a role in determining whether an inherited tendency to become shy is expressed. The Yale-Harvard study revealed that two-thirds of shy children had older siblings who perhaps bullied or belittled them, shaking their self-confidence.

Parental Modeling

Shy parents often produce shy children, but this does not mean shyness is in the genes. Adolescents are prone to fall into the same social styles of their adult models. If they hear their parents discuss others in fearful or mistrustful terms and they see their parents avoid social settings, they may acquire a habit of being quiet and shy.[6] A strict behaviorist would say that shyness is a learned phobic reaction.

Parental Overprotection

Adolescents who have been overly protected by their parents are frequently dependent, passive, and shy. They have been limited in their opportunities to be adventurous, and thus have not learned to trust themselves in dealing with their social environment.

Self-Labeling

A self-perpetuating pattern is set when adolescents perceive and accept themselves as shy.[7] They view the world through timid glasses and don't recognize that they have a choice in eye wear. It is as if they are out to prove that they are shy. Experiences that present contrary findings are warded off. Their belief prevents them from taking actions that could lead them to get what they want and counteract their feelings of inferiority. They have labeled themselves as shy "and that settles it."

✔ HOW PARENTS CAN HELP

The following strategies for helping an adolescent struggling with shyness can be used effectively by parents; however, every parent-child relationship is unique, and some of them may be more pertinent to your situation than others. As with every significant adolescent struggle, it is best for parents to work alongside a competent counselor. With this in mind, the following is offered as a way to help you facilitate the helping process at home with your teenager.

Emphasize Warmth and Acceptance

Although "unconditional positive regard" is taken for granted in most of the sections of this book, shyness demands a reemphasis. The more warmth and acceptance given to shy adolescents the better. If they experience love and acceptance from you, they may then generalize the experience and realize that others can accept them too. Provide them with safe places to let down their social guard, places where they will not be embarrassed or ashamed, where they do not even have to think of being rejected. In doing this you are also modeling effective social interaction. You may find it helpful to review "Characteristics of Effective Helping" and "The Heart of Helping" in Part One.

Encourage Volunteering

Sharing not only feelings, but talents and knowledge as well, according to Zimbardo, helps alleviate shyness.[8] Adolescents do not need to join the Peace Corps, however, to share their abilities. For example, if a shy fourteen-year-old girl has knowledge of photography and enjoys it, urge her to use it to help others. A youth minister, for example, may ask her to chronicle a choir trip on film. This not only increases her self-esteem, but her interest can become an entry into less frightening conversations with others. Encourage shy young people to volunteer for activities. A small job at a party may be a great aid in overcoming social awkwardness. They may be given something to do, such as helping serve or cleaning up. It's their reason for being there. While shy adolescents do not want the spotlight, social assignments or special roles give them reasons to initiate conversation and interaction. These may go a long way in helping them feel good about themselves and secure enough to take more social risks.

Know When to Refer

Refer shy adolescents to a counselor if you find yourself becoming impatient with their seeming inability to master social skills. If you recognize that you are encouraging dependence in an already shy and dependent adolescent, you should also consider referral.

✓ HOW PROFESSIONALS CAN HELP

The following strategies for helping an adolescent struggling with shyness are commonly used by counselors. They are presented here as a way to inform you, as a parent, and help you seek the best possible professional help you can for the adolescent in your care.

Help Them Understand Their Shyness

Adolescents, like all of us, have a need to explain their experiences. Understanding shyness is no exception. Experiments have demonstrated the value of people understanding why they are shy. Three therapy groups of shy people received the same treatment with the exception of an explanation of shyness. Those in one group were helped to understand their shyness by an explanation of the role of their developmental history and childhood experiences. Another group was shown how shyness usually results from their thinking styles and self-perceptions. The third group received counseling that did not focus on finding explanations for shyness. In general, the first two approaches, which helped the shy people understand their shyness, were more effective than the third approach, which did not. When shy adolescents are helped to understand their shyness, they become more amenable to change.[9]

Implement Social Skills Training

Research has shown that social skills are best learned in group settings designed to provide the following experiences: (1) a description and rationale for new behaviors that are to be learned; (2) a demonstration of new behaviors through modeling; (3) practice of new behaviors with feedback about how one is doing; and (4) transfer of new behaviors to the natural environment. These training groups generally proceed gradually to allow clients to progress at their own pace.[10]

If a group setting is not possible, it is still necessary to implement social skill training strategies. Here are some techniques that are often used in counseling shy adolescents.

1. Counselors will help shy teens rehearse what they want to say in specific situations. They will be asked to write out complaints, compliments, and questions, and then read them aloud and role play specific situations. If possible, counselors will have clients use the telephone to express themselves while in the office.

2. Counselors will help teens practice smiling and making eye contact. They will be asked to look in the mirror as practice. They will be given assignments to smile and make eye contact with five strangers each day.

3. Counselors will work to improve teens' speaking voice and volume. They will be taught to experiment with volume levels. Sometimes a tape recorder is helpful in giving them objective feedback.

4. Counselors will ask teens to observe and take notes on behavior patterns of people they respect. They are encouraged to see how others laugh at themselves when things go wrong. They practice modeling behavior. They practice giving compliments, asking questions, and sharing experiences they've recently had.

5. Counselors will guide clients in an exploration of their true selves. Shy adolescents often believe they have to be someone they aren't. They will be encouraged to accept and appreciate their peculiarities as special traits that make them distinctive and interesting (rather than unattractive).

6. Counselors will explore their use of humor. I often find that quiet adolescents have a wonderful sense of humor. Sometimes they need only to be encouraged to try it out. If appropriate, counselors might have clients call a store to ask about a product and have them see if they can make the person on the telephone laugh.

7. Counselors will review their appearance. This idea may sound ridiculous, but research speaks loudly about the importance of physical appearance and social interactions.[11] Physical appearance has a profound impact on first impressions. Dressing appropriately makes young people more appealing to others and helps them feel better about themselves.

Use Relaxation Techniques

Reducing anxiety in social settings involves two basic steps. The first is to develop self-relaxation skills. The second is to use these skills during social interaction. Self-relaxation involves awareness of muscle tension and strategies of deep muscle relaxation. This technique along with others is described in detail in the section on anxiety. Once relaxation techniques have been mastered they may be applied to shyness by having adolescents imagine real-life social situations that cause anxiety and place themselves in these situations as fully as possible. They will then be invited to practice their self-relaxation techniques until they can see themselves in those situations without anxiety.

The use of imagery to promote self-relaxation is based on the procedure of systematic desensitization developed by Joseph Wolpe.[12] The next step is to let them practice these relaxation techniques in actual situations. This will help them reduce their social anxiety and give them control over their seemingly uncontrollable social anxiety.

Teach Positive Self-Talk

Shy behavior is what people do, not what they are. And much of what we do comes from what we think. A very destructive aspect of shyness is young people's acceptance of the idea that they are shy by nature and little can be done to improve things. This belief is supported by numerous irrational assumptions and expectations that have caused them to talk themselves into "being shy." These assumptions include "Everyone must like me," "It is awful to make a mistake in front of others," "I need to be perfect," and "I can't control what I do in a social setting." Consider the thoughts going through the minds of shy adolescents who want to ask someone for a date.

Anxiety is understandable, but young people will multiply the natural apprehension with thoughts like "What if she says no? That would mean I am terrible! I would feel like a jerk and never ask anyone else out again. I can't take that risk. I don't think I will call her."

The challenge facing a therapist is to help a shy young man say something more along the lines of "If she says no, that would be unfortunate, but it certainly wouldn't be the end of the world. What would I have to lose? In fact, I can only gain. If she says yes, great! If not, I still have the satisfaction of knowing I tried and I won't be any worse off." Shyness generally results from viewing social interactions as times when people are evaluating adolescents crippled by shyness. This attitude is bound to make young people feel anxious and appear anxious. With this pattern of thinking, it is not surprising that shy adolescents expect the worst and don't enjoy socializing.

Adolescents who overcome shyness do so with positive self-talk.[13] They see social interactions as opportunities to make new friends and have fun. One previously shy adolescent I worked with did a major shift in his thinking and had a sentence he repeated to himself whenever he started to feel shy: "The party is where I am." This helped him remember that he did not have to depend on another person's evaluation to have self-worth.

Donald Meichenbaum has developed a therapeutic approach built on use of self-statements as coping skills. He presents three major steps for overcoming social anxiety.[14] If a young person wants to meet a stranger, for example, the first step is to prepare for the challenge. This is done through self-statements like "I know how to relax when I get nervous; besides, I am allowed to make mistakes." Next is learning to keep cool during the interaction. The young person may say, "I can handle this. My nervousness is natural and I am doing fine. I am going to focus on the other person, not myself." Finally comes self-reinforcement. Here the adolescent may say, "I survived it and that is success. It is getting easier each time."

Implement Assertiveness Training

Assertiveness is an attitude and a way of acting in any situation where people need to express feelings, ask for what they want, or say no to something they don't want. Several studies have demonstrated the usefulness of this technique with shy adolescents. After a month-long assertiveness-training program, thirteen-year-olds earned higher self-concept scores and became more confident and more willing to speak up in their classes.[15] Even with as little as twelve hours of assertiveness training, high school students had improved their self-esteem and their relationships with teachers. Moreover, students with the lowest self-esteem scores at the outset made the greatest improvements.[16]

Learning to be assertive involves developing nonverbal skills. These include looking directly at other people when addressing them, maintaining an open rather than a closed posture, and literally "standing their ground" by not physically backing away from other people.[17]

Learning to be assertive also involves an expression of feelings and desires. Feelings are neither "right" nor "wrong," but they give people energy. Feelings simply exist. Shy adolescents often evaluate their feelings for appropriateness. They ask, "What should I be feeling?" rather than "What am I feeling?" Once they have learned to identify their feelings, encourage expression of them, first with counselors and then in their environment. Shy adolescents keep their feelings to themselves also because they assume others already know what they want. They need to see that people around them are not mind readers.

Where to Go for Additional Help

Adler, R. B. *Confidence in Communication: A Guide to Assertive and Social Skills.* New York: Holt, Rinehart, 1974.

Alberti, R. E., and M. L. Emmons. *Your Perfect Right: A Guide to Assertive Behavior.* San Luis Obispo, Calif.: Impact Publishers, 1978.

Bower, G., and S. Bower. *Asserting Yourself: A Practical Guide for Positive Change.* Reading, Mass.: Addison-Wesley, 1976.

Bruno, F. J. *Conquer Shyness: Understand Your Shyness and Banish It Forever!* New York: Macmillan, 1997.

Carducci, B. J. *Shyness: A Bold New Approach*. New York: HarperCollins Publishers, 1999.

Daly, J. A., and J. C. McCroskey. *Avoiding Communication: Shyness, Reticence, and Communication Apprehension*. Beverly Hills, Calif.: Sage Publications, 1984.

Emmons, M., and D. Richardson. *The Assertive Christian*. Minneapolis: Winston Press, 1981.

Faul, J., and D. Augsburger. *Beyond Assertiveness*. Waco, Tex.: Word, 1983.

Gilmartin, B. G. *Shyness and Love: Causes, Consequences and Treatment*. New York: University Press of America, 1987.

Simon, G. *How I Overcame Shyness: 100 Celebrities Share Their Secrets*. New York: Simon & Schuster, 1999.

Zimbardo, P. G. *Shyness: What It Is, What to Do About It*. Reading, Mass.: Addison-Wesley, 1977.

_____. *Shyness Clinic*. New York: Biomonitoring Applications, 1978.

_____. *The Shy Child*. New York: McGraw-Hill, 1981.

Notes

1. P. G. Zimbardo, "Shyness," in *Dictionary of Pastoral Care and Counseling*, ed. R. J. Hunter (Nashville: Abingdon, 1990).

2. P. G. Zimbardo, *Shyness: What It Is, What To Do About It* (Reading, Mass.: Addison Wesley, 1977).

3. B. M. DePaulo et al., "Are Shy People Reluctant To Ask for Help?" *Journal of Personality and Social Psychology* 56 (1989): 834–44.

4. Zimbardo, *Shyness: What It Is*.

5. M. E. Seligman, *Helplessness: On Depression, Development and Death* (San Francisco: W. H. Freeman, 1975).

6. S. D. Bradshaw, "I'll Go If You Will: Do Shy Persons Utilize Social Surrogates?" *Journal of Social and Personal Relationships* 15 (1998): 651–69.

7. M. Van Ameringen and J. M. Oakman, "The Relationship of Behavioral Inhibition and Shyness to Anxiety Disorder," *Journal of Nervous and Mental Disease* 186 (1998): 425–531.

8. Zimbardo, *Shyness: What It Is*.

9. M. A. Hoffman and H. Teglasi, "The Role of Causal Attributions in Counseling Shy Subjects," *Journal of Counseling Psychology* 29 (1982): 132–39.

10. R. M. Eisler and L. W. Frederksen, *Perfecting Social Skills: A Guide to Interpersonal Behavior* (New York: Plenum, 1980).

11. R. E. Glasgow and H. Arkowitz, "The Behavioral Assessment of Male and Female Social Competence in Dyadic Heterosexual Interactions," *Behavior Therapy* 6 (1975): 488–98.

12. J. Wolpe, *The Practice of Behavior Therapy* (New York: Pergamon, 1974).

13. N. Eisenberg, S. A. Shepard, R. A. Fabes, B. C. Murphy, and I. K. Guthrie, "Shyness and Children's Emotionality, Regulation, and Coping," *Child Development* 69 (1998): 767–90.

14. D. Meichenbaum, *Cognitive-Behavior Modification* (New York: Plenum, 1977).

15. S. Wehr and M. Kaufman, "The Effects of Assertive Training on Performance in Highly Anxious Adolescents," *Adolescence* 22 (1987): 195–205.

16. J. Stake, C. Deville, and C. Pennell, "The Effects of Assertive Training on the Performance and Self-Esteem of Adolescent Girls," *Journal of Youth and Adolescence* 12 (1983): 435–43.

17. S. D. Bradshaw and M. F. Stasson, "Attributions of Shy and Not-Shy Group Members for Collective Group Performance," *Small Group Research* 29 (1998): 283–307.

SIBLINGS

☑ WHAT THE STRUGGLE LOOKS LIKE

Rivalry between brothers and sisters has been written about from the earliest recorded history. From the biblical account of Cain and Abel to the make-believe world of Cinderella and her stepsisters, sibling conflicts have formed the basis for untold numbers of stories. Our interest in the sibling bond, however, is not limited to literature. Ever since the prominent psychoanalyst of the early 1900s, Alfred Adler, wrote about the firstborn child in a family being "dethroned" by the competition, jealousy, and hostility of a younger brother or sister, sibling rivalry has been the topic of study for numerous researchers.

Growing up in a family context that includes brothers and sisters is an experience that 80 percent of American children share.[1] Children with siblings often spend more time with one another than they do with either parent. Siblings have a tremendous influence on child development. The presence of a second sibling acts as an incentive for change. The first child is pushed to differentiate from the other, usually toward the values of the parents, in order to retain his or her "favored" position. The first child's growth is typically accelerated while the younger child is likely to maintain a more adaptive position, which requires more attention from parents.[2]

According to one study, the most frequent type of aggression occurring in American society is between youthful siblings. These reports indicate that 40 percent of brothers and sisters hit one another with harmful objects at least once during a given year, and more than 80 percent engage in some form of violence against a sibling.[3] Other researchers have found statistics to be less dramatic.[4] Some researchers have found sibling conflict to be the most intense among sibs of the same sex.[5] Others have found close-age spacing to intensify sibling conflict while others have found it to promote stronger ties.[6] Although experts quibble about the exact figures and disagree about research methodology, most agree that sibling rivalry is indeed common, if not normal.

Three forms of sibling rivalry have been identified: *Heir/Heiress*, where siblings perceive that one child is the parents' favorite; *Competitor*, where siblings perceive that the parent-favored child changes depending on current behavior; and *Peers*, where siblings perceive that each is recognized as special to parents and therefore conflicts are minimal.[7]

Failure to resolve rivalry may lead to residual and persistent envy, manipulation, scheming, plotting, grudges, alienation, revenge, sabotage, or even vendettas.[8] Happily, these situations are the exceptions, but effective therapeutic intervention helps to ensure that siblings overcome their inevitable conflicts.

Case Description

Corey, a fourteen-year-old, was engaged in extreme sibling rivalry with his brother Doug, age sixteen. Almost every look and gesture provoked verbal or physical battle. They were in constant competition for attention from others. They argued over who sat where in the family car, what TV shows to watch, who was better at basketball, and on and on. More than once valuable objects were broken as a result of one of their tussles. Doug remembers Corey once cutting the telephone cord with a pair of scissors while he was talking on the phone. Corey recalls Doug threatening him with a hot iron for spilling milk on his homework. During the first session they reeled off their stories of sibling conflict. They were brought into counseling by their mother, a single parent, who simply felt that she had lost control of both of them.

Before exploring the causes and treatment of sibling rivalry it is important to note briefly three unique characteristics of human beings. These traits get to the root of all human conflict. First, each person sees and experiences the world through his or her own perceptual framework. Second, humans are intentional, willful beings with goals to be fulfilled. Third, humans are social beings who live out their identity within the context of family and other relationships. In short, to be human means to have conflict.[9] Siblings do not have an option whether to have conflict, only how to deal with it.

✔ WHY THE STRUGGLE HAPPENS

Many factors lie behind sibling rivalry. The following are just a few of the most commonly cited.

Favoritism

Children depend so much on their parents for love, attention, and fulfillment of their needs that they simply do not like to share their parents with anyone. This is especially true if they perceive, even irrationally, that their parents are playing favorites. Parental favoritism toward one child may spark tremendous resentment in siblings. Joseph and his coat of many colors is a biblical example of jealousy over perceived parental favoritism.

Displaced Anger

Sometimes hostile feelings that originate in other relationships, for example with parents, are taken out on younger siblings. Children may pick fights with siblings as a way to release frustration about matters that are totally unrelated. Brothers or sisters may be convenient marks for a needed physically and emotionally cathartic experience.

Feelings of Inferiority

If children have to live in the shadow of talented siblings' achievements, they tend to feel robbed of their individuality. The competition doesn't seem fair. Adolescents troubled with this problem feel that all of their actions and accomplishments are compared with those of their siblings. One continually hears people say, "You're John's brother? Wow, you have some big shoes to fill." To balance the scales, younger siblings may try, unsuccessfully, to take their rivals down a few notches by showing hostility toward them.[10]

Developmental Changes

Identity issues and self-consciousness add a great deal to the causation of sibling rivalry during adolescence. Teenagers, more than any other age group, may be angered by even a minor assault on their dignity and self-worth. This may include teasing, bossiness, sarcasm, criticism, or unfair treatment. During these years of continual change, the body's chemistry may interact with emotional processing and contribute to short fuses and emotional blowups with siblings. Hormone levels in adolescents, for example, have been shown to be related to anger.[11]

Environment

The structure of some households may promote conflict between siblings. They may compete for property, space, and other tangible goods that they share by virtue of their environment. For example, siblings may become involved in disputes over the use of the bathroom or telephone. Interestingly, when people are placed in situations that create conflict, they are more likely to attribute the origins of conflict to each other than to the situation of which they both are victims.[12]

✅ HOW PARENTS CAN HELP

The following strategies for helping an adolescent struggling with sibling conflict can be used effectively by parents; however, every parent-child relationship is unique, and some of them may be more pertinent to your situation than others. As with every significant adolescent struggle, it is best for parents to work alongside a competent counselor. With this in mind, the following is offered as a way to help you facilitate the helping process at home with your teenager.

Explore Your Part

When young people experience serious conflict with siblings, it is helpful to assess your possible contributions. Are you treating all of your children fairly and still allowing for their uniqueness? Are you avoiding comparing one child with another, as in the question, "Why don't you work hard in school like your sister?" Do you exhibit any subtle signs of favoritism? Do you baby one sibling? Do you call one child by an endearing term? Do you spend more time or money on one child? Do you belittle one child's interests, abilities, or performance? Do you recognize and affirm the uniqueness of each child? Consider spending time alone with each child. Every child should have a meaningful experience, for example, a trip alone with a parent—with no other siblings to compete with. Plan times for one of your children to be your "only" child. Middle children, in particular, tend to suffer from parental neglect, and a focused experience will do much to boost their self-worth.[13]

Uncover the True Source of Conflict

At times sibling conflict is nothing more than the blatant irritation that comes from living with a brother or sister. At other times conflict may be a symptom of an emotion that is buried deep below the surface. Angry adolescents, for example, may be mad at their fathers for embarrassing them in front of their friends, or at teachers for unfair grades. Since adults are more difficult to confront, young people may take out their frustrations on siblings. Examine any potential sources of frustration. The rivalry may be only a guise for the real problem.

Examine Assumptions

People inevitably make assumptions about their siblings' behavior that have no basis in reality, and, in turn, they act on these assumptions without ever checking their validity. For example, one may assume that a brother who forgets to report a phone message does so on purpose, or one may assume that a sister "lost" a favorite cassette tape in retaliation for a real or imagined offense. Adolescents may never reveal these assumptions to others. However, as they keep them from the light of examination they lead only to further destructive conflict. Help them explore whether or not the assumptions they are acting upon are true.

Consider Contracting

When a repetitive and predictable sibling dispute over an issue becomes apparent, a contract may be useful. For instance, if two sisters routinely argue over the use of the stereo, a contract over the shared use of it may ease tension. First, define the goals of the contract. Allow each to voice her concerns. Next discuss an agreed-upon plan to achieve the goals. The two should write the contract together, clearly stating requests, definable behaviors, times, and so on. The contract should be put into writing and signed and dated by each sibling. This signifies their commitment. Post the contract as a visual reminder.[14]

Detect Abuse

It is becoming more apparent that some siblings suffer from the nightmare of a still largely undetected form of abuse from their siblings. It may be physical, emotional, or sexual. If you suspect serious abuse, do not rationalize it away by saying, "Kids will be kids," or, "It's only normal sibling rivalry." Calling sibling abuse nothing more than sibling rivalry is like labeling physical abuse nothing more than a little discipline. For further help in working with these terrible situations you will find the book *Perilous Rivalry* useful.

Model Forgiveness

Angry adolescents who are full of hatred toward siblings ultimately need the healing of forgiveness. They need to forgive brother or sister as well as themselves. Forgiveness holds more promise for aiding effective resolution of chronic sibling rivalry than any therapeutic intervention. The memory of hurtful events will continue to cause anger, bitterness, and resentment throughout adult life. The solution, in these cases, lies not in forgetting or even in conflict-management techniques, but in breaking the power of memories to recreate feelings of hurt at some later date. The solution is found in forgiveness.[15] For techniques and strategies that facilitate this process, see the section on forgiveness.

Know When to Refer

Refer adolescents who struggle with sibling conflict to a competent counselor or psychologist when, over time, they become more out of control and increasingly combative. Refer them if you recognize that you have not dealt with issues regarding your own siblings that may be interfering with how you treat each other.

✔ HOW PROFESSIONALS CAN HELP

The following strategies for helping an adolescent struggling with sibling conflict are commonly used by counselors. They are presented here as a way to inform you, as a parent, and help you seek the best possible professional help you can for the adolescent in your care.

Assign an Anger Log

This assignment is designed to heighten teens' awareness of where, when, why, and how often they get angry. It is a diary-like means of analyzing provocative sibling incidents. In the event of any conflict, counselors will ask teens to record (1) the time, (2) where they were, (3) what happened, (4) who was present, (5) what they did or said, (6) the result, (7) how they felt afterward, and (8) what they would do differently. They will review the log and role-play situations from it with their counselor to learn improvement techniques.

Teach the "Anger Control Chain"

Extensive research has revealed the power that comes from learning anger management. Raymond Novaco has designed a program that centers around "the five links in the anger control chain"—triggers, cues, reminders, reducers, and self-evaluation. This intervention strategy is described in the section on anger.

Teach Conflict Management

When two siblings are in conflict, they have four major choices about the direction they will take. Counselors will help adolescents recognize that *they* make the choice. According to Joyce Hocker Frost and William W. Wilmot, adolescents may choose to (1) avoid the conflict, (2) maintain it at its present level, (3) escalate it, or (4) reduce it.[16] Counselors will explore the tactics of each response. Avoiding the true conflict may be accomplished by postponing or refusing to recognize the conflict. To maintain the conflict siblings may strike a bargain that temporarily maintains the status quo but does not resolve the conflict. They may escalate the conflict by calling each other names, by pulling in other issues that are tangentially related to the real conflict, or by threatening each other. Finally, they may choose to reduce the conflict in the following ways.

- Resist tendencies to attack, criticize, or use emotionally loaded words.
- Break the conflict into smaller issues and deal with them one at a time.
- Ask for more information about the other person's point of view and attempt to empathize with the other's experience.
- Talk about what each is genuinely feeling without accusing one another.
- State the positions of each side clearly and concisely until both can articulate the other's point of view.
- Compromise by agreeing on an alternative that resolves the conflict; each loses something and each wins something.

Another basic guideline for creative conflict management is effective communication. It consists of attentive and reflective listening and sending messages. In sending messages, it is important for young people to remember that all communication is a matter of perceptions and perspectives, not many facts. On the receiving end the key is to avoid distortions. Two things should be practiced for effective receiving of communication. First, listen to both the verbal and nonverbal messages. Second, check with the sender to see whether messages are being understood correctly.

Where to Go for Additional Help

Balswick, J. O., and J. K. Balswick. *The Family: A Christian Perspective on the Contemporary Home.* Grand Rapids: Baker, 1990.

Bank, S. P., and M. D. Kahn. *The Sibling Bond.* New York: Basic Books, 1997.

Clark, B. *The Sibling Constellation.* New York: Penguin Books, 1999.

Collins, G. R. *Family Shock, Keeping Families Strong in the Midst of Earthshaking Change*. Wheaton, Ill.: Tyndale, 1995.

Faber, A., and E. Maslish. *Siblings Without Rivalry: How to Help Your Children Live Together So You Can Live Too*. New York: Norton, 1999.

Lush, J. *Mothers and Sons: Raising Boys to Be Men*. New York: Revell, 1988.

Ostrovsky, E. *Sibling Rivalry: A Guide for Parents Who Want to Understand and Control Conflict Between Their Children*. New York: Cornerstone Library, 1970.

Scarf, M. *Intimate Worlds: Life Inside the Family*. New York: Random House, 1995.

Sloan, H. R. *Stop That Fighting: A Short, Step-by-Step Guide for Turning Sibling Rivalry into Peaceful Coexistence*. Fountain Valley, Calif.: Telesis, 1976.

Sutton-Smith, B., and B. G. Rosenberg. *The Sibling*. New York: Holt, Rinehart, 1970.

Wiehe, V. R. *Perilous Rivalry: When Siblings Become Abusive*. Lexington, Mass.: Lexington Books, 1991.

Notes

1. P. H. Mussen, J. J. Conger, and J. Kagan, *Child Development and Personality* (New York: Harper & Row, 1974).

2. R. Seginer, "Adolescents' Perceptions of Relationships with Older Siblings in the Context of Other Close Relationships," *Journal of Research on Adolescence* 8 (1998): 287–308.

3. R. Felson, "Aggression and Violence Between Siblings," *Social Psychology Quarterly* 46 (1983): 271–85.

4. B. Sutton-Smith and B. G. Rosenberg, *The Sibling* (New York: Holt, Rinehart, 1970).

5. V. G. Cicirelli, "A Comparison of College Women's Feelings Toward Their Siblings and Parents," *Journal of Marriage and the Family* 42 (1980): 111–18.

6. S. Bank and M. D. Kahn, "Sisterhood–Brotherhood Is Powerful: Sibling Subsystems and Family Therapy," *Family Process* 14 (1975): 311–37.

7. C. E. Calladine, "Sibling Rivalry: A Parent Education Perspective," *Child Welfare* 5 (1983): 421–27.

8. E. A. Loomis, "Sibling Rivalry," in *Baker Encyclopedia of Psychology*, ed. D. G. Benner (Grand Rapids: Baker, 1985).

9. D. Lewis, "Conflict and Conflict Management," in *Dictionary of Pastoral Care and Counseling*, ed. R. J. Hunter (Nashville: Abingdon, 1990).

10. J. H. Pfauts, "The Sibling Relationship: A Forgotten Dimension," *Social Work* 21 (1976): 200–204.

11. E. J. Susman et al., "Hormones, Emotional Dispositions, and Aggressive Attributes in Young Adolescents," *Child Development* 58 (1987): 1114–34.

12. K. A. Updegraff and D. A. Obeidallah, "Young Adolescents' Patterns of Involvement with Siblings and Friends," *Social Development* 8 (1999): 52–69.

13. H. Barovick, "Reluctant Referees," *Time* (March 22, 1999): 91.

14. Calladine, "Sibling Rivalry," 421–27.

15. A. Hart, *Unlocking the Mystery of Your Emotions* (Dallas: Word, 1989).

16. J. Hocker Frost and W. W. Wilmot, *Interpersonal Conflict* (Dubuque, Ia.: William C. Brown, 1978).

SLEEP DISTURBANCE

✔ WHAT THE STRUGGLE LOOKS LIKE

Humans spend about one-third of their time asleep. That's about twenty-five years over an average lifetime. Sleep is more than the absence of wakefulness. It is a positive phenomenon that brings rest, restoration, and rejuvenation. Many people, however, are painfully aware that sleep is not always sweet slumber. Disturbed sleep strongly influences waking behaviors and plays a significant role in feelings of well-being. Sleep problems are not trivial and they can no longer be viewed as obscure, even among adolescents.

Toward the end of the 1970s, researchers at Stanford University found evidence to dispute the assumption that sleep disturbance occurs predominantly among adults. They found that approximately 13 percent of adolescents suffer from chronic sleep disturbances. In addition, 38 percent complain of occasional poor sleep. Other research has reported that close to 50 percent of the adolescent population will suffer from mild to severe sleep disturbance. Furthermore, an unknown number of adolescent insomniacs remain undiagnosed and rely on alcohol or habit-forming medication to help them sleep.[1] Without proper intervention, this malady may continue into adulthood and diminish the quality of life and learning.

Sleep disorders include any disruption of the onset or termination of sleep, or any of a number of difficulties occurring during sleep that disrupt normal sleep cycles.[2] A chronic sleep disturbance is defined by three parameters: when a period of forty-five minutes or longer is required to fall asleep on three or more nights a week, when one or more awakenings followed by at least thirty minutes of wakefulness occur on three or more nights a week, and when three or more awakenings occur on three or more nights a week.[3]

One hundred twenty disorders of sleep and arousal have been identified.[4] Most do not merely disrupt sleep; they affect a person twenty-four hours a day. Sleep disorders, according to the *Diagnostic and Statistical Manual* (4th ed.), are divided into two major subgroups: the *Dyssomnias* and the *Parasomnias.* In the Dyssomnias the predominant disturbance is in the amount, quality, or timing of sleep. They include Insomnia (difficulty initiating or maintaining sleep), Hypersomnia (excessive daytime sleepiness), and Sleep-Wake Schedule Disorder (a mismatch between the normal sleep-wake schedule that is demanded by environment and circadian rhythm [twenty-four-hour cycles]).

In the Parasomnias, the predominant disturbance is an abnormal event occurring during sleep. They include Dream Anxiety Disorder (repeated awakenings from sleep with detailed recall of frightening dreams), Sleep Terror Disorder (repeated episodes of abrupt awakening from sleep, usually beginning with panicky screams), and Sleepwalking Disorder (repeated episodes of a sequence of complex behaviors that progress to leaving the bed and walking about, with the person unaware of the episode or not later remembering it).

Other disorders affecting sleep include Sleep Apnea, which is a cessation of breathing that arouses the patient from sleep. Obstructed nasal passages or weak tissue in the throat may restrict the flow of air over the soft palate and trigger an oxygen deprivation. When this occurs, the person then wakes enough only to change positions, often gasping for air, but not enough to remember the disturbance. Sleep apnea may be fatal and should be treated by qualified physicians. Through reconstructive surgery of the nasal passages or soft palate, patients may be completely cured.

Narcolepsy is another sleep disturbance. It is characterized by recurrent sleep attacks appearing abruptly and inappropriately even during the day. For no apparent reason, the person suddenly falls asleep. I strongly recommend referral to a competent neurologist for this problem.

Of all the sleep disorders, insomnia is by far the most common. About 15 percent of the general population consider insomnia a serious problem for which professional help is occasionally sought. It is the sleep disorder that counselors working with adolescents are most likely to see. It is also a common symptom of other problems, such as depression or drug or alcohol abuse.

Sleep complaints among adolescents are usually associated with daytime fatigue, irritability, or depression. They may describe themselves in negative terms such as anxious, tense, or moody. They often experience problems with school attendance and academic performance.[5]

Case Description

Keith is a fifteen-year-old who awakens almost every morning about 2:00 to ruminate on his anxieties. He then has tremendous difficulty resuming his sleep. Keith dreads crawling into bed each night. He is tired of counting sheep, only to find his mind wandering back to the anxieties of the day. He lies there for at least an hour trying to fall asleep. He looks at the clock repeatedly, which, of course, only makes him more anxious. He goes through most days feeling haggard and cranky. Sometimes after school he tries to catch up on his sleep by taking naps. Keith has experienced this pattern for several months. He is not depressed, just tired.

Before exploring causes and treatment strategies for these disorders, it may be useful to quickly review the stages of sleep. The development of the electroencephalogram (EEG) has allowed researchers to measure central nervous system activity during sleep. Sleep can be classified into two major periods or stages: rapid eye movement sleep (REM) and non-rapid eye movement sleep (NREM). REM sleep is characterized by frequent bursts of rapid, jerky eye movements associated with slow, low-voltage brain waves. These eye movements occur infrequently in NREM sleep, which is associated with slow brain waves. NREM stages appear to be important in recovery from muscular fatigue while REM sleep appears to be more important in learning and psychological adjustment. Dreaming usually occurs during REM sleep.

Normal sleep has four or five ninety-minute cycles of NREM sleep alternating with REM sleep in periods lasting an average of fifteen minutes. REM periods get longer later at night, so most of the total REM time is in the last third of sleep. For more on these stages, see the book *Better Sleep.*

✔ WHY THE STRUGGLE HAPPENS

It is impossible to list all the factors contributing to sleep disturbances. The problem is unique for each individual. Nevertheless, many researchers group the causes under the following three major headings.

Physical Influences

Allergies, asthma, or side effects of alcohol, prescribed medications, and illegal drugs may influence sleep patterns. These physical causes are primarily a medical concern and are usually revealed in a careful medical evaluation.[6]

Psychological Influences

A number of psychological influences may affect sleep. Anxiety and depression are two of the most common. Depression is highly correlated with early waking and with inability to return to sleep. Anxiety is associated with difficulty falling asleep upon going to bed. Anxiety, tension, and worry also account for a great deal of poor sleep. Some describe these tendencies as a "fear of letting go." Insomniacs, for example, often have trouble letting go not only of physical tension but also of thoughts (unsolved problems and so on).[7]

Behavioral Influences

Some people have lifestyles, habits, and behavioral patterns that are not conducive to sound sleep. Some of these habits include irregular bedtimes and rising hours, long daytime naps, and the excessive consumption of foods and drinks containing caffeine (such as chocolate, coffee, tea, and soft drinks).[8]

☑ HOW PARENTS CAN HELP

The following strategies for helping an adolescent struggling with sleep disturbance can be used effectively by parents; however, every parent-child relationship is unique, and some of them may be more pertinent to your situation than others. As with every significant adolescent struggle, it is best for parents to work alongside a competent counselor. With this in mind, the following is offered as a way to help you facilitate the helping process at home with your teenager.

Consult a Sleep Expert

Worldwide, only about five or six hundred specialists identify themselves as somnologists (specialists in the study and treatment of sleep disorders). They bring their expertise from the fields of neurology, psychiatry, clinical and experimental psychology, internal medicine, pediatrics, pharmacology, and many other disciplines. While these experts may not be readily available to you for consultation, many practitioners with a wealth of experience work with sleep disorders. Medical institutions are generally the most helpful in guiding you to a sleep disorder expert (also consult the Association of Sleep Disorder Centers noted at the end of this section). Before moving into a treatment plan, you should have your adolescent undergo a careful physical and neurological examinations, even if he or she is obviously experiencing stress. Once physiological problems have been ruled out, psychological counseling can be effective.

Measure Sleeping Patterns

Objective measures of sleep are best achieved in a laboratory. Many major medical schools and hospitals have sleep labs designed for this purpose.[9] However, where this option is impossible or impractical, teens may enlist the assistance of friends or parents to help monitor their sleep. Encourage adolescents to keep accurate sleep diaries, recording approximate bedtime, number of sleep interruptions, and time of arousal. Many may find that they get more sleep than they thought. Monitoring one's sleep provides a useful assessment of the variety of factors related to sleep interference. Continued use of sleep diaries may also help clients monitor their improvement.

Below is an example of a sleep diary page to be completed each day. It is important to let young people know that they should not be concerned with answering the questions perfectly. It is generally best for them to fill in their diaries for at least two to three weeks before a helpful review can be made.

Daily Sleep Diary

- Date: _____
- Approximate total time sleeping: _____
- Approximate time required to fall asleep: _____
- Time I went to bed: _____
- Time I fell asleep: _____
- Number of times I woke up during the night: _____
- Length of time I stayed awake during each uptime: _____
- Time I woke up for the day: _____
- Time and effect of last meal or snack before going to bed: _____
- How rested did I feel this morning, on a scale of 1 to 5? _____
- How free of physical tension was I when I went to bed (1 to 5)? _____
- How free of mental activity was I when I went to bed (1 to 5)? _____
- If I exercised today, did it have a positive or negative effect? _____
- What special circumstances or experiences affected my sleep? _____

Understand Sleep Medications

Because many sleep disorders have been viewed historically as medical problems, the most common treatment has been a variety of prescription and non-prescription drugs. In fact, sleep medications are among the most widely prescribed medications in the United States. It has been reported that 40 percent of insomniacs use sleep medication almost nightly. Another 26 percent use them occasionally. However, studies have shown that most drugs designed to alleviate sleep problems actually make sleep more difficult rather than better because our bodies eventually develop tolerance to the medication.[10] At that point, a cycle evolves in which sleeplessness leads to drug taking, which leads to dependence and more drug taking. This dependency may become a greater problem than the initial insomnia. Medications (1) may alter sleep stages, (2) cause rebound insomnia, (3) increase daytime anxiety levels, and (4) ultimately require increased dosages of medication. Only in the most extreme cases should treatment with sleeping pills be considered. The techniques in this section are designed to prevent adolescents from using and becoming dependent on prescription and nonprescription drugs.

Teach New Sleeping Habits

Adolescents' sleeping environment is critical. The bedroom and normal bedtime may be triggers for troubled youth to start worrying. A teen may have learned negative association through repeated practice, but it can be unlearned with habit-reformation techniques. This strategy involves repeatedly substituting one behavior for another until the new behavior becomes a habit. That is, going to bed at the same time and getting out of bed at the same time consistently. It may mean using the bed and bedroom for nothing but sleep. Ask teens to choose other places to do homework, listen to music, worry, talk on the phone, eat, or do anything else that is not sleep-related. This allows them slowly to learn to associate the bedroom with sleep only.

Successful interventions with adolescents who have poor sleeping habits are common. For example, one researcher reports a typical case of an adolescent insomniac who had the habit of awakening regularly at 2:00 a.m. to ruminate on his worries. He seldom resumed sleep. To break this habit, his counselor simply advised him, upon awakening, to write a list of his worries on a notepad by the bed. By learning to do something constructive with his worries rather than staying awake to ponder them, he was able to alleviate the problem. Within five weeks, his early-morning waking habit was broken and he slept until his alarm went off at 7:00.[11]

Explore Exercise and Nutrition

Effects of exercise on sleep have been studied extensively. Studies have shown that even a simple regular exercise routine helps people sleep better compared to those who are completely sedentary. While exercise may enhance sleep for some, it does not always create a greater need for sleep nor does it produce more sound sleep. The time of exercise seems to be the most important element in determining whether it will adversely affect sleep. Studies indicate that exercise about two hours before bedtime increases metabolic responses that interfere with the onset of sleep. Exercise must be consistent, balanced, and scheduled for several hours before bedtime.[12]

Nutritional requirements must also be consistent for optimal effects. An overabundance of one particular food group may increase sleep disturbances, as will excessive weight change. Coffee, tea, and cola beverages containing caffeine drunk late in the day may also complicate sleep patterns. As a stimulant, caffeine has a peak effect two to four hours after it is consumed, and it may continue to affect a person for as long as seven hours.

Explore Napping

As a general rule, insomniacs should avoid napping. Naps, especially for adolescents, reinforce poor nighttime sleep routines. Studies have shown that napping cannot substitute for a solid night of good sleep. Encourage adolescents who nap to stay up during the day so that they will be more likely to sleep during the night. Sometimes this simple intervention is all it takes to bring relief to insomniacs.

Explore Environmental Factors

Often, a simple consideration of environmental influences will bring some relief to the person struggling with poor sleep. Noise is an obvious problem. If teens are particularly sensitive to noise, take stock of the noise situation with them. While soundproofing a bedroom is usually not an option, an alternative is to experiment with various types of "white noise" such as fans, air conditioners, or audiotapes of ocean waves or rain. Earplugs may be helpful with some people, but they should be used only with a physician's approval because of possible ear infection. If teens are disturbed or awakened by too much light, consider different light-blocking curtains or eyeshades.

Consider the quality of their mattresses as well as their bedroom temperature. When room temperature rises above seventy-five degrees, people become more restless and wake up more often. The optimum bedroom range is between sixty-five and seventy degrees Fahrenheit. Remove watches that beep or clocks that chime on the hour. They cause insomniacs to count each hour that passes and subtly keep them awake as they anticipate the next chime. In short, use a commonsense approach and explore every environmental factor that might influence sleep.

✔ HOW PROFESSIONALS CAN HELP

The following strategies for helping an adolescent struggling with sleep disturbance are commonly used by counselors. They are presented here as a way to inform you, as a parent, and help you seek the best possible professional help you can for the adolescent in your care.

Incorporate Relaxation Techniques

Relaxation techniques may be used to eliminate stress and tension from the skeletal and visceral muscles. Learning to use these techniques has been shown to be an important step in acquiring sound sleep. Invariably, teens who suffer from sleep problems at night are subject to nervousness, anxiety, and worry during the day. At bedtime they often show high levels of physical tension and mental arousal. In these cases, relaxation strategies may be practiced upon retiring to help prepare both minds and bodies for sleep. A high degree of success in treating poor sleepers has been reported by those using progressive relaxation methods.[13] In one published case, a thirteen-year-old male was taught to perform relaxation exercises prior to going to sleep and upon premature waking. His sleep was significantly improved by the eighth week.[14]

Progressive relaxation involves systematically tensing and relaxing the muscle groups in the body. Each time a muscle is tensed and relaxed, the level of tension in the body becomes lower and lower, ultimately eliminating tension. This strategy, along with several others, is described in the section on anxiety.

Use Cognitive Focusing

This cognitive strategy is best used to help adolescents return to sleep upon waking in the night. It is not uncommon for insomniacs to begin worrying that they will not get back to sleep or to begin thinking other negative thoughts once they have awakened prematurely. Cognitive focusing involves thinking positive, calming, reassuring thoughts. Cognitive focusing is often coupled with deep breathing. It is important for young people to develop positive thoughts to replace negative ones. Just trying to stop thinking negatively does not work. Many find it useful to focus their thoughts upon their breathing. For example, upon inhaling they may say to themselves, "I am," and upon exhaling they say, "relaxed." The repetition of these thoughts coupled with breathing calmly helps keep them from negative thinking and allows them to fall back to sleep.[15]

Know When to Refer

Refer adolescents who struggle with sleep disorders to psychologically astute physicians or psychiatrists for complete physical examination at the beginning of treatment. This should occur even if physical symptoms are not present. If over time they suffer increasingly from sleep disturbance, refer them to other competent sleep specialists, counselors, or psychologists.

Where to Go for Additional Help

American Medical Association. *Guide to Better Sleep.* New York: Random House, 1984.

Catalano, E. M. *Getting to Sleep.* Oakland, Calif.: New Harbinger, 1990.

Coates, T. J., and C. E. Thoresen. *How to Sleep Better.* Englewood Cliffs, N.J.: Prentice-Hall, 1977.

Cryer, B., and E. S. Kaplan. *Inside Insomnia: How to Sleep Better Tonight.* New York: Villard Books, 1986.

Lacks, P. *Behavioral Treatment for Persistent Insomnia.* New York: Pergamon Press, 1987.

Nelson, R. *If You Think You Have a Sleep Disorder.* New York: Dell, 1998.

Wiedman, J. *Desperately Seeking Snoozin': The Insomnia Cure from Awake To Zzzzz.* Memphis: Adlard, 1999.

Association of Sleep Disorder Centers (P.O. Box 2604, Del Mar, CA 92014) maintains a list of accredited sleep disorder centers.

Notes

1. J. R. Morrison and B. Storey, "Adolescent Insomnia," *Clearing House* 60 (1986): 110–14.

2. J. H. Jennison, "Sleep and Sleep Disorders," in *Dictionary of Pastoral Care and Counseling,* ed. R. J. Hunter (Nashville: Abingdon, 1990).

3. A. N. Vgontzas and A. Kales, "Sleep and Its Disorders," *Annual Review of Medicine* 50 (1999): 387–400.

4. American Medical Association, *Guide to Better Sleep* (New York: Random House, 1984).

5. T. J. Coates and C. E. Thoresen, *How To Sleep Better* (Englewood Cliffs, N.J.: Prentice-Hall, 1977).

6. M. S. Scher, "Applying Classifications of Sleep Disorders to Children with Neurologic Conditions," *Journal of Child Neurology* 13 (1998): 525–36.

7. J. Vignau, D. Bailly, A. Duhamel, P. Vervaecke, R. Beuscart, and C. Collinet, "Epidemiological Study of Sleep Quality and Troubles in French Secondary School Adolescents," *Journal of Adolescent Health* 21 (1997): 343–50.

8. M. J. Reid, A. L. Walter, and S. G. O'Leary, "Treatment of Young Children's Bedtime Refusal and Nighttime Wakings: A Comparison of 'Standard' and Graduated Ignoring Procedures," *Journal of Abnormal Child Psychology* 27 (1999): 5–16.

9. In 1975 only five medical institutions in the United States had centers devoted to the diagnosis and treatment of sleep problems. Today more than a hundred sleep disorder centers operate under common accrediting requirements.

10. D. R. Anderson, "Treatment of Insomnia in a 13-Year-Old Boy by Relaxation Training and Reduction of Parental Attention," *Journal of Behavioral Therapy* 10 (1979): 263–65.

11. J. R. Morrison, E. Kujawa, and B. A. Storey, "Causes and Treatment of Insomnia Among Adolescents," *Journal of School Health* 55 (1985): 148–50.

12. R. D. Bootzin, "Effects on Self-Control Procedures for Insomnia," in *Behavioral Self-Management: Strategies, Techniques, and Outcomes*, ed. R. B. Stuart (New York: Brunner-Mazel, 1977).

13. Coates and Thorsesen, *How To Sleep Better*.

14. Anderson, "Treatment of Insomnia."

15. R. Pat-Horenczyk, "Changes in Attitudes Toward Insomnia Following Cognitive Intervention as Part of a Withdrawal Treatment from Hypnotics," *Behavioural and Cognitive Psychotherapy* 26 (1998): 345–57.

SPIRITUAL DOUBT

☑ WHAT THE STRUGGLE LOOKS LIKE

Adolescents' quest for identity cannot avoid faith issues. Like trying on different styles of clothing, teenagers question religion and search for a faith that feels right. As a result, they may accuse the church of being a collection of hypocrites and totally reject the family's religious values. By contrast, they may become increasingly committed and involved in their faith. In either case, teenagers are trying to find their own expression of faith, and it often involves a struggle with spiritual doubt.[1]

Spiritual doubt is characterized by an absence of either assent or dissent to a religious proposition. It is not the same as unbelief, which is a conviction that something is false. Psychologically, doubt is often accompanied by anxiety or depression. For some it may become obsessional and especially troubling.[2]

Religious beliefs change as children enter and pass through adolescence. Teens, for example, are less likely than children to believe in literal translations of the Bible. Children report that they believe in God because their parents told them God exists. Adolescents, in contrast, rely more on rational thinking in their faith than on parental precepts. They believe in God, for example, because the universe is orderly.[3]

Among the more extensive studies of how faith changes as people age is the work of James Fowler. From his research, Fowler delineated six stages of faith development.[4] Three of his six stages shed light on the development of adolescent faith and the issues of spiritual doubt.

- *Stage 2: Mythical–literal faith.* This is the level where adolescents begin their journey of faith. Operating at the pre-teen concrete level, they respond to religion according to their cognitive capacity. Persons at this stage view religious stories and music in literal, concrete ways. They perceive God in human form somewhere in the sky. They simply accept their religious heritage and ask no questions.
- *Stage 3: Synthetic–conventional faith.* In early adolescence, with their increased capacity to think abstractly (i.e., formal operations), adolescents' principal task is to relate their own religious views with incompatible views of others. They may conceive of God as a personal advisor and guide, but in a less personalized fashion than previously.
- *Stage 4: Individual–reflective faith.* Not all adolescents reach this stage in their faith development. However, those who do will engage in critical self-reflection and examination of their beliefs and values. Their questioning leads to individual and personal religious beliefs. They view God in more abstract ways, not as a personal advisor, but as a spirit embodying moral truths and personal presence.

The seeds of doubt are usually planted in Stage 3 of Fowler's model, but it is toward the start of Stage 4 that the struggle with doubt shows visible signs of growth and maturity. Spiritual maturity is broached when people have internalized their values and beliefs into an integrated faith by which to live.[5]

Case Description

Russ, seventeen, a thoughtful and articulate high school student, grew up in the church. His parents were strong lay people and active in the life of their local church. Russ couldn't remember the last time he missed a church service. He enjoyed his youth group and was respected as a young leader. Secretly, however, Russ battled spiritual doubt. He questioned everything from the Bible to the existence of God. His prayers had dwindled down to a single word, *why?* Russ was especially concerned that he was a Christian only because he grew up in a Christian home. He was afraid his faith was built on selfish motivations.

☑ WHY THE STRUGGLE HAPPENS

The causes of spiritual doubt are not easily identified. However, some of the following may be contributing factors.

The Nature of Growth

Spiritual development does not progress at a steady direction toward a pinnacle of maturity. Feelings of emptiness are a part of human existence, even on the spiritual journey. Young people may experience an emotional rush during the days, weeks, or even months following a new spiritual commitment, but eventually this energy dissipates and questions arise that may cause doubt. This process is natural. It is endemic to spiritual growth. Some theologians see doubting as a dynamic ancillary to belief and not necessarily in opposition to it. A strong faith is not the result of avoiding questions, but of working with doubt. If there are no mountains without valleys, can there be faith without doubt or answers without questions?

Unsettling New Insights

Swiss psychologist Jean Piaget theorized that in two different ways people come to understand new information: *assimilation* and *accommodation*. Assimilation is the process by which people make an effort to take new information and join it to their existing thinking. The new experience may fit easily, or may require minor adjustment. Accommodation, on the other hand, is necessary when new experiences stretch people beyond their comfortable limits, when they do not fit within their current beliefs, and when they go beyond their structure of thought. A completely new insight regarding God is an example. Radical new ways of thinking about spiritual matters may launch adolescents into debilitating doubt.

Lack of Models

Teenagers need models of vibrant spirituality in whom they have respect and confidence. They need to see faith lived out in peers as well as adults. Unhealthful models in places of spiritual authority only compound the struggle. If young people lack a formative community of friends who share a common faith, they may have difficulty developing religious commitment and therefore struggle with spiritual doubt.[6] Most sociologists believe that faith is kept alive by a human as well as a divine support system. It is hard to keep on believing in a flat earth unless you are surrounded and supported by others who believe in a flat earth.

Idealistic Thinking

Because adolescents are so strongly idealistic, they may easily suffer disillusionment and disappointment with the church. No church can adequately fulfill every ideal of every person. Young people are bound to be disappointed and even critical of their religiously committed parents and church. Difficulty in coping with their own temptations further contributes to their disillusionment. They may begin to think the Christian life is an impossible ideal. This state of mind leads, obviously, to a struggle with doubt.

Unpleasant Church Experiences

Adolescents are more emotional than cognitive. They remember feelings more readily than facts. Concerning their church, they know exactly how they feel about last Sunday's service even when they cannot remember what was said or taught. An unpleasant feeling at church is more important than the sermon content in determining whether young people are drawn to a religious context. If adolescents do not have positive feelings about their churches they may experience spiritual doubt.[7]

☑ HOW PARENTS CAN HELP

The following strategies for helping an adolescent struggling with spiritual doubt can be used effectively by parents; however, every parent-child relationship is unique, and some of them may be more pertinent to your situation than others. As with every significant adolescent struggle, it is best for parents to work alongside a competent counselor. With this in mind, the following is offered as a way to help you facilitate the helping process at home with your teenager.

Examine Your Own Spiritual Growth

It is crucial for those who work with adolescents struggling with doubt (including parents) to know where they themselves stand in their spiritual well-being. Is your personal faith alive and fresh? Are you struggling in Fowler's Synthetic-Conventional stage of faith like adolescents with whom you are working? Are you dealing with unresolved spiritual conflicts that will negatively influence your relationships with adolescents? Modeling how you deal with spiritual struggles may be very useful in helping adolescents, but when your spiritual deficiencies are overwhelming and difficult to articulate, you will probably help doubters most by referring them to spiritually sensitive counselors.

Affirm the Honest Quest

Some people feel uneasy with, or even resent, adolescents with doubts. They lose sight of the fact that faith matures because of, not in spite of, doubt. They forget that serious questions not asked will not produce the richness and depth of an adequate answer. The most destructive thing counselors or parents can do to teenagers passing through periods of honest uncertainty is to attempt to silence their doubts and encourage their repression. "Repressed doubts have a high rate of resurrection," according to John Powell, "and doubts that are plowed under will only grow new roots."[8]

Although the Bible strongly warns against unbelief, not a single passage forbids the asking of critical questions. Doubt and belief are compatible. As odd as this may sound, doubt is not a hazard to faith; it may be the necessary catalyst that will bring a developing faith to maturity. Frederick Buechner put it nicely: "Doubt is the ants in the pants of the seat of faith."[9] Affirm honest adolescents who admit doubt. Your acceptance of their doubts as worthy of serious discussion will lay the foundation for them to construct a stronger faith.

Avoid Pat Answers

Doubting adolescents often ask dozens of questions. It seems that if they only had answers to their questions their doubts would dissipate. Don't be deceived. Doubters who ask for answers do not necessarily expect them or want them. Don't answer doubters' questions prematurely or supply them with heavy books to do the answering for you. Adolescents who struggle with doubt are usually more concerned about having a relationship with God than they are with having answers about God.

Focus on Relationships

Adolescent identity formation takes place in relationships. So does faith development. Creating a place to belong is one of the secrets of the success of youth organizations like Young Life, Youth for Christ, and Fellowship of Christian Athletes. Role models who are living out faithful lifestyles increase the opportunity for young people to integrate a more secure faith into their identity. To help adolescents fighting spiritual doubt, make sure they are part of a vital youth group that embraces healthful faith principles.

If young people are part of religious communities that do not meet their needs for peer relationships and adult role models, they should look elsewhere. An emphasis on relationships is crucial in helping them define their relationship to God. Adolescents who struggle with spiritual doubt are not searching for an explanation. They are longing for a relationship. To locate an area Young Life group, call 719-473-4262. For more information on Youth for Christ, call 913-262-1700, and for Fellowship of Christian Athletes, call 816-921-0909.

Consider the Church Context

Adolescents' religious community must be considered and understood. Research has identified several elements essential to healthful adolescent faith development.[10] To help insure a spiritual commitment, the church must address and satisfy these needs.

1. *Security in freedom.* The church must afford young people opportunities to test values in an atmosphere of respect. It must avoid merely demanding obedience to authority.
2. *Significance and status.* The church must afford adolescents opportunities to earn respect through responsible activity within it.
3. *Idealism and altruism.* The church must embrace the idealism of youth and help them develop altruistic attitudes and behaviors through service.
4. *Love.* The church must discuss all aspects of love, including sexual love, in an open and supportive manner.
5. *Meaning for life.* The church must assist adolescents in discussions about their quest for meaning, including the questions they have about faith.

If it is apparent that adolescents are struggling in their faith because some of these elements are absent in their church, explore alternatives.

Explore Inaccurate Theology

Listen carefully to the comments of young people. Notice what they reveal about their beliefs concerning God. Keith Olson points out that adolescents troubled over issues of faith often hold blatantly incorrect concepts of God.[11] Effective parents and counselors must discover and help correct these beliefs. Some of the most common inaccurate beliefs include: "God will never allow a real tragedy to strike a faithful believer;" "God punishes us by causing accidents;" "God will accept nothing but absolute perfection;" "God is going to destroy the world." Help adolescents avoid faulty theology that will result in their putting God into a box.[12] Christian counselors and parents must correct misinformation in an understanding, gentle, and compassionate manner.

Know When to Refer

Refer adolescents who struggle with spiritual doubt to a competent counselor or psychologist when, over time, they feel more frustrated, depressed, or hopeless. You should also refer teenagers if you recognize that you are uncomfortable with their doubts and even subtly condemn them for their sincere search.

✔ HOW PROFESSIONALS CAN HELP

The following strategy for helping an adolescent struggling with spiritual doubt is commonly used by counselors. It is presented here as a way to inform you, as a parent, and help you seek the best possible professional help you can for the adolescent in your care.

Confront Irrational Thinking

Most adolescents who struggle with spiritual doubt are also burdened with guilt. Counselors are sensitive to these feelings and help them dispute irrational "oughts" and "shoulds." What are their unrealistic expectations about their spiritual development? Perhaps they believe they should never question the Bible or even their pastor. Maybe they think they should never allow their thoughts to be distracted while they are praying. These kinds of distortions and unrealistic expectations are generally unspoken. Counselors must listen carefully to detect them. For additional suggestions on alleviating this component, see the section on guilt.

Where to Go for Additional Help

Barna, G. *Generation Next: What You Need to Know About Today's Youth.* Ventura, Calif.: Regal Books, 1995.
Fowler, J. *Stages of Faith.* New York: Harper & Row, 1981.
Gillespie, V. B. *The Dynamics of Religious Conversion: Identity and Transformation.* Birmingham, Ala.: Religious Education Press, 1991.
Guinness, O. *In Two Minds: The Dilemma of Doubt and How to Resolve It.* Downers Grove, Ill.: InterVarsity Press, 1976.
Nappa, M., A. Nappa, and M. D. Warden. *Get Real: Making Core Christian Beliefs Relevant to Teenagers.* Loveland, Colo.: Group Publishers, 1996.
Parks, S. *The Critical Years: The Young Adult Search for a Faith to Live By.* San Francisco: Harper & Row, 1986.
Shelton, C. *Adolescent Spirituality.* New York: Cross Road, 1989.
Steele, L. *On the Way: A Practical Theology of Christian Formation.* Grand Rapids: Baker, 1990.

Notes

1. D. M. Pedersen, "Validating a Centrality Model of Self-Identity," *Social Behavior and Personality* 27 (1999): 73–85.
2. J. R. Beck, "Doubt," in *Baker Encyclopedia of Psychology*, ed. D. G. Benner (Grand Rapids: Baker, 1985).
3. P. Benson, M. Donahue, and J. Erickson, "Adolescence and Religion: Review of the Literature from 1970–1986," *Research in the Social Scientific Study of Religion* 1 (1989): 153–81.

4.   J. Fowler, *Stages of Faith* (New York: Harper & Row, 1981).

5.   D. Webster, "Fostering the Spiritual Dimension of Education in Young Children," *Early Child Development and Care* 146 (1998): 13–20.

6.   W. Rice, *Junior High Ministry*, rev. ed. (Grand Rapids: Zondervan, 1987).

7.   R. Campbell, *How To Really Love Your Teenager* (Wheaton, Ill.: Victor, 1985).

8.   J. Powell, *A Reason To Live, a Reason To Die* (Allen, Tex.: Argus Communications, 1972).

9.   F. Buechner, *Wishful Thinking* (San Francisco: Harper & Row, 1973).

10.   R. Goldman, *Readiness for Religion* (London: Routledge Kegan Paul, 1965).

11.   G. K. Olson, *Counseling Teenagers: The Complete Christian Guide to Understanding and Helping Adolescents* (Loveland, Colo.: Group Books, 1984).

12.   J. B. Phillips, *Your God Is Too Small* (New York: Macmillan, 1969).

STUTTERING

✔ WHAT THE STRUGGLE LOOKS LIKE

Stuttering is painful and frustrating at any age, but particularly for the teenager who is on a quest for a stable identity. Stuttering is the condition in which the flow of speech is broken by abnormal stoppages, repetitions, or prolongations of sounds and syllables. In addition, stutterers may show unusual facial and body movements associated with their efforts to speak. Some are fluent with friends or when alone, but stutter severely with others, especially with authority figures. While some young people stutter with everyone, many stutter only under certain circumstances. In general stutterers are average or above average in intelligence.[1]

Some stuttering is typical and temporary in young children and is called *developmental* stuttering. The onset is usually between two and four years of age and lasts only a few months. *Persistent* stuttering starts between three and eight years of age and persists unless some effective intervention is employed. Stuttering that appears after age five is considered more serious than stuttering at a younger age.[2]

Several million preschoolers stutter. About 75 percent of ten-year-olds who stutter remain stutterers throughout life, and about 1 percent (two million) of all adolescents struggle with stuttering. At all ages, from four to eight times as many males stutter than females.[3]

Case Description

Ryan is a thirteen-year-old who first began to stutter when he was about six. Within the last few years he has stuttered more and more frequently, and his parents became increasingly concerned about his entering adolescence with this problem. His parents used to try to help him by having him repeat words properly. Rather than getting better, however, Ryan became more anxious and his stuttering increased. He is now seeing a speech and language pathologist. He was brought in for psychological counseling by his parents because he was showing signs of depression and low self-esteem. At the root of his struggle, however, was his problem with stuttering.

✔ WHY THE STRUGGLE HAPPENS

The causes of stuttering are not clear. No single theory of its origin is widely accepted. Here are some of the more commonly noted contributing factors.[4]

Physiological Influences

The likelihood of becoming a stutterer is, in large part, influenced by heredity. The direct physical cause is believed to be an auditory perceptual defect. Stutterers receive delayed feedback from their own speech. Another theory holds that one side of the brain has not achieved the level of influence necessary for smooth speech.

Stressors

Stressful situations like fatigue, school pressures, separation from significant others, and changes at critical stages of development may lead to stuttering. Tension causes susceptible individuals to lose control of their delicate speech muscles, and nonfluent speech becomes their way of indicating fear or reluctance. If the pattern continues, persistent stuttering may result. It is generally understood that proneness to stuttering is increased by stressful situations.

Parental Expectations

Unrealistic parental expectations generate anxiety in children. Stuttering may result from tension caused by parents who try to force young children to speak at levels beyond their normal developmental stage. Perfectionistic parents may also generate this tension by making their children feel compelled to live up to standards that are either impossible or unusually difficult. If parents overreact to normal speech difficulties ("Be more careful when you talk" or "Start again and speak more slowly"), a child may become more self-conscious about speaking. Parents' forceful attempts to reduce children's nonfluency in public may lead to more hesitation and therefore compound the problem.

Expression of Conflict

Unexpressed feelings of anger are thought, by some, to be a cause of stuttering. This idea is analogous to the automobile driver who has one foot pressing the gas pedal while their other foot holds down the brake. Stutterers are seen as wanting to express themselves but at the same time wanting to hold back. While some recognize this internal conflict as a cause, relatively little research is available to support this belief.

☑ HOW PARENTS CAN HELP

The following strategies for helping an adolescent struggling with stuttering can be used effectively by parents; however, every parent-child relationship is unique, and some of them may be more pertinent to your situation than others. As with every significant adolescent struggle, it is best for parents to work alongside a competent counselor. With this in mind, the following is offered as a way to help you facilitate the helping process at home with your teenager.

Provide an Accepting and Calm Atmosphere

It is essential to provide a peaceful and emotionally supportive atmosphere when working with adolescents who stutter. Speak in a soft voice, slowing down your own verbal pace. This helps set the tempo and create a climate that allows stutterers to relax and release tensions that often underlie stuttering. Listen patiently and carefully to what they say, and do not focus on how it is said.

Consult a Specialist

Adolescents who stutter are likely to come to struggle with other problems, such as anxiety, fear, depression, frustration, feelings of inferiority, or guilt. However, these problems are often a result of stuttering. If young people struggle with these kinds of problems and also stutter, consult a specialist. Serious intervention for stuttering requires the specialized treatment of a speech-language pathologist.

Negate Anticipation Anxiety

Anticipation is the worst enemy of stutterers. Give young stutterers "permission" to take chances and be spontaneous. Release the burden of guilt, self-doubt, and inhibition. Stutterers need space and emotional freedom. Try to instill courage in them. Significant others in their environment can be encouraged to help in this way also. This will allow them to "let 'er rip," as a stuttering scholar from the University of Wisconsin says.[5]

✔ HOW PROFESSIONALS CAN HELP

The following strategies for helping an adolescent struggling with stuttering are commonly used by counselors. They are presented here as a way to inform you, as a parent, and help you seek the best possible professional help you can for the adolescent in your care.

Heighten Awareness

Adolescent stutterers are certainly aware of their problem. But it can be helpful to enhance their motivation by reviewing in detail the patterns of speech that result from their stuttering. It is also helpful to discuss the types of words, behaviors, and situations that elicit the most stuttering. Identifying trouble areas can help counselors target helpful treatment strategies (e.g., the relaxation techniques noted below).[6]

Implement Relaxation Techniques

Adolescents with this problem may benefit from a number of relaxation techniques. Once mastered, they provide clients with a sense of control in the midst of a struggle that seems beyond their control. Deep muscle relaxation, biofeedback, deep breathing, guided imagery, and autogenics may all be used. These techniques, along with others, are described in the sections on anxiety and panic attacks.

Consider Group Treatment

Many experts agree that group therapy offers positive experiences to stutterers that cannot be found in individual sessions. For example, in these groups, adolescents share experiences and feelings with others who suffer from the same problem. Young people also find that they are not the only ones having a battle with stuttering and, more importantly, they may benefit from the therapeutic experiences of other stutterers.[7]

Know When to Refer

Adolescents with fluency problems may respond relatively quickly to some of these techniques. However, if they continue to stutter after intervention strategies to help reduce anxiety, consult specialists. Most young people who struggle with stuttering into the teen years do require specialized professional help. The probability of spontaneous remission is practically nonexistent.[8] While general counselors can help adolescents with anxiety issues and self-esteem problems, experts in speech therapy should be consulted. Qualified speech and language pathologists may be obtained through a referral from the American Speech and Hearing Association in Washington, D.C. Speech therapists will evaluate the problem, make recommendations, or treat clients as necessary. Qualified speech-language pathologists are trained at the master's or doctoral degree level, and many hold the Certificate of Clinical Competence (CCC) from the American Speech-Language-Hearing Association (ASHA) and/or a license from your state.

Where to Go for Additional Help

Ainsworth, S. *Stuttering: What It Is and What to Do About It*. Lincoln, Neb.: Cliffs Notes, 1975.

Apel, M. A. *Coping with Stuttering*. New York: Rosen Publishers, 1999.

Bryngelson, B., M. E. Chapman, and O. K. Hansen. *Know Yourself: Guide for Those Who Stutter*. Minneapolis: Burgess, 1966.

Conture, E. G. *Stuttering and Your Child: Questions and Answers*. Memphis: Stuttering Foundation of America, 1999.

Conture, E. G. *Stuttering*. Englewood Cliffs, N.J.: Prentice-Hall, 1990.

Onslow, M., and A. Packman. *The Handbook of Early Stuttering Intervention*. San Diego: Singular Publishers, 1999.

Schwartz, M. F. *Stuttering Solved*. Philadelphia: Lippincott, 1976.

Notes

1. E. G. Couture, *Stuttering* (Englewood Cliffs, N.J.: Prentice-Hall, 1982).

2. C. E. Schaefer and H. L. Millmann, *How To Help Children with Common Problems* (New York: Van Nostrand Reinhold, 1981).

3. Ibid.

4. Ibid.

5. G. F. Johnson, "Ten Commandments for Long-Term Maintenance of Acceptable Self-Help Skills for Persons Who Are Hard-Core Stutterers," *Journal of Fluency Disorders* 12 (1987): 9–18.

6. B. P. Ryan and Van Kirk B. Ryan, "Programmed Stuttering Therapy for Children: Comparison of Four Establishment Programs," *Journal of Fluency Disorders* 8 (1983): 291–321.

7. Couture, *Stuttering*.

8. R. Ladouceur and L. Saint-Laurent, "Stuttering: A Multidimensional Treatment and Evaluation Package," *Journal of Fluency Disorders* 11 (1986): 93–103.

SUICIDE

✔ WHAT THE STRUGGLE LOOKS LIKE

Suicide is a raging epidemic in America. Each year the national statistics on suicide climb—especially for adolescents. Suicide is the third leading cause of death for ten- to twenty-four-year-olds, after car accidents and homicide. Because many suicides, however, are disguised as accidents, it may be the number-one cause of teenage death. Between 1962 and 1996, the teenage suicide rate increased 155 percent.[1]

The problem of adolescent suicides assumes even greater proportions when we consider unsuccessful suicide attempts. Evidence indicates that for every adolescent who commits suicide, fifty to a hundred teenagers attempt it.[2] That adds up to a potential of two million teen-suicide attempts each year.

Sooner or later, people working with adolescents will face the problem of suicide, and this forces them to know what the struggle looks like. The symptoms of suicide are only signals and may not mean that an adolescent is on the verge of committing suicide. However, each sign should be taken seriously.[3] If a young person's symptoms go unnoticed, he or she may resort to drastic measures as a cry for help. Some 90 percent of teenage suicides take place at home between 3:00 P.M. and midnight—the time and place a suicide attempt is most easily discovered.[4] Here are warning signs:

- *A history of problems:* Suicide is a process and rarely an impulsive act.
- *Decline in performance:* Grades drop; the young person no longer wants to compete.

- *A recent traumatic event:* Physical illness, failure in school, breakup of a romance, or divorce of parents may intensify already-present suicidal thoughts.
- *Communication problems:* Suicide may become an inarticulate cry for help by adolescents who have difficulty expressing their feelings.
- *Irrational outbursts:* Suicidal youth may suddenly become quick-tempered, cry easily, or become easily upset by trivial things.
- *Depression:* An enormous sense of sadness is almost always a warning sign.
- *A recent holiday:* Although suicides are fewer than many expect during the Christmas season, the days that follow a holiday show a release of the suppressing effect and contain a significantly higher number of suicides.[5]
- *Change in eating or sleeping habits:* Adolescents begin to sleep or eat much more or much less than they usually do.
- *Talk about suicide:* Experts estimate that about 80 percent of persons who take their lives have talked about it with others.
- *Drugs and alcohol:* When abuse occurs, the possibility of suicide must at least be considered.
- *Withdrawal:* Rather than taking initiative for new experiences, the suicidal teen may spend long hours alone in silence or listening to music.
- *Lack of hope:* "Life just isn't worth living" is the attitude, and the youths see their future as something they cannot control.
- *Tunnel vision:* The suicidal life is often viewed in rigid situations; life is black or white.

✔ WHY THE STRUGGLE HAPPENS

Every suicide is an attempt to say "I need help." A combination of faulty reasoning and a deep sense of hopelessness is nearly always present in young people struggling with suicide. Below are some of the specific motivators that often drive adolescents to take their lives.[6] Keep in mind, however, that usually a combination of several factors makes suicide a serious option.

To Escape

This is perhaps the most common reason we attribute to suicide and it is often a valid assessment.[7] People who consider suicide see no hope for resolution of their life situations. This hopelessness is fueled by irrational thinking that pulls them into deeper despair. The hope that may be obvious to counselors and others may be difficult for suicidal adolescents to see. They view death as the only way to avoid pain. Young people who use sleep to avoid problems are especially at risk, symbolically equating death with prolonged sleep.[8]

To Be Punished

With an overly sensitized conscience, some adolescents devalue themselves. Because of their sins and shortcomings, they believe death is what they deserve. They feel that they have committed the unpardonable sin, and for this they will burn in hell. Whether it be fornication, masturbation, abortion, or simply "evil thoughts," youth who attempt suicide as a means of punishment see no other option for absolving their unbearable guilt.

> ### Case Description
>
> Tim, sixteen, is a "C" student. He has long hair, and most days wears faded jeans and a flannel shirt. His jacket has "Pink Floyd" scrawled on the back in ballpoint pen. Tim lives at home with his mother. His dad left when he was in the third grade. Tim came in for counseling at his mother's insistence. She described him as "a loner, always listening to his music, and never interested in getting a job." Two months earlier Tim had slit his wrists and run into where his mother was sleeping to wave the spurting blood over her bed. Tim's suicide attempt was more of an angry cry for help than anything else. He used this ugly gesture to "get back" at his mom for pressuring him "to be the perfect son." Feeling he had no other means of communication, he resorted to this frightening option.

To Punish Others

Suicide is sometimes directed toward one or more survivors. The eighteen-year-old who overdoses on pills and stabs himself in the abdomen after rejection by his girlfriend really wants, in a distorted way, to make her suffer. In his desire to punish her he says, "She'll know she loves me when I'm dead." It is not always clear, however, whom suicidal adolescents are wanting to punish. The hostility is usually directed toward the person who the adolescent believes will find the body.

To Manipulate Others

When manipulating others is the primary motive for suicide or attempted suicide, adolescents are seeking specific objects or actions. They may feel that attempted suicide will bring about a specific result, like getting mom and dad back together after a stormy separation. While teenagers use threats of suicide to control parents, friends, counselors, or others, threats should be taken seriously. Taking their suicide seriously does not necessarily mean giving in to manipulative demands, but it does mean doing more than simply acknowledging the threat. Manipulators sometimes succeed in taking their own lives.

To Gain Attention

Few behaviors command more attention than suicide. The shocking news of a young life abruptly ended startles us to the core. Even a mere acquaintance suddenly becomes meaningfully important when word of the death is received—"I saw him only yesterday. How can he be dead?" People lavish attention on previously ignored youth who have attempted suicide. Seeing how much concern suicide generates causes other young people to consider the option. It is not uncommon for schools to experience cluster suicides, where one tragedy triggers three or four more. The attention received through death is even reflected in the literature students are often required to read. Nearly every early adolescent identifies with Tom Sawyer's ploy to allow his Aunt Polly to think he has drowned. He delights in the expressions of love he observes as he surreptitiously attends his own funeral.

To Be Reunited with a Deceased Loved One

Suicide is sometimes an attempt to join someone who has died. It is an ancient motive with roots in multiple cultures. In Western culture this idea of joining a deceased loved one persists most commonly among older persons. However, it is by no means limited to the graying population. For this reason, pay careful attention to adolescents' views on death lest suicide attempts follow deaths of loved ones. Suicide for some Christian adolescents with a distorted theology may be an attempt to join Jesus in heaven.

To Express Love

Suicide may also be a tragic way of saying "I love you." Adolescents in love can be extremely loyal and intense. In a distorted and confused way, they may believe that death alone will communicate the great strength of their love. The thought of living without each other is so strong that both partners, like Romeo and Juliet, commit suicide, or a girl may vow to take her life if her boyfriend dies.

To Avoid Being a "Burden"

Some adolescents take their lives to avoid being problems to those around them. If they were out of the way, they believe that things would be better for

everyone. They may see themselves as the root cause of Mom and Dad's fighting. Or they may believe they were unwanted biological "accidents." More than
70 percent of young people who attempt suicide are from broken homes. Even
in homes with stable relationships, adolescents may feel they are an embarrassment or burden to their families. Tragically, this motivation for suicide robs survivors of any opportunity to prove otherwise.

✔ HOW PARENTS CAN HELP

The following strategies for helping an adolescent struggling with thoughts
of suicide can be used effectively by parents; however, every parent-child relationship is unique, and some of them may be more pertinent to your situation
than others. As with every significant adolescent struggle, it is best for parents to
work alongside a competent counselor. With this in mind, the following is offered
as a way to help you facilitate the helping process at home with your teenager.

Focus on Feelings

Getting suicidal adolescents to share their feelings is vital to recovery. The
driving force behind suicidal thought is often buried beneath feelings that the
adolescents have never revealed to anyone. Suicidal youth are usually overwhelmed with guilt, helplessness, and rejection. Arguing about the validity of
these feelings only adds to the load. Troubled adolescents need understanding,
not debate.[9]

Don't Dismiss the Trivial

Teenagers' concerns or problems should never be ignored or played down.
The underlying message of effective suicide intervention must be "I care about
you and I take you seriously." Failing to make the soccer team may seem relatively insignificant to an adult, but teenagers have committed suicide over less
than that. Adolescents' concerns are intensely real and must be respected. They
are never inconsequential.[10]

Take Note of Increased Energy

The greatest danger of suicide is in the first three months following a period
of deep depression. When adolescents seem to be doing better, the danger of
suicide may be greater. Severely depressed teens don't have the ability to do
everyday tasks, let alone kill themselves. However, as the depression lifts, the
ability to act on earlier suicide plans increases.

"Sterilize" the Home of Lethal Means

Although determined suicidal persons can always find a way to kill themselves, there are advantages in clearing the home of easily available lethal materials. Suicidal feelings come and go and the availability of a means for suicide may trigger the attempt. To decrease the likelihood of impulsive suicidal behavior it is best to make the home as safe as possible. Remove poisons, firearms, lethal medications, and razor blades. Restrict driving privileges of suicidal adolescents. Although they may protest these measures, they represent tangible proofs that their parents and their counselors want them to live. This reassurance of parental concern may play a larger role in prevention than cleansing the house of lethal means.

Take Care of Yourself

Few situations drain parents of more energy than working with a son or daughter on the brink of suicide. Paradoxically, ability to help suicidal adolescents is dependent on your ability to maintain personal power, perspective, and vitality for living. You must take care of yourself. These measures include consulting with professionals, exercising, enjoying diversion, and taking time to pray. When you work with a suicidal teen, you do not work alone. God is with you.[11]

Know When to Refer

Refer suicidal adolescents to a competent counselor or psychologist immediately. Also consider with a professional whether hospitalization is needed.

☑ HOW PROFESSIONALS CAN HELP

The following strategies for helping an adolescent struggling with thoughts of suicide are commonly used by counselors. They are presented here as a way to inform you, as a parent, and help you seek the best possible professional help you can for the adolescent in your care.

Explore Personal History

To assess the level of suicide risk, it is helpful to know whether clients have attempted suicide in the past. Four of five young people who kill themselves have attempted suicide more than once.[12] Talking about a previous attempt— how long ago it happened, why it occurred, and its lethality—may help counselors understand the seriousness of the attempt and any possible secondary gains such as attention or new expressions of love. Exploring clients' interpretations of the suicides of friends or family members is also helpful in discerning their perspectives on life and death. When "significant others" deal with stress by attempting suicide, it becomes a viable option to troubled teens.

Discover the Plan

If adolescents express suicidal thoughts, counselors will find out the method they might use. They will simply ask, "Do you have a plan?" They will determine whether their plan includes location and time of day. The risk of actual suicide is probably not so serious without a well-thought-out means. Teenagers who have thought in specific terms about how and when they will commit suicide (with a gun, in the bedroom, on Monday) are much closer to attempting suicide than those who have not. The more specific the plan, the greater the risk. In discussing the plan, counselors will use the past tense. "How were you thinking of going about this?" rather than "How are you thinking. . ." This indicates the adolescent is moving beyond suicide to positive alternatives.

Assess the Lethality of the Plan

If an adolescent does disclose a plan, counselors will assess how deadly the method is likely to be. Using a gun, lying down in front of a moving train, or hanging oneself is a greater danger than slashing one's wrists or taking pills. While these latter methods may be lethal, they often involve less risk. It is also important to understand the adolescent's perception of the deadliness of the chosen method. Swallowing a bottle of aspirin will not normally kill a person. However, if an adolescent thinks a bottle of aspirin is lethal, then one is serious about suicide. Also, the method sometimes symbolizes something privately important to the adolescent. A certain gun, a specific knife, a particular medication may carry a message the youth wants to communicate.

Make a Written Contract

Written contracts with adolescents may be a useful preventive measure, although contracts come with no guarantee. Even if suicidal adolescents seem to have improved, it is important to make the topic easy to talk about. Many counselors have talked with persons threatening suicide who left the session saying, "This really helped; I feel better now," only to learn that they were found dead with a revolver in their hand later that evening. When adolescents are asked to formally sign an agreement to contact counselors if they get suicidal, they are receiving the message that their lives are important.

The contract should emphasize that the teen *will* contact the counselor, not that he or she will just *try* to. This contract is not a mere formality. It meaningfully expresses the value the counselor places upon the adolescent's life. And remember, most teenagers who plan suicide attempts desperately want to be stopped.

Hospitalize If Necessary

Adolescents who have specific plans for carrying out suicide should not be left alone. The revelation of specific plans indicates that clients have already decided to commit suicide.[13] Counselors may use an inpatient-treatment setting until they are sure continued risk of suicide is minimal—sending a clear message to adolescents that their cries for help have been heard and are being taking seriously. Important factors in deciding on hospitalization include the pervasiveness of current stresses, the degree of impulse control, availability of an adequate support system among family and friends, and the willingness and ability of counselors to become involved in crisis management beyond the regular counseling hour.[14]

Where to Go for Additional Help

American Association of Suicidology, 2429 South Ash, Denver, CO 80222. This organization distributes booklets and pamphlets, publishes a journal and newsletter, and conducts educational seminars on suicide prevention.

Blackburn, B. *What You Should Know About Suicide*. Waco, Tex.: Word, 1982.

International Association for Suicide Prevention, 1811 Trousdale Drive, Burlingame, CA 94010. This worldwide organization, with headquarters in Vienna, Austria, trains people and provides information about suicide prevention.

National Committee on Youth Suicide Prevention, 666 Fifth Avenue, 23d Floor, New York, NY 10103. The aim of this organization is to increase public awareness of youth suicide by providing information and developing youth suicide prevention programs in local communities.

Robbins, P. R. *Adolescent Suicide*. Jefferson, N.C.: McFarland & Company, 1998.

Schleifer, J. *Everything You Need to Know About Teen Suicide*. New York: Rosen Publishers, 1997.

Suicide Information Center, 6377 Apopka Place, San Diego, CA 92119. This organization maintains an updated list of materials on suicide and prevention. Free book lists, cassette tapes, and articles are available.

Notes

1.   W. J. Bennett, *The Index of Leading Cultural Indicators: American Society at the End of the Twentieth Century* (New York: Broadway Books, 1999).

2.   www.sanpedro.com/spyc/suicide.html (1999).

3.   A. H. Thompson, R. H. Barnsley, and R. J. Dyck, "A New Factor in Youth Suicide: The Relative Age Effect," *Canadian Journal of Psychiatry* 44 (1999): 82–85.

4.   M. D. Stein and J. K. Davis, *Therapies for Adolescents* (San Francisco: Jossey-Bass, 1982).

5.   T. Sparhawk, "Traditional Holidays and Suicide," *Psychological Reports* 60 (1987): 245–46.

6.   For more detailed descriptions of many of these motivations see B. Blackburn, *What You Should Know About Suicide* (Waco, Tex.: Word, 1982), and G. K. Olson, *Counseling Teenagers* (Loveland, Colo.: Group Books, 1984).

7.   D. S. Lipschitz, R. K. Winegar, A. L. Nicolaou, E. Hartnick, M. Wolfson, and S. M. Southwick, "Perceived Abuse and Neglect as Risk Factors for Suicidal Behavior in Adolescent Inpatients," *Journal of Nervous and Mental Disease* 187 (1999): 32–39.

8.   W. T. Aoki and A. A. Turk, "Adolescent Suicide: A Review of Risk Factors and Implications for Practice," *Journal of Psychology and Christianity* 16 (1997): 273–79.

9.   A. J. Flisher, "Mood Disorder in Suicidal Children and Adolescents: Recent Developments," *Journal of Child Psychology and Psychiatry and Allied Disciplines* 40 (1999): 315–24.

10.   D. Shaffer and L. Craft, "Methods of Adolescent Suicide Prevention," *Journal of Clinical Psychiatry* 60 (1999): 70–74.

11.   R. S. Anderson, *Self Care: A Theology of Personal Empowerment and Spiritual Healing* (Wheaton, Ill.: Victor Books, 1995).

12.   D. Eble, "Too Young To Die," *Christianity Today* (20 March 1987): 19–24.

13.   W. Reid, *The Treatment of Psychiatric Disorders: Revised for the DSM-III-R* (New York: Brunner-Mazel, 1989).

14.   M. Pelkonen, "Adolescent Outpatients' Suicidal Behavior and Inpatients' Twenty-Year Working Capacity," *Psychiatria Fennica* 29 (1998): 50–64.

VICTIMS OF VIOLENCE

✔ WHAT THE STRUGGLE LOOKS LIKE

"I'm so scared." It's a statement being made by more and more kids who have been raped, stalked, stabbed, beaten, or shot by a bullet that was meant for no one in particular. More than one-third of adolescents report having been the victims of violence.[1] It's also the statement being made by kids who have suffered none of these crimes personally but have been almost as traumatized by the chance that they might. With a national string of deadly shootings at schools and teenage violence being reported on in the media month after month, it's not surprising that more and more kids are feeling like victims.[2]

And so are schools. Alarmed by the growing number of violent acts on school grounds, educators are changing the way they go about their mission. They're installing spiked fences, metal detectors, emergency alert systems. They're hiring security guards and imposing searches of students' bags, lockers, and desks. And they're insisting that teachers know how to run lock-down drills and how to strip a student vigilante of his weapon.

As many as 8 percent of school children miss a day of class monthly for fear of being bullied. And in a nationwide survey, 43 percent of children said they were afraid to go to a bathroom for fear of being harassed.[3] Who can deny that educators have a right, even an obligation, to do all they can to protect themselves and the students in their charge from what has become a prime threat to their safety: other students.

Is the violence as bad as most of us believe? After all, the media coverage can make it seem like every single high school in the country is in danger of lethal violence. Truth is these incidents are still very much atypical. Teenagers who use or are prone to use lethal violence in school settings are a very small fraction of all youth. Still, school violence does occur. And the threat of its occurrence is growing. Young people know it.[4] They are a generation who is scared, whether they have personally suffered a violent crime or not. Violence is like a movie, so the common thought goes: it's coming to a theater—or a school—near you. Simply mention the towns and kids know the school-related violence that has shaken them: Pearl, Mississippi; Moses Lake, Washington; Paducah, Kentucky; Jonesboro, Arkansas; Springfield, Oregon; Conyears, Georgia; Littleton, Colorado. By all predictions, the list will go on.

The question is what do we do with scared kids? What do we do to help our young victims of violence?

☑ WHY THE STRUGGLE HAPPENS

When it comes to the reasons kids become victims of violence the answer is clear: Because they were in the wrong place at the wrong time. There are no theoretical explanations or causal factors other than that. Victims of violence are on the receiving end of something they didn't deserve.[5]

Of course, some kids carry many of the same symptoms without being direct victims.[6] And the reason for this is a growing awareness of what has happened to a friend or even a stranger that they identify with. In the case of deadly school shootings that have dotted the country, kids hear, read, and see the reports. They watch interviews with survivors and say "that could be me." Today's kids have seen too many scenes on the nightly news of helicopters flying over yet another school with more running children and fluttering yellow crime tape.

Case Description

Susan, a sophomore in high school, has never been raped. She's never been grazed by a bullet in a drive-by shooting. She's never been stalked or harassed with threatening phone calls. But Susan is scared. One of her girlfriends was threatened by a kid with a gun. It was in the parking lot at a local shopping mall. Susan and her friend were headed to their car after seeing a movie in the mall's Cineplex. That's when her friend realized she left her sunglasses in the theater and headed back to get them while Susan pulled the car around to meet her at the entrance. Five, ten, fifteen minutes passed and Susan was still waiting. Finally Susan turned the car off and walked into the mall to find her friend. It didn't take long. Her friend was curled up on the floor of a phone booth just outside the mall entrance, weeping uncontrollably. Susan's friend had been accosted by a guy with a black mask on, who waved a gun in her face while making threatening comments before getting scared off by pedestrian traffic. It was horrifying. Susan wasn't the direct victim, but you couldn't tell her that. The experience was every bit as real to Susan as it was to her friend. And like her friend, she couldn't sleep at night. She had trouble concentrating in her classes. And normal activities, like going to school, were now riddled with fear.

✔ HOW PARENTS CAN HELP

The following strategies for helping an adolescent who has been a victim of violence can be used effectively by parents; however, every parent-child relationship is unique, and some of them may be more pertinent to your situation than others. As with every significant adolescent struggle, it is best for parents to work alongside a competent counselor. With this in mind, the following is offered as a way to help you facilitate the helping process at home with your teenager.

Prevent Learned Helplessness

It was Dr. Martin Seligman who coined the phrase "learned helplessness" more than two decades ago when he discovered how easy it is for people to give up trying in situations they could make better. One graphic example of this phenomenon was seen near the end of World War II when prisoners in the German death camps were no longer trying to escape because it was "impossible." In actuality, there were many gates and fences that were dilapidated and unprotected near the war's end that would have make it quite easy for some to escape their cruel conditions. But they didn't. All because they believed there was nothing they could do. In less dramatic forms, we all give in to this mentality from time to time. And the youngster who has suffered a violent crime can very easily slip into this frame of mind by believing there is nothing he can do to protect himself from future violence. For this reason, it is important that we help them transcend this kind of negative thinking by focusing on the positive actions they can take to regain control of their life.

Consider Constructive Outlets for Positive Change

The parents of three 1997 murder victims in Paducah, Kentucky, filed a $100 million federal lawsuit claiming a variety of "defective" media products triggered the fatal assault by high schooler Michael Carneal. Named as defendants are the makers of a couple blood-drenched computer games as well as the distributors of a violent movie. In the wake of other school shootings, there have been manifest calls to urge Hollywood and video-game producers to set limits on what they depict and how they do it. With this kind of momentum to take on companies that are feeding our violent youth culture, it can be helpful for some victims of violence to channel their fears and anger into a constructive cause. That certainly doesn't mean filing a lawsuit. It may be a letter-writing campaign to a company or to a person in Congress. It may be sponsoring a small group or a class for educating students about the destructive side of the media or about gun control issues. The point is that the very act of working for positive change is an outlet that helps empower victims to transcend their fear and pain.

Provide for a Stable Peer Group

After World War II, Anna Freud showed that refugee children who had lost their parents in the war survived in relatively good psychological shape when they were allowed to remain with a constant group of peers over a period of years. The presence of a stable peer group that had shared a common traumatic experience was psychologically protective.[7] The lesson to be learned here is that it is vital for survivors of violent crimes to have an opportunity to stay together. Mutual sharing and support of a stable group of peers who have undergone a common, albeit traumatic, experience are critically important to healing and progress.[8]

Prescribe a Gratitude Diary

One of the best ways to help victims of violence make a positive shift in attitude is to get them focused on things they are thankful for. And one of the best ways to do this is by having them start a "gratitude diary." This is a simple strategy whereby they reserve a few minutes at the end of each day to record the things they are grateful for in that day. These can be very small appreciations (a certain person said hello in the hallway) to significant personal accomplishments that may serve as turning points (revisiting the crime scene for the first time with friends who provided strength). The point is to get them looking for the good instead of the bad.

Facilitate a Renewed Commitment to God

After the Columbine High massacre in Colorado, youth workers throughout the country reported a re-energized Christian faith in the kids they minister to. Teenagers in every state set up regular prayer times for the students who suffered the calamity. Its emotional impact transfixed their attention on their need for God. This scenario is not at all unusual at any age, really, but as adults, we need to pay special attention to young people who are victims of violence—whether directly or vicariously—by giving them plenty of opportunity to express their soul's deepest cries. We need to give them ample space to reflect and articulate the spiritual significance of a tragedy. We need to allow their aching hearts to be ministered to by God's presence.

Consider Home Schooling or Private Schooling

One girl who was the victim of a violent scene at her high school says she planned to drop out entirely to begin home schooling. "It's not worth going to school to get shot," said the sixteen-year-old.[9] She's not alone. Plenty of other kids and their parents are making the same decision. And it is a good option to consider. However, this is such an important decision that it certainly cannot be entered into lightly. Home schooling takes an extensive amount of reprioritizing, rescheduling, and often refinancing. Another option along these lines is private schooling. Parents and kids who are frustrated by a public school's lack of security or other policies may find a prep school or a Christian school to be a positive alternative. See the chapter in this book on Schoolwork for organizations that may be helpful in exploring these options.

Encourage Reporting to Authorities

A frightening plot against a school was halted in Port Huron, Michigan, where authorities say a twelve-year-old, a thirteen-year-old, and two fourteen-year-olds, all boys, had been concocting a conspiracy to outdo Eric Harris and Dylan Klebold in Littleton, Colorado. The Michigan boys had stolen a building plan from the custodian's office, knew how they would secure their weapons, and planned to rape some of the girls and shoot many classmates. The boys were caught within a day of a classmate's report to an assistant principal. It is this kind of reporting that empowers victims and would-be victims of violence to take notice and take control. So do what you can to implement a reporting procedure that kids feel safe about. An anonymous tip line, for example, has worked well in many schools.

Be on Watch for Suicide

Research has shown that victims of violence can become depressed and suicidal as a result of feeling helpless.[10] It is therefore imperative that you watch for signs of suicidal ideation. These include tunnel vision, withdrawal, talk of suicide, and lack of hope. Refer to the Suicide chapter in this book for a complete listing of these symptoms.

Know When to Refer

Refer adolescents who have been victims of violence to a psychologically astute physician or psychiatrist when physical symptoms are present or when the resulting anxiety is severe enough to warrant medication. You will also want to refer teenage victims of violence to a competent counselor or psychologist when, over time, the student feels more helpless, anxious, angry, or fearful.

✔ HOW PROFESSIONALS CAN HELP

The following strategies for helping an adolescent who has been a victim of violence are commonly used by counselors. They are presented here as a way to inform you, as a parent, and help you seek the best possible professional help you can for the adolescent in your care.

Pinpoint the Severity

The fear and anxiety that victims of violence experience can be blatantly paralyzing or quite well disguised.[11] For this reason it is especially important to assess the severity of anxiety a young person is experiencing. Of course, a careful assessment can serve as a point from which to measure therapeutic progress. Counselors can use a variety of tools for this.

Increase Confidence

To step over learned helplessness, it is imperative to help young victims repair and increase their level of confidence. After all, the reason for giving up is that they believe they aren't powerful enough to effect any change. So the road to recovery begins by helping them see just how powerful they really are.[12] Counselors may, for example, give victims an assignment to write about the things they can control, the qualities in themselves that work to their advantage. They may be asked to recount their accomplishments and what it took to achieve them. Another effective method for increasing confidence has to do with developing positive self-statements and learning to problem solve. Each of these strategies, and many more, are described in detail in the Inferiority chapter of this book.

Where to Go for Additional Help

Hazler, R. *Helping in the Hallways.* Thousand Oaks, Calif.: Corwin Press, 1998.

Karp, C. L., T. L. Butler, and S. C. Bergstrom. *Treatment Strategies for Abused Adolescents: From Victim to Survivor.* Thousand Oaks, Calif.: Sage Publications, 1998.

Kelly, F. D. *The Psychological Assessment of Abused and Traumatized Children.* Mahwah, N.J.: Lawrence Erlbaum Associates, 1999.

Mintle, L., *Kids Killing Kids.* Altamonte, Fla.: Creation House, 1999.

Skogan, W. G., ed. *Victims of Crime.* Thousand Oaks, Calif.: Sage Publications, 1997.

Notes

1. S. Boney-McCoy and D. Finkelhor, "Psychosocial Sequelae of Violent Victimization in a National Youth Sample," *Journal of Consulting and Clinical Psychology* 63 (1995): 726–73.

2. J. Cohn, "Violations of Human Rights in Children and Adolescents," *International Journal of Adolescent Medicine and Health* 10 (1998): 185–92.

3. N. Gibbs, "Crime: Another School, Another Shooting, *Time* (May 31, 1999): 32–33.

4. I. M. MacDonald, "Violence in Schools: Multiple Realities," *Alberta Journal of Educational Research* 43 (1997): 142–56.

5. D. J. Flannery, M. Singer, L. Williams, and P. Castro, "Adolescent Violence Exposure and Victimization at Home: Coping with Trauma Symptoms," *International Review of Victimology* 6 (1998): 29–48.

6. J. E. Bain and R. T. Brown, "Adolescents as Witnesses to Violence," *Journal of Adolescent Health* 19 (1996): 83–85.

7. W. H. Wist, R. H. Jackson, and K. W. Jackson, "Peer and Community Leader Education to Prevent Youth Violence," *American Journal of Preventive Medicine* 12 (1996): 56–64.

8. P. M. Greenfield and J. Juvonen, "A Developmental Look at Columbine," *APA Monitor* (July/August 1999): 33.

9. J. Cloud, "Just a Routine School Shooting," *Time* (May 31, 1999): 36.

10. S. Stepakoff, "Effects of Sexual Victimization on Suicidal Ideation and Behavior in U.S. College Women," *Suicide and Life-Threatening Behavior* 28 (1998): 107–26.

11. C. K. Berenson, "Frequently Missed Diagnoses in Adolescent Psychiatry," *Psychiatric Clinics of North America* 21 (1998): 917–26.

12. E. De Vos, D. A. Stone, M. A. Goetz, and L. L. Dahlberg, "Evaluation of a Hospital-Based Youth Violence Intervention," *American Journal of Preventive Medicine* 12 (1996): 101–8.

BIBLICAL GUIDANCE FOR STRUGGLING TEENAGERS

GENERAL HELP

Psalm 71:17
Psalm 119:9
Proverbs 3:21–24
Proverbs 4:13
Proverbs 6:20–22
Proverbs 13:20
Proverbs 23:15–16, 19, 26
Proverbs 27:11
Ecclesiastes 11:9
1 Corinthians 15:33
Ephesians 6:2
Colossians 3:20
1 Timothy 4:12

ABUSE

Leviticus 18:6
Romans 6:13, 19
Romans 13:13
Ephesians 5:11–12
James 1:21

ANGER

Psalm 37:8
Proverbs 29: 8, 11
Ecclesiastes 7:9
Ephesians 4:26–27
Hebrews 12:14
James 1:19–20

ANXIETY

Psalm 55:22
Proverbs 12:25
Matthew 6:34
Luke 12:22–23, 25–26
John 14:1
Philippians 4:6–7
1 Peter 5:7

COHABITATION

1 Corinthians 7:7–8, 24–40
2 Corinthians 6:14
Hebrews 13:4

DEPRESSION

Psalm 34:18
Psalm 43:5
Psalm 107:14
Psalm 138:7
Psalm 147: 3
Luke 6:21
1 Peter 1:6–7

DRUGS AND ALCOHOL

Proverbs 4:25–27
Matthew 26:41
Romans 13:14

1 Corinthians 10:13
Ephesians 5:18
James 1:13–15

EATING DISORDERS

Genesis 1:27
Deuteronomy 30:19–20
Job 33:4
Isaiah 40:29
Romans 12:2
2 Corinthians 5:10
Ephesians 2:10

FORGIVENESS

Psalm 34:22
Psalm 103:12
John 3:17–18
Acts 10:43
Romans 5:8
Romans 8:1–2

GOD'S WILL

Psalm 37:5–6
Psalm 40:8
Psalm 143:10
Proverbs 16:3
Luke 22:42
Romans 8:28
Ephesians 5:17
Philippians 2:12–13
Hebrews 10:36
Hebrews 13:20–21
James 4:7
1 John 2:17

GRIEF

Psalm 23:4
Psalm 34:18
Psalm 43:5
Psalm 147:3
Ecclesiastes 3:1–4
Isaiah 25:8
Luke 6:21
1 Peter 1:6–7

GUILT

Psalm 32:1, 5
Psalm 51:1–2
Psalm 65:3
Proverbs 28:13
Isaiah 1:18
1 John 1:9

HOMOSEXUALITY

Leviticus 18:22
Proverbs 5:21
Romans 1:27
1 Corinthians 6:9–10
1 Thessalonians 4:3–5
1 Timothy 5:1–2

INFERIORITY

Deuteronomy 31:8
Proverbs 3:21–24
Ecclesiastes 11:9
Isaiah 58:11
1 Corinthians 15:33
1 Timothy 4:12

INTERNET AND COMPUTER GAME ADDICTION

Psalm 141:4
Ecclesiastes 12:14
Isaiah 5:20
Mark 9:43
Galatians 6:8
1 Peter 1:14

LONELINESS

Psalm 145:18
Matthew 28:20
John 14:18
Acts 17:27
Romans 14:7
James 4:8

MASTURBATION

Romans 6:13
1 Corinthians 6:13, 18–20
Colossians 3:5
1 Thessalonians 4:7
James 1:21

OBESITY

Psalm 139:14
Isaiah 64:8
Romans 12:2
1 Corinthians 15:49
Ephesians 2:10
James 1:18

OBSESSIONS AND COMPULSIONS

Proverbs 1:10
Proverbs 3:21–24
Proverbs 4:14, 25–27
Proverbs 20:11

Proverbs 23:19
Galatians 6:8

OVERACTIVITY AND WORK STRESS

Psalm 127:1
Proverbs 16:2
Proverbs 23:4
Proverbs 28:20
John 6:27
Ephesians 5:15–16

PANIC ATTACKS

Psalm 27:1
Psalm 34:4
Psalm 55:22
Psalm 56:3
Philippians 4:6–7
2 Timothy 1:7

PARENTAL DIVORCE

1 Peter 5:7
2 Corinthians 1:3–4

PARENTS

Proverbs 1:8
Proverbs 6:20–22
Proverbs 15:20, 32
Proverbs 23:25
Ephesians 6:1–2
Colossians 3:20

PEER PRESSURE

Proverbs 24:21
Isaiah 51:7
Matthew 5:11–12
Luke 6:22

James 1:2–3
1 Peter 2:20
1 Peter 3:17

PHOBIAS

Psalm 23:4
Psalm 27:1
Psalm 34:4
Psalm 56:3
Psalm 118:6
Isaiah 12:2
Isaiah 35:3–4
Romans 8:15

PORNOGRAPHY

Proverbs 4:25–27
Proverbs 6:25–26
Matthew 5:27–28
Romans 6:13
Colossians 3:5
James 1:21

PROMISCUITY AND PREMARITAL SEX

Acts 15:29
Romans 6:13
1 Corinthians 6:13, 16, 18–20
Colossians 3:5

RAGE, VIOLENCE, AND GUNFIRE

Leviticus 19:18
Psalm 34:14
Proverbs 14:17
Ecclesiastes 7:9
Ephesians 4:31
James 1:19–20

SCHIZOPHRENIA

Psalm 10:17
Psalm 20:1
Psalm 22:24
Psalm 142:6
Isaiah 41:13

SCHOOLWORK

Psalm 37:5–6
Proverbs 3:13–14
Proverbs 10:14
Proverbs 16:7
Proverbs 18:9
Proverbs 24:14
Ephesians 5:15–16
Colossians 3:23–24

SHYNESS

Psalm 89:15
Ecclesiastes 4:9–10
Matthew 10:27
Mark 16:15
Acts 1:8
Romans 10:15

SIBLINGS

Leviticus 19:17
Psalm 133:1
Philippians 2:14–16
James 4:11
2 Timothy 2:23–24
1 John 4:20
1 John 2:11

SLEEP DISTURBANCE

Psalm 4:8
Psalm 91:1, 4
Ecclesiastes 5:12
Matthew 11:28
James 5:13

SPIRITUAL DOUBT

Psalm 53:1
John 3:36
John 5:39–40
John 20:27
2 Timothy 2:13
1 John 2:28

STUTTERING

Psalm 22:24
Psalm 32:7
Proverbs 13:3
Proverbs 25:15
Isaiah 41:13

SUICIDE

Job 14:5
Psalm 9:9
Psalm 46:1
Psalm 56:13
Psalm 71:20
Galatians 6:8

VICTIMS OF VIOLENCE

Deuteronomy 33:27
Psalm 121:7–8
Psalm 138:7
Psalm 143:11
Proverbs 20:22
Isaiah 58:9

Helpful Web Sites

ABUSE

www.prevent-abuse-now.com

ANGER

www.pp.okstate.edu/ehs/kopykit/anger.htm
www.angermgmt.com

ANXIETY

www.socialphobia.org
www.paems.com.au

COHABITATION

http://members.aol.com/cohabiting

DEPRESSION

www.ama-assn.org/insight/spec_con/depressn/depressn.htm
http://depression.mentalhelp.net/
http://www.depressedanon.com

DRUGS AND ALCOHOL

www.sada.org
www.well.com/user/woa
Online Quiz: www.colby.edu/health.serv/drugs/screen.html

EATING DISORDERS

www.something-fishy.org
www.eating-disorders.com
http://eatingdisorders.mentalhelp.net

FORGIVENESS

www.worldvillage.com/wv/square/chapel/safehaven/forgive.htm
www.forgiving.org
www.intl-forgive-inst.org

GOD'S WILL

http://jesusgift.com
www.seekgod.org
http://www.faithpower.com/index.htm

GRIEF

www.shpm.com/articles/trauma/grief.html

HOMOSEXUALITY

www.narth.com/menus/schools.html

INFERIORITY

www.selfesteem.org

INTERNET AND COMPUTER GAME ADDICTION

www.virtual-addiction.com
www.addictions.com/internet.htm
www.netaddiction.com

LONELINESS

www.solosingles.com/sssudden/lonely.htm
www.creativeye.com/goodnews/loneliness.htm
www.lightdarkness.com

MASTURBATION

www.jesus-connect.net/world/bbs/PPS/Masturbation.html

OBESITY

www.mayohealth.org/mayo/9704/htm/body_ima.htm
www.butler.org/bdd.html
Online Body Image test: www.homearts.com/depts/health/12bodqz1.htm

OBSESSIONS AND COMPULSIONS

http://fairlite.com/ocd
www.sfbacct.com/treatment-ob.html

OVERACTIVITY AND WORK STRESS

www.parentsplace.com

PANIC ATTACKS

www.anxietypanic.com
www.nimh.nih.gov/anxiety/anxiety/panic/pdinfo.htm

PARENTAL DIVORCE

www.divorcecare.com

PARENTS

www.yourteen.com
www.outreach.missouri.edu/parentlink/bethere.htm

PEER PRESSURE

www.tiac.net/users/drmike/peerpress.shtml

PHOBIAS

www.anxietynetwork.com/phobias.html

PORNOGRAPHY

www.no-porn.com/breaking.html
www.helpwithsex.com

PROMISCUITY AND PREMARITAL SEX

www.thewaters.org/columns/premarital.html
www.christiananswers.net
www.abstinence.net

RAGE, VIOLENCE, AND GUNFIRE

www.vpp.com/teenhelp/
www.gangsorus.com

SCHIZOPHRENIA

www.schizophrenia.com
www.schizophrenia-help.com

SCHOOLWORK

www.ed.gov/pubs/parents/Homework/index.html

SHYNESS

www.shyness.com
www.shynesshelp.com

STUTTERING

www.prevent-stuttering.com/Prevention.html
www.stutter.net

SUICIDE

www.sfsuicide.org
www.suicidology.org
www.afsp.org

VICTIMS OF VIOLENCE

www.oz.net/survivor/help.html
www.cause-ut.org/survivor9.htm

INDEX

-T-

-V-

-W-

When Bad Things Happen to Good Marriages

How to Stay Together When Life Pulls You Apart

Drs. Les & Leslie Parrott

Drs. Les & Leslie Parrott understand firsthand that no marriage, no matter how good, is immune to bad things; and as relationship experts, they know how to use the difficult things in life to make a marriage stronger. In *When Bad Things Happen to Good Marriages,* the Parrotts look at five possible reasons why good marriages bump into bad things: unfulfilled expectations, unexamined selves, unskilled couples, unhealthy choices, and unpredictable circumstances. They provide the tools needed to handle everyday problems—such as boredom, drift, and busyness—as well as tough times, such as infidelity, tragic loss, financial debt, and infertility. Throughout, they emphasize that the bad things, when handled wisely and correctly, can actually strengthen and improve a marriage relationship.

Filled with true-life stories and thought-provoking questions, *When Bad Things Happen to Good Marriages* is an insightful and practical guide to finding hope, persevering, and overcoming bad things, resulting in renewed commitment and deeper intimacy.

The *When Bad Things Happen to Good Marriages Workbooks,* with separate editions for husbands and wives, help couples make meaningful connections with the book's content and practice new skills. The *When Bad Things Happen to Good Marriages Workbooks* will help you internalize cutting-edge strategies, skills, and insights to help your marriage stay together when life pulls you apart.

Hardcover 0-310-22459-4
Workbook for Husbands 0-310-23902-8
Workbook for Wives 0-310-23903-6
Audio 0-310-22977-4

Pick up a copy today at your local bookstore!